Preface

It has taken long, far too long, to bring this project to completion. Some of the research was done during the academic year 1977–78 when a fellowship from the National Endowment for the Humanities and a Visiting Fellowship from Wolfson College enabled me to spend a year in Oxford, England, and Poona, India. Parts of the early chapters were written in 1981–82 when I was back in Oxford, again on a Visiting Fellowship from Wolfson College, and in Poona, on a grant from the American Institute of Indian Studies. Many things—administrative burdens and other book projects—postponed its completion. Time has its own rewards: wisdom, one hopes, accompanies gray hairs, and maturity sometimes creates a better product. The long period of gestation, however, has produced its own debts—debts of gratitude to teachers, colleagues, friends, family, and, yes, even institutions.

Much of the writing was done when I was a member of the Department of Religious Studies at Indiana University, Bloomington. The Department and the University provided a rare atmosphere for personal growth and intellectual stimulation. To my colleagues there a heart-felt thank you. The book was completed in my new home at the Center for Asian Studies of the University of Texas, Austin. The Center and the University have provided both good colleagues and fine resources. In India individuals and institutions, too numerous to list, always responded generously to my often importunate requests. I owe a special debt of gratitude, however, to the late Dr. V. V. Bhide and the staff of the Bhandarkar Oriental Research Institute.

Three friends put their friendship to the test by reading the entire manuscript closely and giving invaluable advice: Steven Collins, Anne Feldhaus, and Richard Lariviere. This book would have been much poorer but for their criticisms and suggestions. Gregory Schopen helped by stretching my imagination, if not my mind, in ways only he can. Richard Gombrich read chapter 3 and caught several inadvertent errors. The editorial staff at OUP—Cynthia Read and Peter Ohlin—was, as usual, excellent and obliging. Cynthia Garver, my punctilious copy editor, detected my every careless error and compensated for my sloppy nature. The book is the better for their help and advice. My wife Suman read the entire manuscript—she, like Cynthia Garver, has an eye for the detail. A special thank-you to Suman and my daughter Meera, who for many years have put up with me as I gazed, glassy-eyed, at a computer screen.

Austin, Texas
February 1993

P.O.

The Āśrama System

The Āśrama System

The History and Hermeneutics of a Religious Institution

Patrick Olivelle

Munshiram Manoharlal
Publishers Pvt. Ltd.

ISBN 81-215-1135-6
This edition 2004
© 1993, Patrick Olivelle

This English language reprint edition of The Āśrama System, originally published in 1993, is published by arrangement with Oxford University Press, Inc.

All rights reserved, including those of translation into foreign languages. No part of this book may be reproduced, stored in a retrieval system, or transmitted in any form, or by any means, electronic, mechanical, photocopying, recording, or otherwise, without the written permission of the publisher.

Printed in India.
Published by Munshiram Manoharlal Publishers Pvt. Ltd.,
Post Box 5715, 54 Rani Jhansi Road,
New Delhi 110 055.

Contents

II. THE EARLY PERIOD

III. THE CLASSICAL PERIOD

Abbreviations

NOTE: Complete source information is found in the bibliography to this volume.

Abh	Vedānta Deśika: *Alepakamatabhaṅgavāda* of the *Śatadūṣaṇī*
ĀgG	*Āgniveśya Gṛhyasūtra*
AitĀ	*Aitareya Āraṇyaka*
AitB	*Aitareya Brāhmaṇa*
ALB	Adyar Library Bulletin
AN	*Aṅguttara Nikāya*
ĀnSS	Ānandāśrama Sanskrit Series, Poona
ĀpDh	*Āpastamba Dharmasūtra*
ĀpŚ	*Āpastamba Śrautasūtra*
Artha	Kauṭilya, *Arthaśāstra*
ĀrU	*Āruṇi Upaniṣad*
ĀśG	*Āśvalāyana Gṛhyasūtra*
AV	*Atharvaveda Saṃhitā*
BāU	*Bṛhadāraṇyaka Upaniṣad*
BDh	*Baudhāyana Dharmasūtra*
BG	*Baudhāyana Gṛhyasūtra*
BGp	*Baudhāyana Gṛhyaparibhāṣasūtra*
BhāgP	*Bhāgavata Purāṇa*
BhārG	*Bhāradvāja Gṛhyasūtra*
BhG	*Bhagavad Gītā*
BI	Bibliotheca Indica, Calcutta
BṛD	*Bṛhaddevatā*
BSS	Bombay Sanskrit Series
ChU	*Chāndogya Upaniṣad*
CI	*Corpus Inscriptionum Indicarum*
DN	*Dīgha Nikāya*
EPU	*Eighteen Principal Upaniṣads.* Ed. V. P. Limaye and R. D. Vadekar
GDh	*Gautama Dharmasūtra*
GoB	*Gopatha Brāhmaṇa*
GOS	Gaekwad's Oriental Series, Baroda

HOS	Harvard Oriental Series, Cambridge, Mass.
IHQ	Indian Historical Quarterly
JAAR	Journal of the American Academy of Religion
JAOS	Journal of the American Oriental Society
Jāt	*Jātaka*
JB	*Jaiminīya-Upaniṣad-Brāhmaṇa*
JMV	Vidāraṇya, *Jīvanmuktiviveka*
JRAS	Journal of the Royal Asiatic Society
JU	*Jābāla Upaniṣad*
KauṣU	*Kauṣītaki Upaniṣad*
KKT	Lakṣmīdhara, *Kṛtyakalpataru*
KS	*Kāṭhaka Saṃhitā*
KSS	Kashi Sanskrit Series, Benares
KśU	*Kaṭhaśruti Upaniṣad*
KūrP	*Kūrma Purāṇa*
LiP	*Liṅga Purāṇa*
LSU	*Laghu-Saṃnyāsa Upaniṣad*
MaitU	*Maitrī Upaniṣad*
MatsP	*Matsya Purāṇa*
MBh	*Mahābhārata*
MDh	*Mānava Dharmaśāstra* (*Manusmṛti*)
MK	*Mīmāṃsā Koṣa*
MN	*Majjhima Nikāya*
MNP	Āpadeva, *Mīmāṃsānyāyaprakāśa*
MNU	*Mahānārāyaṇa Upaniṣad*
MS	*Maitrāyaṇīya Saṃhitā*
MuṇU	*Muṇḍaka Upaniṣad*
NpU	*Nāradaparivrājaka Upaniṣad*
NSm	*Nāradasmṛti*
PāM	Mādhava, *Pārāśaramādhavīya*
PārG	*Pāraskara Gṛhyasūtra*
PB	*Pañcaviṃśa Brāhmaṇa*
PMS	*Pūrva Mīmāṃsāsūtra*
PraśU	*Praśna Upaniṣad*
PTS	Pāli Text Society, London
Rām	*Rāmāyaṇa*
RV	*Ṛgveda Saṃhitā*
ŚĀ	*Śāṅkhāyana Āraṇyaka*
ŚāṅŚ	*Śāṅkhāyana Śrautasūtra*

ŚB	*Śatapatha Brāhmaṇa*
SBB	Sacred Books of the Buddhists, London
SBE	Sacred Books of the East, Oxford
ŚG	*Śāṅkhāyana Gṛhyasūtra*
SN	*Saṃyutta Nikāya*
SuN	*Suttanipāta*
SUS	*Saṃnyāsa Upaniṣads.* Ed. F. O. Schrader
SūS	*Sūta Saṃhitā*
SV	*Sāmaveda Saṃhitā*
ŚvU	*Śvetāśvatara Upaniṣad*
TĀ	*Taittirīya Āraṇyaka*
TB	*Taittirīya Brāhmaṇa*
TPU	*The Thirteen Principal Upanishads.* Tr. R. E. Hume
TS	*Taittirīya Saṃhitā*
TU	*Taittirīya Upaniṣad*
VaDh	*Vasiṣṭha Dharmasūtra*
VaiDh	*Vaikhānasa Dharmasūtra*
VaiG	*Vaikhānasa Gṛhyasūtra*
VaiSm	*Vaikhānasa Smārtasūtra*
VāmP	*Vāmana Purāṇa*
VeS	*Vedānta Sūtra*
ViDh	*Viṣṇu Dharmasūtra* (*Viṣṇusmṛti*)
Vin	*Vinaya Piṭaka*
ViP	*Viṣṇu Purāṇa*
WZKS	Wiener Zeitschrift für die Kunde Südasiens
Yād	Yādavaprakāśa, *Yatidharmasamuccaya*
YBh	Vedānta Deśika, *Yatiliṅgabhedabhaṅgavāda* of the *Śatadūṣaṇī*
YDh	*Yājñavalkya Dharmaśāstra* (*Yājñavalkyasmṛti*)
YDhS	Viśveśvara Sarasvatī, *Yatidharmasaṃgraha*
YMtā	Vijñāneśvara, *Mitākṣarā* on YDh
Ypra	Vāsudevāśrama, *Yatidharmaprakāśa*

THE *ĀŚRAMA* SYSTEM

Prologue

The Brāhmaṇical tradition uses the term *āśrama* with reference to what it sees as four distinct and legitimate ways of leading a religious life. The four *āśrama*s are the modes of life of a celibate student, a married householder, a forest hermit, and a world renouncer. Brāhmaṇical theology considers these *āśrama*s as constitutive and interrelated parts of an organic whole made up of the rules (*dharma*s) that govern human conduct; this organic whole is often simply referred to as *dharma.* The two cornerstones of *dharma* are the systems of *āśrama* and *varṇa* ("social classes"). The totality of the Brāhmaṇical *dharma* is often referred to simply as *varṇāśramadharma*, an expression that modern scholars and native interpreters alike have seen as the closest approximation within the tradition to what we have come to call Hinduism: "Even now," observes the eminent Indian sociologist G. S. Ghurye (1964, 2), "Varṇāśramadharma, duties of castes and āśramas, is almost another name for Hinduism."

The system of the four *varṇa*s—Brāhmaṇa, Kṣatriya, Vaiśya, and Śūdra—especially within the context of the related system of castes (*jāti*), has been the subject of repeated study by scholars both Western and Indian. Sociologists and anthropologists, as well as Indologists and historians of religion, have made *varṇa* and caste the focus of intense scrutiny from a spectrum of methodological perspectives.

The parallel system of the four *āśrama*s, on the other hand, has received much less scholarly attention, apart from platitudes repeated in general studies of Indian culture and religion.[1] Nevertheless, the native tradition, as well as modern scholarship, considers the *āśrama* system a pillar of the Hindu edifice. F. Max Müller (1878, 343), for example, with a touch of exaggeration claimed that the *āśrama*s were even more important an institution than caste: "A much more important feature, however, of the ancient Vedic society than the four castes, consists in the four *āśrama*s or stages." Speaking of the *āśrama*s, Paul Deussen (1906, 367) at the turn of the century enthusiastically exclaimed: "The entire history of mankind does not produce much that approaches in grandeur to this thought." Scholarly attention, unfortunately, has not kept pace with scholarly rhetoric. The few studies devoted to the topic are in the form of relatively brief articles and do little justice to the complexity of the subject or the sheer length of its history.

1. Some examples of the way the system is generally presented in such studies are given in section 1.3.1–2 of this volume.

Until now not a single book-length study has been made of the *āśrama* system.[2] In this book, therefore, I have explored a relatively uncharted territory of the Indian intellectual and religious landscape in the belief that if this system is as important as native theology and modern scholarship take it to be, it deserves to be studied seriously and responsibly.

My aim in this book is fourfold: to uncover the origin of the *āśrama* system, to trace its subsequent history, to describe its relationship to other institutional and doctrinal aspects of the Brāhmaṇical world and its position within Brāhmaṇical theology, and to assess its significance within the history of Indian religions.

After dealing with some basic issues of method in chapter 1, I provide in chapter 2 the theological and historical context within which the *āśrama* system was created.[3] In the classical texts of Brāhmaṇism and in modern studies of Hinduism alike, the four *āśramas* are presented as specific modes that a man is expected to assume during successive periods of his life. Accordingly, the very term *āśrama* is most frequently translated as "stage of life." I demonstrate in chapter 3, however, that the *āśrama* system originated as a theological scheme that presented four alternative paths of religious living to adult males, any one of which they may freely choose. The *āśramas*, furthermore, were conceived as lifelong vocations and not temporary stages of a man's life. In chapter 4 I examine the historical and theological factors that may have influenced the radical change that converted the original system into its classical formulation. Chapter 5 examines the classical system within which the *āśramas* came to be considered stages of life through which each individual should ideally pass, and chapter 6 discusses further developments and modifications that the classical system underwent in the course of history. In the final two chapters, 7 and 8, I explore the growing interrelation between the *āśrama* system and other central institutions of Brāhmaṇism, as well as medieval theological disputes and controversies surrounding that system.

The *āśrama* system was created as a structure for inclusion—for finding a place within the Brāhmaṇical world to ideologies and ways of life that challenged many of the central doctrines and values of that world. The classical system in a special way was intended to blunt the opposition between the two value systems—the one centered around the married householder and the other around the celibate ascetic. The success of the scheme in resolving that basic conflict in Indian culture has been taken for granted by many scholars. I hope to demonstrate that a closer examination of the history of the system will show that the issue was never fully settled and that old battles had to be fought over and over again throughout the Middle Ages and down to modern times even after the *āśramas* had become part of the mainstream of Brāhmaṇical theology.

2. Liebich's (1936) study—the inaugural lecture at his *Habilitation* at the University of Breslau in 1892—contains just 40 pages, and, although published in a monograph form, it can hardly be considered a major work.

3. In chapter 2 of this volume I reproduce in an expanded and modified form some material contained in the introduction to my translations of the Saṃnyāsa Upaniṣads (Olivelle 1992).

I

INTRODUCTION

1

Meaning and Method

At the beginning of this study I want to deal explicitly and in some detail with the problems of meaning and method—the meaning of the term *āśrama* and of the *āśrama* system and the proper ways to study it—because serious and pervasive methodological errors have impaired most previous scholarly works on the history of the *āśrama* system. Failure to understand the meaning of the *āśrama* system within the tradition of Brāhmaṇical theology[1] and institutions and to evaluate properly the earliest available data are at the root of most problems in modern scholarship on the *āśrama*s. They have led to the mishandling of evidence and inevitably to wrong conclusions.

I will argue that the *āśrama* system is primarily a theological construct. The system and its history, therefore, should be carefully distinguished from the socio-religious institutions comprehended by the system and from their respective histories. The history of the *āśrama* system, moreover, should be firmly located within the history of Brāhmaṇical hermeneutics (*mīmāṃsā*)—that aspect of Brāhmaṇical theology engaged in interpreting received sacred texts. During the long period of research and reflection leading up to the writing of this book, it became apparent to me that writing a history of the *āśrama* system is indeed an exercise in tracing the hermeneutical controversies and developments within Brāhmaṇism.

Hermeneutics and exegesis, as Jonathan Z. Smith (1982, 43–52) has convincingly argued, is at the heart of both religious traditions and, consequently, the task of all historians of religion, not just those of Christianity. He offers the telling example of food and cuisine. Human cultures reduce the vast number of potential sources of nutriment to an extremely small number of permissible food items and then use great ingenuity to prepare a bewildering variety of dishes from that limited number of permitted ingredients: "If food is a phenomenon characterized by limitation, cuisine is a phenomenon characterized by variegation" (Smith 1982, 40). Religions, likewise, limit the number of texts and stories that are considered authoritative, thereby forming "canons," whether they

1. Throughout this work I have used the term "theology" to refer to the systematic study of religious doctrines and practices carried out within the native Brāhmaṇical tradition. I am aware that some may accuse me of using a term with strong Christian overtones. The reluctance to use this term in a value-neutral and cross-cultural manner, I would argue, may indicate a desire among some to uphold a privileged position for Christian theology. Taken as the intellectual effort by a tradition to understand and explain its religious beliefs and practices, "theology" comes closest—certainly closer than "philosophy"—to defining what Brāhmaṇical intellectuals, both the anonymous authors of the *dharma* texts and later systematizers such as Śaṃkara, were actually engaged in doing.

are relatively fixed and bounded as in the Judeo-Christian traditions or left vague and open as in most others. Hermeneutics, like cuisine, extends this arbitrary limit, applying the canon according to well-defined rules of interpretation to every conceivable human situation.

Within Brāhmaṇism the hermeneutical enterprise is at the heart of law and theology. Early in the history of Brāhmaṇical theology the theory arose that *dharma* is revealed solely and completely in the Vedas. The Smṛtis, which comprise the other class of authoritative literature, were interpreted as deriving their authority from the fact that they are based on the Vedas. Novelty in doctrine, institution, or practice was not recognized. When new ideas and practices arose,[2] as they were bound to, they challenged the hermeneutical ingenuity of theologians to find a basis for them in the known rules of Vedas and Smṛtis. The fact that most of the major theological and legal works within the Brāhmaṇical tradition consist of commentaries bears testimony to the centrality of interpretation in theology and law. Here I hope to demonstrate that the creation of and later developments within the *āśrama* system are striking examples of Brāhmaṇical hermeneutics.

1.1 The Meaning of Āśrama

If we are to properly evaluate the meaning of the *āśrama* system, it is necessary to investigate first the meaning of the word *āśrama* and of cognate terms within the broader vocabulary of the Indian religious traditions in general and of the Brāhmaṇical tradition in particular. Clearly the authors of the system operated within that linguistic world and shared that vocabulary, even when they stretched the meaning of the term in new and significant directions.

Āśrama is a relatively new term in the Sanskrit vocabulary. The word does not occur in the vedic Saṃhitās and Brāhmaṇas or even in the early Upaniṣads. This term, I believe, originated as a neologism, a word coined at a particular time in Indian history to express a novel idea or to indicate a novel phenomenon or institution.

Etymologies are not always helpful guides to the meanings of words in actual use. Indeed, even the Indian hermeneutical tradition considered the conventional meaning of a word to have greater force than any meaning that may be derived from its etymology.[3] In a neologism like *āśrama*, however, where use has not determined the meaning, its etymology may provide us with helpful insights into its original use and meaning. This is especially true in the case of Sanskrit where early grammarians had accurately described the verbal roots, the function of suffixes, and the derivation of nouns and adjectives. We can be fairly certain that those who coined this word knew the function and meaning of the cognate term *śrama*, which appears frequently in the early vedic literature, and of the verbal root √*śram* from which both *śrama* and *āśrama* are etymologically derived. In

2. On the way myths perform the hermeneutical function of understanding the new and the incongruous, see Smith 1982, 90–101.

3. Compare *rūḍhir yogam apaharati* —"the conventional meaning ousts the etymological" and *rūḍhir yogād balīyasī*—"the conventional meaning has greater force than the etymological." Cf. MK 6, 3327; MNP 98.

determining the meaning of the term *āśrama* and consequently of the *āśrama* system, therefore, it will be useful to examine first its etymological roots.

1.1.1. The Meaning of Śrama

In this section I will examine the semantic history of both the verb √*śram* and its nominal derivative *śrama*. They appear frequently in the early literature with two related meanings. The first meaning is "to become weary, tired, or exhausted," and this usually carries a negative connotation. Weariness is something one seeks to avoid or at most to endure patiently; one does not welcome it or willingly accept it. The term is used frequently with this meaning in the context of traveling. Gods, for example, became weary (*śramayuvaḥ*) after pursuing Agni (RV 1.72.2). A bird became tired after flying (AitB 3.25: *aśrāmayat;* BāU 4.3.19: *śrāntaḥ*). The rivers, made to flow by Varuṇa, feel no weariness although they never cease to run (RV 2.28.4: *na śrāmyanti*). Similarly, the Soma juices flow unwearied (RV 9.22.4: *na śaśramuḥ*).[4] The weariness, however, need not be physical; it may also be mental, as when it is associated with the fear of an enemy.[5] The negative connotation of *śrama* as weariness is revealed very clearly in the *Śatapatha Brāhmaṇa* (6.3.3.7), where it is equated with evil (*pāpman*). Weariness may finally result in death; thus in the *Bṛhadāraṇyaka Upaniṣad* death is said to approach in the form of *śrama*.[6]

The second meaning is "to labor, to toil, or to exert oneself." It implies strenuous activity or exercise which is directed at achieving a positive result or for which a reward is expected. The *Ṛgveda* (10.114.10), for example, states that horses receive a recompense for their toil (*śrama*). The term is used most frequently in the vedic literature, however, to express the toil inherent in religious, especially ritual, exertions.

Śrama is closely related to the vedic sacrifice (*yajña*), and hence it is frequently associated with two other ritual activities: austerity (*tapas*) and praise (*arcana*).[7] A man toils (*śaśramāṇaḥ*) in bringing fuel for sacrifice (RV 4.12.2). The Ādityas bestow wealth "on the wearied presser of Soma" (*śrāntāya sunvate:* RV 8.67.6). Manu labored (*aśrāmyat*) at cooking the sacrificial oblation (TS 1.7.1.3). The *Śatapatha Brāhmaṇa* (12.3.3.1) states that when the gods performed a thousand-year sacrifice, all the creatures became worn out (*śaśrāma*) after the first 500 years. It is probably within the context of sacrificial toil that the *Ṛgveda* (4.33.11) declares that when toil is absent (*ṛte śrāntasya*) the gods are not inclined to friendship.

As the toil inherent in the sacrifice, *śrama* is associated in a special way with three primordial and archetypal activities: the gaining of heaven by the gods, the discovery of sacrificial knowledge by the vedic seers, and the creation of the world. The gods won

4. In a similar sense, the gods are told at RV 2.29.4: "Of kinsmen such as you never let us be weary" (*mā śramiṣma*). At RV 2.30.7 the author prays: "Let it not vex me, tire me (*śramat*), make me slothful; and never let us say 'Press not the Soma.'"

5. RV 8.4.7: *mā bhema mā śramiṣma*—"may we not fear, may we not become weary." Sāyaṇa commenting on this verse interprets the term to mean "oppressed" (*pīḍita*). See also RV 10.105.3 where weariness (*śaśramāṇaḥ*) is associated with the fear of an enemy.

6. BāU 1.5.21; see also BāU 4.3.19.

7. On the meaning of *tapas* in the Vedas, see Blair 1961. On the relation between *tapas, śrama*, and the ritual, see Lévi 1898; Knipe 1975, 90–137; Kaelber 1989.

heaven by *śrama* (AitB 2.13). When the nectar of immortality absconded, they searched for it by means of *śrama* and *tapas* (ŚB 9.5.1.2). The seers likewise discovered the meters and the sacrificial bricks through *śrama* and *tapas* (TB 5.3.5.4).[8] Both gods and seers searched for Speech (*vāc*) in the same manner (TB 2.8.8.5). Then there is the story (ŚB 1.6.2.1–3) of the gods who managed to get to heaven by means of the sacrifice. Prior to that they had lived on earth in the company of humans. In an effort to prevent humans from following them to heaven, the gods erased all traces of the sacrifice on earth. The seers, however, searched for the sacrifice by praising (*arcantaḥ*) and toiling (*śrāmyantaḥ*), "for by toil (*śrama*) the gods indeed gained what they desired to gain, and so did the seers." Here *śrama* is used clearly as a synonym for sacrifice.

The most significant aspect of *śrama*, however, emerges in the descriptions of the creative activities of Prajāpati. To create the world Prajāpati toiled (*aśrāmyat*) and tortured or heated himself (*tapo 'tapyata*). As he was thus worn out (*śrāntaḥ*) and heated (*tepānaḥ*) he brought forth the creatures, which are his offspring (*prajā*). This paradigm is repeated constantly in creation stories.[9] Evidently the priestly imagination patterned the creative acts of gods after the sacrificial acts of priests:

> Most of the creation-legends in the Brāhmaṇas begin in the same way. As the magician must prepare himself for his magic, and the priest must prepare for the sacrifice, by means of self-torture and mortification, so Prajāpati, too, has to prepare himself in the same way for the great work of creation. (Winternitz 1927, I, 220, n. 2)

The toil and exertion of Prajāpati's creative act carry clear sexual connotations; creation is procreation. The *Taittirīya Saṃhitā* (7.1.5.1), for example, explicitly refers to the sexual intercourse between Prajāpati and earth. He spread her out and "in her Prajāpati labored" (*tasyām aśrāmyat*).[10] The result of such toil is offspring, the goal alike of the creative and the procreative act. So when the gods, whom he had just engendered, tell Prajāpati, their father, that they too would like to have children, he advises them to imitate him in *śrama* and *tapas* (TS 7.1.5.2).

The association of *śrama* with sexual activity is not limited to the gods. After the great flood had wiped out all creatures, Manu, the sole survivor, desirous of offspring, engaged in praise and toil.[11] The toil of the aged couple Agastya and Lopāmudrā (RV 1.179) is also associated with sex and the desire for progeny.

The two meanings of *śrama*—weariness and labor—we have discussed have been noted also by Indian grammarians and lexicographers. The *Dhātupāṭha*, the ancient list

8. See also ŚB 1.7.2.23; 1.7.3.2, 14. Agni, Indra, and Sūrya gain superiority over the other gods by praising and toiling (ŚB 4.5.4.2). In the same manner, the gods strengthen Prajāpati when he is exhausted after creation (ŚB 4.6.4.1).

9. See AV 4.35.2; 6.133.3; 10.7.36; 12.5.1; TS 7.1.5.1–2; ŚB 2.2.4.1; 2.5.1.1; 3.9.1.4; 6.1.1.8, 13; 6.1.3.1; 10.6.5.2–6; 11.1.6.1, 7; 11.5.8.1; TB 1.1.3.5. At ŚB 6.1.1.1 the seers create the universe through *śrama* and *tapas*. After the birth of Rudra, Prajāpati asks him why he cries "when you are born out of toil and torture" (ŚB 6.1.3.9). At TB 3.12.2.2–5 and 3.12.4.2–6 Prajāpati is asked to toil (*śrāmyasi*) by various means; all his activities, indeed, appear to involve *śrama*. See also BāU 1.2.2.6; GoB 1.1.1–2, 5, 6, 8.

10. The same expression is used in BāU 1.2.2. See also ŚB 1.8.1.10. On the creative power of heat and its sexual connotations, see O'Flaherty 1973, 40–41.

11. ŚB 1.8.1.7: *so 'rcaṃśchrāmyaṃś cacāra prajākāmaḥ*—"desirous of offspring, he engaged in praising and toiling." The same expression is used in the case of Prajāpati at ŚB 11.1.6.7, making clear the parallel between divine and human acts.

of Sanskrit verbal roots, for example, explains that the verb √*śram* is used with reference to both religious austerity and fatigue.[12]

In the legend of Śunaḥśepa *śrama* is associated with a life of wandering away from human habitats, a meaning that may be a precursor of the later association of *śramaṇa* with wandering ascetics. Rohita has wandered in the forest for a long time in order to escape being killed in sacrifice by his father. When he returns Indra advises him to wander more:

> "Manifold is the prosperity of him who is weary,"
> So have we heard, O Rohita;
> Evil is he who stayeth among men,
> Indra is the comrade of the wanderer.
> Do thou wander.[13]

As in other passages, here too the fruitfulness of *śrama* is emphasized, but the activity is here related to wandering, whereas the opposite, namely the sedentary mode of life, bears no fruit. This connection of *śrama* with wilderness and wandering, as we shall see, has significant implications for the semantic history of both *śramaṇa* and *āśrama*.

1.1.2 The Meaning of Śramaṇa

Śramaṇa is another important term in Indian religious history that is etymologically derived from the verb √*śram*. Because of its etymological relationship to *āśrama* and because several scholarly studies have attempted to establish a link between the historical realities underlying these two terms,[14] it will be useful to examine briefly the meaning of *śramaṇa*.

This term is used frequently in post-vedic literature and in inscriptions with reference to various types of ascetics. Buddhist and Jain canonical texts use it frequently to designate Buddhist and Jain monks.[15] It appears that at least by the time of Aśoka (middle of the third century B.C.E.) *śramaṇa* was used principally, if not exclusively, with reference to non-Brāhmaṇical ascetics. The compound word *śramaṇa-brāhmaṇa* is used in Aśokan inscriptions to indicate the double class of religious people worthy of honor and donations.[16] A century or so later the grammarian Patañjali uses the same phrase as an example to illustrate the rule of Pāṇini about compounds in which the component words refer to objects that are opposed to each other.[17] The same com-

12. *Dhātupāṭha*, 4.95: *śramu tapasi khede ca*. For an assessment of its authorship and age, see Cardona 1976, 161–64. See also Bhānuji Dīkṣita on Amarasiṃha's *Amarakośa*, 2.7.3.

13. AitB 7.15 (Keith's translation): *nānā śrāntasya śrīr astīti rohita śuśruma / pāpo nṛṣadvaro jana indra ic carataḥ sakhā caraiveti //*

14. See, for example, Winternitz 1926, 226. Thapar (1982, 276) writes:"The śramaṇa, therefore, is one who labours towards an objective and āśrama was the process of doing so. Eventually the place where the śramaṇas gathered was also called āśrama."

15. For the Buddhist use of the term see Dutt 1960, 31–53. See also Pande 1978; Deo 1956; and Olivelle 1974b.

16. See *Edicts of Aśoka*, Rock Edicts 3, 4, 8, 9, 11, 13; Pillar Edict 7.

17. Pāṇini, *Aṣṭādhyāyī*, 4.9: *yeṣāṃ ca virodhaḥ śāśvatikaḥ*. The rule establishes that a coordinative compound (*dvandva*) of words signifying animals between whom there is permanent enmity is declined in the singular. See Patañjali, *Mahābhāṣya*, I, p. 476, l. 9.

pound is also used in the Pāli Canon with a reference similar to that of the Aśokan inscriptions.[18]

An examination of early Brāhmaṇical texts, several of which in all likelihood predate Aśoka,[19] however, indicates that the clear distinction and even opposition between *brāhmaṇa* and *śramaṇa* may have been a later semantic development possibly influenced by the appropriation of the latter term by non-Brāhmaṇical sects such as Buddhism and Jainism.

The *Taittirīya Āraṇyaka* belonging to the Black Yajurveda contains the earliest reference to *śramaṇa* in Brāhmaṇical literature:

> The *vātaraśana* seers (*ṛṣi*) were *śramaṇas* and celibates (*ūrdhvamanthinaḥ*). The seers went to them in supplication, but they absconded, entering the Kūṣmāṇḍa verses one after another. (The seers) found them there by means of faith and austerity.[20]

In this text *śramaṇa* is associated with three other terms: *vātaraśana*, *ṛṣi*, and *ūrdhvamanthin*. An examination of these may shed further light on the meaning of *śramaṇa* in the early Brāhmaṇical vocabulary.

The term *vātaraśana* appears first in the Ṛgvedic hymn (10.136) that celebrates an enigmatic figure called *muni*, a title applied in later literature to any holy or ascetic person, but whose original meaning is far from clear.[21] He is given the epithet *keśin*, "the long-haired one." The very first verse regards him as participating in cosmic functions: "The long-haired one supports Agni and moisture, and heaven and earth. He is all sky to look upon. The long-haired one is called this light." The long hair of the *muni* is mentioned seven times in the hymn. In the second verse the *munis* (now in the plural) are called *vātaraśanāḥ* ("girdled with the wind"), and they are said to wear dirty clothes (*malāḥ*). Some scholars have seen in the term *vātaraśana* a reference to their naked condition; it would then be a synonym of the later term *digambara* ("sky-clad" = naked) commonly used with reference to ascetic nudity.[22] It is, however, inconsistent for these men to be described in the same verse both as naked and as wearing dirty clothes. The term is more appropriately interpreted in the light of the *munis*' association with the wind, a recurrent theme in the hymn. The second half of the verse in which the term appears reads: "They follow the wind's swift course and go where the gods have gone before." Other verses echo the same theme: (3): "we have pressed on into the wind"; (4): "The *muni* . . . flies through the atmosphere"; (5): He is "the steed of the wind and the friend of the wind"; (7): "The wind has churned for him." Flying through the air and

18. MN I, 285–86, 400, II, 54; AN I, 180, III, 228.; Jāt I, 57, 187. The two terms also appear in the Greek and Latin accounts of India: Majumdar 1960, 425–48.

19. The *Taittirīya Āraṇyaka* and the *Bṛhadāraṇyaka Upaniṣad* probably predate Aśoka by at least a couple of centuries. The Dharmasūtras of Baudhāyana and Gautama also are probably somewhat older than Aśoka. For the dates of their composition, see section 3.4.

20. TĀ 2.7: *vātaraśanā ha vā ṛṣayaḥ śramaṇā ūrdhvamanthino babhūvus tān ṛṣayo 'rtham āyaṃs te nilāyam acaraṃs te 'nupraviśuḥ kūṣmāṇḍāni tāṃs teṣv anvavindañ chraddhayā ca tapasā ca..* For a detailed discussion of this text see Malamoud 1977.

21. See Keith 1925, 402; Bhandarkar 1940, 53; Pande 1957, 258–61; Ghurye 1964, 11f; Singh 1972, 182–83.

22. Geldner (1951, III, 369, n. 2) remarks: "D.h. nackten." Similar interpretations are given by Ghurye 1964, 12; Pande 1978, 23–25; Malamoud 1977, 73. Sāyaṇa, on the contrary, in his commentary on this verse, explains it as a patronymic: "sons of Vātaraśana." It is doubtful that the term designates a class within the Ṛgvedic context.

being carried by the force of the wind are characteristics of a *muni*'s state. When the term is interpreted within this context, "girdled with the wind" probably means that the *munis*' garments are swirled or blown by the wind or that the wind swirled around their bodies, rather than that they went about naked.

The third verse of the hymn states that the *munis* are *unmaditā maunyena*. The term *unmadita*, frequently used in later literature with reference to ascetic behavior,[23] can refer to madness, intoxication, frenzy, or trance. The *munis* are thus intoxicated, frenzied, in a trance, or out of their mind as a result of or by the power of their "munihood." This may indicate that their status as *muni* was closely associated with special psychic states or powers that they exhibited. "The prattle of the *muni* Aitasa" (*aitasapralāpa*) in the *Aitareya Brāhmaṇa* (7.33) also suggests the irrational quality of a *muni*'s trance. In the latter episode his son covers Aitasa's mouth while he was prattling and remarks, "our father has gone out of his mind." The *munis* are said to roam wild areas, to tread the path of beasts, Gandharvas, and Apsarases. They drink from the same cup as Rudra, a god associated with asceticism and the wilderness.[24]

By the time of the *Taittirīya Āraṇyaka*, however, the meaning of the term *vātaraśana* appears to have undergone some changes. The author of this text uses the term no longer as an adjective but as a noun denominating a class of *ṛṣis*.[25] In an earlier passage the same text (TĀ 1.23) describes how three classes of *ṛṣis*—Aruṇa, Ketu, and Vātaraśana—originated from the flesh that fell off when Prajāpati shook his body after he had performed austerities (*tapas*). The *ṛṣis* ("seers") are regarded as the founding fathers of the Brāhmaṇical tradition. They discovered the knowledge contained in the Veda as well as in all other branches of learning. This title is one of the highest honors that the authors of Brāhmaṇical texts bestow on a person. Its use here indicates that the Vātaraśanas were considered to have belonged to that elite class of Brāhmaṇical ancestors. It is highly significant, therefore, that the terms *śramaṇa* and *ūrdhvamanthin* are used to describe them.

The latter term is clearly an adjective qualifying *ṛṣi*. The ambiguity of the term *manthin* makes the meaning of the compound word unclear. *Manthin* can refer to the penis as well as to the sperm (Malamoud 1977, 73). If it refers to the penis, the compound means "ithyphallic." It would then be a synonym of *ūrdhvaliṅga*, the more common term in later literature, and would confirm the *muni*s' relationship to the ithyphallic god Rudra-Śiva already hinted at in RV 10.136.7. If, on the other hand, *manthin* means sperm, the compound means "one who retains his sperm." It would then be a synonym

23. See, for example, JU 69: *anunmattā unmattavad ācarantaḥ*—"although they are sane, they behave like madmen." The NpU (154) says that an ascetic "acts like a fool, a lunatic, or a goblin" (*bālonmattapiśācavat*).

24. The information on the muni in other early vedic texts is extremely meager. The RV 8.17.14 (= SV I.275) calls Indra "the friend of *munis*," and the RV 7.56.8 says that the wind roars like a *muni*. The AV 8.6.17 lists "*muni*'s hair" among the evil ones exorcised from a woman. In verse 5 of the same hymn an *asura* ("demon") is called *keśī* ("long-haired"). See also AV 7.74.1; Bloomfield 1899, 98; Malamoud 1977, 73.

25. The point the TĀ text (2.7) wants to make is not that these *munis* were girdled with the wind, but that the Vātaraśana class of *munis* were *śramaṇas* and *ūrdhvamanthins*. Malamoud's (1977, 72) translation—"Les ceinturés de vent étaient des *ṛṣi* sramanes pleins de continence"—does not take into account this change in meaning of the term or its use as a class name earlier in the text. Sāyaṇa (on TĀ) with greater perspicacity takes it as a patronymic and refers to the earlier chapter of the text that distinguishes the three classes.

of the more common *ūrdhvaretas*. In either case, however, the adjective appears to indicate that the Vātaraśana *ṛṣis* practiced sexual control of some kind. This does not necessarily imply, however, that they practiced total continence or celibacy.[26]

Now the syntax of this passage clearly demands that *śramaṇa* should have the same syntactical function as *ūrdhvamanthin;* both should be taken as adjectives that describe the seers. Those who interpret *śramaṇa* to indicate a class of ascetics to which the seers belong are assigning to this term a meaning derived from other, and possibly later, contexts.[27] The meaning of this term, moreover, should not be simply assumed to be the same as in these later ascetical contexts. We need to search for its meaning within the context of the vedic use of the related terms √*śram* and *śrama*. *Śramaṇa* in that context obviously means a person who is in the habit of performing *śrama*. Far from separating these seers from the vedic ritual tradition, therefore, *śramaṇa* places them right at the center of that tradition. Those who see them as non-Brāhmaṇical, anti-Brāhmaṇical, or even non-Aryan precursors of later sectarian ascetics are drawing conclusions that far outstrip the available evidence.[28]

The use of the title *ṛṣi*, moreover, demonstrates that the Vātaraśanas were not only regarded as Brahmins but also as part of the elite group of mythical ancestors who were the founders of the Brāhmaṇical tradition. The use of the term *śramaṇa* to describe them, however, indicates that they were a group of special people given to practices and a life style far from common. Taken together with the term *vātaraśana* and its historical link to the *muni*, we may not be too wrong in concluding that the adjective *śramaṇa* referred to their uncommonly strenuous way of life.

We come across this term also in a text of the White Yajurveda, the *Bṛhadāraṇyaka Upaniṣad*, generally regarded as one of the earliest of the Upaniṣads. Describing the state of deep sleep in which there are no dreams or desires and in which the individual is in the embrace of the self, the Upaniṣad declares:

> In this state a father is a not a father, a mother is not a mother, worlds are not worlds, gods are not gods, the Vedas are not Vedas, a thief is not a thief, an abortionist is not an abortionist, a Cāṇḍāla is not a Cāṇḍāla, a Paulkasa is not a Paulkasa,[29] a *śramaṇa* is not a *śramaṇa*, and a *tāpasa* is not a *tāpasa*. (BāU 4.3.22)

In this passage the two terms *śramaṇa* and *tāpasa* are clearly nouns denoting classes of people, just as the other words of the list. It is unclear, however, whether these two terms refer to well-established and identifiable groups, in the same way as do, for example, the terms gods, Vedas, and Cāṇḍālas, or whether they indicate broad categories into which individuals fall because of their behavior, as in the case of thieves and abortionists. I prefer to interpret them in the latter sense, which corresponds to the understanding of *śrama* and *tapas* in the vedic literature, than to read into them the later classification of ascetics

26. This interpretation is made by Malamoud 1977, 72, when he translates the term as "pleins de continence." See also Sharma 1939, 19.

27. See, for example, Malamoud 1977, 73; Sharma 1939, 19.

28. For such interpretations, see Bhandarkar 1940, 53; Chakraborti 1973, 14; Barua 1921, 242; Chanda 1934, 98; Sharma 1939, 18–20; Pande 1978.

29. A Cāṇḍāla is an outcaste at the lowest end of the social hierarchy. Even his touch pollutes an upper-caste person. A Paulkasa is a similar social outcaste, the offspring of a low-caste father and an upper-caste mother.

into hermits (*tāpasa*) and wandering ascetics.[30] It is clear, however, that as in the *Taittirīya* passage, so here too *śramaṇas* belong to the Brāhmaṇical tradition.

The relationship of *śramaṇa* to the vedic ritual tradition is underscored by the use of the related term *śrāmaṇaka* in the Dharmasūtras with reference to the sacred fire of a hermit. The expression *śrāmaṇakenāgnim ādhāya* ("having installed the fire according to the *śrāmaṇaka* procedure") occurs in three Sūtras.[31] Contrary to Bühler, it is clear that *śrāmaṇaka* does not refer to a text but to a special procedure for establishing the sacred fire.[32] The *Vaikhānasa Dharmasūtra* uses the compound word *śrāmaṇakāgni* where *śrāmaṇaka* appears to be the designation of the hermit's fire rather than of the procedure for its establishment.[33] The *Vaikhānasa* also contains a description of the procedure for installing the *śrāmaṇaka* fire, although it is highly unlikely that the authors of the early Sūtras had in mind the procedure described in this rather late text.

The significant point for our discussion, however, is that the Dharma texts use this term not only within the context of what is obviously a Brāhmaṇical institution but also with specific reference to the ritual fire and the ritual activity of a hermit. This relationship between *śramaṇa* and ritual activities is further confirmed by the *Baudhāyana Śrautasūtra* (16.30), which, in describing a sacrificial rite of *munis*, refers to the performer of this sacrifice as *śramaṇa*.[34]

From the use of *śramaṇa* in the early Brāhmaṇical literature we can draw the following conclusions. The term is used predominantly in an adjectival sense to describe a special way of life of certain seers, although the literature does not provide details of that life. It is reasonable to assume, however, that this mode of life was considered in some way extraordinary and that it incorporated the ritual exertions indicated by the term

30. Śaṃkara, for example, in his commentary on this passage interprets the former as a *saṃnyāsin* and the latter as a *vānapratha*. It is always a temptation to read earlier texts in the light of later classificatory schemes in imitation of the commentators, a temptation that historians must clearly guard against. The terms *śrama* and *tapas*, as we have seen (section 1.1.1), are often coupled in early texts to refer to two closely related sets of activities. The derivative nouns, *śramaṇa* and *tāpasa*, very likely are similarly coupled in this passage.

31. BDh 2.11.15; GDh 3.27; VaDh 9.10.

32. At GDh 3.27 and VaDh 9.10 Bühler translates *śrāmaṇakena* as "according to the (rule of the) Śrāmaṇaka (Sūtra)," whereas at BDh 2.11.15 he translates it as "according to the Śrāmaṇaka (rule)." Bühler probably followed the explanations of Maskarin and Haradatta (on GDh 3.27) who take the term to refer to the "Vaikhānasa Treatise" (*vaikhānasaśāstra*). Govinda Svāmin (on BDh 2.11.15) more accurately explains: *śrāmaṇo nāmādhānavidhir asti vaikhānasaśāstre, tenāgnim ādhāya*—"in the Vaikhānasa Treatise there is a procedure named *śrāmaṇa* for establishing a fire; having established the fire according to that." See also MBh 1.81.12; 12.9.11; 12.21.15; 15.25.13; 15.35.4.

33. VaiDh 1.6,7; 2.1,4,5. See also VaiG 1.8. At the offering of clarified butter (*āghāra*) in the *śrāmaṇaka* fire, special mantras are recited. These are given in the *Vaikhānasa Saṃhitā* and they include the phrase *śrāmaṇakayajñam āvāhayāmi*—"I invite the *śrāmaṇaka* sacrifice." See Caland's translation of the VaiDh 8.6, p. 188–89. The *Āgniveśya Gṛhyasūtra* (2.7.10), again a rather late work, uses the term *śramaṇa* with reference to this fire.

34. The *Mahābhārata* (12.21.14) contains the expression *vidhinā śrāmaṇena* ("according to the *śrāmaṇa* rule") with reference to the manner in which a king should live in a forest after he has abdicated in favor of his son. We can also find instances in the epic literature where the term *śramaṇa* is used with reference to a variety of Brāhmaṇical ascetics: Rām 1.1.46; 1.13.8; 3.69.19; 3.70.7; 4.18.31 (where the reference is uncertain); MBh 12.50.18; 13.135.104 (where it is one of Viṣṇu's epithets). It is uncertain whether the naked *śramaṇa* in MBh 1.3.136 is a Brahmin.

śrama. The term in its use in the Brāhmaṇical documents, however, implies no opposition to either Brahmins or householders; in all likelihood it did not refer to an identifiable class of people, much less to ascetic groups as it does in later literature.

1.1.3 Āśrama *as a Place and as a Way of Life*

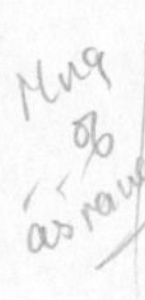

Ancient Indian literature reveals two meanings of the term *āśrama.* The first is that of a residence where holy people live and perform religious austerities. When it refers to such a residence, the term is commonly translated as "hermitage." This is by far its most common meaning; it is so used in Brāhmaṇical, Buddhist, and Jain literary sources, as well as in what might be called non-religious texts such as drama, poetry, and fables. The second meaning of the term is that of a religious or holy way of life. The latter is, in all likelihood, a technical usage, as it occurs exclusively in Brāhmaṇical literature and mainly within the context of the *āśrama* system.

Although there appears to be a scholarly consensus that *āśrama* refers to a place or a mode of life associated with religious exertion,[35] there is a minority opinion which takes *āśrama* to mean a place of rest.[36] Under this hypothesis the prefix "*ā*" would have to be construed as the strong vowel grade (*vṛddhi*) of the privative prefix "*a*". *Śrama,* moreover, would have to be taken in its first meaning, namely fatigue, which has no religious connotation. According to this hypothesis, therefore, *āśrama* is derived from *a-śrama* ("lack of fatigue"). The *Rāmāyaṇa* (4.13.16) appears to support this derivation when it calls the hermitage (*āśrama*) of the Saptajanāḥ sages "a place that destroys fatigue" (*śramanāśana*).[37] In all likelihood, however, the poet is here only attempting to draw a picture of one aspect of a hermitage, the peace and quiet of its surroundings and inhabitants, by the use of what I would call "phonetic etymology," a frequent practice in Indian literature, often amounting to nothing more than a play on the phonetic similarity between words.[38] If this were the original meaning it is difficult to explain how the term could have been used with reference to religious modes of life which the tradition considers as entailing ceaseless effort and toil.[39] The Indian grammatical tra-

35. Gonda 1960–63, I, 287 n. 11; Sprockhoff 1976, 5; Winternitz 1926, 227; Sharma 1939, 14–15; Deussen 1909, 128; Rhys Davids 1903, 249; Kane 1974, II.1, 425.

36. Macdonell and Keith 1912, I, 68, translate it as "resting place," and they are followed by Prabhu 1954, 83. Miller and Wertz (1976, 6) more explicitly regard the word as a negative: "*Āśrama,* the negative of the Sanskrit root *śram* (to exert oneself), means 'a place of peace.'" Strictly it could not be the negative, since the privative suffix is not "*ā*" but the short "*a*".

37. A similar expression occurs also in the MBh 3.82.*423: *āśramaṃ śramaśokavināśanam*—"an *āśrama* that destroys fatigue and sorrow."

38. Quite frequently Indian authors draw etymological relationships between words that have phonetic similarities. They then proceed to uncover semantic equivalences based on such phonetic etymologies. This is clearly a pedagogical strategy, and the authors' intent is not to teach etymologies but to draw out what they regard as the innermost and the most significant meaning of a term. Given the advances made by Indian grammarians, it is quite likely that these authors usually know the grammatically correct etymologies of the terms whose meanings they seek to elucidate through phonetic equivalences.

39. Those who wish to exalt the householder often use the argument that the householder's life is far more difficult (*duṣkara*) than those of the other *āśramas*: MBh 12.20.6–14; 12.23.6; 12.261.58. Renouncers have an easy life (*śramasyoparama*: MBh 12.261.10), whereas the householders toil (*śrama*: MBh 12.261.59). See also MDh 2.168 where *śrama* as "religious exertion or toil" is used probably with reference to the *āśramas.*

dition, moreover, clearly considers the suffix to be the particle "*ā*" rather than the privative.[40]

The exact modification of meaning that the prefix "*ā*" imparts to the term *śrama*, however, is unclear. The modification is certainly not as radical as, for example, when this prefix is used before verbs of motion.[41] Indeed, outside the lexicons I have not found a single example of the prefix "*ā*" used with a verbal form of √*śram*.[42] The compound occurs only in the nominal form *āśrama* and in its derivatives such as *āśramin*. The only explanation of the prefix "*ā*" to be found among commentators is that it indicates emphasis and intensity.[43] The lexicographers, moreover, are unanimous in explaining *āśrama* as religious exertion.

Āśrama, we may conclude, refers to religious exertion. The term, however, is used in ancient Indian literature with two distinct but related meanings: it refers to both a residence for and a mode of life devoted to religious exertion. Which of these is the root meaning from which the other is derived? Winternitz (1926, 227) gives priority to the latter:

> The word *āśrama* (from the same root *śram* as *śramaṇa*) probably denoted at first "the religious exertion" of *śramaṇas*, ascetics and forest dwellers, and consequently it also received the meaning "place for religious exertion," "hermitage."

Sharma (1939, 14) agrees with Winternitz. Sprockhoff[44] also gives priority to a mode of life. According to him, however, the term originally referred to the life of a householder, and he strongly—and properly—objects to Winternitz's association of *āśrama* with the life of *śramaṇas*.

The evidence, however, appears to point the other way; the more basic meaning of *āśrama*, I believe, is that of a residence for religious exertion. The term is used with reference to a mode of life mainly within the confines of the *āśrama* system.[45] The latter

40. The term is derived from *ā* + √*śram* by adding the *ghañ* suffix (= *a*), according to Pāṇini, *Aṣṭādhyāyī*, 3.3.19. The *vṛddhi* of the radical vowel, which should normally occur here (e.g., *ārāma*, *āvāsa*) is suppressed according to Pāṇini, ibid., 7.3.34. See also the lexicographical references in the following notes.

41. In verbs of motion the prefix changes the direction of the motion, thus imparting a meaning opposite to that of the simple verb: e.g., √*gam*—"to go," and *ā*-√*gam*—"to come"; √*dā*—"to give," and *ā*-√*dā*—"to receive."

42. The verb *āśrāmyati* is used by lexicographers to explain the etymology of *āśrama*, but it is probably an artificial term serving a grammatical purpose: *asmiṃś catuṣṭake āśrāmyanti tapasyanty asminn āśrame pratyekaṃ vartate*—"in these four they toil, they do austerities; in this *āśrama* a person lives, in one at a time" (Kṣīrasvāmin on Amarasiṃha's *Amarakośa* 2.7.3). Bhānuji Dīkṣita (on *Amarakośa* 2.7.3–4) indicates the double meaning as place and way of life: *āśrāmyanty atra anena va*—"they toil here or by means of it." Haradatta (on ĀpDh 2.21.1) appears to follow the lexicographers: *āśrāmyanty eṣu śreyo' rthinaḥ puruṣā ity āśramāḥ*—"*āśramas* get their meaning by the fact that people who seek bliss toil in them." The *Gaṇapāṭha* (on Pāṇini, *Aṣṭādhyāyī*, 2.4.31, no. 117) lists the term among those that can be declined either as a masculine or as a neuter noun. See also Amarasiṃha's *Amarakośa* 2.7.4; Durgasiṃha, *Liṅgānuśāsana*, 66.

43. Bhānuji Dīkṣita on Amarasiṃha's *Amarakośa* 2.7.3–4 explains: *ā samantāc chramo 'tra*—"there is toil all around (or completely) here." A similar explanation of "*ā*" in the term *ānīla* ("dark") is given by Mallinātha in his commentary on Kālidāsa's *Raghuvaṃśa*, 3.8.

44. Sprockhoff 1976, 5, 54; 1979, 412 n. 139; 1981, 82. Deussen (1909, 128) gives the two meanings and enigmatically remarks: "It may be doubted which of the two meanings is the original."

45. I shall discuss below the few occurrences alluded to by Sprockhoff and Meyer in support of the hypothesis that the term first referred to the life of a householder.

should be regarded, therefore, as a technical use. When the term is used outside that context it invariably refers to a residence. In the *Bṛhaddevatā* (5.64; 6.99), in the *Gopatha Brāhmaṇa* (1.2.8), and with great frequency in the two epics and in Sanskrit belles lettres and fables, the term is used with reference to the residence of a special type of Brahmin.[46] This, moreover, is the only meaning of the term in all non-Brāhmaṇical literature, including the Pāli Canon. It is difficult to see how such a common and broad use of the term could have been derived from its more technical and narrow use. The presumption clearly has to be that the latter must be a secondary and derived meaning.

Within the Indian context, however, the distinction between these two meanings and the priority of the one over the other are not issues as important as they might appear to be. Ancient Indian thought closely associated a definite pattern of behavior or conduct with a specific place or region. A good example of this tendency is the claim that the customs prevailing in a region of north-central India called Āryāvarta ("region of the Āryas") are to be regarded as authoritative on questions of *dharma*.[47] Indeed, even the Indian grammarians defined the cultured elites (*śiṣṭa*) who spoke proper Sanskrit "by their place of residence (*nivāsa*) and their way of life (*ācāra*). And that way of life is found only in Āryāvarta."[48] Manu (MDh 2.22–24) goes as far as to advise the Āryas to live only in that region. A tale containing a discussion between a jackal and a tiger recorded in the *Mahābhārata* (12.112) is instructive with regard to the common Indian association between proper conduct and proper place. The jackal, whose normal place of residence is a cemetery, a place universally regarded as impure, argues against that common association between virtue and geography. One can attain contemplation even in a cemetery, the jackal argues, while an *āśrama* (probably a hermitage) is not necessarily a mark of righteousness.

> One kills a Brahmin in an *āśrama*,
> One gives a cow in a non-*āśrama*.
> Does the former not constitute a sin?
> And that gift, has it been given in vain?
> (MBh 12.112.14)

Given the close association between place of habitation and way of life, it did not require a giant semantic leap to call by the name *āśrama* the life of those who lived in *āśramas*. Conversely, we find that the modes of life of those belonging to the *āśramas* of student, householder, and hermit are often referred to by their respective residences: teacher's house, home, and forest or wilderness.[49] The verb √*vas* ("to dwell"), more-

46. In the *Rāmāyaṇa* I have been able to find only one instance (2.98.58) where the term is used with reference to a mode of life, that too clearly within the context of the *āśrama* system (see section 3.4.1). Residence is, of course, the common meaning of the term in later Sanskrit belles lettres (*kāvya*) and drama.

47. BDh 1.1.2.9–12; VaDh 1.8–15. With reference to the Brahmāvarta, a similarly holy region, Manu (MDh 2.20) advises: "All people on earth should learn their respective mores from a Brahmin born in that country."

48. Patañjali, *Mahābhāṣya* on Pāṇini, *Aṣṭādhyāyī*, 6.3.109 (Kielhorn edition, III, 174). On this question see the interesting comments of Deshpande 1985: 131–36.

49. ĀpDh 2.21.1 calls the first simply *ācāryakulam* ("teacher's family or house") and the MBh 12.174.8(2) uses the expression *gurukulavāsaḥ* ("dwelling at the teacher's house"). Manu (MDh 4.1; 6.33) speaks of living at the teacher's house, at home, and in the forest. The householder's state is often called *gṛhāśrama* ("house-*āśrama*"): MDh 6.1; ViDh 33.2; 58.1; 59.1, 27, 28, 29; MBh 1.3.83; 3.2.59; 12.61.4,12; 12.66.18; 12.184.17. Cf. also YDh 3.56; JU 64.3; MDh 6.33.

over, is used regularly with reference to the pursuance of an *āśrama*, reinforcing again the association between conduct and place.[50] The *Mahābhārata* (3.134.10), for example, calls the four *āśrama*s "four houses" (*niketana*).

1.1.4 The Original Meaning of Āśrama

Irrespective of whether its root meaning is residence or mode of life, the crucial question for our study is *whose* residence or way of life was at first characterized as *āśrama*. On the basis of the available evidence it is not possible to give a precise or certain answer to that question. It is even unclear whether during the earliest period of its use the term referred to an identifiable class of people.

It is nevertheless possible, I believe, to answer the question in a general way by showing what the term certainly did not mean and, more positively, by indicating the types of people and activities that the term may have comprehended. In what follows I expect to demonstrate that (1) *āśrama* did not refer to ascetic habitats or modes of life, if by ascetic we understand values and institutions that oppose the Brāhmaṇical value system centered around the householder;[51] (2) on the contrary, *āśrama* is fundamentally a Brāhmaṇical concept and refers to habitats and life styles dedicated to the principal obligations of a Brāhmaṇical householder; (3) originally and outside the context of the *āśrama* system, nevertheless, the term did not refer to simply any householder but to exceptional Brahmins who dedicated their lives in an extraordinary manner to religious exercise (*śrama*), living, in all likelihood, in areas somewhat removed from villages and towns.

There is no evidence to support Winternitz's (1926, 227) view that *āśrama* "denoted at first 'the religious exertion' of *śramaṇa*s, ascetics and forest dwellers." The etymological connection between the two terms is clearly insufficient evidence to draw such a conclusion. *Āśrama* is fundamentally a Brāhmaṇical institution and, as we shall see, it is depicted as such even in non-Brāhmaṇical sources. We have seen, moreover, the use of the term *śramaṇa* within strictly Brāhmaṇical contexts. We have also seen the use of the term *śrāmaṇika* with reference to the ritual fire of Brāhmaṇical hermits whose residence many sources identify as *āśrama*.[52] In the epics, too, residents of *āśrama*s are occasionally identified as *śramaṇa*.[53] These, however, are not sufficient grounds for concluding that *āśrama* originally meant the residence or life style of Brāhmaṇical *śramaṇa*s, if this is taken to mean Brāhmaṇical ascetics living celibate lives in the wilderness. Indeed, within the Brāhmaṇical context both *śramaṇa* and *āśrama* are associated with the activity central to the Brāhmaṇical view of *dharma*, namely the sacrifice.

One reason why scholars have attempted to find a connection between *āśrama* and anti-Brāhmaṇical ascetical institutions is the prevalent but mistaken view (see section 3.3.1) that the *āśrama* system was created by Brahmins to stem the tide of the ascetical movement by coopting into the Brāhmaṇical system the very institutions that opposed it

50. VaDh 7.3 (*āvaset*); MDh 4.1 (*uṣitvā gurau*); 5.169 (*gṛhe vaset*); 6.1 (*vane vaset*); ViDh 51.66 (*gṛhe gurāv araṇye vā nivasan*); MBh 12.235.1; 12.313.17–20.

51. For the major aspects of this value system, see section 2.1.

52. BDh 3.3.20; VaiDh 2.2, 3.

53. Rām 1.1.46; 1.13.8; 3.69.19; 3.70.7; MBh 12.150.18; 13.135.104. Cf. also MBh 1.3.136, where the reference may be to a non-Brāhmaṇical ascetic.

(Heesterman 1964, 24). If *āśrama* was an ascetic concept, the argument goes, then its use with reference to the Brāhmaṇical householder is meant to indicate that a householder's life is as good as an ascetic's. The very opposite, as we shall see (section 3.3.4), appears to have been the case. The authors of the *āśrama* system were coopting a good Brāhmaṇical term to indicate that the ascetic life was as good as the ideal Brāhmaṇical life expressed by the term *āśrama*.

Our discussion of the meaning of *śrama* also supports the association of *āśrama* with the central values and activities of Brāhmaṇism, values and activities that form the basis of the Brāhmaṇical theology of the householder. In several of his recent writings Sprockhoff[54] has argued strongly for this position. According to Sprockhoff, *āśrama* originally referred to the life of a householder. This view was already put forward by Meyer (1927, 316–17) in his discussion of the *pariṣad* ("Brāhmaṇical council": see section 7.4).

One problem with Meyer's and Sprockhoff's interpretations is that they take *āśrama* to refer to a householder's life in general and not merely to extraordinary householders who dedicated their life totally to the Brāhmaṇical ideals. I think this is too broad an application. If such a generic use was current in the Brāhmaṇical tradition we should expect to find it in discussions about marriage and about the duties of a householder. As we have noted, it is absent in the early Brāhmaṇa texts, and even the Dharmasūtras never use it in their discussion of the householder outside the narrow confines of the *āśrama* system. The term is conspicuous by its absence in the early Gṛhyasūtras, which deal specifically with domestic rites including marriage. If it was a common term for a Brāhmaṇical householder, moreover, we may expect to find it with that meaning in Buddhist and other non-Brāhmaṇical sources.

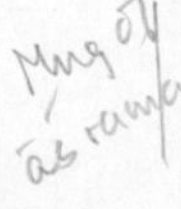

The very newness of the term *āśrama* argues against the contention that it meant simply the life of a householder. Neologisms are rarely coined to refer to well-known ideas or institutions; they are mostly resorted to when people are groping for a way to express something new, or at the very least, a new aspect of something old. It makes more sense, therefore, to see it as a term coined to indicate the extraordinary life and dwelling adopted by some exceptional Brahmins.

The evidence from Brāhmaṇical and Buddhist sources, in fact, indicates that *āśrama* probably had just such a restricted meaning. It appears that the term was applied not to just any householder but to the place and/or life of a very special category of Brāhmaṇical householders. These householders did not constitute a uniform category of people. There was, for example, quite an ancient distinction between Brahmins devoted to learning and scholarship (*śrotriya*) and those who performed household duties (*gṛhamedhin*). The early literature on *dharma* also establishes distinctions between householders on the basis of their livelihood.[55] It appears that those who were associated with the *āśrama*s constituted a similar special class different from common householders.

The Pāli term *assama* (Sk. *āśrama*) is used with some frequency in the Buddhist Canon. Given the uncertainty of the dates of the various texts that form the Pāli Canon, it

54. Sprockhoff 1976, 1979, 1981, 1984. On the interpretation of *vṛddhāśrama* ("*āśrama* of the aged"), see Sprockhoff 1987, 250.

55. JB 2.225. See Heesterman 1964, 11; Sprockhoff 1984, 21–25; and section 6.1.1–2.

is difficult to draw accurate historical conclusions from the Pāli usage of the term. A wide spectrum of texts in the Canon, however, use this term with a very similar, if not identical, meaning.[56] This consistency may permit us to conclude that it must correspond at least roughly to the dominant meaning of the term also in the Brāhmaṇical society to which these texts refer.

Assama is used in the Pāli Canon invariably with reference to a residence not of any Brahmin householder but of a special type of Brahmin. Such Brahmins are often, but not always, called *jaṭila*, indicating that they were distinguished by their matted hair.[57] These *assamas* were located in the wilderness, that is in the uninhabited area outside a village or town.[58] There are indications that they were located not far from a village; when Ānanda, for example, asks the Buddha to visit Rammaka's *assama* after begging in the city of Sāvatthi, he says that it is not very far (*avidūra:* MN I, 160).

A constant feature of an *assama* is the presence of the sacred fire. Some texts speak of a fire stall in which the sacred fire was kept and *jaṭilas* are given the epithet "fire-worshipping."[59] A dominant feature of the life of these Brahmins, as depicted in the Pāli sources, was the worship of the sacred fire. Furthermore, they did not always live solitary or celibate lives. We hear of families, possibly groups of related families, living in an *assama*. Sexual activity clearly took place within these communities. When Sela[60] visits Keṇiya, for example, and sees all the residents of the *assama* busy preparing a feast he thinks that there is going to be a marriage. The terms *paṇṇakuṭī* and *paṇṇasālā* ("hut made with leaves"), it appears, are used as equivalents of *assama*.[61]

Several Buddhist texts note that living in an *assama* was the normal life of the earliest Brahmins who were dedicated to holiness. The Brāhmaṇical seers (*ṛṣi*, Pāli *isi*) are said to have followed this mode of life. The term *isipabbajja* ("the *ṛṣi*'s mode of going forth") is used to indicate the undertaking of this mode of life. These holy ancestors are contrasted by the Buddhists with the unholy life of present-day Brahmins who live in villages (DN I, 104; III, 94).

The Buddhist admiration for Brahmins living in *assamas* is clear. They were exempted, for example, from the probationary period (*parivāsa*) of four months prior to their initial admission into the Buddhist monastic order (Vin 1, 71). The story of the conversion of the three Kassapa brothers (Vin 1, 24–38), who were *jaṭila* Brahmins living in *āśramas*, is probably intended to demonstrate the victory of the Buddha over the best that Brāhmaṇism had to offer. The encounter of the Buddha in the company of Uruvela Kassapa, the most senior of the three, with King Bimbisāra of Magadha is instructive. Bimbisāra wonders aloud whether the Buddha has become Kassapa's disciple or vice versa. Then follows the verse account of the Buddha's question and Kassapa's reply:

> What knowledge have you gained, O inhabitant of Uruvelā, that has induced you, who were renowned for your penances, to forsake your sacred fire? I ask

56. For a listing of these occurrences, see *Critical Pāli Dictionary*, pp. 521–22, and *Pāli Tipiṭakaṃ Concordance*, p. 295.

57. Vin 1, 24–38; DN II, 339. The *jaṭila* manner of wearing the hair—either matted or braided—is closely associated with Brahmins. It is prescribed in ĀpDh 1.2.31–32 for even Brāhmaṇical students.

58. DN II, 339.

59. See Vin 1, 71; DN II, 339; MN 1, 501.

60. See the *Selasutta* in SuN p. 102–12; MN II, 146. For a variant of the story see Vin 1, 245.

61. See, for example, Jāt II, 283–85; MN II, 154–55; DN II, 339.

> you, Kassapa, this question: How is it that your fire sacrifice has become deserted?
>
> It is visible things and sounds, and also tastes, pleasures and woman that the sacrifices speak of; because I understood that whatever belongs to existence is filth, therefore I took no more delight in sacrifices and offerings.[62]

These verses highlight both the centrality of the fire sacrifice in the life of these Brāhmaṇical holy men and the significance attached to its abandonment in Buddhist asceticism.

The Buddhist accounts are corroborated by Brāhmaṇical evidence. The *Bṛhaddevatā,* which is assigned to the fifth century B.C.E., uses the term *āśrama* in two episodes. The first is the story of Śyāvāśva (BṛD, 5.50–81), the son of the *ṛṣi* Arcanānas and the grandson of the *ṛṣi* Atri. All three are said to have lived in an *āśrama* (BṛD 5.64). Arcanānas and Śyāvāśva once went to king Rathavīti Dārbhya's palace to perform a sacrifice for the king. When they saw the king's daughter, Śyāvāśva promptly fell in love with her, while Arcanānas, for his part, thought she would make a perfect daughter-in-law. The story ends with Śyāvāśva marrying the king's daughter. The second story is about a girl named Apālā, who is the daughter of Atri and lived in the *āśrama* of her father (BṛD 6.99). Here it is the god Indra who falls in love with her and cures her skin disease.[63]

Several points of these stories are significant for our investigation. All these *ṛṣi*s, who lived in *āśrama*s, were married and had children; indeed, Arcanānas used the occasion of the sacrifice to obtain a good wife for his son. They not only performed the fire rituals, but also officiated at sacrifices for important people in society.

The two epics are also full of references to and descriptions of *āśrama*s,[64] the inhabitants of which were married and had children. The sacred fire and fire rituals were the major focus of their lives.

One point clearly emerges from the above discussion: the inhabitants of these *āśrama*s are depicted as following a life style radically different from that of forest hermits (*vānaprastha*) described in later literature within the context of the *āśrama* system. The latter were celibates who often assumed this life style only in their old age. The confusion that one sees in the epic and later literature is caused by the conflation of several types of eremitical asceticism into a single institution. At some point, moreover, the *āśrama* mode of life must have become idealized, an ideal that was projected back to the ancient *ṛṣi*s, the founding fathers of the Brāhmaṇical tradition.

What is significant for our study, however, is that the life of the *āśrama*-dwelling Brahmins was much closer to that expected of all Brāhmaṇical householders than to later ascetic modes of life, and that in its early usage *āśrama* defined more the ideal life of a Brahmin householder than that of an ascetic. This is the real significance of Meyer's and Sprockhoff's insights. This meaning, furthermore, closely follows the meaning of *śrama* in the vedic literature, lending further support to its priority.

62. Vin 1, 36. Rhys Davids and Oldenberg's translation, p. 138.

63. The *Gopatha Brāhmaṇa* is the only one to use *āśrama*. There also it is a place of residence of *ṛṣi*s. The *Gopatha,* however, according to Keith (TS, tr. I, p. ciii), "is certainly the latest of the Brāhmaṇas."

64. For a long description of *āśrama*s in the *Rāmāyaṇa* see Vyas 1967, 266-73.

In this context, Sprockhoff's[65] explanation of the compound words *āśramapāra* and *atyāśramin* makes much better sense than those of earlier scholars who attempted to explain them within the context of the *āśrama* system. The former term occurs in the *Laghu-Saṃnyāsa Upaniṣad* (15.2). With reference to a Brahmin who has maintained the vedic fires and who has recovered after being at the point of death, the text states: *svastho vāśramapāraṃ gaccheyam iti*—"or if he recovers he resolves: 'I wish to go beyond the āśrama.'" The reference here is not to the *āśrama* system. What is meant here, as Sprockhoff (1976, 54) points out, is that the person decides to go beyond his *āśrama*, namely the life of a householder, or more generally the life of sacrifice and procreation. A similar "going beyond" is also the likely meaning of the term *atyāśramin*, which occurs in the *Śvetāśvatara Upaniṣad* (6.21); the term refers to people who have gone beyond the householder's life and not to enlightened people who are not comprehended by the *āśrama* system.[66] In these compounds we already note the expansion of the semantic range of *āśrama* to include all Brahmin householders and not just the exceptional ones living in *āśramas*, an expansion that is evident also in the *āśrama* system.

Even in later times we observe the use of similar compounds that assumes *āśrama* to be the life of a householder. For example, Vasiṣṭha (VaDh 17.52) uses the expression *āśramāntaragatāḥ* to refer to people who have proceeded to an *āśrama* different from that of the householder. The compound *āśramāntara* is used with the meaning "other than a householder" in the *Mahābhārata* and even by medieval authors such as Śaṃkara and Kumārila.[67] This is clearly a vestige of the old meaning ossified in a common compound and further corroborates our conclusion that the term in its earliest usage must have referred to some type of householder.

What conclusions then can we draw from the above discussion with regard to the original meaning of *āśrama*? Two uncertainties make any conclusion extremely tentative. First, we are uncertain about the dates of both the Buddhist and the Brāhmaṇical documents. Second, we are not sure whether the documents we have examined reflect the actual historical conditions prevalent at the time of their composition, or whether they are describing an ideal type according to established literary canons.

With all these caveats, however, I feel we can draw a few safe conclusions with

65. See Sprockhoff 1976, 5, 54; 1979, 412, n. 139; 1981, 82. In the *Laghu-Saṃnyāsa Upaniṣad* (18.1) the term *āśramin* is used to describe a student who has completed his vedic study. It is unclear whether this use supports Sprockhoff's thesis, because in the same passage at 17.12, for example, studentship is called *āśrama*. Sprockhoff's general interpretation of these terms, however, is plausible, even if *āśrama* may not have been a common term for all householders.

66. See Deussen 1906, 368; Winternitz 1926, 217; Weinrich 1929, 83; Silburn in her edition of the ŚvU (Paris, 1948), pp. 1, 75. The term occurs also in the *Kaivalya Upaniṣad*, 24. The same Upaniṣad (5) uses the related term *atyāśramastha*. In later literature that I will discuss in section 8.2, this term is used regularly to mean "beyond the *āśramas*" with reference to the highest type of renouncers or to enlightened renouncers. But in those contexts *āśrama* does not mean merely the householder's state but the usual four *āśramas*.

67. MBh 12.63.21; 12.66.3; 12.308.44; Śaṃkara on VeS 3.4.17–20 (where the compound is used frequently); on BāU 4.5.15 (p. 717); on TU 1.12 (p. 41); Kumārila, *Tantravārtika* on PMS 1.3.4 (p. 110).

regard to the original meaning of *āśrama*. (1) It referred to the place and by extension the life of exceptional Brahmins. (2) The life of these Brahmins centered around the maintenance of and the offering of oblations in the sacred fire. They are also depicted as performing *tapas* ("austerities"), a concept that we saw was closely associated with *śrama*. (3) They were married and had children. The presence of a wife, as we shall see (section 2.1.2) is absolutely necessary for the performance of the fire sacrifice. (4) They lived apart from normal society, even though it is not altogether certain whether the *āśrama*s were always located in the wilderness.

1.2 The Meaning of the Āśrama *System*

I have chosen to call the teaching regarding the four *āśrama*s "the *āśrama* system." I use the term "system" to highlight two of its significant aspects. First, the system seeks to classify or arrange under four rubrics a variety of observable life styles and thereby to make them integral parts of *dharma*. Second, the system links these parts to show a logical plan and establishes an orderly and methodical way of assuming one or several of these life styles. The system, as I have used it, operates primarily at the theological and normative levels. I do not use the term in the sense of an organic whole existing in the world as a physical or a social reality, such as the solar system or the caste system.

1.2.1 The System as a Theological Construct

I stated at the outset that confusion regarding the meaning of the *āśrama* system has impaired most studies of this subject. A major question and the source of much confusion regarding its meaning is whether the *āśrama* system is a social institution that parallels the system of classes and castes (*varṇa* and *jāti*: see section 7.2) with which it is commonly coupled in Brāhmaṇical literature, or whether it is a theological construct designed to impart a theological meaning to social institutions. By social institution I mean an institution that is out there in the world; it may be, of course, at the same time a religious institution. The distinction I wish to draw is not between social and religious institutions—most Indian institutions share characteristics of both—but between such institutions and theological constructs. The latter are not institutions in themselves; they are rather theological discourses regarding social institutions and operate on the plane of ideas.[68]

The following assumptions regarding the meaning of the *āśrama* system govern the method and content of this study. (1) The system originated as a theological construct and *āśrama* in its technical usage within the system is a theological concept. The system,

68. I am aware that social institutions themselves, such as marriage, are cultural constructs. The distinction here is between such cultural constructs and their further theological definitions and evaluations. The primary cultural construct, e.g., marriage, may exist as a social institution shared by all in a given society, whereas the theological construct, e.g., marriage as an *āśrama*, may be accepted by only a subgroup within that society. The one cannot be equated with the other. A similar process of theological evaluation occurs in the Christian sacrament of marriage.

therefore, is only indirectly related to the institutions which are the subject of its theological evaluation. (2) Over time the *āśrama* system underwent significant changes as it evolved from its original formulation to its classical formulation enunciated in the law book of Manu. (3) In both formulations, but especially in the classical, the theological evaluations resulted in legal prescriptions that sought to regulate both the social institutions comprehended by the system and the manner in which individuals lead their lives. The system thus assumed some characteristics of a social institution within the confines of the Brāhmaṇical mainstream.

The justifications for these premises will be developed fully in the course of this volume. Here I wish to highlight a few significant points. The major implication of our first premise concerns the relationship between the four *āśramas* and the corresponding social institutions. All the evidence indicates that they are not coextensive. The institutions of the vedic student and the married householder, and in all likelihood also those of the forest hermit and the wandering mendicant, existed prior to the creation of the *āśrama* system. Even after its creation these institutions continued to exist in large sections of Indian society quite independently of that system.

Within the Brāhmaṇical tradition itself in which it originated, we see ambiguity and ambivalence toward the *āśrama* system during the early period of its history represented by the Dharmasūtras and Gṛhyasūtras. The discussions of vedic initiation, the duties of a student, marriage, and the duties of a householder are carried out in these early Brāhmaṇical documents with no reference to the *āśrama* system.[69] Indeed, many significant Brāhmaṇical texts of this period, such as the Dharmasūtras of Baudhāyana and Gautama, explicitly rejected the theological basis of the system. Even the proponents of the system, moreover, regarded these four institutions as *āśramas* only with reference to Brahmins, or at the most with reference to twice-born Āryas. It is clear, for example, that these early proponents did not regard the condition of a Śūdra householder as an *āśrama*.[70] The same is true even in later periods with regard to lay members of sectarian traditions, such as Buddhists and Jains.

In the last two *āśramas* the coextensiveness is lacking at two levels. On the one hand, there are several ascetical modes of life to which the term *āśrama* does not apply. There is no evidence that Buddhist, Jain, and other non-Brāhmaṇical ascetics regarded their way of life as constituting an *āśrama*. Indeed, the term in this technical sense is conspicuous by its absence in the vocabulary of these sects. Even its proponents would clearly exclude such non-Brāhmaṇical ascetics from the system. On the other hand, it is simply not possible to reduce the variety of ascetical modes that existed in ancient India to just two patterns as envisaged by the *āśrama* system (Sprockhoff 1976, 294; 1979). These two *āśramas* bring under two classificatory rubrics a variety of concrete life styles on the

69. Pandey (1969, 8) is clearly wrong when he says that "the Dharmasūtras deal with the Varṇas (castes) and the Āśramas (stages of life). It is under the Āśrama-Dharmas that the rules about the Upanayana [initiation] and Vivāha [marriage] are given exhaustively." This is an example, as we shall see by no means unique, of reading into older texts classificatory systems from a much later period.

70. This is, of course, all the more true in the case of foreigners (*mleccha*). It was at a much later period that the *āśramas* were distributed among the four classes and the Śūdras were made eligible for membership in the second *āśrama*. See VaiDh 1.1 and section 7.2.

basis of some common features. It is a mistake to regard the *āśramas* themselves as specific social institutions. The classificatory nature of the *āśramas*, especially of the last two, is indicated, moreover, by the numerous subclassifications they were subjected to in later literature (see section 6.1.2).

Unlike its companion terms *varṇa* ("class") and *jāti* ("caste"), therefore, *āśrama* neither is coextensive with nor refers directly to social institutions. The former terms are universally recognized in India; they are not confined to a sect or a tradition. Caste, just like a personal name, is a term of both self-identity and social identity. Persons belonging to a particular caste will be recognized as such by themselves and by others in society, irrespective of their religious or ideological affiliations. *Āśrama*, on the contrary, is a concept that operates within the confines of Brāhmaṇism, and even within those confines the *āśrama* system was aimed at imparting a theological meaning to and at making a theological evaluation of several Brāhmaṇical modes of life. The self-identity or the social identity of the individuals in the institutions encompassed within the system is not necessarily determined by this theological evaluation of those institutions. The theological nature of the system is underscored, moreover, by the total lack of reference to it in non-Brāhmaṇical sources.[71]

At first, as we have seen, the term *āśrama* in all likelihood indicated the place and, by extension, the life style of a very special type of Brahmin who epitomized the ideal religious life of Brāhmaṇical theology. The association of the *āśrama* life with the mythical founders of Brāhmaṇical culture, the *ṛṣis*, must have given it added strength as the mode of life that best conformed to the ideal *dharma* of a Brahmin. Long before the creation of the *āśrama* system, *dharma* had emerged as the pivotal concept of Brāhmaṇical theology.[72] *Dharma* within the mainstream of Brāhmaṇical theology referred to the spectrum of vedic injunctions and prohibitions that regulated the ritual, social, and ethical life of twice-born Āryas. For an adult Brahmin, as we shall see in the chapter 2, the three central features of *dharma* were sacrifice, procreation, and study. These were practiced to the highest degree by those Brahmins and *ṛṣis* given to *śrama*, to religious toil, in *āśramas*.

The *āśrama* system, it appears, sought to bring rival and often mutually exclusive life styles within the orbit of *dharma* by extending the use and meaning of *āśrama*. To call a mode of life an *āśrama*, therefore, was to give that life a theological meaning within the context of *dharma*. It meant more specifically that vedic injunctions provided for such a mode of life and that it was as legitimate and as ideal a life style as the primordial *āśrama* of the *ṛṣis*. The proponents of the system, in effect, were telling their Brāhmaṇical audience that the life of a celibate ascetic or student is as good as the life of a holy householder.[73]

In common Indian pattern, the theological evaluation of these institutions was car-

71. Buddhist sources are completely silent with the exception of the twelfth-century Pāli lexicon *Abhidānappadīpikā* by Moggallāna, v. 928 (p. 150). See *Critical Pāli Dictionary*, I, 521.

72. For an illuminating discussion of the history and of the scholarly studies of *dharma*, see Halbfass 1988, 310–33.

73. In later literature there are examples of a similar extension of *āśrama*, this time from its normal meaning within the system to other non-āśramic behavior. Thus the *Mahābhārata* (12.65.6–7) says that the *dharma* of a Kṣatriya is truly *an āśrama*.

ried out by classification.[74] Baudhāyana (BDh 2.11.9), one of the earliest sources for the *āśrama* system, calls the *āśramas* "a fourfold division of *dharma*," and throughout its history the system has been regarded as a classification of *dharma* that parallels its older classification into the four *varṇas*.[75]

The semantic extension of terms to entities not covered by their original meanings is a phenomenon not unique to *āśrama*. As we shall see (sections 2.1.3–4), similar extensions are found in the famous doctrines of the three debts and the five great sacrifices. Such semantic extensions are meant to impart new theological meanings and values to activities and institutions by associating them with other well-known elements of the Brāhmaṇical world. Calling something a sacrifice, for example, gave it a specific value and required those who shared that world to relate to it as they would to a sacrifice. Similar semantic extensions occurred when Buddhists appropriated the word *dharma* and when Buddhist and Brāhmaṇical theologians wrote about the "true Brahmin." The architects of the *āśrama* system appear to have put the term *āśrama* to similar use.

1.2.2 The System as a Social Institution

Even though the *āśrama* system was primarily a theological construct, it was not totally divorced from the institutions it attempted to classify and evaluate. It did not, in other words, operate in a historical vacuum. We must, of course, distinguish the system from the institutions; nevertheless, we need to examine the history of these institutions and their relationship to rival religious ideologies if we are to understand the origin and the historical development of the theological system.

Theological schemes, moreover, tend to assume legal dimensions. Proponents of such schemes seek to control and to regulate social mores. The treatment of *āśramas*, for example, in the legal texts clearly aims at regulating these institutions. The system's relation to actual life styles is also evident in the further classifications that individual *āśramas* were subjected to in the course of history;[76] the multiplicity of observed life styles had to be reconciled with the simple fourfold system, just as the multiplicity of castes with the four *varṇas*.

The regulatory dimension is much more evident in the classical formulation of the system. In the original formulation, the four *āśramas* were considered as four legitimate modes of life open to adult men, any one of which could be freely chosen. In the classical formulation, however, the system becomes prescriptive. Modeled after the sacramentary (*saṃskāra*) system, the successive passage through all *āśramas* at appointed times is viewed if not as obligatory then at least as an ideal to be aspired after.

Even though these prescriptive rules are found in normative texts such as the Dhar-

74. Classification is the enumeration of the components that constitute a whole. This was the principal method also in philosophical investigations, as exemplified by Sāṃkhya and Buddhism. We shall have occasion later to comment on the relationship between Sāṃkhya and the *āśrama* system (section 3.3.3).

75. For a discussion of "four" in these classificatory systems, see sections 3.5 and 7.6.

76. See section 6.1.2 for these subclassifications. It is, of course, possible that not every subdivision represented a real difference in observed life styles. In later scholasticism such classifications often became an intellectual game, as in the case of the ten types of drama. Cf. Senart 1930, 104–05.

maśāstras, their influence in shaping the thought and practices of later generations should not be underestimated.[77] In later Hinduism, therefore, the *āśrama* system assumed the function of regulating the life of individual members of society and thus in some ways became a social institution consciously adhered to at least as an ideal by a segment of society.[78]

1.3 Issues of Method

The nature of its object, we would readily agree, should determine the method of our study. In the preceding discussion (and in the second part of this book) I argue that the *āśrama* system is primarily a theological construct aimed at a theological evaluation of several socio-religious institutions, and that *āśrama* in its technical usage within the system is a theological concept. Four major points regarding method emerge from that discussion. (1) It is necessary to distinguish carefully the history of the *āśrama* system from the histories of the several institutions comprehended by that system. Conversely, it is methodologically improper to assume the existence of the *āśrama* system whenever a source happens to mention one, some, or even all of these institutions. (2) In investigating the origin of the *āśrama* system and the motives for and the historical circumstances surrounding its creation, we should take as our basis solely the earliest known formulation of the system. Later formulations may provide insights into the development of the system but not into its origin. (3) Given the theological nature of the system, normative and overtly theological texts are proper sources for tracing its history. We must be careful, I repeat, not to confuse the history of the system with that of the institutions, for whose histories the evidence contained in those sources should be used with great caution. (4) The theological scheme of *āśrama*s follows the general conventions of Brāhmaṇical hermeneutics. It is necessary to pay sufficient attention to the hermeneutical bases of the system if we are to properly evaluate the history of the system and its relationship to other Brāhmaṇical institutions.

1.3.1 The System and the Institutions

The four *āśrama*s, as we have seen, are not coextensive with the respective social institutions classified by the system. It is indeed quite likely, as it will become apparent during

77. I am referring here to a trend among some scholars to dismiss the Dharmaśāstras as unrelated to social reality. As Halbfass (1988, 333) notes: "It is easy to argue that *Mīmāṃsā* and *Dharmaśāstra* do not represent the totality of the Hindu tradition; but it is also easy to underestimate their central and paradigmatic role." See Lingat 1973, 137–42. Derrett (in an appendix to Lingat 1973, 274), citing two medieval inscriptions that demonstrate the use of Dharmaśāstras in actual litigations, observes: "Such instances dispose at once of the extreme notion, once commonly heard, that śāstric texts never played a practical role, or that if they did, they did so only when it pleased some individuals to invoke them." Richard Lariviere has recently argued that the contents of Dharmaśāstras did in fact reflect local customs and constituted "real law" ("Dharmaśāstra, Custom, 'Real' Law and 'Apocryphal' Smṛtis," unpublished manuscript).

78. For the identification of *āśrama*s with the corresponding social institutions in later theology, see section 7.2.1. The *āśrama* system and the prescriptions regarding *āśrama*s in the Dharmaśāstras are appealed to even in the courts of modern India. See, for example, the very interesting case regarding the legitimacy of a Śūdra ascetic, Mathura Ahir, who was the head of a monastic establishment, heard by the Indian Supreme Court: *All India Reporter 1980, Supreme Court*, 707–26.

the course of this volume, that each class of the system does not correspond to a single social institution, and that the system imposes its own tidy classification on an ill-defined mass of institutions and observed behaviors.

The history of the system, therefore, is quite distinct from the history of these institutions taken individually or collectively, and the study of the former should not be confused with that of the latter.[79] It is thus improper to claim as many scholars do, for example, that the first two *āśrama*s are known from early vedic times; it is not these *āśrama*s but the institutions of vedic studentship and marriage that are so known.[80] This confusion is also at the root of many studies that seek to uncover the gradual evolution of the *āśrama*s from the original two, through the intermediary three, to the final four.[81] Kane's (1974, II.1, 418) comments exemplify this common error:

> The word āśrama does not occur in the Saṃhitās or Brāhmaṇas. But this cannot be stretched to mean that the stages of life denoted by this word in the sūtras were unknown throughout the Vedic period. It has been shown above . . . that the word brahmacārī occurs in the Ṛgveda and the Atharvaveda and that brahmacarya is mentioned in the Tai[ttirīya] S[aṃhitā], the Śat[apatha] Br[āhmaṇa] and other ancient Vedic works. So the stage of brahmacarya was well-known in the remotest past. The fact that Agni is said to be 'the gṛhapati of our house' (Ṛg. II.1.2) and the fact that in the famous verse (Ṛg. X.85.36) which is employed even today in the marriage ceremony the husband says to the bride when taking hold of her hand that the gods gave her to him for gārhapatya (for attaining the position of a house-owner or householder) establish that the second stage of the householder was well-known in the Ṛgveda.

If this line of thought were to be followed to its logical and absurd conclusion, we would have to assume that the second *āśrama* was known to the ancient Egyptians and that it continues to be practiced by twentieth-century Americans![82]

A further corollary follows from our conclusion that the *āśrama* system is a theological scheme. The system is not necessarily implied whenever the term *āśrama* occurs in a text. The same applies, a fortiori, to the use of terms such as *tapas* ("austerity"), *yajña* ("sacrifice"), and *adhyayana* ("study"), which are assumed by some to be code words for the *āśrama*s of hermit, householder, and student, respectively (Sprockhoff 1981,

79. The confusion between the *āśrama*s and the social institutions is evident, as we shall see (section 3.5), in the works of Ludwik Skurzak 1948, 1958, 1967-68.

80. This methodological error is so pervasive that it can be found in most studies. Pande (1978, 5): "The first two *āśrama*s are implied in the whole Vedic religion." Ghosh Chaudhury (1967, 130): "Brahmacarya and Garhasthya—these two stages of the Asrama system were originally prevailing in the Vedic life. Dispute arises about the origin of the 3rd and 4th Asramas." Lingat (1973, 47): "The first two stages, however, are known from the Vedas onwards." Basu (1969, 225): "In the Saṃhitā and the Brs. [Brāhmaṇas] we do not find explicit mention of the third and fourth orders, viz,—forest life and the life of a recluse. The remaining two orders, viz, studentship or brahmacarya and the domestic life, gārhasthya have been mentioned in clear terms." The entire argument of Gangadharan 1976 for the antiquity of the *āśrama* system is based on this confusion. A similar confusion, likewise, underlies Kakar's (1968) study.

81. Deussen 1906, 60f, 366–82; 1909; Winternitz 1926; Skurzak 1948; 1958; 1967–68; Macdonell and Keith 1912, I, 68–69; Sharma 1939, 15; Gonda 1976, 123; O'Flaherty 1973, 78–82. See section 3.5.

82. Indeed, one scholar (Chanda 1934, 89) appears to draw just such a conclusion: "The orders of students and householders are universal. The order of the forest-dwellers and religious mendicants probably originated in India."

76–83). Thus, the famous passage of the *Chāndogya Upaniṣad* (2.23) regarding the "three branches of *dharma*" has been regularly interpreted as referring to the *āśrama* system (see section 3.5). Haug in his translation of the *Aitareya Brāhmaṇa* (7.13) interprets dirt, antelope skin, beard, and austerities, as referring to a householder, a student, a hermit, and a renouncer, respectively. Basu (1969, 225) is even more emphatic:

> The four terms used in this couplet [i.e. AitB 7.13.4], viz, mala (filth), ajina (skin of the black antelope), śmaśru (beards) and tapaḥ (penance) have been taken by the commentator Sāyaṇācārya and all Vedic scholars of the east and the west to allude to the four orders of life [i.e. *āśramas*]—domestic life, studentship, forest life and the hermit life, respectively.

Neither the mention of any of the four institutions nor, a fortiori, some presumed reference to them through code words, I want to repeat, can be interpreted as a reference to the *āśrama* system. Especially in the more ancient texts, even the explicit use of the term *āśrama* is no sure indication that the *āśrama* system is meant; the term may well be used in its original meaning outside the context of the system. The assumption that *āśrama* always implies the system, as we have seen (section 1.1.4), has led to the misinterpretation of such significant expressions as *atyāśramin* and *āśramapāra*.[83]

1.3.2 The Original Formulation and the Origin of the System

Our second point regarding method—that in investigating the origin of the system we should take into account solely the earliest known formulation of the system—is so obvious that it requires little defense or explanation. Yet it is rare to find a modern discussion of the *āśrama*s that does not violate this principle, a violation exemplified by the common translation of *āśrama* as "stage of life."[84]

According to the most ancient formulation of the system presented in the Dharmasūtras, a formulation that I will examine in the third chapter, the *āśrama*s are not stages but rather permanent modes of life open to any young adult who has completed his period of vedic education. Within this formulation the temporary period of studentship following vedic initiation was not considered an *āśrama*. It was four or five centuries later, around the beginning of the common era, that the classical formulation of the system appeared (see section 5.1), and it was only within that formulation that the *āśrama*s came to be considered stages of life through which a person was expected to pass.[85]

83. For example, Macdonell and Keith (1912, I, 68) cite the passage of the *Śvetāśvatara Upaniṣad* (6.21) that contains the expression *atyāśramin* as the earliest use of *āśrama* "denoting the stages of a Hindu's life." See section 8.2.

84. See for example: Müller 1878, 343; Deussen 1909, 129–30; Kane 1974, II.1, 421; Apte 1951, 493; Ghurye 1964, 3; Banerjee 1962, 132; Gonda 1976, 123. In German also the common translation is "Lebensstufen" or "Lebensstadien"; Winternitz 1926, 215; Eggers 1929, 10; Liebich 1936, 9f; Sprockhoff 1979, 374.

85. It is highly anachronistic to interpret passages or terms in earlier documents in the light of this rather late development in the *āśrama* system. An example is Keith's translation of the *Aitareya Āraṇyaka* passage 5.3.3—*na vatse na ca tṛtīya iti*—as "not to a child or a man in the third stage of life." The division of human life into different periods such as youth, adulthood, and old age surely could have taken place outside the context of the *āśrama* system, as evidenced by the ChU 3.16.1–6, which

Many scholars have taken the classical formulation as their point of departure.[86] Kakar (1968, 128), in his comparison of the system with modern psychological theories of human development, writes: "The *āśrama* theory, which was evolved some two and a half thousand years ago in India by men like Manu and Gautama, also saw human development in terms of distinct stages of life." Even a historian of the calibre of Thapar falls into the same trap. In examining the social causes of the *āśrama* system, Thapar assumes that it was "a theory towards ordering of the individual life-cycle" (1982, 277) and concludes that it was invented to blunt the opposition between renunciation and married life by blending the two into a single lifetime:

> Thus whereas the Buddhist and the Jaina traditions, for example, encouraged the dichotomous categories in the role of the gahapati [householder] and bhikkhu [religious mendicant], the Brahmanical tradition sought to weaken it by weaving it into a single life-cycle. (1982, 296)

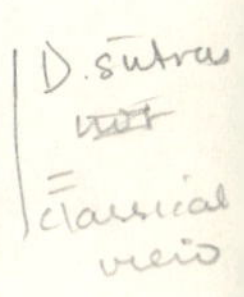

Lingat (1973, 47), in an otherwise excellent study, also assumes that the classical formulation is found in the Dharmasūtras, although the evidence clearly shows the contrary: "It is only in the *dharma-sūtras* that the four *āśrama*s appear as successive stages of life."[87]

This error is also the likely background of the romantic view of some scholars regarding the origin and purpose of the *āśrama* system. Max Müller (1878, 343) was one of its earliest advocates:

> The whole course of life was traced out in India for every child that was born into the world; and, making every allowance for human nature, which never submits entirely to rules, we have no reason to doubt that, during the ancient periods of Indian history, this course of life, as sanctioned by their sacred books and their codes of law, was in the main adhered to.

The romantic view of the *āśrama* system finds its most eloquent voice in Deussen (1909, 131), who paints an idyllic portrait of the system:

---

divides the human life span into three parts of 24 years, 44 years, and 48 years, homologizing them with the sacrificial libations of Soma offered in the morning, afternoon, and evening, respectively. A similar threefold division of life unrelated to the *āśrama*s is found in Vātsyāyana's *Kāmasūtra*, 1.2.1–6. See section 5.1.

86. Most introductions to Indian religion, law, and culture merely present this classical formulation in their discussion of the *āśrama* system as if it were the only formulation of the system: Jolly 1928, 320–27; Bloomfield 1908, 288–89; Barnett 1913, 130–31; Chakladar 1962, 559–63; Biardeau and Malamoud 1976, 32–36; O'Flaherty 1973, 78–82; Radhakrishnan1929, I, 132; Zaehner 1966, 113. Smart (1970, 108) in his article on *āśrama* merely enunciates the classical formulation. See also Mees 1935, 74; Bhagwat 1939b, 126–27; Renou and Filliozat 1947, I, n. 768; Gangadharan 1976. Miller and Wertz (1976, 3) assert without any references that "asceticism goes back to the four stages (*āśrama*) of life described in the Vedas." Even Heesterman (1964, 24) uses the classical theory of stages in his structural comparison between the *āśrama*s and the modes of life assumed by a sacrificer. More recent examples include Klostermaier 1989, 320–21, and Tilak 1989.

87. Gopal (1959, 483), likewise, confidently asserts that "according to the scheme of life envisaged in the Dharmasūtras, the entire life of an Ārya is divided into four stages (*Āśrama*s)." So also Tilak (1989, 27).

> If it is true that the highest aim of mankind is not to be found in this worldly existence, but in the realm beyond, however closed to our knowledge this may be, it is none the less true that the attempt, as we have it in the four *āśramas*, to transform the whole earthly existence into a preparatory school for eternity, merits recognition and admiration even from those who have reached the highest degree of civilization. The Indian system does not demand what is impossible; it does not tear men away roughly and abruptly from that attachment to the world which is innate in them. It offers the opportunity in the stage of *grihastha* [householder] to enjoy life, and by enjoying it to convince oneself of its futility. It then, in an advanced age, in the stage of *vānaprastha* [hermit], tends to a systematic mortification of sensuality, and it describes in the *sannyāsin* [renouncer] a man who, approaching the end of his days, has become free from all worldly fetters, and is best prepared for departure.

Deussen (1906, 367) exclaims: "The entire history of mankind does not produce much that approaches in grandeur to this thought."

Acceptance of the classical formulation as the sole representative of the *āśrama* system by the scholarly community is illustrated by the statements found in *The New Encyclopaedia Britannica*, which defines the *āśrama*s as "any of the four spiritual abodes, or stages of life, through which the 'twice-born' Hindu ideally pass."[88]

This lack of historical judgement on the part of so many scholars is all the more disconcerting when we find that the distinction and the historical distance between the two formulations were pointed out as far back as 1920 and by as well-known a scholar as Farquhar.[89] Writing about the formulation in the Dharmasūtras, Farquhar (1920, 40) observes:

> It is well to note that in the time of these sūtras each man chooses his own *āśrama*, i.e. whether he is to remain a student, or become a householder, a hermit, or a sannyāsī: these modes of life have not yet become a series through which each man is expected to pass.

Elsewhere Farquhar (1920, 29) specifies the time of this choice: "When a student had completed his education, he was allowed either to remain with his teacher for life, or to marry and settle down as a householder, or to retire to the woods as a hermit." Farquhar also comments on the late origin of the classical formulation and suggests correctly that its origin must not have been far removed from the date of composition of Manu's law book:

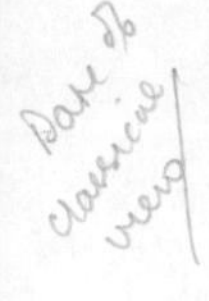

88. *The New Encyclopedia Britannica*, 15th ed. (Chicago, 1990), I, 627. This statement in the Micropedia is no doubt influenced by the statements in the article on Hinduism written by Wendy Doniger, A. L. Basham, and J. A. B. van Buitenen: Vol. 20, 520 and 523.

89. Others also have pointed out this distinction: Gonda 1960, I, 287–88; Apte 1951, 493–94. With reference to the *Arthaśāstra* (1.3.9–12), Kangle (1960–65, III, 151) observes: "It would, in fact, appear that the four *āśrama*s are represented as four different ways of life to be adopted according to one's aptitude and bent of mind, rather than as successive stages in the life of the same individual." Even Chakladar (1962, 563), citing the relevant sections of the Dharmasūtras, notices this distinction: "In fact, according to some social legislators, on the completion of the duties of studentship, one is declared free to enter any of the *āśrama*s at one's pleasure."

> It was at a much later date that there came into use the ideal rule for the life of the twice-born man, that his life should be lived in four stages, *āśramas*, as a student, householder, hermit and monk. (1920, 29)
>
> This great code [Manu] registers several advances in Hindu religious law. Here, and also in the contemporary didactic Epic, the ideal is laid down, though it is not made compulsory, that the twice-born man should pass through the four *āśramas* in order, i.e. the life of the celibate student, the householder, the hermit, and the monk. (1920, 81)

This example illustrates the disconcerting fact that advances in the human sciences take generations to be incorporated into general scholarship, and that errors assume the quality of undisputed facts when they are repeated a sufficient number of times in influential works.

1.3.3 The Sources

The final point regarding method concerns the sources of our information. The function of normative and theological texts in historical reconstruction has been a constant problem in the study of religious history. It is foolhardy to dismiss them completely and naive to accept their evidence as historical fact.

My use of sources is determined by the object of my study. Given that the *āśrama* system is a theological construct, it is appropriate to use theological and normative sources in reconstructing its history. It is simplistic to assume that only "events" are historical. Attempts at theoretical and theological self-understanding are as much a part of the history of a culture as wars and dynasties. With reference to this aspect of cultural history, Halbfass (1988, 181–82) strikes a salutary warning about dismissing offhand the normative and technical literature: "It would be quite wrong to deny that these texts have 'real' historical value, or that they can provide insights into the realities of Indian thought and life. They may be 'theoretical'; nevertheless they are significant historical documents of Indian self-understanding."

The problem with many previous studies of the *āśramas* is not their use of normative literature but that they confuse the *āśramas* with the corresponding social institutions and attempt naively to reconstruct the history of these institutions using theological sources that deal with the *āśrama* system.

Theological texts, furthermore, in spite of their normative intentions, are documents composed by human beings within specific historical settings. Clearly the authors of these, however theologically motivated they may have been, were children of their times, and their writings should provide some clues to the social context in which they lived and wrote. Irrespective of the intentions of their authors, therefore, these texts are in fact historical documents and contain evidence regarding the time in which they were composed. If they are read with some sophistication they can and do provide historically valuable information regarding dogma and institutions about which they pretend to provide normative and often atemporal information and rules. Those who dismiss theological and religious literature as irrelevant for historical purposes are throwing out the baby with the bath water.

Even a theological construct such as the *āśrama* system, however, is not completely divorced from social reality. It can be understood adequately only within its own historical context. For the study of this context non-normative literary and non-literary sources are essential, and I have made use of them to the fullest extent possible.[90]

1.3.4 The Āśrama *System and Brāhmaṇical Hermeneutics*

I have already made reference to the centrality of hermeneutics within Brāhmaṇical law and theology in general and the *āśrama* system in particular. When we examine the writing of any theologian with regard to a point of doctrine or practice, we encounter a general pattern of argument. First, the writer will adduce a vedic or smṛti text that supports it either explicitly or through the use of established hermeneutical principles. The need for such a proof text is based on the doctrine that the Vedas and the Smṛtis, which are assumed to be based on and derive their authority from the Vedas, are the sole authority in matters of *dharma*. Second, the writer will attempt to show that similar proof texts put forward by opponents to support their doctrines and practices do not actually support them. Here again the writer would use sophisticated hermeneutical arguments.

As we study the early history of the *āśrama* system, we find that it is indeed presented within the context of interpreting vedic and smṛti passages. The issue around which the entire system revolves is surely one of the most central in Brāhmaṇical hermeneutics: the resolution of conflicts that arise when vedic injunctions contradict each other. There are three ways of resolving these conflicts, all of which are represented in the history of the system. First, one may dismiss all but one of the conflicting injunctions. This may be done either by showing that the rejected injunctions do not have the same force or power (*bala:* see section 3.1.1) as the one accepted or by demonstrating that they are actually not found in the Vedas or Smṛtis (Olivelle 1986, 57–76). This hermeneutical strategy is technically called *bādha* (see section 3.2.1.1). Second, one may accept the equal authority of all and admit an option. Thus an individual may choose to follow any one of the injunctions in conflict. This strategy is called *vikalpa.* Third, one may accept the equal authority of all and the obligation to follow all of them. This course calls for a strategy, technically called *samuccaya,* that would make it possible for all the obligations to be fulfilled by the same individual (see section 5.2). The great medieval theologian Vijñāneśvara (on YDh 3.56–57) in fact presents the history of the *āśrama* system as a history of the hermeneutical strategies of *bādha*, *vikalpa*, and *samuccaya.*

The history of the *āśrama* system, therefore, is primarily the history of a theology. And the history of this theology is primarily the history of Brāhmaṇical hermeneutics as applied to alleged conflicts between vedic injunctions that serve as the basis for the legitimacy of alternate modes of life.

90. The information on the *āśramas* contained in epigraphical and other non-literary sources, unfortunately, is meager: see section 7.3.1.

2

Background and Context

The theological scheme of the *āśrama* system originated against the background and within the context of several religious, social, and economic developments.[1] If we are right in assigning the creation of the system to a period during or soon after the fifth century B.C.E. (see section 3.4), its socio-religious background would include the fully developed vedic tradition represented by the Brāhmaṇas and the ritual Sūtras. Its immediate context would include the socio-economic changes that gave rise to cities, monarchies, and a merchant class, as well as the emergence of rival religious ideologies and life styles both within and outside the vedic tradition. An understanding of these changes is especially significant in studying an institution such as the *āśrama* system, because, as I shall argue, it was created as a hermeneutical device to incorporate socio-religious changes within the vedic world. In this chapter, therefore, I briefly examine these three major elements of the background and context of the *āśrama* system.

2.1 The Vedic Ideal of Religious Life

In chapter 1 we saw that the original meaning of the term *āśrama* referred to the life of a Brahmin who epitomized the ideal of religious living as formulated in the Vedas. This point is amply demonstrated by the retrospective projection of such a life style to the *ṛṣi*s who received and promulgated vedic knowledge. An examination of the vedic texts will provide us further details regarding this ideal, which was intended not only for religious virtuosi but also for ordinary people.

At the outset, however, I want to make a few comments regarding the Vedas which may be useful in properly assessing the information contained in these documents. The early vedic literature presents on the whole a fairly coherent view regarding religious duties and obligations. It would be a mistake, however, to conclude either that that view was shared and those ideals practiced uniformly by all the people who lived during the vedic period or that they remained unchanged over the many centuries during which these documents were composed.

On the one hand, vedic society was highly heterogeneous, containing not only vari-

1. It may be useful to reiterate here (see section 1.3.2) that in examining the social and theological context within which the *āśrama* system originated, we focus exclusively on its original formulation as described in chapter 3.

ous social classes within the Aryan population but also non-Aryan elements.[2] The geography of the vedic society was also changing continuously. It was expanding into new regions of the east and the south, bringing into its orbit new peoples, customs, beliefs, and languages. On the other hand, vedic literature was produced by and, for the most part, intended for the Brāhmaṇical elite.[3] This literature, therefore, provides us with just one, and a somewhat narrow, window into that complex society. The vedic documents reflect the priorities and concerns of that elite priestly class and reveal principally its customs and beliefs. As Gonda (1965, 200) rightly observes: "Neither the Ṛgveda nor the other parts of the Vedic literature give us a complete idea of the spiritual life of ancient India or a complete vocabulary of the language of its population in general."[4] Even within the confines of the priestly community, moreover, these documents deal principally with men (Gonda 1965, 206). Males occupy the central position within the religious framework of the Vedas; for the most part, females are ignored and enter theological discourse only as they relate to men as wives, mothers, or daughters.

Although it is just one narrow peephole, however, given the paucity of other literary and non-literary evidence, vedic literature is the only window of any significance we have into this ancient period of Indian history. The Brāhmaṇical elite, moreover, did not constitute a monolithic entity; there were differences of opinion among different schools and teachers discernible even in the extant corpus of the vedic texts. With due regard to the above caveats, therefore, this literature, if it is examined with some care and sophistication, can provide valuable information, not only regarding the dominant views of the Brāhmaṇical tradition but also about that society in general and especially about dissident voices and minority opinions within that tradition.[5] This information is especially valuable for the study of the *āśrama* system because it is a product of precisely that Brāhmaṇical tradition.

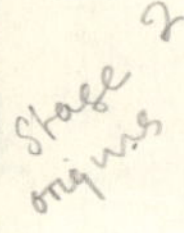

The ideal and typical religious life within vedic ideology is that of a married householder. The normative character of that life is related to the two theologically central religious activities: offering sacrifices and procreating children. Only a married householder, according to that theology, was entitled and qualified to perform either of them. It is accurate, I believe, to say that the vedic world revolved around the married householder. I want to examine at the outset, therefore, the vedic theology of sacrifice and pro-

2. The Aryans immigrated into northwestern India during the second millennium B.C.E. Their descendants, who composed the vedic literature and who constituted the dominant classes within vedic society, had lost all memory of that immigration by their ancestors. The term Aryan is used here as a cultural and linguistic rather than a racial designation. Intermarriage surely wiped out any "racial purity" at a very early period. Even though occasionally there are racial overtones, I believe that the term is used principally as a cultural rather than a racial demarcation in the vedic and other Indian literature.

3. See Rau 1957, 61; Sprockhoff 1979, 375–76.

4. See also Gonda 1965, 349; Collins 1982, 30–33.

5. Collins (1982, 32) uses the concept of "cultural hegemony" in an imaginative way to demonstrate the significance of Brāhmaṇical ideas and texts for the study of even anti-Brāhmaṇical institutions: "The intellectual influence of developed Brahmanical thought on Buddhism is due to the undoubted fact of the former's playing in India . . . a 'culturally hegemonous' role. That is, although the texts of that tradition by no means portray the historical reality of early Indian religion in its entirety, still they came to be taken as culturally prestigious, and provided an inescapable conceptual paradigm for speculative thought."

creation in relation to the married householder and some of the theological schemes created to reinforce the central and obligatory nature of these acts.

2.1.1 Marriage and Sacrifice

The vedic sacrificial theology came to be fully articulated in the liturgical texts known as the Brāhmaṇas.[6] This theology is based on two significant claims: creation resulted from the sacrifice, and gods attained immortality through the sacrifice.

In the later stratum of the *Ṛgveda* the sacrifice is already depicted as a cosmogonic principle. The *Puruṣasūkta* (RV 10.90) describes the sacrifice of the primeval male (*puruṣa*), from whose dismembered body the several elements of creation, including the four classes (*varṇa*) of human society, originated.

The Brāhmaṇas identify the sacrifice with a new and somewhat artificial creator god, Prajāpati.[7] He is both the sacrifice personified and the performer of the sacrifice from which the whole of creation proceeds.[8] Not just humans and the physical universe but even gods derive their being from Prajāpati and the sacrifice (TS 7.1.5.1).

The efficacy of the sacrifice, however, does not depend on anything or anyone other than the sacrifice itself. The sacrifice, like magic, when performed properly and accurately produces an automatic effect (Keith 1925, 454; Lévi 1898, 129). The most important issue with reference to the sacrifice, therefore, is knowledge—knowledge of the proper ritual formulae (*mantra*) and of the correct procedure for performing the sacrificial acts.[9]

As the source of creative power, the sacrifice is also the source of immortality.[10] The gods, it was believed, were the first creatures to obtain knowledge of the sacrifice. The gods at first were mortal like us and lived on earth with humans. By performing the sacrifice correctly they attained heaven and immortality.[11] Further, in the primordial battle between gods and demons (*asura*), both of whom were children of Prajāpati and were produced by the sacrifice, gods gained the upper hand because their knowledge of the

6. Within the scope of this study I can deal only with a few significant points. For more complete accounts, see Lévi 1898; Keith 1925, 257–78, 454–67; Basu 1969, 137–71; Biardeau and Malamoud 1976; Smith 1989. Even though there was a wide variety of vedic sacrifices, vedic theology regarded them as reflections of a hypostatized cosmic sacrifice. It is to this theological concept of *yajña* that I refer when I use the term sacrifice.

7. "The basis of the whole system is the identification of the sacrifice with Prajāpati, who is the creator par excellence" (Keith 1925, 445). On the role of Prajāpati in vedic theology, see Gonda 1984, 1986; Lévi 1898, 13–35; Oldenberg 1919, 26–32; Biardeau 1969, 14–23; Smith 1989, 54–69.

8. See ŚB 2.2.4.1; 2.5.1.1; 6.1.1.8, 13; 6.1.3.1; 10.6.5.2, 6; 11.5.8.1; TB 1.1.3.5; 1.6.2.1; 2.3.8.1; AitB 2.33. On Prajāpati's identification with the year, which represents the "all," see Gonda 1984.

9. It is this "sacrificial knowledge" that will be contrasted with the new types of mystical knowledge leading to liberation in the new religions, including the Upaniṣads: see section 2.3.1.

10. The exact meaning of "immortality" (*amṛta*) is not clear. As Collins (1982, 42–44) points out, in this context the term probably means the freedom from death and the indefinite continuation of existence, which is different from the deathless state envisaged within the later concept of *mokṣa* (absolute freedom). *Mokṣa* transcends both life and death, which as inseparable correlatives constitute *saṃsāra* (life subject to repeated births and deaths), a concept that by definition assumes the indefinite continuation of existence.

11. TS 7.2.4.1; MS 2.2.2; 3.4.7; ŚB 2.2.2.8–14; 11.2.3.6; 10.4.3.3–8; PB 24.19.2. See also Lévi 1898, 36–76; Keith 1925, 456–57.

sacrifice was superior to that of the demons (Lévi 1898, 36–76). The sacrifice, indeed, is portrayed as the very self or body of gods.[12]

The gods, having obtained immortality through the sacrifice, left humans behind on earth. They wanted to make sure, however, that people did not follow them to heaven. One delightful story (ŚB 2.3.4.4) informs us that the gods decided to leave earth after becoming disgusted with humans who importuned them constantly for favors. To prevent those people from following them, the gods obliterated all traces of the sacrifice on earth. They were determined to deny humans access to the knowledge of the sacrifice. The vedic seers (*ṛṣi*), however, discovered that knowledge and through the medium of the Vedas handed it down to future generations.[13]

The sacrifice, then, is the source of immortality for humans as it was for gods. It is connected, furthermore, with the archetypal activity of the creator god Prajāpati, as well as of gods and seers. This activity recorded in myth and reinforced by Brāhmaṇical theology, therefore, becomes doubly paradigmatic for humans. Humans should sacrifice both because they are expected to follow the example of gods and seers and because they seek immortality. That humans must imitate gods is a recurrent theme in the Brāhmaṇas.[14]

The obligation to imitate gods is grounded in a practical concern: humans seek to be like gods, to attain the world of gods (or divine space: *loka*).[15] This is tantamount to becoming immortal, a belief reflected in the later concept of the "path of gods" (*devayāna*).[16] The sacrifice is intimately connected with the concept of *loka;* the performance of sacrifices assures a heavenly *loka* after death.[17] The sacrifice indeed is identified with the heavenly world; heaven is actually localized on earth on the ground where the sacrifice is performed.[18]

The sacrifice is considered a new birth for the sacrificer.[19] The ceremony of consecration (*dīkṣā*) for a sacrifice symbolically represents the sacrificer's death and new

12. "The sacrifice is the very self [or the body] of the gods"—*yajña u devānām ātmā*: ŚB 8.6.1.10. "The sacrifice is the self of all the gods"—*sarveṣāṃ devānām ātmā yajñaḥ*: ŚB 14.3.2.1. See Lévi 1898, 38.

13. TS 6.3.10.2; 6.5.3.1; AitB 2.1; ŚB 1.6.2.1–3; 3.1.4.3; 3.2.2.2, 11, 28; 3.4.3.15; 3.7.1.27. See Lévi 1898, 143–44.

14. TS 6.1.1.5; MS 3.6.3; TB 1.5.9.4; ŚB 1.2.2.9; 1.7.2.9; 3.1.2.4–5; 3.1.3.14; 3.2.2.16; 7.2.2.6; 11.1.2.13. See Lévi 1898, 85–87.

15. On the important concept of *loka* in the Vedas and its various meanings, see Gonda 1966.

16. See section 2.3.2, and BāU 6.2.2; ChU 4.15.5; 5.3.2; 5.10.2; MuṇU 3.1.6.

17. "He thus makes the sacrificer attain union with the gods and obtain the same form and the same world as the gods"—*devānāṃ yajamānaṃ sāyujyaṃ sarūpatāṃ salokatāṃ gamayati*: AitB 2.24. See Gonda 1966, 87–95.

18. "The sacrifice is truly the heavenly world"—*svargo vai loko yajñaḥ*: KS 14.1. The *āhavanīya* fire is said to be the heavenly world: ŚB 9.3.4.12. Heaven is where they immolate the victim: ŚB 3.2.8.5; 13.2.8.5. See Gonda 1966, 90. Because heaven is unlimited, it can only be gained by an unlimited sacrifice: AitB 6.23.12; PB 9.8.14; 17.12.3; GoB 2.6.5. The unlimited nature of the sacrifice is often connected with the giving of a thousandfold sacrificial fee (*dakṣiṇā*), for "thousand" is equivalent to "all": Gonda 1966, 88. See ŚB 4.5.1.11; 13.4.1.6.

19. "La vie du sacrifice est donc une série infinie de morts et de naissances": Lévi 1898, 81. Heesterman (1957, 6–7) sees a cosmic dimension in this death-rebirth process: "They [birth and death] are the two poles of cosmic life; and the sacrificer, realizing through the ritual symbols his identity with the universe, performs through the sacrifice the cyclical rhythm of the universe in a series of deaths and births; again and again he enters as an embryo upon the dīkṣā to be reborn out of the sacrifice."

birth. The man undergoing consecration (*dīkṣita*) is called a fetus. The shed in which he sits represents the womb.[20] The sacrificial fire, likewise, is considered the womb and the sacrificial victim the seed. From that union the sacrificer is born anew.[21] Gods attained immortality by establishing the sacred fire in the innermost part of their being (ŚB 2.2.2.8–14). The *Jaiminīya Brāhmaṇa* (3.14.8) states explicitly that a man remains unborn until he has sacrificed and has been born through the sacrifice: "Unborn, indeed, is a man so long as he does not sacrifice. It is through the sacrifice that he is born, just as an egg first burst." The final sacrifice of a man—the cremation of his body in his sacrificial fire—is similarly viewed as a new birth in which Agni, the fire god, becomes his father (ŚB 2.3.3.5; 12.5.1.13). The *Śatapatha Brāhmaṇa* (11.2.1.1) thus refers to the three births of a man: the first from his parents, the second from the sacrifice, and the third from the cremation fire.

Offering sacrifices, therefore, constitutes the primary religious obligation of twice-born men. Thus far we have looked at this obligation from the standpoint of the individual sacrificer. Although the vedic sacrifice is intended primarily for the benefit of a single sacrificer (*yajamāna*), the obligation to sacrifice has also a cosmic dimension. The piling of the fire altar (*agnicayana*), for example, is a ritual re-creation of the cosmos (ŚB 10.1.1.1–3; 10.1.3.5). As Biardeau (1976, 24–25) points out:

> L'interdépendence du ciel et de la terre est donc totale. Ils ne se maintiennent qu'ensemble. L'ordre que permet à ce tout de subsister et où chacun a son role à jouer est le *dharma:* notion fondamentale et inséparable de celle de sacrifice, puisque l'un ne peut exister sans l'autre. Le drame cosmique se joue donc sur terre, en ce monde où l'on sacrifie.

The *Śatapatha* (3.6.3.1–2) likewise declares that the sacrifice is all and that he who is initiated for sacrifice (*dīkṣita*) sets free all creatures. A much later text echoes the same theme: "He who is diligent in the performance of sacrifices, supports both the movable and the immovable creation" (MDh 3.75).

The king, as the hub of the social cosmos and as the chief sacrificer in society, occupies a central position in the sacrificial recreation of the cosmos. With reference to the cosmic function of the king and the sacrifices peculiar to him, Heesterman comments:

> The rājasūya [royal consecration] seems to be an abridgment of what originally must have been an unremitting series of yearly ceremonies with the object of regenerating the universe. The king took a central place in it. The universe had yearly to be recreated and so had the king who, like the common śrauta sacrificer, incorporated the cosmos. (1957, 10)
>
> At the centre of the cyclical regeneration of the universe, set in motion and regulated by the ritual proceedings at the place of sacrifice, stands the king. When, standing with raised arms, he receives the unction, the king manifests himself as the cosmic pillar, the path between heaven and earth along which the fertilizing unction waters take their circular course from sky to earth and back again. The king is, however, not only the centre and pivot of the universe, he is the universe itself; he has been seen to

20. TS 6.1.3.3; 6.2.5.3–5; AitB 1.3. On *dīkṣā* see Gonda 1965, 313–77.

21. ŚB 6.6.2.16; 10.4.1.1–2; 11.1.2.2; 12.5.1.13. Gonda 1965, 331. The fire of cremation has the same ritual effect: ŚB 11.2.1.1.

encompass, like the cosmic man Prajāpati, the universe in respect both to space and to time. (1957, 223–24)

The theology with respect to the obligatory nature of performing sacrifices developed especially with reference to the *agnihotra*, the daily fire sacrifice. Most vedic sacrifices were offered on special occasions or on specific days of the ritual calendar. Given their elaborate nature and the enormous expense they entailed, few in all likelihood could have afforded to perform the major vedic sacrifices. The relatively simple daily offering of *agnihotra* thus began to assume an ever increasing importance among theologians and ritual experts who speculated on the significance of the sacrifice and who were intent on discovering ever new ritual equivalences.[22]

According to the *Jaiminīya Brāhmaṇa* (1.3–4), the *agnihotra* is what the gods produced when they contracted the thousand-year sacrifice of Prajāpati.[23] It is, therefore, unsurpassed (MNU 527). As night and day follow each other and have no limit, so the *agnihotra*, which is performed in the morning and in the evening, has no limit.[24]

The obligation to perform the *agnihotra* is also related to its association with the archetypal activities of gods and seers:

> This *agnihotra* Brahman offered during twelve days. During twelve days Prajāpati, during twelve days the gods and the seers (also offered it). Having offered it during twelve days each time they obtained their wishes and desires.[25] How much more (will he obtain these) who offers thus during his whole life.[26]

The obligation to maintain the sacred fires and to offer the daily *agnihotra* in them during one's entire life is stated unambiguously in the Brāhmaṇas. A passage occurring in both the *Śatapatha Brāhmaṇa* (12.4.1.1) and the *Jaiminīya Brāhmaṇa* (1.51) declares: "It is assuredly a long sacrificial session upon which they enter who offer the *agnihotra*, a session to be broken off only through old age, for it is old age or death that absolves a man from it."[27] With reference to the sacred fire another text records the prayer of a sac-

22. On the *agnihotra* and its later development in the *prāṇāgnihotra* ("offering in the vital breaths"), see Bodewitz 1973, 215–343, 1976. Bodewitz rightly criticizes Varenne's interpretations in his edition of MNU II, pp. 69–114.

23. To state that a rite, an activity, or even a text is an abridgement of a much larger and more complex primordial equivalent was a common strategy in ancient India and served to highlight the importance of that rite or text. Given the human condition, divine archetypes can only be duplicated on earth in abridged forms, which nevertheless capture the essence of their archetypes. On the origin of the *agnihotra*, see Bodewitz 1976, 14–29.

24. See Bodewitz 1973, n. 19 on JB 1.4.

25. Twelve is associated with the year of twelve months. Just as the year, therefore, twelve represents totality, the all, the unlimited: Gonda 1984, 62–63. See TS 2.2.5.1–5; 2.2.6.1–5; 5.1.9.5; 5.4.7.6–7; 5.5.1.6–7; ŚB 2.2.2.3–5; 2.6.3.1; 10.4.3.1–2; 5.2.5.14–15; 6.2.1.35–36.

26. JB 1.37. Bodewitz's (1973) translation.

27. Regarding the term *jarāmarya* (translated here as "to be broken off only through old age"), see Bodewitz 1973, 155, n. 2. He rightly rejects Deussen's and Varenne's interpretations and remarks that "having old age as its limit (*maryā*) is the only tenable" meaning. Eggeling's translation (at ŚB 12.4.1.1)—"ensuring death in old age"—is clearly inaccurate, although he acknowledges the possibility of the other meaning in a footnote. The *agnihotra* is a lifelong obligation irrespective of whether one maintains the *śrauta* ("vedic") or the *gṛhya* ("domestic") fires. See Gonda 1980, 415; MNU 547. Later legal texts also comment on the obligation to offer the *agnihotra*: GDh 8.19–20; BDh 2.4.23; VaDh 11.46; MDh 4.25; YDh 1.97, 124–25; ViDh 59.2–9. On the use of a similar injunction as an argument against the *āśrama* system, see section 8.5.

rificer: "For a hundred years may I kindle you."[28] A man who extinguishes his sacred fire is called "the slayer of the hero among gods; Brahmins desirous of righteousness did not formerly eat his food."[29]

Although every twice-born man had the obligation to sacrifice, yet not every man was entitled or qualified to perform it. Only a married man accompanied by his legitimate wife was qualified to be a sacrificer; the husband and the wife constituted a single sacrificial persona. The obligation to sacrifice, therefore, implies the obligation to get married. "A man who has no wife," the *Taittirīya Brāhmaṇa* says, "is not entitled to sacrifice."[30] The wife is "the hind half of the sacrifice."[31] The *Ṛgveda* (1.72.5; 5.3.2; 5.28.3) declares that the husband and wife should cooperate in worshipping gods. In the celebrated marriage hymn the bridegroom tells the bride: "I take your hand for prosperity so that you may grow to old age with me, your husband. The gods Bhaga, Aryaman, Savitṛ, and the wise Pūṣan have given you to me for performing the duties of a householder."[32] The *Taittirīya Brāhmaṇa* echoes the same theme: "May the wife unite with her husband by means of good deeds; they become yoked like oxen to the sacrifice."[33] The intimate and unbreakable union between husband and wife in the sacrifice, the *Śatapatha Brāhmaṇa* (12.8.2.6) says, is like that between truth and faith, and between mind and speech: wherever the husband is there also is the wife. "It is on account of this close association of the wife in all sacrifices (either śrauta ["vedic"] or smārta ["domestic"])," says Kane (1974, II.1, 558), "that the wife if she dies before her husband is burnt with the sacred fire or fires and with the sacrificial vessels and implements [of her husband]."

2.1.2 Marriage and Procreation

Next to sacrifice, the obligation to procreate is central to the Brāhmaṇical theology of religious life. In his final instruction the teacher reminds the pupil who has completed

28. TS 1.7.6.5. So also the *Īśa Upaniṣad* (2): "Let a man desire to live a hundred years here while he continues to perform sacrifices." A hundred years is considered the full life span of humans: TS 1.5.2.2; 1.5.7.6; 1.6.6.3; 2.3.2.1; 2.3.11.5; 3.2.6.3; 7.2.1.4; 7.5.9.2; AitB 2.17; 6.2; ŚB 2.3.3.6; 4.3.4.3; 5.4.1.13; 5.5.4.27; 13.1.1.4. The ŚB (11.1.2.1–13) states that gods became immortal by gaining the year (= all) and that humans can do the same by performing the new- and full-moon sacrifices for at least 30 years.

29. TS 1.5.2.1; KS 9.2. In the later legal texts extinguishing or neglecting to kindle the sacred fires is regarded as a sin resulting in the loss of caste (*upapātaka*): MDh 11.66; YDh 3.234, 239; ViDh 37.28; 54.13. GDh 15.16 states that the destroyer of the sacred fire should not be fed and at 2.11 says that such a person defiles those who dine with him (*paṅktidūṣaka*) and that his sin is an *upapātaka*. Cf. VaDh 11.45–46.

30. TB 2.2.2.6; 3.3.3.1. The need for the wife to be present at the sacrifice is illustrated by the tale of Rāma, who sacrificed with a golden image of Sītā by his side during the period she was held captive by Rāvaṇa: Rām 7.91.25. See Kane 1974, II.1, 428–29, 556–58.

31. ŚB 5.2.1.8. TB 3.7.1 states that "half of the sacrifice is destroyed in the case of that sacrificer whose wife is unavailable [e.g., due to her menses] on the day of sacrifice."

32. RV 10.85.36. Again at 3.53.4 the RV states: "Wife is the true home"—*jāyed astam*. The MBh (12.144.66) echoes the same thought: "The home is not the house, they say, but the housewife"—*na gṛhaṃ gṛhaṃ ity āhur gṛhiṇī gṛham ucyate*.

33. TB 3.7.5.11. See also KS 5.4; MDh 9.96. On the cooperation between husband and wife in the sacrifice in later Mīmāṃsā theology, see PMS 6.1.6–21. The ĀpDh sees this cooperation as the reason why there can be no partition of property between a husband and a wife (2.14.16-17) and why a husband cannot take a second wife when his first is able to participate in the ritual (2.11.12–14). The grammarian Pāṇini (*Aṣṭādhyāyī*, 4.1.33) likewise says that the title *patnī* ("wife") is reserved for a wife who shares in the husband's sacrifices. Patañjali, commenting on this *sūtra*, observes that the wife of a Śūdra, who is not entitled to sacrifice, is not a true *patnī*, but is so called by analogy.

his vedic studies and is about to assume the responsibilities of adulthood of this obligation: "Speak the truth. Follow the Law (*dharma*). Do not neglect the daily vedic recitation. Bring a generous gift for the teacher, and then do not cut off the line of progeny" (TU 1.11.1).

Procreation, just like sacrifice, is a religious duty that presupposes marriage. Indeed, the complete religious persona, according to this theology, is constituted by the triad of husband/father, wife/mother, and son.[34] The wife is one half of the husband (TS 6.1.8.5), because so long as a man is without a wife he remains childless and incomplete:

> A full half of one's self is one's wife. As long as one does not obtain a wife, therefore, for so long one is not reborn[35] and remains incomplete. As soon as he obtains a wife, however, he is reborn and becomes complete. (ŚB 5.2.1.10; cf. ŚB 8.7.2.3)

"When he finds a wife, therefore," the *Aitareya Āraṇyaka* (1.2.5) remarks, "a man considers himself to be, as it were, more complete."

The fully complete person, however, includes not just the married couple but also the fruit of their union, the son, in whom the father is reborn and who constitutes the father's immortality. A later legal text puts it plainly: "Wife, self, and offspring: that, (the Vedas say), is the true extent of a man. Learned Brahmins, likewise, maintain: the husband is said to be the same as the wife."[36]

Apart from her indispensable role in ritual activities, the wife's importance is directly related to her being the mother of her husband's son. The marriage hymn of the *Ṛgveda* invokes the blessing of ten sons on the bride.[37] One of the common Sanskrit terms for wife, *jāyā,* is derived from the verbal root √*jan* ("to beget") and indicates that procreation is her essential and defining function. It is, however, not just the child that she begets; the husband is born again in her as the son. A wife's role in this rebirth and continuation of her husband is said to be her true "wifehood" (*jāyātva*):

> The husband enters the wife;
> Becoming an embryo he enters the mother.
> Becoming in her a new man again,
> He is born in the tenth month.

34. Son refers not merely to a single male child but represents male progeny regardless of number. Cf. AV 6.112.2; TS 6.5.6.3; Gonda 1976, 14. Copulation or pairing (*mithuna*) is said to consist of three: TS 5.3.6.2; TB 1.1.9.4; 1.6.3.1; 3.11.9.5; JB 2.123. Although "son" often refers to offspring in general, the male child is the offspring par excellence: "the wife is a friend, a daughter brings grief, but a son is a light in the highest heaven" (AitB 7.13). On the importance attached to the begetting of a son in the Brāhmaṇas, see Keith 1925, 579–80.

35. The author plays on the double meaning of *prajāyate*: "to be reborn" and "to beget." Without a wife one cannot beget a son and thereby make oneself reborn in the son.

36. MDh 9.45. Yājñavalkya (YDh 1.78), likewise, states that sons, rites, service, pleasure, and heaven for oneself and for one's ancestors depend on the wife. The wife is one half of the husband: MDh 1.74.40; Bṛhaspati quoted Aparāditya's commentary on YDh, p. 740.

37. RV 10.85.45. See also RV 1.91.20; 1.92.12; 3.1.23. A sonless wife is said to be possessed of ill luck (*nirṛti*): ŚB 5.3.2.2. See MS 1.10.11; 3.6.3; JB 1.98f. Later legal texts also agree that women are created to produce offspring: MDh 9.96. ĀpDh 2.11.13–14, for example, permits a man to take a second wife if the first is unable to bear a son.

A wife is called "wife,"
Because in her he is born again.[38]

"The father," says the *Śatapatha Brāhmaṇa* (12.4.3.1), "is the same as the son, and the son is the same as the father." Consequently, a man should desire a good wife, thinking "let my self come into existence in something good," and guard her continuously "lest in my womb, in my world somebody else come into existence."[39]

The *Ṛgveda* (5.4.10) already expresses the belief, later to become a cardinal point in the Brāhmaṇical theology of religious life, that the son constitutes the immortality of the father: "Through offspring, O Agni, may we attain immortality."[40] The *Taittirīya Brāhmaṇa* (1.5.5.6) forthrightly exclaims: "In your offspring you are born again; that, O mortal, is your immortality." A father is born a second time in his son (AitĀ 2.5), and he attains immortality when he sees the face of his living son (AitB 7.13.1).

The vedic conceptions of immortality as freedom from death[41] and of the family as the true and complete person are reflected in the belief that a man's immortality is found in his son. The family line continues in the son despite the death of the father; the son inherits the paternal estate and replaces the father as the ritual and economic head of the family. As the son survives after the father's death, so the father in his son survives his own death. This appears to be the meaning of the statement that a father is born again in his son. This new birth frees him from the death that must eventually end the life begun at his first birth. In a very significant way, therefore, the family is what guarantees human immortality.

The belief that the son continues the existence of the father finds ritual expression in the ceremony of transmission (*saṃpratti* or *saṃpradāna*), which is performed when the father's death is imminent.[42] According to the *Kauṣītakī Upaniṣad* (2.15) account, the son lies on top of the father touching each limb and organ of the father with his own. The father then delivers all his faculties to the son and the son accepts them. The father, as he departs, enters the son and through him stands firm in the world. The son assists the father as he departs and procures him a world (*loka*).

Gonda (1966, 70) observes that there is "a close association between the possession of a son and the *loka* ['world' or 'living space'] concept."[43] The long eulogy of a son

38. AitB 7.13. MDh 9.8: "The husband enters the wife and, becoming an embryo, is born again here. That he is thus born (*jāyate*) again by her constitutes the true wifehood (*jāyātva*) of a wife (*jāyā*)." See also YDh 1.56; MBh 1.68.36. TS 5.6.8.4 speaks of three seeds: father, son, and grandson. MBh 12.179.14–15 declares that as a tree survives only in the seed, so a man survives only in his seed, the son. See also TB 3.12.9.7; ŚĀ 4.11; ĀśG 1.15.3; Keith 1925, 579–80.

39. JB 1.17. Bodewitz's (1973) translation. See also BDh 2.2.3.34; ĀpDh 2.13.7; MDh 9.7–9; YDh 1.81.

40. This passage occurs also in TS 1.4.46.1 and VaDh 17.4. It is associated with the theology of debts in the BDh 2.6.11.33. TS 7.1.1.1 equates offspring with light (*jyotis*). On securing immortality through a son, see ĀpDh 2.24.1; VaDh 17.1–5; MDh 9.107, 137; YDh 1.78; ViDh 15.45–46; O'Flaherty 1973, 76–77; Gonda 1957, 8–14.

41. See section 2.1.1, n. 10.

42. BāU 1.5.17–20; KauṣU 2.15. For a discussion see Sprockhoff 1979, 385–98, and section 4.3.2.

43. In the *saṃpradāna* ceremony also the son is called the world. See BāU 1.5.17: "Through a son he conquers the worlds, through a grandson he obtains immortality, but through his son's grandson he gains the world of the sun." VaDh 17.5; MDh 9.137; ViDh 15.46; YDh 1.78. In JB 1.17 the husband calls the womb of his wife in which his son will be conceived "my world."

from the *Aitareya Āraṇyaka* (7.13) cited below says that "A sonless man has no world." According to the *Bṛhadāraṇyaka Upaniṣad*, "this world of men is to be obtained only by a son and by no other means" (1.5.16); a son is "world-procuring" (*lokya:* BāU 1.5.17). The continuation of life and of the world requires the begetting of sons (AitĀ 2.5; JB 1.85). Aṣṭādaṃṣṭra, who had grown old without sons, thought that he had "torn asunder these worlds" (PB 8.9.21; Gonda 1966, 72):

> That the possession of offspring and livelihood, i.e. the double aspect of continuance of life, might be considered the essential elements of a *loka* appears from TB 2.2.3.1f *ṛtavaḥ saṃvatsaraḥ; prajāḥ paśava ime lokāḥ* "the year is (consists of) the seasons, these 'Räume' [expanses or worlds] are (consist of) offspring (creatures) and cattle." (Gonda 1966, 70–71)

A conversation between King Hariścandra, who had a hundred wives but still failed to obtain a son, and Nārada (AitB 7.13) provides perhaps the clearest and boldest enunciation of the theological significance of a son and, by implication, of a wife, although, as we shall see below, it also contains hints that significant challenges to this theology were brewing. Hariścandra asks:

1. Now, since they desire a son,
Both those who are intelligent and those who aren't;[44]
What does one gain by a son?
Tell me that, O Nārada.

Nārada replies:

2. A debt he pays in him,
And immortality he gains,
The father who sees the face
Of his son born and alive.

3. Greater than the delights
That earth, fire, and water
Bring to living beings,
Is a father's delight in his son

4. By means of sons have fathers ever
Crossed over the mighty darkness;
For one is born from oneself,
A ferry laden with food.[45]

5. What is the use of dirt and deer skin?
What profit in beard and austerity?
Seek a son, O Brahmin,
He is the world free of blame.[46]

44. As the commentator, Sāyaṇa, points out, the meaning appears to be that both rational beings such as humans and gods and non-rational animals desire progeny. Keith's translation, "Since now men desire a son," misses this point, which is mentioned also in verses 10–11.

45. The father is born from himself as the son (see verse 7), who is like a ship full of provisions that will ferry the father to safety.

46. The meaning is uncertain. I follow Sāyaṇa's interpretation, which accords with the general belief that the son procures a happy world for the father. Keith translates: "This is the world's advice." Haug:

6. Food is breath, clothes protect.
Gold is for beauty, cattle for marriage.
The wife is a friend, a daughter brings grief.
But a son is a light in the highest heaven.

7. The husband enters the wife;
Becoming an embryo he enters the mother.
Becoming in her a new man again,
He is born in the tenth month.

8. A wife is called "wife,"
Because in her he is born again.[47]
He is productive, she is productive,
For the seed is placed in her.

9. The gods and the seers
Brought to her great luster.
The gods said to men:
"She is your mother again."[48]

10. "A sonless man has no world."
All the beasts know this.
Therefore a son mounts
Even his mother and sister.

11. This is the broad and easy path
Along which travel men with sons, free from sorrow;
Beasts and birds see it;
So they copulate even with their mothers.

In this connection it is noteworthy that, as we have seen, the creative act of Prajāpati has all the features of the procreative act. The Sanskrit term for creature and offspring is the same: *prajā*. Prajāpati ("lord or protector of *prajā*") is not only the creator of creatures but also the father of offspring. Human procreation thus follows the archetypal activity of creation and, therefore, is likened to a sacrifice. The sexual act is called a fire sacrifice (*agnihotra:* ŚB 11.6.2.10). The *Bṛhadāraṇyaka Upaniṣad* (6.4.3) homologizes the various parts of a woman with elements of the sacrifice: "Her vulva is a sacrificial altar; her pubic hairs, the sacrificial grass; her skin, the soma-press, and her labia, the fire in the middle." Sexual intercourse is a Soma sacrifice: "As great indeed as the world gained by one who performs a Soma sacrifice, is the world gained by one who, with this knowledge, engages in sexual intercourse" (BāU 6.4.3). The same idea is present in the famous doctrine of the five fires (*pañcāgnividyā*), which seeks to explain the rebirth process. The final step in a person's return to earth is sexual intercourse. At this sexual

"Thus people talk of them." Dirt, deer skin, beard, and austerity are references to some type of ascetic life that challenged the values of marriage and children.

47. See above (especially n. 38) for an explanation of this etymology of "wife" (*jāyā*).

48. In this extraordinary passage that, if he had known it, would have have delighted Freud, the wife is presented to the men as their mother, because in their sons they will be born again by her and become, in effect, her children.

sacrifice the woman is the fire in which the man offers the semen; the result of this sacrifice is the birth of a child.[49]

The belief that a son saves or rescues (*trāti*) his father is expressed in etymologies, often far-fetched,[50] of *putra*, the Sanskrit term for son. In this context the son rescues the father not from death but from evil worlds in which he may end up after death. It is already hinted at in the transmission (*sampratti*) passage of the *Bṛhadāraṇyaka Upaniṣad* (1.5.17): "Whatever wrong has been done by him, his son frees him from all that. Therefore, he is called *putra* ('son')." Later literature takes the term *putra* to be a compound word made of *put* and *trā* ("to rescue"). *Put* is said to be the name of a hell, although the term does not occur outside this context.[51] A son (*putra*) receives his name, therefore, because he saves his father from the Put hell.[52]

2.1.3 The Theology of Debts

In the foregoing discussion we saw a significant aspect of what Peter Berger (1969) has called world construction, the social creation of a common conceptual framework within which individuals can understand and find meaning in their discrete experiences of themselves and of the social and physical world. Sacrificial and procreative theology addressed in a special way the marginal situation of death when the socially constructed world is threatened with ultimate meaninglessness. In explaining death and the means of overcoming it, moreover, this theology legitimized the central social institution of marriage and, by extension, society itself.

All culturally created worlds, however, are intrinsically unstable (Berger 1969, 29). They are constantly challenged by new experiences and by individuals and groups seeking new meanings. We will discuss some explicit challenges to the Brāhmaṇical theology later in this chapter. A couple of examples will suffice to illustrate that even within the Brāhmaṇical tradition not everyone appears to have agreed with the centrality given to sacrifice and procreation and that some segments of that society were seeking new meanings of life and death. A challenge to sacrifice, for example, forms the likely background of a significant passage in the *Śatapatha Brāhmaṇa* (1.2.5.24), even though it is presented within the context of a minor ritual violation:

> Then unbelief (*aśraddhā*) took hold of men. They said: "Those who sacrifice become more sinful, while those who do not sacrifice become more excellent." Thereupon no sacrificial oblations reached the gods from here, for the gods subsist on what is

49. BāU 6.2.9–13; ChU 5.5–9; JB 1.18. At ChU 3.17.5 also the sacrificial analogy is apparent: *soṣyati* ("he will procreate") also means "he will press out (the Soma juice)," and *asṛṣṭa* ("he has procreated") also means "he has pressed out." This activity is called the father's rebirth, which is true with reference to both procreation and sacrifice. Conversely, sexual symbolism is evident within the sacrifice, as in the parallelism between the sexual act and the generation of fire by means of the fire drill. See Gonda, 1957, 23.

50. See my comments on "phonetic etymology" section 1.1.3, n. 38.

51. Cf. Sprockhoff 1979, 388, n. 53; Mayrhofer II, 303.

52. Cf. GoB 1.1.2; MBh 1.68.38; 1.129.14; Rām 2.115.12; MDh 9.138; ViDh 15.44. Yāska in *Nirukta*, 2.11) gives two possible etymologies: *putraḥ puru trāyate niparaṇād vā pun narakaṃ tatas trāyata iti vā* —"a son is so called because he rescues often by offering oblations to the manes, or because he rescues from the hell called Put."

> offered from here. Now, the gods said to Bṛhaspati Āṅgirasa: "Unbelief indeed has taken hold of men. Ordain the sacrifice for them."

The sacrifices, these "unbelievers" may have argued, are more important to gods than to men, for gods depend on them for their subsistence. It is precisely such an "unbelief" that the *Bṛhadāraṇyaka Upaniṣad* (1.4.10) supports:

> In the beginning this was just Brahman, and it knew only itself, thinking "I am Brahman." Therefore it became all. Whoever among the gods came to realize this, only he became that. So also is it in the case of seers and men. . . . So even now whoever knows that, thinking "I am Brahman," becomes all this. Even the gods cannot prevent his becoming that, for he is their very self. So whoever worships another divinity than himself thinking "I am one and he is another," he knows not. Just as an animal is for men, so is he for the gods. As indeed many animals serve a man, so does each man serve the gods. Even if one animal is taken away, it causes displeasure; how much more, if many? It does not please the gods, therefore, that men should know this.

With regard to procreation, the long discourse of Nārada (AitB 7.13) cited above is clearly directed against those who belittled the religious significance of a son, as when he asks rhetorically:

> What is the use of dirt and deer skin?
> What profit in beard and austerity?
> Seek a son, O Brahmin,
> He is the world free of blame.

The initial response of the experts of the old religious world to such challenges commonly is to create new and more sophisticated schemes of legitimation (Berger 1969, 31f). The two theological schemes we are about to discuss appear to be such efforts at legitimizing the centrality of sacrifice and procreation and, consequently, of the married householder.

The first scheme uses the concept of debt to characterize certain major religious obligations centered on the householder and presents these debts as innate traits of every individual.[53] The second extends the meaning of sacrifice to cover five daily obligations of a householder (see section 2.1.4).

There are two formulations of the theology of debt in the vedic literature. The first and perhaps the older formulation (Sprockhoff 1979, 389) is found in the *Taittirīya Saṃhitā* (6.3.10.5):

> A Brahmin, at his very birth, is born with a triple debt—of studentship to the seers, of sacrifice to the gods, of offspring to the fathers. He is, indeed, free from debt, who has a son, is a sacrificer, and who has lived as a student. This (debt) he satisfies (*avadayate*) by these cuttings (*avadāna*). That is how the cuttings get their name.

The formulation in the *Śatapatha Brāhmaṇa* (1.7.2.1–6) reads:

53. For a detailed discussion of this doctrine see Malamoud 1980. The entire issue of *Puruṣārtha* (1980, n. 4) in which Malamoud's study is published is devoted to the concept of debt in South Asia. On the debt to the seers, see Malamoud 1977, 24–44.

Now, whoever exists is born indeed as a debt at his very birth to the gods, to the seers, to the fathers, and to men.[54] Because he has to sacrifice, he is born as a debt to the gods; and he pays it to them when he sacrifices to them and when he makes offerings to them.

Because he has to study the Veda, furthermore, he is born as a debt to the seers; and he pays it to them, for they call a person who has studied the Vedas "the guardian of the seers' treasure."

Because he has to desire offspring, furthermore, he is born as a debt to the fathers; and he pays it to them when he has children that provide the continuity of their lineage.

Because he has to provide shelter, furthermore, he is born as a debt to men; and he pays it to them when he offers them shelter and food.

Whoever does all these things, has done what he has to do; he obtains everything, and he conquers everything. So, because he is born as a debt to the gods, he satisfies (*avadayate*) them when he sacrifices and when he makes offerings in the fire. Therefore, whatever they offer in the fire is called *avadāna* [the portion cut for sacrificial offering].

Before I discuss these two formulations of the doctrine, it may be useful to examine the vedic concept of debt and its relationship to religious duties and obligations. The concept of debt in the earliest strata of the vedic literature is rather complex. "Debt" refers first and foremost to the acceptance of a loan with the promise of future payment (RV 8.47.17). There are, for example, frequent references to the debts incurred by gamblers (RV. 10.34.10; AV. 6.118). Even these common debts, however, appear to have broader implications; debtors will remain bound by their debts even after death. Bergaigne (1878, III, 163–65) and Renou (1955–69, VII, 89; XV, 179) have noted the ambiguity of the term *ṛṇa* ("debt"), which can mean a debt in the strict sense as well as fault, crime, or guilt. These two meanings are often present together as components of a single concept.[55]

Indebtedness is considered a grave state and gods are frequently petitioned to eliminate one's debt.[56] The Apsarases, for example, are asked in AV 6.118 to discharge debts incurred in gambling, while in the very next hymn (AV 6.119) Agni Vaiśvānara is requested to remit debts not related to gambling. A suppliant prays: "Debtless in this (world), debtless in the higher, debtless in the third world may we be; the world traversed by the gods and traversed by the fathers—in all the paths may we abide debtless" (AV 6.117.3). The remitting of a debt by gods clearly does not refer to the actual payment of the sum owed to a creditor, but rather to the release from the inner state of

54. Eggeling (ŚB tr. I, p. 190, n. 1) considers the wording of this sentence ambiguous "so much so indeed, that it could also be taken in the sense that 'whoever exists, is born as (one to whom) a debt (is owed) from the gods,'" and refers to ŚB 1.1.2.19 where the gods are said to be indebted to the sacrificer. This ambiguity, however, disappears if we consider the context, for, although the gods may be viewed as indebted to man, the seers, fathers, and men cannot be so considered. On the ŚB version see Devasthali 1965, 100.

55. Malamoud (1980, 41), citing Renou (1955–69, XV, 179), considers the "stricter sense" of the term connected with the social contract to be its primordial meaning. Such attempts to establish semantic priority are hazardous at best. The dual aspect of the term is also present in the German "Schuld." On the uncertain etymology of *ṛṇa*, see Malamoud 1980, 42–43.

56. Petitions are directed, among others, at Varuṇa (RV 2.28.9), Ādityas (RV 2.27.4), Soma (RV 9.47.2), Uṣas (RV 10.127.7), Indra (RV 4.23.7), and Maruts (RV 1.169.7).

bondage and obligation which indebtedness creates. It is to this inner state that the second meaning of debt, namely guilt, refers. When people are in debt they lack something; they are wanting in fullness. Significantly, the term *ṛṇa* is used in mathematics to indicate the "minus."

Already in the *Ṛgveda* human ritual obligations are referred to as debts. Brahmaṇaspati, for example, is asked to accept the debt, which in the context clearly refers to the sacrificial oblation.[57] Agni is requested not to accept the debt from an insincere brother (RV 4.3.13), where again "debt" refers to the sacrificial offering. Brahmins who offer Soma are not in debt (RV 8.32.16). At AV 6.119.2 Agni Vaiśvānara is petitioned to remit the debt owed to gods in general and to break the nooses—namely the state of bondage—that it creates. Besides the general debt to gods, the vedic texts refer frequently to a specific debt to Yama, the god of death (Malamoud 1980, 50–52): "At his very birth, indeed, a man is born as himself a debt to death. When he sacrifices he redeems himself from death" (ŚB 3.6.2.16). It is Agni once again who is petitioned to cancel this debt to Yama.[58]

There is one place in the *Ṛgveda* (6.61.1) where debt is associated with the acquisition of a son: "She [Sarasvatī] gave to the donor of oblations, Vadhryaśva, a son, Divodāsa, endowed with speed and acquitting the debt (*ṛṇacyutam*)." Although the passage does not specify to whom the debt is owed, it appears likely that the author has in mind the debt of a son to the forefathers.[59]

It appears, therefore, that already in the time of the *Ṛgveda* the category of debt with the accompanying notion of guilt was extended to human obligations vis-à-vis significant persons of the vedic world. The view that considered sacrifice and offspring as debts to gods and forefathers, therefore, was considerably older and more widespread than the two texts of the *Yajurveda*—the *Taittirīya Saṃhitā* and the *Śatapatha Brāhmaṇa*—in which it finds systematic formulation.

The context in which the theology of debts is discussed in these two texts also suggests that they were recapitulating a common doctrine rather than enunciating a new one. Neither expressly sets out to teach this doctrine. Both allude to it in the course of explaining the etymology and thereby the significance of *avadāna*, the sacrificial portions cut from a single sacrificial cake (in ŚB) or from the sacrificial animal (in TS). *Avadāna*, these texts point out, receives its name from the fact that it is offered to the gods as payment of a debt, thereby satisfying (*avadayati*) the gods.[60]

57. RV 2.24.13. Sāyaṇa explains by noting that the portion offered has the nature of a debt (*avadānasya ṛṇatvam*), namely that it is a debt owed to the gods, and refers to the passage TS 6.3.10.5 cited here, which also develops the doctrine of debts within the context of explaining the meaning of *avadāna*.

58. AV 6.117.1 (cf. parallels in Whitney's translation.). Cf. also TS 3.3.8.1; TB 3.7.9.8; ŚB 10.4.3.9.

59. Sāyaṇa explains that a son pays the vedic debt relating to fathers, as well as the secular debt, no doubt referring to the obligation of children to pay the debts incurred by their fathers. Chatterjee (1971, 86) sees here only a reference to the obligation of a son "to discharge debts incurred by father." See also Sprockhoff 1979, 389.

60. This is another example of what I have called "phonetic etymology" (section 1.1.3, n. 38). The term *avadāna* is etymologically derived from *ava-√do* ("to cut"), but its phonetic similarity to words derived from *ava-√day* ("to satisfy") provides the opportunity for the authors to explain the sacrifice as the payment of a debt to the gods. Cf. Eggeling, ŚB tr. I, p. 191, n. 1; Malamoud 1980, 45–46.

The doctrine of debts, moreover, was known also to the author of the *Aitareya Brāhmaṇa,* which belongs to the *Ṛgveda.* In one passage he defines an *anaddhāpuruṣa*[61] cryptically as *na devān na pitṝn na manuṣyān iti* (AitB 7.9). Keith translates the phrase: "One who (offers) neither to gods nor to the fathers nor to men."[62] Although he does not use the term "debt," it is very probable that the author in fact was referring to the doctrine of debts, especially because in the same passage there is a reference to being free from the debt to one's mother and father (*mātāpitṛbhyām anṛṇārthāt*). Another reference to debts occurs in the long passage of the same text praising a son that we have already cited (AitB 7.13). There the reference to the debt of procreation is clear:

> A debt he pays in him,
> And immortality he gains,
> The father who sees the face
> Of his son born and alive.

An important feature of the theology of debts is that a man becomes indebted by the mere fact of his birth. This stands in sharp contrast to the normal understanding that a debt is contracted by a deliberate action of an adult. Sāyaṇa (on ŚB 1.7.2.1) recognizes the new definition of debt in this theology when he says that "birth alone is the cause of indebtedness" (*ṛṇatve jananam eva nimittam*). The texts do not throw any light on the mechanism through which a man falls into debt at birth. There is no myth of origin that would give us some clues. Unlike the Judeo-Christian doctrine of original sin, the debts one incurs at birth, on the one hand, are not caused by some act committed by one's ancestors, and, on the other, affect only twice-born males. The manner in which debts are inherited, furthermore, contradicts the ideology of *karma.*[63] While the doctrine of *karma* insists that people reap what they sow, the doctrine of debts asserts that twice-born men become burdened with debts without any deliberate act on their part. Further, even though debts are incurred immediately upon birth, the tradition is unanimous that their payment can only be made when the individual is able and qualified to do so: the payment of the debt to the seers requires vedic initiation, and the payment of the debts to gods and forefathers presupposes marriage.[64]

It appears, therefore, that the concept of debt was given a new meaning in this theology and that it was used to illustrate and define the obligations of ritual actors—namely adult males—in the context of their relationship to significant individuals who play central roles in the vedic world. The inhabitants of this world—including gods, ancestors, seers, and other human and non-human beings—live in a web of interdependent relationships which create reciprocal rights and obligations. The obligations of twice-born adult males, who are the principal actors in the social world, are here singled out and defined as debts.

61. The term probably approximates "a good-for-nothing fellow." Malamoud (1980, 57, n. 72) translates it as "homme <de manière incertaine>" and sees his condition as resulting from his refusal to perform rites. He is therefore useless for gods, fathers, and men.

62. Haug (AitB tr. II, 455, n. 12) also takes the phrase to mean one who "does not discharge his duties towards the gods, ancestors and men."

63. In all likelihood, the theology of debts predates the origin of *karma* and rebirth as significant explanatory concepts in Indian theodicy.

64. For the use of this fact as an argument against those who rejected the legitimacy of the *āśrama* system on the basis of the theology of debts, see sections 6.2.2 and 8.5.

Let us now turn to the two formulations given in the *Taittirīya Saṃhitā* (TS) and the *Śatapatha Brāhmaṇa* (ŚB). Although both teach basically the same doctrine, there are several significant differences in the two formulations (Malamoud 1980, 47–48).

The most obvious difference is that the TS enumerates only three debts, whereas the ŚB gives four, with the addition of the debt of hospitality to men. The exegetical tradition and the later legal literature, however, take into account only the three debts of the TS and generally ignore the ŚB formulation.[65] The significance of the ŚB formulation, as I shall point out later, is its relation to the theology of the great sacrifices.

The person who incurs the debts is a Brahmin in the TS and "whoever exists" (*yo'sti*) in the ŚB (Sprockhoff 1979, 389). Malamoud expresses his astonishment at the cruel paradox of the ŚB where all are born in debt while only the twice-born can pay the debts to gods and seers. One does not have to be an Indian exegete to see that this is a false dilemma caused by reading too much into the wording of the ŚB. It is quite unlikely that the priestly author of the ŚB wanted to make a statement about human beings or human nature in general. Vedic authors, just like their later dharmaśāstric counterparts, normally address only the twice-born males, who alone are qualified to participate fully in the vedic religion. Sentences 2–5 of this passage, moreover, suggest that the existence of the debts is revealed by the obligation or the propensity of men to perform these tasks. Now, the obligations to sacrifice and to study the Vedas exist only for twice-born men; other men and all women are forbidden to undertake these activities. It appears more likely, therefore, that the ŚB uses the expression "whoever exists" to complement the expressions "is born" (*jāyate*) and "at his very birth" (*jāyamāna eva*), highlighting thereby the fact that the very existence, the very birth of a man creates his condition of indebtedness.

The word "Brahmin" in the TS version, likewise, has been interpreted by Indian exegetes such as Śabara (on PMS 6.2.31) as including all three twice-born classes. This need not be viewed as a purely scholastic interpretation, because in most Brāhmaṇical texts the terms *brāhmaṇa* and *dvija* ("twice-born") are used interchangeably. The main object of these injunctions is the Brahmin, although mutatis mutandis they refer to other twice-born men as well (Biardeau and Malamoud 1976, 32).

The TS says that a man is born "indebted" (*ṛṇavā*), while the ŚB says that he is born "a debt" (*ṛṇam*). Here too I am not sure how much we should read into this wording. The ŚB, however, appears to make a stronger statement: man is not just affected by debts, he is defined by them.

The TS, furthermore, declares that when one has performed the three duties one becomes freed from debt (*anṛṇa*). The ŚB makes no mention of freeing oneself from debt. According to the ŚB, the obligation to perform the four duties is correlated to the fourfold debt; the one cannot exist without the other. If a man is freed from debt at any time during life, he would not have to perform those duties thereafter. It appears, therefore, that the ŚB envisaged the four duties as lifelong obligations; one is freed from debt only at death. This supports Malamoud's (1980, 48) opinion that the ŚB formulation is related to the doctrine of the great sacrifices (*mahāyajña*), to which I shall turn presently. The TS, on the other hand, sets specific times when a man can be regarded as freed from

65. A notable exception is the MBh. At 1.111.12–14 it speaks of four debts—to gods, seers, ancestors, and men—and at 12.174.13 it alludes to the duty to please gods, ancestors, seers, and Prajāpati. Guests replace seers in the three debts at 12.25.6. Twice the MBh refers to five debts (12.281.9–11; 13.37.18).

debts at least with reference to seers and forefathers. He achieves this freedom after he has finished the period of studentship and after he has had a son (*putrī*). The *Aitareya Brāhmaṇa* (7.13) also suggests that the birth of a son constitutes the total payment of one's debt to the fathers. The time when one is freed from the debt to the gods is left vague; the term *yajvā* ("sacrificer") used by the TS may mean a person who has offered one or many sacrifices, and may imply a lifelong obligation to engage in sacrifices.

The debt of procreation raises several questions. First, it is remarkable that the ŚB relates this debt not to any extrinsic obligation but to the internal and innate longing for children. We saw a similar view in the AitB (7.13) where even incest among animals is justified on these grounds. The ŚB, moreover, speaks only of children or progeny in general (*prajā*), whereas the TS, as also the AitB (7.13), refers specifically to the birth of a son. Second, it is unclear whether the debt is simply abolished at the birth of a son cr whether it is passed on to the son. The problem is created by the ambiguity of the term *saṃnayati* (meaning both "bestow" and "pay") used in the AitB 7.13 and in later literature (VaDh 17.1; MDh 9.107). Geldner (1951–57, II, 368) argues, on the basis of RV 8.47.17, where the same term is used with reference to the payment of a debt, that it means "aufbringen" or "zusammenbringen," that is, "to pay up completely." Bühler, in his translations of VaDh 17.1 and MDh 9.107, takes it to mean "to throw on." The father, according to this interpretation, passes his debt onto his son (Malamoud 1980, 54–55). Later legal texts appear to favor the latter interpretation. The obligation to assume this vedic debt of the father, they reason, is the basis for a son's obligation to assume his father's secular debts and to pay them after his father's death.[66]

The final, and perhaps the most significant, question is whether the debt to the forefathers is paid just by the first son. The TS and the AitB (7.13) are ambivalent, although they can be interpreted to mean that the oldest living son constitutes that payment.[67] Later legal texts, however, opt for this interpretation and make it the basis of primogeniture:[68] "That son alone on whom he throws his debt and through whom he obtains immortality [cf. AitB 7.13] is begotten in fulfillment of the Law [*dharmaja*]; others they consider the offspring of desire [*kāmaja*]" (MDh 9.107). It is open to question, however, whether this view was shared by the vedic authors. The obligation, and indeed the desire, to procreate do not end with just the first son. The *Ṛgveda* (10.85.45) invokes the blessing of ten sons on the bride. The husband is also required to have sexual relations with his wife during the proper season, that is, soon after her monthly period.[69] Nevertheless, as we shall see (section 6.2.1), the view that the first-born satisfies the debt to the fathers played an important role in the history of the *āśrama* system.

One other difference between the two formulations relates to the action that consti-

66. See Kane1973, III, 442–54; Chatterjee 1971, 87–134.

67. The term *putrī* in the TS can mean a person who possesses one or several sons. Similarly, the AitB passage need not necessarily refer only to the first-born son. It may mean that the birth of every son constitutes a payment of a debt to the fathers.

68. Manu (MDh 9.106) is clear: "Immediately on the birth of his first-born a man becomes the father of a son and is freed from the debt to the fathers. That son, therefore, is entitled to the whole estate."

69. See MDh 3.45–46; 9.4; GDh 5.1; ĀpDh 2.1.17; BDh 4.1.18–21; VaDh 12.21; ViDh 69.1; YDh 1.79–81; ŚG 4.11.16; PārG 1.11.7–8. Besides the obvious economic ones, there are many religious reasons for the desirability of having many children. "One should desire to have many sons in the hope that one of them may repair to Gayā" (ViDh 85.70). Cf. MatsP 207.39.

tutes the payment of the debt to the seers. The TS specifies residence at the teacher's as a student, whereas the ŚB speaks more generally of studying, which can refer to both the period of formal studentship and the daily recitation of the Veda (*svādhyāya*) obligatory on all, including householders (Malamoud 1977, 1–89). This wording again fits with the ŚB view that the debts are lifelong duties and confirms the connection within the ŚB between the debts and the great sacrifices.

The ŚB, furthermore, gives the positive result obtained by performing the duties inherent in the debts: "Whoever does all these things, has done what he has to do; he obtains everything, and he conquers everything." Winning everything is a common expression in the Brāhmaṇas to indicate the attainment of one's final goal: heaven and immortality (Gonda 1984, 62–63).

In spite of these significant differences, the doctrine of debts became an important theological device for legitimating several central religious and social obligations of the vedic world, especially sacrifice and procreation entailing marriage and domestic life.

2.1.4 The Theology of the Great Sacrifices

Like the theology of debts, the theology of great sacrifices also appears to represent an attempt to present systematically and to legitimize theologically the major religious duties of a twice-born man.[70] As the former extends the meaning of debt, so the latter extends the meaning of sacrifice to provide a new theological evaluation of five daily duties of a married householder.

Every day he is obliged to offer (1) a fire oblation as a sacrifice to gods; (2) the private recitation of the Veda as a sacrifice to Brahman; (3) oblations of food and water as a sacrifice to the forefathers; (4) hospitality as a sacrifice to human beings; and (5) *bali* offerings as a sacrifice to beings (*bhūta*).[71] The great sacrifices are mentioned in the *Śatapatha Brāhmaṇa* (11.5.6.6–7) and the *Taittirīya Āraṇyaka* (2.10.1). According to several Gṛhyasūtras and nearly all the Dharma texts, these sacrifices form the central daily duties of a householder.[72]

Devasthali (1965, 100) and Malamoud (1980, 48) have noted the analogies between the great sacrifices and the ŚB version of the debts.[73] The debts to gods, seers, and men correspond exactly to the sacrifices to gods, Brahman, and men, respectively. The sacrifice to the fathers, however, consists of food and water offerings, whereas the debt to them relates to begetting offspring. These two duties, nevertheless, are connected with

70. On the great sacrifices, see Gonda 1980, 413–21; Malamoud 1977, 11–21; Kane 1974, II.1, 696–704; Basu 1969, 220–23; Biardeau and Malamoud 1976, 40–48.

71. *Bali* is a food offering made to a sundry group of beings, including "certain gods, semi-divine beings, spirits, household divinities, animals, all sorts of other creatures, and even undefined deities (beings) or lifeless objects." Gonda 1980, 417.

72. BG 2.9.6; BGp 2.4.8–13; BhārG 3.15; ĀśG 3.1.1–5; PārG 2.9.1–12; VaiG 6.17; ĀgG 3.12.2; GDh 5.3,9; BDh 2.6.11.1–7; ĀpDh 1.12.15–16; 1.13.1; MDh 3.69–83; 4.21; ViDh 59.20–25; YDh 1.102; KūrP 2.18. For the different orders in which they are enumerated see Malamoud 1977, 13.

73. Biardeau (in Biardeau and Malamoud 1976, 40) ignores the ŚB version when she relates the five sacrifices to the three debts: "On a ici une nouvelle formulation des <trois dettes> congénitales dont doit s'acquitter le <deux-fois-né>. Les trois dettes sont devenues cinq, mais ce qui est plus remarquable est qu'elles soient exprimées en termes du sacrifice."

each other, because one of the principal reasons for keeping the line unbroken (ŚB 1.7.2.4) is to ensure that these offerings, on which depends the felicity of the forefathers, are carried out without interruption. Thus, the *Mahābhārata* (1.111.14), speaking of the same four debts as the *Śatapatha Brāhmaṇa*, states that the debt to the fathers consists of both sons and food offerings (*śrāddha*). Elsewhere the *Mahābhārata* says that this debt consists of just the food offerings.[74] The sacrifice to the *bhūta*s is something completely new. It appears to be an extension of the debt of hospitality from human to non-human beings.

The other significant feature of the great[75] sacrifices is that they are considered sacrifices. This theology is one more instance of the common tendency in Brāhmaṇism to conceive any activity of value in terms of sacrifice. We have seen already the extension of the concept of sacrifice to procreation. "Sacrifice" becomes the currency for appraising the value of an activity. In later literature many religious and devotional acts, and even acts of military heroism, are measured by that currency; one practice may be worth a hundred Soma sacrifices, and another a thousand horse sacrifices!

The number five is derived probably from the ancient fivefold division of the sacrifice.[76] The *Aitareya Brāhmaṇa* (2.3.3) relates this classification of sacrifices to the fivefold nature of a human being, who consists of earth, air, ether, water, and light. The year, which is often identified with the sacrifice (Gonda 1984, 67–71), is similarly considered as fivefold, consisting as it does of the five Indian seasons.[77] At a much later date, Manu (MDh 3.73–74) gives each of the five great sacrifices a specific sacrificial appellation mostly derived from the verbal root √*hu* ("to sacrifice"): *ahuta* ("not offered in the fire" = vedic recitation), *huta* ("burnt oblations to gods"), *prahuta* ("offered by scattering" = *bali*), *brāhmyahuta* ("offered in Brahmins" = hospitality), and *prāśita* ("eaten" = oblation to the manes).[78]

A major difference between the two theologies of debts and great sacrifices is that the former refers in a general way to ritual obligations of twice-born men, whereas the latter deals with the duties of a householder that have to be performed every day. As we

74. MBh 12.281.9–11. At MBh 12.174.13 the fathers are said to be satisfied with offerings and Prajāpati with offspring. The reference in the MBh to five debts also supports the connection between debts and sacrifices: MBh 12.281.9–11; 13.37.18.

75. The *Āpastamba Dharmasūtra* (1.4.12.15) says that these are called "great" by way of laudation. The ŚB, in which the expression first appears, uses it with reference to the Soma sacrifice (11.7.2.2). By extension the ŚB (2.4.4.14) says that one gains as much reward from a full- and new-moon sacrifice as from a Soma sacrifice, and concludes that the former "is indeed a great sacrifice." It is possible that these five acts are called great sacrifices through a similar extension from the Soma sacrifice.

76. TS 5.4.7.2; 6.1.1.8; 6.1.5.2; 6.1.9.5; 6.2.1.3; ŚB 1.5.2.16; 4.5.1.14.

77. "There are five utterances . . . ; fivefold is the sacrifice, fivefold the animal victim, five are the seasons of the year: this is the one measure of the sacrificial rite, this its completion" (ŚB 1.5.2.16). Cf. ŚB 3.1.3.17; 3.1.4.5, 20; 3.3.3.5; 3.4.1.14; 3.9.4.11. In India the rainy season is added to the four seasons. Another parallel is the doctrine of the five fires (*pañcāgnividyā*): see n. 49. On the significance of five, see Gonda 1970, 41, 45–48. See also section 8.3.

78. See Kane 1974, II.1, 698–700. The reason given by Manu for these sacrifices reveals the growing importance of the ethic of non-injury (*ahiṃsā*): "A householder has five slaughter houses—the hearth, the grinding stone, the broom, the mortar and pestle, and the water pot—by using which he is bound. In order to expiate successively (the offenses committed by means) of all these the great sages have prescribed for householders the daily (performance of the five) great sacrifices" (MDh 3.68–69). Cf. ViDh 59.19–20; MatsP 52.15–16.

have seen, the daily fire sacrifice was considered not only a daily but also a lifelong obligation. Given the sacrificial context in which the five duties are enumerated, it is not farfetched to assume that they were similarly regarded as daily and lifelong obligations.

The theologies of debts and of great sacrifices show a significant change in the views regarding the nature of the obligation to sacrifice and to procreate. At first these acts were regarded as benefiting their performers either in this world or after death. In these theologies, however, gods and fathers are viewed as dependent on the services of men. They are harmed when sacrifices and oblations are not offered.[79] This dependence, of course, is mutual, because humans depend on gods and ancestors for rain, successful crops, and the like. The TS (3.2.9.7) puts it in a nutshell: "Gods live on what is offered from here. Men live on what is offered from there."

The householder thus stands at the center of the cosmic and the social food cycles.[80] He offers food to gods and ancestors, assuring thereby the continuity and success of the cosmic food cycle. He offers food not only to his immediate dependents but also to other human beings who depend on him for food on a temporary or permanent basis: beggars, religious mendicants, travellers, and guests. In the *bali* he extends the orbit of his food offering to include all known beings. Later Brāhmaṇical literature, as we shall see (sections 3.2.2.1–2), makes this a central point in the argument for the superiority of the householder.[81]

The married householder, therefore, represents the ideal religious life within the vedic world. We can sum up this ideal as follows. A twice-born man, following his vedic initiation, studies the Vedas at the house of his teacher; after returning home he marries a suitable wife and establishes his sacred fires; he begets offspring, especially sons, by his legitimate wife; and during his entire life offers sacrifices, recites the Veda, offers food and water to his deceased ancestors, gives food to guests and mendicants, and offers food oblations to all creatures. It is this theology of religious life which was rejected by the ascetical traditions and which was challenged and modified by the *āśrama* system.

2.2 The Socio-Economic Context

The period roughly between the sixth and the fourth century B.C.E.. was a time of radical social and economic changes in northern India, principally along the upper Ganges valley. It is doubtful whether the new religious ideologies and modes of life both within and outside the Brāhmaṇical tradition, ideologies that presented serious challenges to the vedic theology we have just examined and that were the catalysts for the creation of the *āśrama* system, could have arisen without those socio-economic changes. Although

79. The BDh 2.6.11.28 implies this when it says that the author of the division of *dharma* according to *āśramas* was "striving with the gods" (see section 3.2.1.2). Gods depend on the food offered in sacrifice: ŚB 8.1.2.10; 1.2.5.24–26 (see section 2.3.1). The MBh offers a number of examples of the dire state of the fathers when a descendent of theirs fails to beget a son and thus to assure the continuation of food offerings: 1.41.4–11; 3.94.11–15; 9.49.55.

80. On Indian food cycles, see Khare 1976; Olivelle 1991.

81. Āpastamba (ĀpDh 2.7.1–13), for example, equates the hospitable reception of guests with a sacrifice to Prajāpati, and goes on to draw close parallels between various elements of the hospitality rite and significant aspects of the sacrificial rite.

the dates cannot be established with precision, archaeological evidence suggests that these changes occurred roughly during the period—fifth century B.C.E..—that saw the creation of the *āśrama* system (see section 3.4).

The Aryans who migrated into India during the second millennium B.C.E. were nomads. They lived in tribes whose economy was based principally on cattle rearing. This tribal organization persisted even after these people had settled down in the upper Gangetic plane and agriculture had become their principal economic activity (Apte 1954, 52f; Gonda 1969, 1). They lived in small village communities, and the vedic civilization remained village based until at least the sixth century B.C.E. The early vedic views of religious life we have examined, therefore, reflect a village culture with an economy based on agriculture and animal husbandry. Such cultures generally tend to be conservative, jealously guarding their traditions and traditional values (Thapar 1979, 182).

The Indus Valley civilization, of course, boasted an urban culture centered around the two principal cities of Harappa and Mohenjo Dāro. This civilization came to an end sometime in the second millennium B.C.E., however, and it is impossible to estimate whether or to what extent it influenced the vedic culture and religion.[82] As Ghosh (1973, 2) points out: "For her next cities, her 'second urbanization', India had to wait for over a thousand years after the disappearance of the Indus cities—till the middle of the sixth century B.C., which saw simultaneously the beginnings of her historical period." The rise of cities in the Gangetic plain is clearly the most significant aspect of the socio-economic changes that we want to examine. Although precise dating is impossible with the available archaeological data, there appears to be a consensus that an urban culture and political structures of states emerged during the period from 600 to 350 B.C.E. Erdosy (1988, 116)[83] summarizes the archaeological evidence:

> Even the meagre evidence at our disposal suggests important changes occurring in the 6th–4th centuries B.C. Settlement patterns show the emergence of a four-tiered hierarchy with clearly defined functions for its elements, fulfilling the tenent of Central Place Theory that higher order sites have all the functions of lower order ones in addition to some unique to themselves. Craft specialisation, monumental architecture, rapid rates of population growth and agglomeration, and intensification of production as shown by the large-scale use of iron tools in agricultural operations have also been noted, as well as a tendency towards the regular spacing of towns and cities, and a primate rank-size curve. If the previous period's findings indicated a chiefdom, here we may justifiably argue for the first emergence of a state level political organization.

The states of the period were largely monarchical, and many of the emerging cities were also the royal capitals. Along the Ganges valley in a region commonly referred to

82. Attempts to reconstruct the non-Aryan contributions to ancient Indian culture are for the most part educated guesswork, without much foundation on evidence: see section 2.3.3.

83. The Allchins (1982, 358–61) are in broad agreement with Erdosy's assessment, adding that "the social, economic and intellectual concomitants of this near sudden flowering of city life are striking" (1982, 360). Regarding the rise of states, as opposed to the village or regional political structures that existed in the vedic period, see Thapar 1984.

as the "Middle Country" relatively large kingdoms began to be consolidated under the absolute authority of kings, who were constantly seeking to expand their power and territories through aggression and alliance.

The military capability of the kings assured a relatively efficient and safe network of roads and waterways, a necessary prerequisite for maintaining a central government and for administering a large territory. The facility of travel that enabled religious mendicants to travel freely over a large region and to disseminate new ideas and customs also permitted a merchant class to flourish. Archeological evidence supports the growth of trade and the development of trade networks during this period (Erdosy 1988, 114–16). Although there is much controversy regarding the date of the first coins, recent evidence suggests that they may have been in use by the fifth century B.C.E.[84] Merchants established the first professional organizations in India. The merchant guilds had their own laws and government, which were respected by the civil authority (Thapar 1966, 109–135).

Throughout the vedic period we detect a movement of the population to the lower regions of the Ganges valley where the land was very fertile and rain was more abundant. Rice cultivation on wet lands became the major agricultural activity. Some scholars argue that it was the discovery of iron and the invention of the iron axe and plough that made possible the clearing of the forests and the large-scale colonization and cultivation of that fertile land (Kosambi 1965; Sharma 1983). Others, however, point to the lack of archaeological evidence for the widespread use of iron tools during this period and question their need for successful farming or for creating urban cultures (Gombrich 1988). Erdosy (1988, 125–26) argues that state formation was well advanced by the time iron tools were introduced on a large scale and concludes:

> While iron tools undoubtedly played an important part in the colonisation of the Ganga Valley, and helped to intensify the production of surplus, their introduction appears rather to be a response to prevailing pressures, than their originator. Their role as a catalyst in no way diminishes their importance, only places it on a different plane.

Whatever its causes, however, wet-land rice cultivation gave rise to an agricultural surplus that permitted both an increase in the population and urbanization.[85] The concentration of populations during this period is revealed in Erdosy's (1988, 113) estimate that 20,000 people working for 250 days were needed to build the rampart at Ujjain.

Cities, kings, and the merchant class contributed to the rise of individualism, a factor of great significant for our study. Dumont (1960) has argued that vedic thought lacked

84. For an assessment of data and further bibliography, see Erdosy 1988, 115. It is a matter of controversy whether writing was used during this period. See Ghosh 1973, 27; Gombrich 1988, 53.

85. On the archaeological evidence for population growth during the period, see Erdosy 1988, 129, where he estimates the rate of rapid growth at 0.41 to 0.455% per annum. On the correlation between rice as the staple diet and the increase of population, see Ling 1976, 49–51, where further bibliography is also given. Ghosh (1973, 19–21) has argued convincingly that a food surplus does not arise spontaneously even when the technical and ecological conditions for a surplus exist (see also Erdosy 1988, 126). Cities and urban social organizations are not merely the result of a pre-existing food surplus but the instruments that creates such surpluses. Food surplus is, thus, not just a technical but also a social product.

the concept of the individual; it was the group that gave the individual conceptual reality. Caste ideology stressed the centrality of the group at the expense of the individual. Even though Dumont's dichotomy between the lack of the individual in the world and the centrality of the individual in the institution of world renunciation may not present a totally accurate picture of the individual in Indian history, nevertheless he is right in pointing out the marginal status of the individual in the mainstream of vedic thought. Among the factors that contributed to the discovery of the individual as a central concept in religious and social thought both within and outside the institution of world renunciation was undoubtedly the emergence of urban culture.[86] The king, of course, was the supreme individual in society. His belonging to the noble class was pure theory; there was no one like him in his kingdom. Ambition, strategy, and intrigue all played a role in a man's becoming a king and in his expanding his realm. A similar individualistic mentality was surely prevalent among the merchants, whose success depended on initiative, enterprise, and the willingness to take risks rather than on merely following an established pattern of conduct.

Urbanization also created a climate that permitted the rise of rival religious ideologies and modes of life. Cities and the courts of the kings located within them attracted nobles, priests, philosophers, and leaders of religious sects. The breakdown of the strict family and kinship networks that urban life usually entails and the resultant freedom for individual initiatives clearly encouraged both the ideological and the practical challenges to traditional Brāhmaṇism. The many religious movements that arose about this time were primarily urban in nature.

The individualistic spirit permitted also the creation of the first voluntary organizations in India. The Buddhist and Jain monastic orders are the earliest available examples of such organizations. People entered them because they wanted to, because they had taken a personal decision regarding how they wanted to live their lives. They were not following a set pattern for correct living ritualized in life-cycle ceremonies. They exercised the same individual initiative at the religious level that kings and merchants exercised in the political and economic fields. Such non-conformity and voluntarism are less likely to appear within village communities, and the institutionalization of non-conformist modes of life in mendicant orders was certainly facilitated by the new urban environment. Food surplus, which is at the heart of city life, also made possible the rise of these economically unproductive organizations which were maintained by the surplus and generosity of the population. The freedom to choose is at the heart of both the challenges to the vedic religious ideal and the theology of the original *āśrama* system that permitted a choice (section 3.1.1) among several modes of religious life.

2.3 Rival Views of Religious Life

Not all was well, however, during that period of social change and economic prosperity, and there appears to have been a growing sense of dissatisfaction and unease. It is reflected in the ideologies of many religious movements, such as Buddhism and Jain-

86. Thapar 1978, 70; 1979, 179–82; Ling 1976, 72–77. Weber (1964, 80–85) also sees the urban elites as the careers of ethical rationalization in most societies, including the ancient Indian.

ism, born during that time of upheaval, which proved to be a watershed in the history of Indian culture and religion. These ideologies shared the view that human life was essentially suffering, which even death could not end, for death was a mere interlude in a never-ending cycle of rebirth (*saṃsāra*). Many adopted life styles of intense mortification, separating themselves completely from social, economic, and even familial ties, in search of an escape from the bondage of life.

In discussing how an urban environment may have contributed to these radical changes in outlook and life style, Gombrich (1988, 57–58) summarizes Ghosh's (1973, 37) conclusions:

> The movement from village to town to city entails a more complex division of labour and professional specialization; social organization less in terms of kinship groups and more in terms of goal-oriented associations; less stringent control over the individual and greater dependence on impersonal institutions of control (bureaucracy, police, etc.); greater individual freedom and mobility and hence some disintegration of the traditional culture and social order. . . . The general picture is familiar: a move away from the closed community towards a more open society, an increase in the individual's power to choose and hence doubt about choosing rightly.

Others, such as Mary Douglas, have argued against such a correlation between maladjustment created by urban life and the rise of non-ritual and ecstatic forms of religion:

> When the social group grips its members in tight communal bonds, the religion is ritualistic; when this grip is relaxed, ritualism declines. . . . The most important determinant of ritualism is the experience of closed social groups. The man who has that experience associates boundaries with power and danger. The better defined and the more significant the social boundaries, the more the bias I would expect in favour of ritual. If the social groups are weakly structured and their membership weak and fluctuating, then I would expect low value to be set on symbolic performance. Along this line of ritual variation appropriate doctrinal differences would appear. With weak social boundaries and weak ritualism, I would expect doctrinal emphasis on internal, emotional states. Sin would be more a matter of affect than of transgression; sacraments and magic would give way to direct unmediated communion, even to the sacralisation of states of trance and bodily dissociation. (Douglas 1982, 13–14)

Although such socially weak groups can be found, as Douglas's examples show, even in tribal societies, they are, nevertheless, more likely to emerge in urban settings. Indeed, it is precisely the type of religion that Douglas predicts—non-ritual, ecstatic, individualist, and upholding an ethic centered on internal virtue rather than on ritualistic rules and taboos—that emerged in north India during this period.

These new religious ideologies and the increasingly widespread ascetic life styles stood in sharp contrast to the vedic religious world centered around the householder and his duties of sacrifice and procreation. What is significant for our study, moreover, is that the challenges to the vedic world came not just from those outside the Brāhmaṇical tradition, such as the Buddha, but also from people within that tradition.

There appear to have been tensions and rivalries between the traditional Brahmins of the villages, who were the heirs and guardians of the vedic world, and the newly urbanized Brahmins. Several Dharmasūtras, which generally reflect the mentality of the conservative tradition, advise Brahmins not to visit cities (ĀpDh 1.32.21; BDh 2.6.31–34).

Some establish a permanent prohibition against reciting the Vedas in a town or a city.[87] As the Upaniṣads show, other Brahmins had no qualms about attending and officiating at court rituals and participating in disputations conducted in royal assembly halls:

> In fact, the ethos pervading the law-texts is definitely oriented towards ruralism, with strong kinship bonds not possible in the city. . . . In contrast, the Brahmins who gathered round royal courts in various capacities—as ministers, priests, astrologers—could not have borne the inhibitions of their rural co-castemen. This dichotomy in the Brahmin fold, not necessarily based on affluence [or] lack of it (for there might have been rich rural Brahmins as well), is not explicitly recognized in the law-texts but was inherent in the very state of things. What mobility existed between the two groups we do not know, but there could be only one-way traffic—from the village to the town. (Ghosh 1973, 53–54)

New sects that spawned during this time became increasingly influential socially and politically. Kings and rich merchants were attracted by their "ethic for the socially mobile"[88] and became their patrons. The exclusive privilege enjoyed by Brahmins in the area of religion was broken. A new religious elite, the ascetic virtuosi, competed with the Brahmins for allegiance, influence, and economic support.

Within Brāhmaṇism itself, it was the urban Brahmins who, in all likelihood, were most influenced both by the dramatic socio-economic changes of urbanization and by the rising prestige and influence of non-Brāhmaṇical religious movements. Most urban Brahmins probably remained within their tradition, but challenged and changed it from within. It is these changes, and not primarily the threat posed by non-Brāhmaṇical groups as assumed by many scholars, that I believe were the catalysts for the creation of the *āśrama* system (sections 3.3.1–4). In the following discussion, therefore, I focus mainly on the challenges to the vedic world posed by the changes occurring within Brāhmaṇism itself, even though the ideas and modes of life we examine were not exclusive to Brāhmaṇism.[89]

The sources I examine are mainly the early Upaniṣads. They are difficult documents to analyze because they are anthologies that contain texts of diverse nature and different provenance. Moreover, these texts were composed over a long period of time. They contain sections dealing with sacrificial theology and symbolism that are very similar to the liturgical texts of the Brāhmaṇas and reflect the old vedic ideology. There are other sections, however, that share the new symbolic world we are about to discuss. The ideas and attitudes expressed in them, especially their anti-ritual and pro-celibacy stance,

87. GDh 16.43; VaDh 13.11. ĀpDh 1.9.4 prohibits the recital of the Veda in a *nigama*, which Ghosh (1973, 46) has clearly shown to mean a market town.

88. For an excellent presentation of the new Buddhist ethic aimed at merchants, financiers, and politicians, see Gombrich 1988, 78–86. This ethic encouraged saving and reinvestment, discouraged ostentatious consumption, and posited wealth and success as moral goals and as the result of moral living.

89. I want to note in passing that dissenting voices may have been there even before this time. The vedic documents themselves contain evidence of life styles different from that of the typical householder. We have examined the *muni* in our discussion of *śramaṇa*. Other categories include *yati, vrātya, vaikhānasa, vālakhilya*. Information on them is extremely meager and permits no firm conclusions. Ghurye 1964, 11–35; Chanda 1934; Singh 1972, 79–80; Hauer 1927; Heesterman 1962.

make it likely that they originated within a socio-economic background similar to that of Buddhism and Jainism. In other words, I think that the new doctrines of the Upaniṣads were urban products.[90]

The internal evidence of the early Upaniṣads, especially the larger collections of the *Bṛhadāraṇyaka* and the *Chāndogya*, appears to support such a conclusion. Many scholars have long argued that the major upaniṣadic doctrines were the product of the nobility. The Upaniṣads themselves present several doctrines as known only to the nobility and record many instances when kings became teachers of Brahmins, inverting the established ritual pattern. Deussen articulates this position clearly:

> We are forced to conclude, if not with absolute certainty, yet with a very high degree of probability, that as a matter of fact the doctrine of the ātman, standing as it did in such sharp contrast to all the principles of the Vedic ritual, though the original conception may have been due to Brāhmans, was taken up and cultivated primarily not in Brāhman but in Kshatriya circles, and was first adopted by the former in later times.[91]

Frauwallner (1973, I, 35), in this context, draws a parallel between this and the fact that the Buddha and Mahāvīra, the founder of Jainism, were also of noble descent.

I think, however, that the proper, and certainly the more significant, questions are not why these upaniṣadic doctrines were created by kings and whether the Buddha and Mahāvīra were indeed nobles—it is impossible to answer these questions with any degree of historical certainty—but why the proponents of these upaniṣadic doctrines ascribed them to kings and why the adherents of Buddhism and Jainism portrayed the founders of their respective traditions as nobles.

It is not possible here to investigate these questions fully and in detail. I think, however, that the proponents of these doctrines must have found it advantageous to align their doctrines with the nobility in general and with kings in particular. We do not have sufficient historical data regarding the position of the various kings named in the upaniṣadic texts to identify why their names were used. In general, however, I think the alignment with the nobility must have served to distinguish these doctrines from the vedic doctrines that were identified with Brahmins. The very term "Veda" signified "knowledge" par excellence; the three Vedas were referred to simply as *trayī vidyā*, "the triple knowledge." It may not be too farfetched to imagine that this "knowledge" was closely associated with the old village culture. In a positive way, therefore, the identification of a doctrine with a king may have served to show that it was a doctrine of and for the new age, an urban doctrine suitable for the new urban culture.

It is also noteworthy that the divine incarnations (*avatāra*), such as Kṛṣṇa and Rāma, who were the teachers of the new religions centered on the love of god (*bhakti*) are also depicted as of royal descent.

In this light, what appeared a problem for those scholars who upheld the noble provenance of upaniṣadic doctrines, namely why Brahmins should have preserved and handed down these stories that belittled them, ceases to be a problem at all. I would

90. This does not mean, however, that the upaniṣadic collections themselves or their transmission within the vedic schools were carried out in urban settings. I refer only to the new doctrines contained in these complex documents.

91. Deussen 1906, 19. See also Frauwallner 1973, I, 34–35, and 359 for further bibliography.

argue that it was precisely the Brahmin partisans of these doctrines who stood to gain by such stories. Aligning with kings gave their doctrines a new status and prestige and served to distinguish them from the old doctrines. What these stories of kings teaching new doctrines to Brahmins point to, I believe, is the divide that existed within the Brahmin tradition between the village Brahmins clinging to the old ritual religion and urbanized Brahmins[92] who were part of an emerging new symbolic world. Both the anti-ritual doctrines of the Upaniṣads and, as we shall see, the *āśrama* system probably originated within the latter class of Brahmins.

2.3.1 The Emergence of a New World

The challenge to the old vedic views was made at two interrelated levels: theology and practical life style. On the theological plane a set of ideas came into being that shaped a new symbolic world markedly different from the vedic world. This new symbolic world is so well known by anyone familiar with Indian culture that it is unnecessary to describe it here in detail.

Its principal components were the following: (1) *saṃsāra:* human existence is subject to rebirth and it is a state of bondage and suffering; (2) *karma:* ritual and moral actions determine the rebirth process and contribute to the continuation of human bondage; and (3) *mokṣa:* liberation from *saṃsāra* is the ultimate goal to which all religious efforts should be directed. Most religious traditions of India accept these as axiomatic; their disagreements center on the nature of human bondage and release. This is not the place to discuss these doctrines in detail, but one can detect two rival viewpoints. One claims that the human predicament is due to a lack of understanding, and freedom can come only from acquiring the proper gnosis. The other locates the problem in human actions (*karma*) and/or intentions, and prescribes a path of self-control and asceticism. Elements of both viewpoints are usually found in the same tradition.[93]

A couple of significant conclusions, however, flow from this new framework for understanding human life and death. The two central religious activities of the vedic world—offering sacrifices and begetting offspring—come to be considered obstacles to achieving liberation, the ultimate religious goal of the new world; they are activities that an individual who pursues the new religious ideal should seek to avoid. Liberation, the new equivalent of immortality, is a meta-ritual (according to some even a meta-ethical) state with regard to which ritual activity is ineffective. Sacrifice, the *karma* par excellence, far from being the source of immortality, is in fact a cause of human bondage and suffering. Ritual activity, therefore, is not only devalued but also acquires a negative connotation. Scholars have tended to ignore the close relationship between the theologies of *karma* and sacrifice.[94] Within the Brāhmaṇical tradition, the most common, the most basic, and the most significant dimension of *karma* is the ritual act. We have seen how vedic theology elevated the sacrificial *karma* to the level of a cosmogonic principle

92. By "urbanized Brahmins" I do not mean Brahmins who actually lived in cities, but those who had come under the influence of the new urban civilization, irrespective of where they actually resided.

93. See the introduction to van Buitenen's (1981) translation of the *Bhagavad Gītā* for a lucid presentation of this changing world view and its impact on the vedic world.

94. For an exploration of this relationship, see Tull 1989.

and the source of immortality. When translated into the theology of *saṃsāra*, however, ritual acts, because of their very power and efficacy, become the principal *karma* that causes the continuation of the rebirth process. Within the Brāhmaṇical theology of renunciation (*saṃnyāsa*), consequently, the elimination of *karma* means principally the elimination of rites, and renunciation is defined precisely as the abandonment of ritual activities.[95] The theology of *karma* in the new world is thus at total variance with the theology of sacrificial *karma* in the vedic world.

The heavenly worlds that formed the context of the sacrificial theology are now reduced to being components of *saṃsāra*. Rebirth follows upon death for both gods and humans, and sons and funeral offerings cannot assure ultimate bliss. This is an individualist ideology in which both the situation after death and final liberation are determined by what an individual does and knows and not by intermediaries, whether priests or heirs.

I have already cited (section 2.1.3) the *Bṛhadāraṇyaka* passage (1.4.10) according to which gods desire to keep humans ignorant in order that they continue offering sacrifices. The *Muṇḍaka Upaniṣad* (1.2.6–10) has an interesting and satirical passage regarding the inefficacy of the sacrifice and the delusion that constitutes the sacrificial theology contained in the vedic texts. After describing (1.2.1–5) the efficacy of sacrifices, the author puts these words in the mouth of the offerings personified:

> "Come! Come!" say the oblations shining bright,
> as they carry their offerer on the sun's rays of light,
> praising him, telling him flattering things:
> "This is yours, this Brahmā's world,
> the reward of good deeds (*puṇya*) and rites well done (*sukṛta*)."

The author then exposes the guile of sacrificial theology:

> These surely are rickety boats, the eighteen types of sacrifice,[96]
> which, they say, are the lower type of rites (*karma*).
> Those who revel in them as the path to final bliss (*śreyas*), the fools,
> return again and again to old age and death.
>
> Wallowing in ignorance but calling themselves wise,
> thinking they're learned, tormenting themselves,
> the fools go around like blind men
> led by one himself blind.
>
> Wallowing in ignorance time and again,
> these ignorant men
> imagine they have reached their life's aim.
> Because of their passions they do not understand,
> the people who perform rites.
> So they fall from those worlds,[97]

95. For more detailed discussions of this topic, see Olivelle 1975; 1981; 1992, 58–67.

96. The identity of these 18 forms is unclear. They may refer to the three classes of texts in the four Vedas, which make 12, and the six auxiliary sciences. Cf. MuṇU 1.5.

97. The meaning is that they fall to lower levels of existence when they have exhausted the reserve of merit that had won them the heavenly worlds.

these unhappy souls,
once their merits are gone.

Sacrifices and good deeds are the best, they deem;
none other the path to final bliss, they think,
utter fools!
They enjoy themselves in the highest heaven
won by rites well done,
and then enter this world
or one worse still!

Several significant points are made in this passage. Those who perform rites (*karma*) gain, or perhaps make for themselves,[98] a heaven after death. They live in the realm of ignorance (*avidyā*) and consider this heaven as *śreyas*, a term which means the ultimate good or bliss.[99] But this heaven will one day come to an end, and the performers of rites will return once again to earth. Such people are referred to repeatedly as fools pretending to be wise. They are the guardians of the old sacrificial religion. I am tempted to think that the author of the *Muṇḍaka* is satirically referring to the Vedas, the "knowledge" par excellence for the ritualists, as "ignorance." The ritualists who daily study the Vedas and follow their directions are wallowing in ignorance. Could it be that the blind man who leads other blind men is indeed the Veda? The *Muṇḍaka Upaniṣad* (1.1.4–5) elsewhere denies the authority of the Vedas:

> Two kinds of knowledge are to be known, as, indeed, the knowers of Brahman declare—the higher as well as the lower. Of these the lower is the Ṛgveda, the Yajurveda, the Sāmaveda, the Atharvaveda, phonetics, ritual, grammar, etymology, metrics, and astrology. And the higher is that by which the Undecaying is apprehended.

Vedic knowledge deals only with the ritual. It is useful only for worldly existence (MuṇU 1.2.1–6). It is not the knowledge that leads to final liberation, and from that perspective it is ignorance masquerading as knowledge.

2.3.2 The Householder and the Celibate

As the sacrificial ideology promoted the married householder as the paragon of religious life, so the new world view minimized the religious significance of marriage and children and advocated the value of celibacy and the control of sexual passion.

From the perspective of the new framework for understanding the human individual, the claim that a son constitutes a person's immortality (see section 2.1.2) would have seemed downright silly. At a sacrifice of King Janaka, Yājñavalkya, a proponent of the new theology, compares a human being to a tree and questions the assembled priests: "Now, a tree, when it is cut down, grows anew from its root. From what root does a man

98. The heaven is said to be *sukṛta*. It probably means that the heaven is made by performing correctly (*su*) the ritual acts.

99. The *Kaṭha Upaniṣad* (2.1–2) opposes *śreyas* to *preyas*, the fleeting delights. The wise choose the former, and the fools the latter.

grow, when he is cut down by death? Do not say 'from the semen,' for he produces it while he is alive" (BāU 3.9.27.4–5). A son issues from his father's semen, but he is not the continuation of his father's existence. Individuals are now considered complete in themselves, with personal continuities of their own from one life to another. The doctrine of rebirth posits the individual as an entity that transcends its transient relationships to a particular body, family, and social group and that receives its identity not from those relationships but from itself. The family is no longer needed to transform the individual into a complete person. The son is then not the continuation of the father's self but the result of the father's desire.

We saw that in the early vedic cosmology Prajāpati's desire for progeny is regarded as the impetus for creation. The human desire for offspring is a continuation of that creative impulse. In the new theology, however, such a desire results from ignorance and prolongs saṃsāric existence. For a person seeking liberation, overcoming desire and attachment is the major goal, and ascetic celibacy is the only path to achieve it:

> The great unborn self, indeed, is he who among the senses consists of knowledge. In the space within the heart lies the controller of all, the lord of all, the ruler of all. He does not increase by good acts (*karman*) or decrease by evil acts. He is the lord of all, he is the ruler of beings, and he is the protector of beings. He is the causeway that separates and keeps these worlds apart. It is him that Brahmins seek to know by reciting the Vedas, by sacrifices, by gifts, by penance, and by fasting. It is he, on knowing whom, one becomes a silent sage (*muni*). It is he, desiring whom as their world, wandering ascetics wander forth. When they came to know this, indeed, the men of old had no desire for offspring: "We possess this Self, this world; what is the use for us of offspring." Rising above the desire for sons, the desire for wealth, and the desire for worlds, they lead a mendicant life. (BāU 4.4.22)

This passage associates three central features of ancient Indian asceticism—celibacy, homeless wandering, and mendicancy—with those who aspire after the knowledge of the Self.[100] The householder is replaced by the celibate ascetic as the new religious ideal.

The rejection of the religious primacy of the householder is found also in other traditions sharing the new world view. The Buddhist literature is emphatic in its rejection of the salvific value of both the sacrifice and the householder's life. The following stock phrase, repeated frequently in the Pāli Canon, clearly shows the Buddhist attitude to home life:

> The household life is a dusty path full of hindrances, while the ascetic life is like the open sky. It is not easy for a man who lives at home to practice the holy life (*brahmacariya*) in all its fullness, in all its purity, in all its bright perfection.[101]

The *Majjhima Nikāya* (I, 483) contains one of the clearest statements on the inability of householders to attain liberation. There the Buddha declares that he knows of no house-

100. Elsewhere (BāU 3.5.1) the ascetic and celibate life is presented as the natural outcome of knowing Brahman. See also MaitU 6.8.28; MuṇU 3.1.5; 3.2.6.

101. DN I, 63; MN I, 179; Cf. SuN 406. On the superiority of the renouncer over the householder, see also MN II, 197–205; SuN 18–34, 393.

holder who has made an end of his suffering without giving up the household life.[102] The *Munisutta* of the *Suttanipāta* (SuN 207–21) also dwells on the great disparity between the renouncer and the householder.[103] The desire for children is singled out as one of the chief obstacles to holiness. When Māra, the evil god of death, declares: "A father [*puttimā*: lit. 'man with sons'] rejoices in his sons" (SuN 33), the Buddha retorts: "A father suffers on account of his sons" (SuN 34). The *Khaggavisāṇa Sutta* of the *Suttanipāta* also dwells on this theme. One should not desire a son, how much less a companion (SuN 35). Care for wife and children makes one like a bamboo tree entangled with other bamboos. Without such cares one becomes like a bamboo shoot, not clinging to anything and growing straight upward (SuN 38).

The Upaniṣads express the contrast between the ideals of the new theology and of the vedic tradition in terms of the opposition between wilderness (*araṇya*) and village (*grāma*).[104] Here again we have an example of the close association between way of life and place of residence that we discussed with relation to *āśrama* (section 1.1.3). In two parallel passages, the *Chāndogya* (5.10.1–2) and *Bṛhadāraṇyaka* (6.2.15–16) Upaniṣads apply the doctrine of the two paths along which the dead travel—path of the gods and path of the fathers—to the two classes of people: those who live in the wilderness and those who dwell in villages.[105] I cite the *Chāndogya* version, which is probably the older[106] and where the opposition between wilderness and village is drawn most sharply.

> Now, those who know thus and those in the wilderness here who worship with the thought "Faith is our austerity," pass into the flame, and from the flame into the day, from the day into the fortnight of the waxing moon, from the fortnight of the waxing moon into the six months when the sun moves north, from these months into the year, from the year into the sun, from the sun into the moon, from the moon into lightning. There is a person there who is not a man. He leads them to Brahman. This is the path leading to the gods.
>
> But those in a village here who worship with the thought "Sacrifice and good works are our gift," pass into the smoke, and from the smoke into the night, from the night into the latter [i.e., dark] fortnight, from the latter fortnight into the six months when the sun moves south—they do not pass into the year—from these months into the world of the fathers, from the world of the fathers into space, from space into the moon. . . . They live there until (their merits) are exhausted and return by the same course along which they went.

The *Bṛhadāraṇyaka* version states explicitly that those who live in the wilderness do not

102. Elsewhere, however, it is said that laymen and laywomen can attain liberation: MN I, 490–91; Vin I, 17; SN V, 94; AN III, 451. Cf. Rhys Davids, DN III, 5 n. The *Milinda Pañho*, 264, attempts to resolve this conflict by stating that when a layman becomes an Arhat, that very day he either becomes a monk or dies.

103. Elsewhere (SuN 1043–47) the Buddha emphatically denies that sacrifices can assure immortality; people sacrifice merely to prolong life. On sacrifices and their inability to liberate a person, see DN I, 141–42; II, 352–53; MN I, 343–44, 411–12; SuN 463–77.

104. For a detailed discussion of the wilderness-village opposition see Sprockhoff 1981, 32–67, where all the relevant upaniṣadic data are examined. Cf. also Rau 1957, 51–54; Malamoud 1976b; Olivelle 1990.

105. See also KauṣU 1.1–7; Frauwallner 1973, I, 38–41.

106. See Sprockhoff 1981, 51, and note 86 there for additional secondary literature. On the importance of the wilderness, see also MNU 508; MaitU 1.2.

return, while those who win worlds by sacrifice return the same way they went. The central activities of those who live at home in a village, especially sacrifice, are associated with return—that is, with prolongation of the rebirth process. Cessation of that process is associated with the activities of those who have left home and village and live in the wilderness.

The corresponding passages of the *Muṇḍaka* and *Praśna* Upaniṣads appear to follow the *Chāndogya* version (Sprockhoff 1981, 51), although their emphasis is on the inability of sacrifice and good works to procure liberation. The *Muṇḍaka* verse follows immediately after the verses cited earlier (section 2.3.1) regarding the inefficacy of sacrifices and the foolishness of those who perform them: "Those in the wilderness who practice austerity and faith, tranquil, wise, and living a mendicant life, pass without stain through the sun's door to where that immortal person, the imperishable self, dwells" (MuṇU 1.2.11). The message is clear. Those who live in a village perform sacrifices and do good works, and they are subject to rebirth. The *Praśna* passage notes further that village people also desire offspring. Those who live in the wilderness attain liberation. The *Muṇḍaka* identifies life in the wilderness with religious mendicancy, while the *Praśna* observes that such people practice chastity.[107]

Most discussions of the contrast between village and wilderness have assumed that "village" symbolized society and civilization. That may well be true, but still it is the village and not the town or city that is so contrasted. This point becomes significant because the literature that contains this contrast was probably of urban origin, and the ascetics and the ascetic ideologies that were identified with the wilderness had urban associations. Ghosh (1973, 55) observes:

> How the urban population regarded the rural one we do not know. Later literature is replete with references to the naiveté and crudeness of the rural folk. The word grāmya came to mean 'vulgar'; the attitude of the townsmen was one of mockery, condescension and even unfriendliness.

It may not be too farfetched to detect a hidden meaning in these texts: the activities of the village are not only unprofitable but vulgar and not fit for the elite, whether it be urban or ascetic.

The central position assumed by the wilderness in these rival views of religious life becomes even more significant when we consider the negative value ascribed to the wilderness vis-à-vis the village within the vedic mainstream (Sprockhoff 1981, 32–43; Malamoud 1976b). The revaluation of the wilderness symbolizes the revaluation of a wide spectrum of places, practices, and life styles. In every case the value system of the vedic world is inverted: wilderness over village, celibacy over marriage, economic inactivity over economic productivity, ritual inactivity over ritual performance, instability over stable residence, inner virtue and experience over outward observance. Both in ideology and in life style these reversals represented a radical challenge to the vedic world.

107. The Pāli Canon is also full of references to the wilderness as the ideal residence of monks and the best place for meditation. The following is a stock phrase: "One chooses a solitary abode—the wilderness, the foot of a tree, a mountain brae, a grotto, a rock-cavern, a cemetery, a woodland, an open field, or a haystack." DN II, 77, 242, 284; II, 49; MN I, 181, 440; III, 3, 35, 82, 115–16. See also DN III, 38, 195; SuN 958–59; MN I, 16–20, 323, 333, 335, 425.

2.3.3 The Aryan and the Non-Aryan in Indian Asceticism

The causes of the radical changes both in ideology and life style that took place between the sixth and the fourth century B.C.E. have been the subject of much speculation and conjecture. Several scholars have argued that these changes were precipitated by the rising influence of non-Aryan beliefs and practices as the center of vedic civilization shifted further down the Gangetic valley to present-day Bihar.

Belvalkar and Ranade (1927, 401), for example, postulate "an extraneous influence" on the rise of renunciation and consider that "it is more natural to suppose that we have here to do with a contact of the Aryans of the Brāhmaṇa period with peoples of a different culture whom they encountered in the course of their march into the interior of India" (p. 81). Pande (1957, 251–61) likewise advances the theory that the vedic *muni*, *śramaṇa*, and *yati* were non-Aryan figures possibly coming from the Indus civilization.[108] He claims that Aryans knew only the *pravṛtti-dharma* ("*dharma* of action") and that *nivṛtti* ("non-action") came from the non-Aryans but was later accepted by the Aryans (1957, 322–25; 1978, 30).

Singh expands on Pande's ideas and tries to discover the "ethno-geographic basis of the *āśrama*s" (1972, 176–85). He claims that the *āśrama* system "owes its origin to the commingling of several ethno-geographic currents" (p. 176–77) during a period that saw the fusion of different ethno-geographic elements, both Aryan and non-Aryan. He identifies *vaikhānasa*, *yati*, and *vrātya* with the forest tribes of Kirātas and Mongoloids, and *muni* with Niṣādas or Austics (pp. 184–85).[109]

These hypotheses are clearly untenable if we confine ourselves to the available evidence. It is obvious that vedic society contained large numbers of people whose roots were non-Aryan and that their customs and beliefs must have influenced the dominant Aryan classes. It is quite a different matter, however, to attempt to isolate non-Aryan customs, beliefs, or traits at a period a millennium or more removed from the initial Aryan migration. The vedic literature, as Gonda (1965, 200) observes, does not give us a complete account of the religious life of the Aryans. That some aspects we observe at a later period are absent in earlier texts is no proof of their absence at that time or of their non-Aryan provenance.

The Brāhmaṇical religion, furthermore, like any other historical phenomenon, developed and changed over time not only through external influences but also by its own inner dynamism and because of socio-economic changes, the radical nature of which we have already discussed. New elements in a culture, therefore, need not always be of foreign origin.[110] We need to pay more heed to Gonda's (1965, 206) caution:

108. Many scholars posit a distinction between *yati* and *muni*. The former is assumed to be non-Aryan (*asura*) and the latter Aryan: Sharma 1939, 17–20; Bhandarkar 1940, 80. Kane (1974, II.1, 419–20) concludes: "So it appears that even in the times of the Ṛgveda persons who led a life of poverty, contemplation and mortification were known, and were honoured and called munis, while persons corresponding to them among non-vedic people were probably called yatis." Dutt (1960, 60–63; 1962, 39) also considers religious mendicancy to be a non-Aryan institution. For a survey of opinions, see Chakraborti 1973, 4–12.

109. Sarkar (1917) proposes a similar thesis. This article, in spite of its title, deals only with caste. In a more recent article, Peter Della Santina (1989) likewise subscribes to the idea that the *śramaṇa* movement was associated with pre-Aryan Indus Valley civilization. See also Chanda 1934.

110. Regarding the possible development of renunciation through the inner development of the Brāhmaṇical tradition, see Heesterman 1964.

> These considerations may suffice to prevent us from nourishing too great hopes of reaching definite results in attempting to unravel the problem of the extent of the Aryan and non-Aryan contributions to a considerable number of Indian social and religious phenomena.

In the absence of an adequate definition of orthodoxy within the Brāhmaṇical tradition, moreover, the division of these conflicting theologies and life styles into "orthodox" and "heterodox" is not very useful either for historical purposes or for a phenomenological description of the data. The challenges to the traditional vedic view are found across a broad spectrum of religious literature, including some of the most authoritative texts of Brāhmaṇism. Opposition to accepted views of a tradition, after all, can and often does come from within that tradition.

The theological debates that we have discussed took place as much within the Brāhmaṇical circles as between the so-called orthodox Brāhmaṇism and the heterodox sects. The intense discussion between Krisṇa and Arjuna in the *Bhagavad Gītā* on the thorny issue of the relative value of renunciation and engagement in one's socially appointed duties is a classic example of such controversy and debate. An interesting and significant passage in the *Mahābhārata* presents in the clearest fashion what Heesterman (1985) has termed "the inner conflict of tradition" within the bosom of Brāhmaṇism. Bewildered by the array of expert opinions regarding the true *dharma*, the seers ask the creator god, Brahmā:

> To which, indeed, of the *dharma*s should a person here most closely adhere? What do they have to say about this? Tell us, for the course of *dharma* appears to us to be diverse and contradictory.
>
> Some claim that there is life after death, while others maintain that there is not. Some express doubt about everything, while others claim certainty.
>
> Things are impermanent according to some and permanent according to others, unreal according to some and real according to others. Some believe that the one reality appears as dual, while others think that it is mixed;[111] some teach unity, others separateness, and yet others multiplicity.
>
> Thus do Brahmins who are wise and perceive the truth argue.[112] Some wear matted hair and deer skin, others shave their heads, and still others go naked.
>
> Some say that one should not bathe, while others insist on bathing. Some favor eating, while others are given to fasting.
>
> Some praise rites and others the cessation from them. Some assert the influence of both place and time, while others deny it.[113] Some extol liberation and others diverse pleasures.

111. The meaning is unclear. The Nīlakaṇṭha, in his commentary on MBh, explains that the one reality is taken as both identical with and different from the phenomenal multiplicity.

112. Nīlakaṇṭha ascribes some of the opinions referred to in this passage to Buddhists, Jains, materialists, and the like. This verse, however, makes it clear that the author is describing the vast diversity of opinion among learned Brahmins themselves. The text, in fact, deals with the problem of discovering the true *dharma* amidst such a variety of opinions. The opinions of heretics, at least in the eyes of the author, would have no authority in matters relating to *dharma*.

113. The meaning is unclear. "Place and time" is a reference to the astrological tradition. Nīlakaṇṭha's explanation of the expression *naitad asti* as a reference to the idealist tradition that denied the existence of the material world is, I think, far-fetched, occurring as it does in the next two verses.

> Some desire wealth, while others strive after poverty. Some maintain the efficacy of worship, while others deny it.
>
> Some are devoted to non-injury (*ahiṃsā*) and others to injury.[114] Some claim that one attains glory through good deeds, while others deny it.
>
> Some delight in certainty as to the truth,[115] while others adhere to skepticism. Suffering is the motive for some and pleasure for others.
>
> Some assert the primacy of meditation, other wise men that of sacrifice, and still others that of giving gifts. Some assert the existence of everything, while others deny that anything exists.
>
> Some praise austerity, while other people extol vedic study. Some assert that knowledge comes from renunciation, while nature philosophers claim that it comes from nature.
>
> With so much disagreement regarding *dharma* leading in so many directions, we become bewildered, O god supreme, unable to reach any certainty.
>
> "This is ultimate bliss," "No, that is ultimate bliss": so thinking, people charge on, for one always praises the *dharma* that one loves.
>
> In this regard our judgment is confounded and our minds bewildered. This we want you to tell us, O lord: what is ultimate bliss? (MBh 14.48.14–27)

It is this conflict between two contradictory symbolic worlds and the theological debates and controversies that it engendered within the Brāhmaṇical tradition that forms the background for the creation of the *āśrama* system.

114. This may well be a reference to the sacrificial killing of animals, a practice condemned by the ascetic traditions.

115. This is a rather lengthy translation of *sadbhāva*, but the rest of the statement appears to indicate that it means the opposite of uncertainty.

II

THE EARLY PERIOD

The early period in the history of the *āśrama* system is marked by several features that distinguish it from what I shall call its classical period. During the early period the theological legitimacy of a system that permitted the repudiation of married life and the adoption of celibate modes of life was the subject of intense controversy. Discussions of the system centered exclusively around its original formulation within which the *āśramas* are regarded as adult vocations unrelated to either adolescence or old age. The classical formulation, which required a person to pass from one *āśrama* to the next at specific times in one's life, was then unknown. The *āśramas* as a province of *dharma*, moreover, were not integrated into the systematic expositions of *dharma* carried out in the Dharmasūtras; discussions of such central institutions as vedic initiation and marriage are conducted in the Dharmasūtras and the Gṛhyasūtras without any reference to the *āśramas*.[1] The term *varṇāśramadharma* used at a later period as a code for the totality of *dharma* is completely absent in the literature of this period.

Given the difficulty of dating ancient Indian texts, it is impossible to fix the upper and lower limits of this early period with any degree of certainty or precision. I shall discuss later (section 3.4) the probable date of the creation of the system, a date that would mark the upper limit of this period; we would not be far wrong in placing it around the fifth century B.C.E. Its lower limit may be placed in the first century B.C.E. The *Vasiṣṭha Dharmasūtra*, the last Dharma work to record exclusively the original formulation, was composed probably during or slightly before that century. The classical formulation, which signals the end of this period and the more complete integration of the system into the Brāhmaṇical theology of *dharma*, is recorded for the first time in the *Mānava Dharmaśāstra*, which was composed probably during the first two or three centuries of the common era.

It is this period, then, consisting of the last four or five centuries prior to the beginning of the common era, that will be the focus of this part of our study.

1. Pandey (1969, 8) is clearly wrong when he says: "The Dharmasūtras deal with the Varṇas (castes) and the Āśramas (stages of life). It is under the Āśrama-Dharmas that the rules about the Upanayana [initiation] and the Vivāha [marriage] are given exhaustively." The earliest of these texts do not mention the *āśramas* at all in their presentations of these rules.

3

The Origins

A major problem in studying the origins of the *āśrama* system stems from the sources. There are no extant texts composed by the creator(s) of the system or by anyone belonging to the tradition or milieu within which the system was created. The earliest descriptions of the system we possess are made by the authors of the Dharmasūtras, who either explicitly rejected its legitimacy or had serious doubts regarding some of its ramifications. Gautama and Baudhāyana, two of the earliest authors to record the system, present it as an opponent's position—a *pūrvapakṣa* in traditional terminology—which they set out to refute. Āpastamba appears to accept the legitimacy of the system, but with deep reservations.

It is unclear, furthermore, whether the descriptions of the system contained in these documents are actual fragments from texts composed by those who created or supported the system, or whether they are the authors' own presentations of their opponents' views. In any case, the earliest information regarding the *āśrama* system comes to us from sources not favorably disposed toward it. We are forced, therefore, to look at the earliest articulations of the system through the eyes of its opponents.

Such a situation, however, is by no means unusual in India or elsewhere and is not as hopeless as it may seem; ancient dharmaśāstric authors by and large present the views of their opponents without deliberate distortions. The probable date of the creation of the *āśrama* system (see section 3.4), moreover, is not far removed from the dates of composition of the Dharmasūtras of Gautama, Baudhāyana, and Āpastamba, suggesting that they were reacting to a comparatively new theory within Brāhmaṇical theology. This conclusion is also supported by the near total silence regarding the *āśrama* system in the early Upaniṣads and the *Rāmāyaṇa* (see section 3.4.1). We can be somewhat certain, therefore, that the information they provide belongs to a period close to the creation of the *āśrama* system.

Lacking hard evidence on the origin of the system, however, we are forced to glean as much information as we can from the available clues. The most one can expect under the circumstances is to construct hypotheses that are plausible within the context of the available evidence and the general history of ideas and institutions of ancient India.

3.1 The Original Formulation

The earliest expositions of the *āśrama* system are found in the Dharmasūtras of Gautama, Baudhāyana, Āpastamba, and Vasiṣṭha, which are the four oldest documents of the technical literature dealing with the subject of *dharma.*[1] They present substantially the same formulation of the system, even though Baudhāyana and Gautama take a position opposite to that of Āpastamba and Vasiṣṭha regarding the legitimacy of the system.

I will examine these early debates regarding legitimacy in the next section (3.2). Here I want to describe the system as formulated in these documents, a formulation as close to that of the creators of the system as we have. We can never be absolutely sure, of course, that this was in fact the original formulation of the system. I have termed it the "original formulation," nevertheless, because it is the earliest we possess and as close to the original as we are ever likely to get, and to distinguish it from the "classical formulation" that became the standard from about the beginning of the common era.

The original formulation of the system, like its classical successor, posits four *āśramas*, those of student, householder, hermit, and renouncer. These modes of life, which existed as independent social and religious institutions both before and after the creation of the system, are given a specific theological valuation and legitimacy within the system by being named and regarded as *āśramas*. Unlike its classical counterpart, however, the original formulation regards these *āśramas* not as temporary stages of a person's life but as four alternate and permanent modes of life open to an individual, one—and only one—of which he may freely choose. The person competent to make this choice is a young male adult who has undergone vedic initiation and who has completed his course of vedic studies under a teacher.

There are several major and unique features of this early theology of the *āśramas* that both distinguish it from the classical system and provide significant insights into the theological reasoning that led to its creation. (1) The *āśramas* are permanent modes of life. One is expected to live in one's *āśrama* of choice all one's life. (2) They are also adult vocations and are unrelated either to adolescence or to old age and retirement. (3) They are envisaged as alternate and equally legitimate modes of life. (4) A person is permitted to choose freely one of those modes. (5) The person competent to make that choice is a young adult male who has completed his vedic studentship. (6) The period of temporary studentship following vedic initiation is not considered an *āśrama.* The *āśrama* of a student, like all others, is also a permanent choice made after completing the temporary studentship and is carefully distinguished from the latter in these documents. I shall examine in detail these major features of the original system in the rest of this chapter

3.1.1 Choice of Āśrama

All the authors of the early Dharmasūtras present the four *āśramas* as alternate and parallel vocations open to a young adult male who has undergone vedic initiation and completed the period of study that follows. Such a person is referred to as a *snātaka*, one who has taken the ritual bath that signals the completion of studies with a teacher and returned home from the teacher's house. I shall call this temporary period of study "ini-

1. For the dating of these documents, see section 3.4. The Dharmasūtras are written in pithy and often aphoristic prose, and are distinguished from the later verse compositions on *dharma* referred to as Dharmaśāstra.

tiatory studentship" to distinguish it from the permanent studentship which alone, according to the original formulation, constitutes an *āśrama.* The subject to whom the system addresses itself, therefore, is the same young adult who, after his return home, would be expected, under the normal scheme of *dharma,* to marry a bride chosen by his parents. The *āśrama* system, it would indeed have appeared to theologians upholding the traditional scheme, was putting a monkey wrench into the nice and clean scheme so carefully nurtured in the set of life cycle rites. To this young man, the system says that it is not necessary for him to marry and that he may legitimately seek out other options for leading a good religious life as an adult. The vedic theologians—and I assume most parents—were not amused.

Vasiṣṭha presents the provision of the *āśrama* system in clear and unambiguous terms. After enumerating the four *āśramas*, he states: "After studying one, two, or (all) the Vedas, a person who has not violated his *brahmacarya* may enter whichever of these (*āśramas*) he prefers."[2] The term *brahmacarya* here refers to the vows that a student has to observe, and more specifically to chastity (Gonda 1965, 290f). The meaning, therefore, is that the person making the choice of an *āśrama* should have completed his studies and, until the moment of that choice, should have continued to observe chastity. The author's intent appears to be to foreclose the possibility of choosing to enter another *āśrama* after a person has married and become a householder. In addition, this provision would also foreclose the possibility of choosing a celibate *āśrama* by a person who has broken his vow of chastity as a student.

Āpastamba makes the same point when he uses the expression "only after that, maintaining his *brahmacarya,* he goes forth,"[3] with reference to becoming both a renouncer and a hermit. "Only after that" refers to the completion of vedic studies. Right at the beginning of his discussion of the *āśramas*, Āpastamba states explicitly that the completion of the initiatory studentship is a requirement for all *āśramas*: "To live at the teacher's house following vedic initiation is (a duty) common to all (*āśramas*)."[4] Furthermore, Āpastamba's entire exposition presupposes such a choice, and the above statement clearly presents the young man who has completed his initiatory studentship

2. VaDh 7.3: *teṣāṃ vedam adhītya vedau vedān vāviśīrṇabrahmacaryo yam icchet tam āvaset.* Altekar (1955, 186) commenting on this passage states: "After mentioning the four Āśramas, Vasiṣṭha says that one should study the Vedas and then follow any of the remaining three Āśramas." This is a good example of reading an ancient text in the light of the classical formulation of the system. The text says that one may choose any one of the *āśramas*, not "any of the remaining three." Altekar confuses the initiatory studentship with the *āśrama* of a student, which is permanent studentship, and which may also be chosen by the candidate. This is a common confusion. Lingat (1973, 51), for example, says about the authors of Dharmasūtras: "They forbid the Ārya to become an ascetic or a hermit before he has passed through at least the *brahmacarya* stage," and cites ĀpDh 2.21.2–4, 8 and GDh 3.1 in support. These sources, as we shall see, have no conception of stages of life.

3. ĀpDh 2.21.8, 19: *ata eva brahmacaryavān pravrajati.* "Going forth" is a common expression for the departure from home and village of a person becoming an ascetic. In his discussion of the time of renunciation Deutero-Baudhāyana (BDh 2.17.2; see 3.2.1.2 for an explanation of the term Deutero-Baudhāyana) cites this statement verbatim as the opinion of some (see section 4.2.2). The commentators Haradatta (on ĀpDh 2.21.8) and Govinda (on BDh 2.17.2) agree that according to this statement only a student who has completed his studies and has not broken his vow of chastity is entitled to renounce.

4. ĀpDh 2.21.3: *sarveṣām upanayanaprabhṛti samāna ācāryakule vāsaḥ.*

as the subject who is competent to make that choice. His assertion of the equality of all *āśramas*: "Remaining steadfastly in any of these (*āśramas*), one attains bliss,"[5] makes sense, moreover, only within the context of choice. A significant statement (ĀpDh 2.21.5) that I will discuss in section 3.1.4, moreover, appears to consider vedic studentship as a period of preparation for all the *āśramas* and to explictly permit a vedic student who has has completed that preparation to choose the *āśrama* he prefers. Āpastamba's major aim, however, is to prevent the deck from being stacked in favor of the celibate *āśramas*, so that the choice may be made in the knowledge that all *āśramas*, including that of the householder, are equally good and lead to the same final goal (see section 3.2.2.1).

Gautama presents the *āśrama* system as the doctrine of an opponent. He introduces the topic at the beginning of chapter three with the statement: "For him, some assert, there is a choice of *āśramas*."[6] Chapter two deals with the duties of a student during his initiatory studentship, and Gautama concludes that chapter by saying that the student after completing his studies should give the customary gift to the teacher and, with the teacher's permission, take the ritual bath that concludes the period of studentship. The expression "for him" (*tasya*) that opens the third chapter, therefore, undoubtedly refers to the student who has completed his studies.

Gautama is the only author of a Dharmasūtra to use the term *vikalpa* ("option" or "choice") with reference to the choice of an *āśrama*. It is certain that he uses this term in its technical meaning within the vedic exegetical tradition of Mīmāṃsā, because at the very beginning of his treatise Gautama defines this term: "An option arises when (injunctions) of equal authority are in conflict with each other."[7] A conflict arises when what is enjoined by one authoritative text makes it impossible to carry out what is enjoined by another. The classical example of such a conflict is the differing injunctions regarding the grain used for making sacrificial cakes, some enjoining rice and others barley. The use of the one type of grain precludes the use of the other; a conflict ensues, allowing a person the option to use either rice or barley (Kane 1962, V.2, 1249f).

The conflict, however, has to be between injunctions of equal authority or force. Now, in matters of *dharma* three authoritative sources were recognized: Veda, traditionally authoritative texts known as Smṛti, and the behavior and customs of learned and virtuous people (*śiṣṭa*).[8] Already during the time of the Dharmasūtras it was recognized that

5. ĀpDh 2.21.2: *teṣu sarveṣu yathopadeśam avyagro vartamānaḥ kṣemaṃ gacchati*. The expression *teṣu sarveṣu* literally means "in all these" or "in every one of these." It is clear, however, that the locative plural is used here in a partitive sense and that Āpastamba's intention is to show that each one of the *āśramas* is equally productive of the identical result. The *āśramas*, as we shall see, are taken by Āpastamba as permanent states, and hence it is impossible for a person to remain in all of them. The author's intent is to assert the equality of all *āśramas* by stating that each and every *āśrama* leads to final bliss. Āpastamba uses the term *kṣema* in his discussion of yoga and the knowledge of the self (*ātman*): 1.23.3; 2.5.18; 2.21.2, 14, 16. The term appears to signify a beatific state after death, although it is unclear whether it is a synonym of *mokṣa*.

6. GDh 3.1: *tasyāśramavikalpam eke bruvate*.

7. GDh 1.5 (1.4 in Bühler's trans.): *tulyabalavirodhe vikalpaḥ*. For the technical meaning of the term in the later Mīmāṃsā literature, see PMS 12.3.10 and Śabara on PMS 10.6.33. On the knowledge of Mīmāṃsā principles among the authors of the Dharmasūtras, see Kane 1962, V.2, 1154–55. An option may also arise when a text explicitly permits one (see section 5.1), but this appears not to have been the argument of the proponents of the system.

8. Cf. ĀpDh 1.1.1–3; GDh 1.1–2; BDh 1.1.1–6; VaDh 1.4–5.

vedic statements have greater authority than either custom or the statements of Smṛtis (ĀpDh 1.4.8). Thus, if customs or the provisions of Smṛtis contradict vedic injunctions, then the former are to be rejected as unauthoritative in favor of the vedic provisions.

As we have seen in the last chapter, the Vedas contain numerous and explicit injunctions regarding the householder's life. Implicit in the assertion that there is an option among the four *āśramas*, therefore, must be the claim that similar vedic injunctions are found also for the other three *āśramas*. The resultant conflict, the proponents of the system appear to argue, is the basis for the option and thus for allowing a student who has completed his studies to choose an *āśrama*. At least this is what we gather from Gautama's refutation of their argument.

Baudhāyana, indeed, opens his discussion of the *āśramas* with precisely such a vedic text. The proponents of the system, according to Baudhāyana, cite the following *Taittirīya* passage as the vedic basis of the four *āśramas*: "Four paths leading to the gods traverse between heaven and earth. Place us on that among them, all ye gods, which will bring us unfailing prosperity."[9] On the basis of this text, Baudhāyana says, "some propose a fourfold division of this very same *dharma*."[10] Baudhāyana does not state explicitly either that there is a choice of *āśramas* or when that choice should be exercised. He bases his argument against the *āśrama* system (see section 3.2.1.2), however, on vedic texts that assert the obligation to procreate, an obligation that presupposes marriage. Such an argument is valid only under the assumption that entering any other *āśrama* necessarily precludes marriage, which is precisely what happens when an *āśrama* other than that of the householder is chosen immediately after completing one's studies.

The conflict between injunctions that is the foundation of choice also shows why in the case of the *āśramas* that choice had to be exercised at that particular time. A choice is properly exercised only at a time when conflicting injunctions open alternative courses for the performance of an imminent action. For example, the choice of rice or barley can only be made just prior to performing a sacrifice. Once a person decides to use rice, for example, a choice is no longer open to the sacrificer; he cannot at a later time during that sacrifice opt to use barley. In the case of the *āśramas*, the normal time for marriage is when a young man has returned home after completing his initiatory studentship. If alternatives to marriage are possible because of the option (*vikalpa*) resulting from conflicting injunction, then the time for exercising that choice between those alternatives coincides with the normally prescribed time for marriage. Once a person has married, a choice of alternate life styles is no longer open to him even though they may be legitimately prescribed in the Vedas.

Two significant points emerge from this discussion. First, the theology of the original *āśrama* system appears to follow closely the pre-existing theological model of marriage and the assumption of household responsibilities, except that the *āśrama* system extends the latter model to cover other modes of life. Second, the system is described and discussed within the standard exegetical format of Brāhmaṇical theology, and it is presented as a hermeneutical necessity emerging from that exegesis.

9. TS 5.7.2.3: *ye catvāra pathayo devayānā antarā dyāvāpṛthivī viyanti / teṣāṃ yo ajyānim ajī tim āvahāt tasmai no devāḥ pari datteha sarve //* See BDh 2.11.9, 11, 29. This scriptural basis of the system is also mentioned in MBh 12.260.14; 14.35.34.

10. BDh 2.11.9: *tasya he vā etasya dharmasya caturdhā bhedam eka āhuḥ.*

3.1.2 The Āśramas *as Permanent and Adult Vocations*

Apart from choice, the other central feature of the original formulation of the system that stands in sharp contrast to its classical formulation is that all the *āśrama*s are regarded as permanent states of life intended for adults.[11] There is no provision in the original system for a person to change his *āśrama* or to go from one *āśrama* to another. The prescribed time for their selection, moreover, demonstrates that they are adult modes of life. I have called them vocations because, as Vasiṣṭha (VDh 7.3) states explicitly, a person chooses the one toward which he is attracted by inclination or conviction.

The permanent nature of the *āśrama*s was taken so much for granted by these authors that they apparently did not feel the need to discuss it explicitly. The one exception is the *āśrama* of a student, with regard to which the authors saw the possibility of some confusion. The terms *brahmacārin* ("student") and *brahmacarya* ("studentship") were used with reference to both the *āśrama* and the temporary period of study that follows a boy's initiation. In the original formulation this temporary period of what I have called initiatory studentship is not considered an *āśrama* at all.[12] The completion of the initiatory studentship, we saw, was the prerequisite for choosing an *āśrama*. All the authors, therefore, make it a point to state explicitly that a person who chooses the student's *āśrama* has to remain a student for life.[13] Āpastamba observes: "Following the rules of a temporary student (*vidyārtha*), a student (*brahmacārin*) shall serve (his teacher) until death and leave his body in his teacher's house."[14] By using two different terms for the two types of student Āpastamba is clearly making an effort to signal the difference between the two. Others are more brief but make the same point. Baudhāyana: "A student shall serve his teacher until death."[15] Gautama: "He shall remain obedient to his teacher until death."[16] Vasiṣṭha: "A student shall serve his teacher until death."[17] Gautama goes on to say that if his teacher dies, a student should continue to serve his teacher's son until death, and, if there is no son, an older fellow student or the sacred fire.[18]

11. Kakar's (1968, 128) lament that the *āśrama* theory "does not pay any attention to early childhood" can be given historical perspective when we consider that the creators of the system had no intention of propounding a theory of the "psycho-social development" of humans and that the system in no way bases itself "on the biological development of man," as supposed by Kakar. The accurate delineation of the historical development of the system, moreover, will throw considerable light on why, as Kakar himself admits (168, 131), the system does not fully correspond to Erik Erikson's psychological theory of human development.

12. There has been a lot of confusion in modern scholarship regarding this point. I have already mentioned (n. 2) the views of Altekar and Lingat. Banerjee (1962, 133) likewise states: "The entrance to this stage [studentship] is marked by the ceremony of initiation to vedic studies (*upanayana*)." No such initiation ceremony is prescribed for entry into the *āśrama* of a student in these early sources. See also Sharma 1939, 22.

13. For a detailed discussion of Brāhmaṇical studentship, see Gonda 1965, 284–314. Aparāditya (p. 76), a medieval commentator of the YDh, observes that when a student decides to remain a student forever he does not take the ritual bath (*avabhṛta*) that marks the conclusion of studentship.

14. ĀpDh 2.21.6: *yathā vidyārthasya niyama etenaivāntam anūpasīdata ācāryakule śarīranyāso brahmacāriṇaḥ.*

15. BDh 2.11.13: *brahmacārī guruśuśrūṣy ā maraṇāt.*

16. GDh 3.5: *ācāryādhīnatvam āntam.*

17. VaDh 7.4: *brahmacāry ācāryaṃ paricared ā śarīravimokṣaṇāt.*

18. GDh 3.7–8. The VaDh (7.5–6), on the other hand, merely says that when his teacher dies a student should serve the sacred fire.

The institution of permanent studentship was not the creation of the *āśrama* system; it preexisted the system. In the well-known passage regarding "three divisions of *dharma*" of the *Chāndogya Upaniṣad* (2.23.1) which I shall discuss later (section 3.5), the third division consists of "a vedic student living at his teacher's house . . . who settles himself permanently in his teacher's house." The Buddhist literature also uses the term *brahmacarya* with reference to the permanent celibate mode of life of Buddhist monks. This extension would have been more difficult if within the older vocabulary the term had referred simply to the life of an adolescent boy engaged in a temporary period of study.

From the famous hymn on the *brahmacārin* in the *Atharvaveda* (11.5) and from other vedic texts on the subject, Gonda concludes both that such a student was an adult and that he is associated with travel in search of knowledge.[19] Heesterman sees the *brahmacārin, vrātya,* and *dīkṣita* as originally variants of the same basic type; they are all, of course, adults, and he argues that "the meaning of brahmacārin was certainly not yet limited to that of a young man learning the Vedas."[20] It is this adult and permanent, or at least not specifically temporary, institution associated with learning—an institution whose early history is admittedly vague and only partially understood—that appears to be at the root of the first *āśrama* and not the initiatory studentship associated with adolescence.

Āpastamba's statement that "remaining steadfastly (*avyagra*) in any of these (*āśramas*), one attains bliss" (ĀpDh 2.21.2) shows that he regarded all the *āśramas* to be permanent states and lifelong vocations. Using the term *avyagra*, Āpastamba intends to show that each *āśrama* can lead to ultimate bliss if one does not deviate from its path.

I have already drawn attention to Gautama's use of the technical term *vikalpa* ("option") in presenting the view of the proponents of the *āśrama* system and to the fact that in the exegetical tradition the choice of one alternative necessarily excludes the others. Such an option is viable only within the context of the permanence of the *āśramas* and the consequent impossibility of belonging to more than one *āśrama* during one lifetime. If the *āśramas* were not permanent and if they could be assumed successively, scriptural texts enjoining them would not be in conflict with each other, and, consequently, there would be no room for an option. Rather, all the *āśramas* would become equally obligatory. This is the opposite of option and in the Mīmāṃsā tradition is technically called *samuccaya* ("aggregation"), which, as we shall see (section 5.2), is the position advocated by the proponents of the classical system.[21] The permanence of the *āśramas*, moreover, is at the basis of the arguments of Gautama and Baudhāyana against the validity of the *āśrama* system that I shall discuss in detail in sections 3.2.1.1–2.

19. "That the ambulatory life was regarded as typical for the brahmacārin may be inferred from TB, 3,4,1,16 where a certain correlation is supposed to exist between him and the way (*adhvan-*), and from TĀ, 7,4,2 *ā mā yantu brahmacāriṇaḥ . . . vi mā yantu . . . pra mā yantu.* The frequent use of the verbs *eti* and *carati* in AV, 11,5 (st. 1; 6) may point in the same direction." Gonda 1965, 285.

20. Heesterman 1964, 25, n. 45 and also pp. 24–25; Bloomfield 1899, 94.

21. For a discussion of *vikalpa* and *samuccaya,* see Kane 1962, V.2, 1249–53, 1328–29. The exegetical tradition treated choice with deep suspicion (see section 5.2), and later texts allude to the six faults inherent in a choice. Every effort should be made to find a way out of a choice, and it is permitted only when no other way could be found to interpret the conflicting injunctions.

3.1.3 The Three Celibate Āśramas

According to the original formulation, all *āśramas* except that of the householder are regarded as celibate.[22] This assumption underlies all the discussions and debates about the *āśrama* system in these early documents. A Brāhmaṇical student, the subject of the first *āśrama,* is by definition celibate. We have seen, moreover, that the person choosing any *āśrama* is expected not to have violated the vow of chastity incumbent on a student. Āpastamba (2.21.8, 19) reiterates this requirement with regard to both the hermit and the renouncer. Their celibacy, moreover, is implied by Āpastamba (2.23.3–9) when he presents the view of those who claim that these *āśramas* are superior to marriage. According to Āpastamba, the backers of celibate *āśramas* cite two verses of a Purāṇa that praise chastity:

> Those eighty thousand sages who desired offspring went along Aryaman's path to the south and obtained burial grounds.
>
> Those eighty thousand sages who did not desire offspring went along Aryaman's path to the north and attained immortality. (ĀpDh 2.23.4–5)

On the basis of such texts, Āpastamba observes, they "say that these *āśramas* are superior" (ĀpDh 2.23.9).

The celibacy of *āśramas* other than that of the householder is also implied in Baudhāyana's assertion that the householder's is the only valid *āśrama* because others do not produce offspring (BDh 2.11.27: see section 3.2.1.2). The same reason is adduced by Gautama to show that the householder is "the source" (*yoni*) of the others (GDh 3.3).

It is this characteristic of the non-householder *āśramas* that makes the arguments regarding the system I will presently examine finally boil down to a debate on the merits of the householder versus those of the non-householder.[23]

3.1.4 Initiatory Studentship as Preparation for the Āśramas

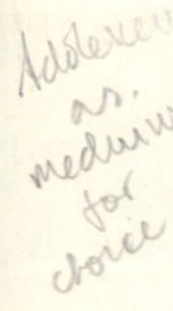

We have seen that a person was required to complete his studies before being permitted to choose an *āśrama.* The proponents of the *āśrama* system appear to have envisaged this period of an adolescent's life as a preparation or a novitiate which would teach him the duties of the various *āśramas* and thereby enable him to make a wise choice.[24] The idyllic picture that emerges, therefore, is something like this. Vedic initiation separates a boy from his carefree childhood in preparation for assuming adult responsibilities. This period of separation and preparation takes place in the house of a teacher. There he is taught the vedic lore as well as the alternate ways of leading a good and religious life as an adult, that is, the duties of the four *āśramas.* At the conclusion of this period, the boy,

22. The Sanskrit term *brahmacarya* has the meanings of both celibacy, by which I mean a state socially defined as different from marriage and free from sexual activity, and chastity, which relates more to individual morality. Clearly all these discussions refer primarily to celibacy, although people in the celibate *āśramas* are evidently expected to be chaste.

23. In the literature that deals with liberation and asceticism, on the contrary, the dichotomy is between the renouncer and the non-renouncer.

24. For more detailed information on vedic initiation and studentship, such as the proper age for initiation, the length of studentship, and the duties of a student, see Kane, 1974, II.1, 268–415.

who is now a young adult, is given the option of choosing a vocation—an *āśrama*—that he would like to follow during his adult life.

Such a picture, for example, is presented by Āpastamba—although in the cryptic fashion of a *sūtra*—who, after mentioning the obligation to study under a teacher following one's initiation, says: "Having learned the rites he may undertake what he pleases."[25] Even though the initiatory studentship is always described as a time devoted to vedic study, that is, memorizing the vedic hymns and formulae, it appears that in fact the boys were taught many other subjects, including the duties and responsibilities of adult life.

That the duties of a householder were part of the normal curriculum is also evident from the comments of Āpastamba in his discussion of initiatory studentship outside the context of the *āśrama* system. With reference to the initiation of a person whose father and ancestors have not been initiated, Āpastamba states that after an appropriate penance he may be initiated and that "he may then be taught the duties of a householder, but not receive vedic instruction" (ĀpDh 1.2.7–8). Although one cannot be absolutely certain, it appears the entire curriculum of a student consisted of instruction in both the Veda and the duties of household life. A boy coming from a family that has neglected initiation and vedic study for several generations should be taught only a part of that curriculum, vedic study being too sacred to be imparted to such a person.

If the hypothesis that the initiatory studentship outside the context of the *āśrama* system was a period of preparation for assuming the duties of a householder is correct,[26] then what the creators of the system did was to extend its curriculum—at least at the level of theory—to include the duties of the other *āśrama*s as well.

3.1.5 Who was Entitled to Choose an Āśrama?

The Dharmasūtras do not explicitly discuss the question of the qualifications of those for whom the *āśrama* system was designed.[27] The context within which the system is presented, however, makes it possible for us to discover them fairly easily.

During the time of these texts, initiation and studentship were meant exclusively for adolescent boys.[28] The choice of an *āśrama*, therefore, was meant to be exercised by a young man. There is no discussion of women within the context of the system, and it appears extremely unlikely that any of its provisions were intended for women.

With reference to social class (*varṇa*), vedic study and initiation were the prerogatives of the twice-born classes of Brahmins, Kṣatriyas, and Vaiśyas. The *āśrama* system, like most other provisions of these texts on *dharma*, were addressed to male members of these three classes. Even though Kṣatriyas and Vaiśyas are not excluded, the discussion

25. ĀpDh 2.21.5: *buddhvā karmāṇi yat kāmayeta tad ārabheta.* It is clear from the context that the rites or activities (*karmāṇi*) refer to the duties of the various *āśramas*.

26. The exhortation to a student who is about to graduate contained in the *Taittirīya Upaniṣad* (1.11.1–6) also implies this.

27. I will discuss in sections 7.1–2 the later discussions and debates on these issues—especially gender and caste—with specific reference to the classical formulation.

28. There is some evidence that girls were also initiated in ancient times: see section 7.1 and Kane 1974, II.1, 293–95. In the Dharmasūtras, however, a boy is assumed to be the subject of both initiation and studentship.

nevertheless appears to center on the Brahmin.[29] In this early period, however, there is no attempt to distribute the *āśramas* among the social classes (see sections 7.2).

Even though the theology of the *āśramas* did not take into account women or Śūdras, we cannot conclude from it that women and/or Śūdras did not participate in the institutions comprehended by that system. As I pointed out earlier, we need to keep the *āśrama* theology and the *āśrama* system distinct from the institutions. Clearly both women and Śūdras got married and raised families. There is plenty of evidence, moreover, to suggest that they also became ascetics (see sections 7.1–2). Their life in those institutions, however, was not given the specific theological evaluation and significance that come from incorporation into the *āśrama* system.

3.1.6 The Order of Āśramas

An issue that has drawn a fair amount of scholarly attention concerns the order in which the *āśramas* are enumerated in these early documents. In later texts the usual order is student, householder, hermit, and renouncer, reflecting the sequence of the passage from one *āśrama* to another, an order that scholars have often assumed to be the normal and the norm, any deviations from which would require an explanation.

In the Dharmasūtras, however, only Baudhāyana and Vasiṣṭha follow that order. Āpastamba lists the householder first and the student second, while Gautama follows the usual order with regard to these two. Both, however, place the renouncer third and the hermit last.

Commentators and scholars alike have attempted to discover the reasons for this departure from the "normal order."[30] Kane (1974, II.1, 416), for example, observes:

> Āp. [Āpastamba] places the householder first among the āśramas, probably on account of the importance of that stage to all other āśramas. Why he should mention the stage of forest hermit last is not clear. Gaut. [Gaútama] also (III.2) enumerates the four āśramas as brahmacārī [student], gṛhastha [householder], bhikṣu [mendicant] and vaikhānasa [hermit]. Here also Gaut. speaks of bhikṣu before vaikhānasa and Haradatta [see note 30] explains this departure from the usual sequence of āśramas as due to the words in Gaut. 28.47.

This order, however, is "normal" only within the context of the classical formulation. A specific order becomes insignificant when the *āśramas* are taken as four alternative adult vocations. The specific order in each author may be purely accidental, or it may reflect the structure of his literary work. Thus, Āpastamba may list the householder first because his treatment of the householder immediately precedes the section on the *āśramas*. Gautama, on the other hand, introduces the *āśramas* immediately after his discus-

29. The tendency of these authors to use the terms *brāhmaṇa*, *dvijottama*, and *vipra* (all synonyms for Brahmin), in their injunctions indicates that, de facto, these provisions were addressed to Brahmins. See Biardeau and Malamoud 1976, 32.

30. Both Haradatta and Maskarin on GDh 3.2 comment that Gautama departs here from the normal order (*kramabheda*) and lists the hermit last so as to exclude him from the constituents of an assembly (*pariṣad*), which, according to GDh 28.47 (28.49 in Bühler's tr.), includes three men belonging to the three *āśramas* before the last. See also Bhagwat 1939b, 126–27; Meyer 1927, 317. I shall deal with the question of *pariṣad* later (section 7.4).

sion of initiation and studentship. Listing the student first permits him to be brief regarding the duties of a student; he just says: "(The duties) of a student have already been given" (GDh 3.4). It is a fruitless enterprise, therefore, to attempt to discover the motives for the departure from a non-existent "normal order."

To sum up, then, according to the original formulation of the system, the four *āśrama*s are permanent and adult modes of life. Any one of them may be chosen by a young man who has returned home after completing his period of study with a teacher following his vedic initiation. The choice appears to be irrevocable, for no provision is made for changing one's *āśrama.*[31] All, except the *āśrama* of a householder, are celibate. The *āśrama*s of a hermit and a renouncer, moreover, are not associated with old age, as they are in the classical formulation of the system.

3.2 Controversy and Debate

Brāhmaṇical controversies and debates, especially in matters of ritual and conduct, were carried out within a framework that included canons of exegesis and interpretation and rules of logic and debate. To properly understand and evaluate the arguments of Brāhmaṇical scholars recorded in their literature, therefore, we must enter their conceptual world and comprehend their technical vocabulary; we must understand the rules of their game.[32] If some of the following discussion appears abstruse, it is because I am attempting to unfold the arguments and counterarguments regarding the *āśrama* system within their original frame of reference.

The four Dharmasūtras we have examined make it abundantly clear that during this early period the legitimacy of the *āśrama* system was a highly controversial issue. It was not universally accepted as part of the vedic *dharma* in the specialized Brāhmaṇical schools within which these documents were produced, studied, and handed down. Even among those who accepted its validity there were disputes regarding the relative excellence and superiority of the four *āśrama*s. These disputes provide us with significant insights into the origin and early history of the system.

3.2.1 The Legitimacy of the Āśrama *System*

Gautama and Baudhāyana, two of the earliest authors of Dharmasūtras, reject the legitimacy of the *āśrama* system as it is enunciated in its original formulation. They present the system as the view of an opponent (*pūrvapakṣa*) and put forward arguments against its acceptance. I will deal with Gautama's position first, both because his is probably the oldest document (see section 3.4) and because he presents the most radical argument against the system from the perspective of Brāhmaṇical hermeneutics.

3.2.1.1 Gautama

As we have seen, Gautama introduces the *āśrama* system not as his own but as the opinion of "some" (*eke*): "For him, some assert, there is a choice of *āśrama*s" (GDh 3.1).

31. I will discuss in section 4.1.1 the exception Āpastamba makes in the case of a forest hermit.

32. For a discussion of Brāhmaṇical hermeneutics within a literary debate, see Olivelle 1986, 57–76.

"Some" is a favorite term of Gautama; he uses it over 40 times in presenting opinions different from his own.[33] In every instance the opinion of "some" follows the view presented by Gautama as his own; Gautama does not refute the other opinions and appears to present them to the reader as possible but inferior alternatives. The only exception is the *āśrama* system, where the opinion of "some" precedes Gautama's own view, which he gives at the very end of the discussion: "But the Venerable Teacher (prescribes) a single *āśrama*, because the state of the householder is prescribed in express (vedic texts)."[34]

Gautama uses 35 *sūtra*s or aphorisms to present the opinion of "some" concerning the *āśrama*s. The length of this presentation contrasts with the other instances of "some," in which Gautama presents their opinions in one or two *sūtra*s. The length and the fact that he presents it before giving his own view appear to indicate that Gautama intended to present this opinion on the *āśrama*s as the *pūrvapakṣa*, literally "the first position or thesis." In literary debates an author presents in the *pūrvapakṣa* the position of an opponent, and then goes on to refute it and to establish the true position, which is referred to as *uttarapakṣa* or "the later or final position." From the structure of Gautama's presentation it is very clear that he intended to refute the view that permitted a student who had completed his studies to choose one of four *āśrama*s. "But the Venerable Teacher,"[35] he says, "(prescribes) a single *āśrama*." In keeping with the practice of authors who wrote in the *sūtra* style, Gautama probably intended this *sūtra* to be syntactically related to the opening *sūtra* (3.1). The word *tasya* ("for him") from that *sūtra* is understood here also. The meaning, therefore, appears to be that the Venerable Teacher prescribes "for him"—that is, for a person who has completed his vedic studies—a single *āśrama*, namely that of the householder. In other words, a student who has completed his studies and returned home has no other choice but to get married and become a householder.

The most significant part of Gautama's argument for the history of the *āśrama* system is the reason for his position. A student who has completed his studies is obliged to become a householder, Gautama says, "because the state of the householder is prescribed in express (vedic texts)." In our discussion of the hermeneutical concept "option" (*vikalpa*), we saw that an option is allowed only when injunctions of equal authority prescribed different things that cannot be carried out simultaneously. In rejecting an option with regard to the *āśrama*s, Gautama points out that such equality of authority is lacking in injunctions on *āśrama*s by saying that "express (vedic texts)" enjoin the householder's *āśrama*.

The term "express" (*pratyakṣa*) undoubtedly refers to *pratyakṣaśruti* ("express vedic text"), which is a technical term in Brāhmaṇical hermeneutics. *Pratyakṣa* literally means perception; *pratyakṣaśruti*, therefore, is a vedic text that is perceivable. Given that the Vedas were not available in written form during this period—the very term *śruti* after all relates to hearing—it meant a vedic text that was actually recited and heard in a vedic

33. GDh 1.19; 2.9, 34, 51; 3.1, 19; 4.15, 18–21; 6.6; 7.5, 23; 10.25, 45, 52, 65; 11.16; 12.30; 13.12; 14.33, 36; 15.11, 20, 30; 16.14, 27, 39, 45; 18.7, 19, 23; 19.4–5; 21.6, 8, 14; 23.13, 29; 24.4, 5, 6; 27.14; 28.19, 26, 40. See Kangle 1968, 422. Both Haradatta and Maskarin in commenting on many of these passages interpret "some" to mean that these opinions are clearly not shared by Gautama.

34. GDh 3.36: *aikāśramyaṃ tv ācāryāḥ pratyakṣavidhānād gārhasthyasya.*

35. The plural *ācāryāḥ* in all likelihood is either honorific (cf. Bühler's note on GDh 3.36) or it is meant to refer to teachers in general or to most teachers (Meyer 1927, 261). The use of this term, however, clearly indicates that Gautama shared this view. See Kane 1942.

school. Its opposite is *anumitaśruti* ("inferred vedic text").[36] These two categories result from the theological reasoning regarding the sources of *dharma.* The Vedas constitute the single authoritative source of *dharma.* Authoritative texts of tradition called Smṛtis and the conduct of virtuous people are, however, recognized as authoritative with respect to points which are not covered by any vedic injunction. These secondary sources of *dharma,* nevertheless, possess no independent authority: in theory at least they are based on vedic authority; they derive their authority from vedic injunctions on which they are founded. If a vedic text cannot be located within the extant corpus (*pratyakṣaśruti*) to support a provision recognized by Smṛtis or custom, then one can *infer* that such a vedic text must have existed in the past, although it is now lost. That the theory of inferring a lost vedic text on the basis of a Smṛti or custom was known within the intellectual milieu to which Gautama belonged is demonstrated by the fact that it is clearly enunciated by Āpastamba: "All injunctions were (originally) taught in the Brāhmaṇas. Those sections of theirs that have been lost are inferred on the basis of custom" (ĀpDh 1.12.10). Thus all provisions of *dharma* are based on either express vedic texts, that is, texts that are currently available, or on vedic texts whose existence is inferred on the basis of Smṛtis or custom.

One can see the parallel between these two types of vedic evidence and the two basic sources of knowledge and means of proof (*pramāṇa*) in Indian logic, namely perception (*pratyakṣa*) and inference (*anumāna*). As perception outweighs inference, so when verbal authority is the means of knowledge (*śabdapramāṇa*) an express or "perceived" vedic text annuls an inferred one.[37] Now, this hermeneutical principle was not unknown during the period of the Dharmasūtras; Āpastamba enunciates it clearly: "For an (express) vedic text has greater force than a custom from which (the existence a vedic text) is inferred."[38]

Gautama's argument, therefore, boils down to this. There cannot be an option regarding the *āśramas* because there is an inequality in the texts that enjoin them. Only the householder's *āśrama,* according to Gautama, is the subject of an express vedic injunction; with regard to the others the existence of vedic texts has to be inferred on the basis of Smṛtis or custom.[39] Consequently, an option cannot be permitted, because

36. On these terms and on the whole question of the vedic basis of *dharma,* see Kane 1962, V.2, 1255–82; Jha 1964, 157–24.

37. This principle is enunciated by Jaimini in the PMS 1.3.3: "When there is a conflict (between a vedic and a smṛti text, the smṛti) should be disregarded, because only when no such conflict exists is there an inference (of a vedic text)."

38. ĀpDh 1.4.8: *śrutir hi balīyasy ānumānikād ācārat.* On Āpastamba's knowledge of Mīmāṃsā principles, see Bühler's introduction to his translation of ĀpDh, xxviii–xxix.

39. In comparing this *sūtra* of Gautama with the corresponding passage of Baudhāyana, to which I will turn presently, Kangle (1968, 420) observes: "It seems that the discussion in B. [Baudhāyana] is original, G. [Gautama] ignoring it and contenting itself with the taking over of the main s. [i.e., *sūtra*]. It is also obvious that the reason stated in B. *aprajananatvād itareṣām* ['because others do not beget offspring'] is more natural, being germane to the discussion, than the reason stated in G. which is very lame. If *gārhasthya* [householder's state] is prescribed in the sacred texts, so are the other *āśramas.* Clearly G.'s s. [*sūtra*] is secondary and derived from elsewhere, most probably from B." Kangle clearly has failed to understand the force of Gautama's argument from the perspective of vedic hermeneutics. Far from being "very lame," Gautama presents a much more radical argument against the *āśrama* system than Baudhāyana. Irrespective of whether Gautama is older or younger than Baudhāyana, it is not possible to conclude that this *sūtra* is in any way secondary to that of Baudhāyana.

although there may be a conflict, the conflict is not between injunctions of equal authority. The provisions of Smṛtis and custom that support other *āśramas* should hence be rejected as unauthoritative. The *āśrama* system as proposed by "some," therefore, is illegitimate.[40]

The hermeneutical position which rejects the authority of a "weaker" scriptural text in favor of a "stronger" one is referred to by the technical term *bādha.*[41] Within the history of the *āśrama* system itself, the views of Gautama and Baudhāyana rejecting the validity of *āśramas* other than that of the householder are referred to also as "the *bādha* position" by medieval theologians such as Vijñāneśvara.[42]

Within the structure of Gautama's literary work, the discussion of the *āśrama* system appears as a long parenthetical digression. He concludes his exposition of initiation and studentship in the first two chapters. In chapter three he refutes the opinion of some that, upon the completion of his studies, a student may choose a mode of life different from that of a householder. After that digression, he picks up the thread of his argument again in chapter four where he begins the discussion of marriage and the duties of a householder. Contrary to what many scholars assume, the structure of Gautama's works shows that the *āśrama* system was not yet integrated into the exposition of *dharma.*

3.2.1.2 Baudhāyana

The Dharmasūtra of Baudhāyana poses special problems for the historian of the *āśrama* system. It deals with topics relating to the system in two separate sections—2.11.9–34 and 2.17–18—that provide different and often contradictory information. Bühler, more than a century ago, expressed his doubts regarding the authenticity of the last two books (*praśna*) of the Sūtra which deviate substantially from the first two.[43] It is clear that the work has undergone repeated alterations. Even with regard to the first two books, Kane (1968, I.1, 43) observes that "there are many repetitions even in the first two praśnas, which therefore make one rather doubtful about the authenticity of the first two praśnas in their entirety."

I believe that BDh 2.17–18, constituting the last two sections (*kāṇḍa*) of the second book, is such an interpolation. These two *kāṇḍas*, dealing with the duties of a renouncer and the procedure for becoming one, come just prior to the first three sections of the

40. It is not altogether clear whether Gautama rejected the system outright or merely asserts that for the student who has completed his studentship only one *āśrama*, namely the householder's, is open. He refers to the *āśramas* at three other places (11.9, 29; 19.1). In an earlier work I expressed the opinion that the above evidence makes the second alternative more likely (Olivelle, 1984, 86). I am not as certain now, because of the likelihood that Gautama's text, which is not part of a larger Kalpasūtra, may have undergone emendations over time. If the *āśramas* are permanent vocations, moreover, the choice of marriage by a student would preclude the possibility of his entering any other *āśrama*, thus rendering them, if not illegitimate, at least irrelevant.

41. The term means "suspension" or "annulment," in this case the setting aside of the provisions of a rule. This is the opposite of the hermeneutical position called *samuccaya*, which I will discuss in section 5.2. For a discussion of *bādha*, see Kane 1962, V.2, 1327–31.

42. See his *Mitākṣarā* on YDh 3.56–57 (p. 443) and section 5.4.5.

43. See the introduction to his translation of the BDh, pp. xxxiii–xxxv. Kane (1968, I.1, 42–43) also expresses similar doubts: "The extant Dharmasūtra does not appear to have come down intact. The fourth *praśna* is most probably an interpolation. . . . The third *praśna* also is not free from doubt."

third book that also deal with holy types of householders and hermits. These five sections thus appear to go together and to constitute a later addition from ascetic literature.[44]

The view of the *āśramas* presented in BDh 2.17–18 and the discussion therein of the proper time for renunciation could not have been written by the same person who wrote the account of the system at 2.11.9–34. Five opinions are given at BDh 2.17.1–6 on who is entitled to renounce. They permit householders, hermits, widowers, and old people to become renouncers. The *āśramas* are clearly not considered in this passage as permanent and lifelong vocations,[45] and renunciation is related to old age. On the other hand, the view of *āśramas* in BDh 2.11.9–34, as we shall see, corresponds exactly to that presented by Gautama.

The author of BDh 2.17–18, moreover, regularly refers to renunciation as *saṃnyāsa*, a term that is not found in the first part of Baudhāyana or in any other Dharmasūtra and, as I have shown elsewhere, becomes common only at a relatively late date.[46] It is apparent that he was favorably disposed toward the life and goals of asceticism, in marked contrast to the hostility shown in the earlier section. Specifically, at BDh 2.11.30 two verses from the *Taittirīya Brāhmaṇa* (3.12.9.7) are cited, verses that were used by some to prove the superiority of ascetic celibacy. In the very next *sūtra* Baudhāyana cites two other verses from the same Brāhmaṇa to demonstrate the opposite. At BDh 2.17.7, however, the same two verses in praise of celibacy are cited in support of not an opponent's but the author's own view.

It appears, therefore, that only the discussion of *āśramas* contained in BDh 2.11.9–34 belonged to the original Sūtra and that BDh 2.17–18, just like the last two books, are later additions. For the sake of convenience, I shall use the term "Baudhāyana" only with reference to the former and call the latter "Deutero-Baudhāyana."[47]

Baudhāyana, like Gautama, presents the *āśrama* system as the opinion of "some," and, again like Gautama, he goes on to refute this *pūrvapakṣa* view. Whereas Gautama's refutation consists of a single *sūtra*, Baudhāyana's is long and detailed, and it offers us significant insights into the intellectual climate surrounding this controversial issue.

Baudhāyana, just like Gautama, makes no attempt to integrate the discussion of *āśramas* into the structure of his literary work. He introduces the topic of *āśramas* almost as a digression in the course of his discussion of the five great sacrifices. This framework provides an excellent background for Baudhāyana to reject outright any conces-

44. Indeed, BDh 3.3 appears to have been taken from a treatise on forest hermits (a Vaikhānasasūtra) and shares much in common with the VaiDh. The Baudhāyana tradition in general seems to have been influenced by texts dealing with renouncers. Baudhāyana's is the only Pitṛmedhasūtra (3.11; ed. in BG) to deal with the funeral of a renouncer. The *Baudhāyana Gṛhyaśeṣasūtra* (ed. in BG), moreover, devotes two sections to the renouncer: one (4.16) contains a procedure of renunciation according to Kapila (*kapilasaṃnyāsavidhi*), and the other (4.17) is a verse account of the funeral of a renouncer.

45. This is confirmed by BDh 2.17.15–16 in which the expression "having proceeded from *āśrama* to *āśrama*" (*āśramād āśramaṃ gatvā*), reminiscent of MDh 6.34, is repeated twice. Even though the passage from one *āśrama* to another in a regular sequence is not explicitly stated, the image of the *āśramas* in this section of the BDh is closer to the classical than to the original formulation.

46. See Olivelle 1981; 1984, 127–136.

47. I use this term merely to distinguish the older unitary section of the Dharmasūtra (i.e. Proto-Baudhāyana) from later additions. I do not intend to suggest that these later additions form a unitary whole or that they were composed by a single author.

sion to ascetic celibacy and to assert the preeminent position and the obligatory nature of a householder's life.

He introduces the topic by referring to the opinion of some according to which *dharma* contains a fourfold division, namely the four *āśramas*: "Some maintain that there is a fourfold division of this very same *dharma* " (BDh 2.11.9). They base their assertion, Baudhāyana says, on the vedic text (TS 5.7.2.3) regarding the four paths leading to the gods that I cited previously: "Four paths leading to the gods traverse between heaven and earth. Place us on that among them, all ye gods, which will bring us unfailing prosperity." In the light of our discussion of Gautama's argument, this statement of Baudhāyana is very revealing. According to Baudhāyana, the proponents of the system did indeed present express vedic texts in support of the division of *dharma* in terms of *āśramas*.

The expression "paths leading to the gods" (*devayāna*), as we have seen (section 2.3.2), indicates both the path that the dead will take to reach the world of permanent bliss and the activities in this life that will place one along that path. The proponents of the *āśrama* system interpreted the "four paths" of this passage to mean the latter—that is, the modes of life that are conducive to attaining the world of the gods. The four are considered parallel paths: because they all lead to the same goal, they should be regarded as equally good; and because they are mentioned in the same vedic text, they should be viewed as equally legitimate. Marriage, in other words, is neither compulsory nor essential to reach the world of the gods or, to put it differently, to attain beatitude after death. These four paths authorized in the Veda, they contended, are the four *āśramas*.[48]

At the conclusion of his presentation of the opponent's view on these *āśramas* Baudhāyana refutes it: "But the Venerable Teacher (prescribes) a single *āśrama*, because one does not beget offspring in the others."[49] The main clause of this sentence agrees verbatim with the corresponding passage of Gautama; the reason for there being only one legitimate *āśrama*, however, is different. It is possible that one of these may have borrowed the phrase from the other. It appears to me more likely, however, that both are reproducing a stock phrase of the conservative tradition—what I would call the *aikāśramya* ("the single-*āśrama*") school—that recognized the legitimacy of only the householder.

Baudhāyana's reason for rejecting the legitimacy of the *āśramas* besides that of the householder is that their adherents are celibates and therefore do not beget offspring. Gautama (GDh 3.3), on the other hand, gives this as the reason for the superiority of the householder. Although Baudhāyana's argument against the legitimacy of the *āśrama* system appears to be different from Gautama's, the two are based on the same premise.

48. The *āśramas* are frequently referred to as "paths" (*panthānaḥ*) in later literature: MBh 12.18.4; 12.260.12–14; 12.269.19; 12.292.20; 14.35.28, 34. For the opposite image of the ladder associated with the classical formulation, see section 5.1

49. BDh 2.11.27: *aikāśramyaṃ tv ācāryā aprajanatvād itareṣām.* Gautama (GDh 3.3) uses the latter expression to show that the householder is the font of all other *āśramas*: *teṣāṃ gṛhastho yonir aprajanatvād itareṣām*—"the householder is their source, because one does not beget offspring in the others." It is unclear whether this is Gautama's own statement, or whether it is part of his description of his opponents' position. We will encounter similar statements on the superiority of the householder among authors who support the *āśrama* system (see sections 3.2.2.1–2; 5.3.1).

Baudhāyana's argument would go somewhat like this. There are express vedic injunctions requiring every man to beget offspring. Baudhāyana himself says that there are an innumerable number of such texts, and cites two. The first is the Ṛgvedic verse: "Through offspring, O Agni, may I obtain immortality" (RV 5.4.10; TS 1.4.46.1). The second is the *Taittirīya Saṃhitā* (6.3.10.5; see section 2.1.3) passage on the three debts. One of these debts, of course, is that of a son, a debt that one owes to one's ancestors. Since a person can beget offspring legitimately only as a householder, these texts implicitly enjoin everyone to become a householder.[50]

Baudhāyana, like Gautama, appears to deny any express vedic text that enjoins the other *āśrama*s, for that would result in an option. This is the likely conclusion from Baudhāyana's discussion of the vedic text on the "four paths," which its proponents adduced in support of the *āśrama* system. This text is not without ambiguity, because the term *āśrama* or the names of the four institutions are not mentioned in it. It is, therefore, open to differing interpretations. Baudhāyana rejects the interpretation offered by the proponents of the system. According to him, the four paths refer not to *āśrama*s but to four different types of sacrifices. He offers this interpretation both at the beginning (BDh 2.11.9–10) and at the end (BDh 2.11.29) of his discussion of the *āśrama*s. In the latter instance Baudhāyana prefaces his statement with the elliptical term *adṛṣṭatvāt*, which Bühler translates: "Because no (other meaning is) perceptible." It appears to me more likely, however, that the term refers to the fact that a vedic text regarding the fourfold division of *āśrama*s is not perceived; the term *dṛṣṭa* ("seen or perceived") here parallels *pratyakṣa* ("perception") that we examined earlier. What Baudhāyana wants to say is that the interpretation of "four paths" as referring to the four *āśrama*s is illegitimate without an explicit vedic text enjoining the four *āśrama*s.[51] "Because (such a text) is not seen," the four paths must refer to the four types of sacrifices.

Another significant point that emerges from Baudhāyana's polemics is his use of the theology of debts as a powerful argument against the legitimacy of the *āśrama* system. It is, of course, impossible to know whether the theology of debts was actually formulated within such a polemical setting or whether it was later used by theologians such as Baudhāyana for this purpose. In any case, the argument from debts would remain a powerful weapon against asceticism throughout the history of Brāhamaṇical theology. Baudhāyana's argument, however, makes sense only within the original formulation in which the assumption of one *āśrama* precludes the assumption of the others. As we shall see,[52] at a later time when the classical formulation becomes dominant the same theology of debts is given as an argument in support of the *āśrama* system and against those who permitted renunciation prior to marriage.

After asserting that there is only one *āśrama*, Baudhāyana cites a saying condemning the fourfold division of *āśrama*s:

50. The connection between the duties of a householder and the three debts is also explicitly mentioned by Vasiṣṭha (VaDh 11.47–48).

51. Technically, such an injunction would be what is called *apūrvavidhi*—that is, a rule that prescribes something new and otherwise unknown. The text on the four paths cannot be such a rule, because the institutions are not mentioned and, at best, presupposed. To interpret this passage in the manner the proponents of the system want, Baudhāyana would say, requires an *apūrvavidhi* on which that interpretation could be based.

52. See sections 5.3.1 and 6.2.1–2.

> With reference to this matter they adduce (this statement): "Now, there was once a demon named Kapila, the son of Prahlāda. It was he who made these divisions, while contending with the gods. A wise man should pay no heed to them." (BDh 2.11.28)

This again was probably a story current in the tradition that opposed the *āśrama* system.[53] Saying that something is the work of the devil, of course, is always a good way to reject religious innovations; but there appears to be something more to this statement. The assertion that Kapila was contending or struggling with the gods indicates that the opponents of the *āśrama* system saw it as an affront to the gods. Here we are reminded of the texts we examined in chapter 2, which claim that sacrifices are more important to gods than to humans.[54] It appears that, according to Baudhāyana, the proponents of the system were similar anti-ritualists or at the very least did not accord to rites the centrality they had in the Brāhmaṇical mainstream.

This conclusion is confirmed by a vedic text that, according to Baudhāyana, these proponents cite in support of their position: "This eternal greatness of a Brahmin is neither increased nor decreased by rites. The self knows the nature of his (greatness), and knowing it he is not stained by evil deeds" (TB 3.12.9.7–8; = BāU 4.4.23). According to their interpretation of this text, rites, or good and evil acts, do not touch the true self; they can neither harm nor benefit a person. Such a theological position would undoubtedly diminish the importance of married life, which as we saw was defined by ritual and procreative activities.

To refute this conclusion Baudhāyana cites a passage that occurs right before the former in the *Taittirīya Brāhmaṇa*:

> At his death a man who does not know the Veda does not think of that great, all-perceiving self, through which the sun, resplendent with brilliance, gives warmth, and through which a father comes to have a father[55] by the son at his birth from the womb. (TB 3.12.9.6)

Baudhāyana then cites a verse from the *Ṛgveda* (10.71.9) that reproaches those who merely use the words of the Veda without understanding their meaning.[56] This appears to be directed at the proponents of the *āśrama* system who cite vedic texts in support of their view without truly understanding their meaning.

Baudhāyana concludes his argument against the system by citing a verse probably taken from an ancient Smṛti, a verse that Āpastamba (2.24.8) also cites in praise of the householder's life and which he ascribes to Prajāpati: "We are with those who do the following: (study of) the three Vedas, vedic studentship, procreation, faith, austerity, sacrifice, and giving gifts. He who praises anything else becomes dust and perishes" (BDh 2.11.34). This verse condemns all practices that do not conform to the traditional

53. Kane (1968, I.1, 45) detects in the language of this citation a similarity to that of the Brāhmaṇas. On Kapila as the founder of the *āśrama* system, see section 3.3.3.

54. Sections 2.1.3 and 2.3.1–2. See ŚB 1.2.5.24; BāU 1.4.10; MuṇU 1.2.4–10.

55. In an interesting reversal, the son here is depicted as his father's father, because the father receives a new existence in the son. For a parallel statement about the wife, see section 2.1.2.

56. For an explanation of this difficult verse, see Sāyaṇa's commentary and Bühler's comment on BDh 2.6.11.32.

duties associated with a married householder and clearly supports Baudhāyana's position that there is only one *āśrama.*

Baudhāyana returns to his main argument against the *āśrama* system, namely the vedic obligation to procreate, in other sections of his treatise as well. "When sacrifices are not offered, when marriages are not performed, when the Veda is neglected, and when Brahmins are slighted," he says, "families become degraded" (BDh 1.10.26). Baudhāyana devotes an entire section (2.16) to the need to beget offspring, where he repeatedly points out that this is a debt which every man must pay:

> Through a son one wins the worlds, through a grandson one attains eternal life, and through one's son's grandson one ascends the very summit of heaven. . . . A man saves himself by begetting a virtuous son. A man who obtains a virtuous son saves from the fear of sin seven generations—that is six others with himself as the seventh—both before him and after him. . . . Therefore, he should assiduously beget offspring. (BDh 2.16.6, 8, 9, 11)

3.2.2 The Debate over Relative Superiority

The debate shifts its focus in Āpastamba and Vasiṣṭha, who, unlike Gautama and Baudhāyana, accept the legitimacy of the *āśrama* system. Their main aim is to deny a privileged status to the celibate *āśrama*s by establishing the equality of all *āśrama*s and, for good measure, by extolling the virtues of the householder.

3.2.2.1 Āpastamba

At the very beginning of his discussion, Āpastamba[57] asserts the equality of all *āśrama*s with regard to the final goal of human life; a person who lives steadfastly in any one of them will attain that goal. In his discussion of the renouncer, moreover, he rejects the claim of anti-ritualists that one attains final bliss (*kṣema*) by knowledge alone, because that goes against the provisions of *śāstra,* by which term he probably means the Veda. The vedic injunctions regarding rites and offspring are the cornerstones of Āpastamba's argument.

He opens the section (ĀpDh 2.13.3–6) on the relative superiority of *āśrama*s with two verses from a Purāṇa, which we have cited above and which the supporters of the celibate *āśrama*s present as scriptural evidence for the superiority of these *āśrama*s.[58] The gist of their argument is that, according to scripture, those who desire offspring "went along Aryaman's path to the south and obtained burial grounds"—that is, they are condemned to rebirth—whereas those who practice celibacy attain immortality. They also claim that celibates acquire superhuman powers even on earth: "Furthermore, they accomplish what they want by mere thought, for example, (producing) rain, bestowing the gift of a child, seeing distant objects, travelling by mere thought, and other similar

57. ĀpDh 2.21.2. For a discussion of this text, see section 3.1.1, n. 5.

58. ĀpDh 2.23.4–5. See section 3.1.3. Versions of these two verses occur in later Purāṇas: see Bühler's introduction to his translation of the ĀpDh, pp. xxxi–xxxii. An argument from the expression "burial grounds" is found also in the MBh 12.19.14.

things."[59] "Therefore, because of such vedic texts and because of visible results,"[60] Āpastamba concludes, "some say that these *āśramas* are superior" (ĀpDh 2.23.9).

Āpastamba's argument against the superiority of the celibate *āśramas* parallels Baudhāyana's argument against the *āśrama* system as such. At the outset Āpastamba gives a reasoned argument in favor of marriage and ritual activity:

> It is, however, the firm view of those who are well versed in the triple Veda that the Vedas are the authority.[61] They declare that it is obligatory to perform those (rites) prescribed therein, which are performed in the company of the wife, using rice, barley, animals, ghee, milk, and potsherds, and with the recitation of loud and muttered (mantras), and that any practice opposed to them is without authority.[62] (ĀpDh 2.23.10)

Āpastamba next turns to the two verses about the 80,000 sages that form the scriptural basis in the opponents' argument for the superiority of celibacy. He explains that the term "burial grounds" in the first verse is only meant to prescribe the funerary rites for those who have performed many sacrifices.[63] For such people the Vedas assure "heaven," which Āpastamba (2.23.12) explains as "an unending reward," and therefore not different from the immortality that awaits the celibates. After refuting their interpretation of the first verse, Āpastamba turns to the second. His argument here is based on the vedic injunctions regarding procreation. Since celibacy contradicts the Veda, the provisions of this verse have no validity. He says: "The Vedas, furthermore, declare that offspring constitutes one's immortality" (ĀpDh 2.24.1), and cites the well-known passage from the *Taittirīya Brāhmaṇa* (1.5.5.6): "In your offspring you are born again; that, O mortal, is your immortality." It is children, not celibacy, that assure human immortality.

Āpastamba goes on to show that even perception, the other central means of knowledge besides vedic scriptures, lends support to the revealed doctrine, because sons even look like their fathers: "One, moreover, knows through perception that (the son) is a distinct reproduction (of the father). One observes, moreover, their resemblance; only the bodies are different" (ĀpDh 2.24.2). Express vedic texts and human perception, the two main sources of knowledge that invalidate all other sources which contradict them, oppose the argument for the superiority of celibacy.

59. ĀpDh 2.23.7–8. The *Chāndogya Upaniṣad* (8.2) expresses a similar belief: when a person who knows the self merely thinks of something he wants, it immediately comes into being. Such powers are, of course, commonly associated with yogins and holy people in Indian culture.

60. The argument from "visible results" (*pratyakṣaphala*) reminds one of the famous *Sāmaññaphala Sutta* of the *Dīgha Nikāya* in which King Ajātasattu asks the Buddha about the visible results of an ascetic's life.

61. The term *pramāṇa* indicates both authority and means of knowledge; here it refers to the source of authoritative knowledge regarding *dharma*. For the sources of *dharma*, see ĀpDh 1.1.1–3. This argument is very similar to the one we discussed earlier with reference to the term *pratyakṣa* ("express vedic text") of Gautama.

62. *Apramāṇam* ("without authority") means that such conduct lacks a valid means of knowledge—it is not sanctioned by the Veda, which is the only means of knowledge with regard to *dharma*.

63. A verse of Yājñavalkya (YDh 3.186), whose work on *dharma* was probably composed a millennium or so later around the fourth century C.E., recapitulating these verses says explicitly that the 80,000 sages who lived at home were subject to rebirth (*punarāvartinaḥ*). The interpretation of the supporters of celibacy appears to have won out.

Āpastamba (ĀpDh 2.24.3–6) cites several verses from a text called *Bhaviṣyat Purāṇa* which show that offspring contribute to the glory of their departed ancestors. He then anticipates a possible objection: if children are the same as the father, then the sins they commit should affect the father. Resorting to the doctrine of *karma*, Āpastamba (2.24.7–10) says that the sins of children do not affect their parents. Those who commit sins perish alone; parents are not held responsible for the crimes of their children.

Even though the arguments used by him are similar to those of Gautama and Baudhāyana, Āpastamba draws a very different conclusion. He does not reject outright the legitimacy of the four *āśrama*s or the appropriateness of choosing a celibate *āśrama*. His fight is not with the system itself but with those who claim a superior status to the celibate *āśrama*s. His aim is to defend the equality of all *āśrama*s. He began the argument with it (ĀpDh 2.21.2), and he returns to it in his closing statement:

> It may well be that someone [namely a celibate] while still in his body may gain a heavenly world through austerity or by means of a portion of merit (acquired in a former life), or that someone may accomplish what he wants by mere thought. But it does not follow from that that one *āśrama* is superior to another. (ĀpDh 2.24.14)

3.2.2.2 Vasiṣṭha

Vasiṣṭha's is the latest extant Dharmasūtra, and by his time the controversies surrounding the *āśrama* system had by and large ceased. He does not defend the equality of the *āśrama*s as explicitly or as vigorously as Āpastamba, but some concern regarding the alleged superiority of the celibate *āśrama*s must underlie his eulogy of the householder:

> A householder alone offers sacrifices. A householder afflicts himself with austerities. Of the four *āśrama*s, therefore, the householder is the best.
>
> As all rivers and rivulets ultimately end up in the ocean, so people of all *āśrama*s ultimately end up with the householder. (See section 5.3.1, n. 23)
>
> As all creatures depend on their mothers for their survival, so all mendicants depend on householders for their survival. (VaDh 10.14–16)

Another implicit affirmation of the equality of *āśrama*s is found in Vasiṣṭha's statements at the end of his discussions of the householder, the hermit, and the renouncer regarding the final reward of the respective *āśrama*s. A householder will not fall from the world of Brahmā (8.17), a hermit will attain endless bliss in heaven (9.12), and a renouncer will not fail to attain the world of Brahmā (10.31).

The *āśrama* system must have gained sufficient acceptance within the mainstream of the *dharma* tradition by the time of Vasiṣṭha, because he is the only author of a Dharmasūtra to integrate the system fully into his discussion of *dharma*. It is no longer a parenthesis or an afterthought. Vasiṣṭha discusses the duties of students, householders, hermits, and renouncers within the framework of the *āśrama* system, devoting one chapter to each *āśrama*. We detect thus a significant shift with regard to the system within the *dharma* tradition during the period of three to four centuries that separate Vasiṣṭha from his predecessors.

The debates and arguments regarding the *āśrama*s we have examined are incomplete because the evidence comes only from the authors of the Dharmasūtras and not from their opponents, whose arguments we see only as our authors present them. It is impossible to gauge how completely they present the views of their opponents. The debate on both sides, however, was conducted according to the rules of logic and exegesis that were current within the Brāhmaṇical tradition. An analysis of these arguments and the changing attitudes of these authors to the system will provide some clues to the important questions of authorship and date of the *āśrama* system.

3.3 Authorship

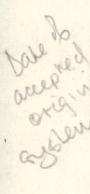

The *āśrama* system as presented in the early Dharmasūtras has the characteristics of a novel doctrine. Gautama and Baudhāyana deal with it almost parenthetically and question its legitimacy. Even Āpastamba, who accepts the system, does not integrate it into the body of his treatise. Gradually, however, it received acceptance—grudgingly at first no doubt, as seen in Āpastamba—within the mainstream of the *dharma* tradition. By the time of Vasiṣṭha around the second century B.C.E. it had become part of the mainstream itself. The Dharmasūtras thus bear witness to the early attitude of the mainstream to the system: from outright rejection to total acceptance and integration into the framework of the treatises. We can be fairly certain, moreover, that the evidence provided by the early Dharmasūtras is not too distant in time from the creation of the system itself. The two questions that I want to deal with here are who were the inventors of this system and what was the purpose of that invention?

3.3.1 Was the Āśrama *System a Defense of Orthodoxy?*

Two common assumptions have prevailed among scholars regarding the authorship and intent of the *āśrama* system: it was created by conservative Brahmins with the intention of resisting the new religious movements and of safeguarding the Brāhmaṇical religion by incorporating the renunciatory life style into a scheme that would lessen its impact and reduce or eliminate the conflict between it and the life of the householder. Thus, for example, T. W. Rhys Davids (1903, 249–50) writes:

> Unable therefore, whether they wanted or not, to stay the progress of newer ideas, the priests strove to turn the incoming tide into channels favorable to their Order. They formulated—though this was some time after the rise of Buddhism—the famous theory of the *Āśramas*, or Efforts, according to which no one could become either a Hermit or a Wanderer without having first passed many years as a student in the brahmin schools, and lived after that the life of a married householder as regulated in the brahmin law-books.

These remarks typify the danger I noted earlier of using the classical formulation to discover the origin and purpose of the *āśrama* system.

Winternitz (1926, 226) also sees the system as an attempt to reconcile the two different ideals of the householder and the renouncer within "orthodox" Brāhmaṇism, a view shared by most scholars.[64] The view expressed by Lingat (1973, 50–51) is representative:

64. See Weinrich 1929, 80–81, 88, 92; Sharma 1939, 20; Apte 1951, 442–43, 447, 493; O'Flaherty 1973, 78–82.

> As for the fourth *āśrama*, it is doubtless the result of a defensive policy on the part of our Brahmins *vis-à-vis* the ascetics who competed with them in the field of religion. . . . Their [renouncers'] way of life placed them outside Brahminical precepts. Hence the Brahmins thought of canalising and damming up this current of mysticism by making it into a fourth *āśrama*.

Belvalkar and Ranade consider the willingness to incorporate any new doctrine so long as it did not question the authority of the Vedas or the theology of sacrifice as a general characteristic of Brāhmaṇism, and cite the *āśrama* system as a good example:

> If the newer philosophy was willing to allow full scope to the cult of the Vedic sacrifice during the first two stages, then Brāhmaṇism was prepared to give, in the case of those duly qualified for the task, full scope for abstract meditation on *Brahman* and on the other problems of life as propounded by the new school. This compromise, so far as it went, was largely successful. (Belvalkar and Ranade, 1927, 84)

Thapar (1979, 182) agrees: "That the theory of the four *āśramas* functioned to some extent as a safety valve would seem evident from the placing of *saṃnyāsa* in old age, after the completion of social obligations."

One can readily agree with one point in this thesis: as I have attempted to demonstrate in the preceding chapter, the background against which the *āśrama* system came into being was the conflict between the doctrines and institutions of the vedic world and those of an emerging new world with an alternative definition of reality. Following the ideals of the one meant rejecting those of the other. With reference to such conflicts between worlds, Berger and Luckmann (1967, 106–7) observe:

> The group that has objectivated this deviant reality becomes the carrier of an alternative definition of reality. It is hardly necessary to belabor the point that such heretical groups posit not only a theoretical threat to the symbolic universe, but a practical one to the institutional order legitimated by the symbolic universe in question.

The initial response of the guardians of the threatened world is the outright rejection of the new and the implementation of strategies for suppression, coupled with theoretical legitimations of the old world. Such, as we have seen, was the response of the early experts of *dharma* represented by Gautama and Baudhāyana.

It is the second stage that represents the more interesting phase of this conflict, however. As Berger and Luckmann (1967, 115) observe:

> [It] involves the more ambitious attempt to account for all deviant definitions of reality *in terms of* concepts belonging to one's own universe. . . . The deviant conceptions are not merely assigned a negative status, they are grappled with theoretically in detail. The final goal of this procedure is to *incorporate* the deviant conceptions within one's own universe, and thereby to liquidate them ultimately.

In religious traditions the incorporation of the new into the structures of the old takes place primarily through the hermeneutical process so prominent in the history of the *āśrama* system. Berger and Luckmann believe that this process is initiated and carried out by the guardians of the old world; it represents the reaction of the old to the new. In this they support the conclusion of the scholars cited above that the creation of the *āśrama* system represents such an attempt to include and thereby liquidate a threat that could not otherwise be suppressed or avoided.

The evidence of the Dharmasūtras, I expect to show, does not support such a hypothesis.[65] Contrary to Berger and Luckmann, I would argue that the initiative to find ways of grafting the new onto the old can and often does come from the leaders of the deviant world who seek acceptance, patronage, and economic advantage within the broader society. The creation of the *āśrama* system provides a good example of such an initiative.

3.3.2 The Āśrama *System as a Theological Innovation*

A close reading of these early texts leads us to the conclusion that the *āśrama* system was created not by the conservative mainstream in order to encompass in a stifling embrace new ideas and institutions that it had failed to suppress but by Brahmins who shared those ideas and ideals and who sought exegetical loopholes to introduce them into the Brāhmaṇical mainstream. From our examination of the debate on the *āśrama* system within the Dharmasūtras we can draw the following conclusions with some confidence. (1) The authors of the system were Brahmins who were supporters of or sympathetic toward the ideals of celibacy and renunciation, and who belonged to what may be termed the "liberal"[66] segments of the Brāhmaṇical community. (2) Their purpose in creating the system was to legitimize the modes of life different from that of the householder by providing a place for them within the sphere of *dharma*, thereby stretching this central concept in new directions.[67]

Baudhāyana, we have seen (section 3.2.1.2), makes several statements that give us a glimpse into the views of those whom he considered the authors or, at the very least, the proponents of the *āśrama* system. They cite a vedic text (TB 3.12.9.6–7) in support of their position, a text that indicates that the authors believed rites or moral norms to be of little use with regard to the ultimate goal of humans. Their anti-ritualist position is also revealed in the statement that the Asura Kapila devised the system as part of his strategy in his struggle with the gods (BDh 2.11.28). That this struggle involved the rejection of sacrifice is made clear by Baudhāyana's reinterpretation of the vedic text on the "four paths," the vedic basis for the *āśrama*s in the eyes of the proponents of the system, as referring to sacrifices (BDh 2.11.29). We have seen elsewhere also that such struggles with gods involved the non-performance of sacrifices (sections 2.1.3; 2.3.1–2).[68] Baudhāyana's own argument against the supporters of the system centers on the obligation to

65. It needs to be pointed out that scholars who see the *āśrama* system as a defense of orthodoxy invariably take as their point of departure the classical formulation of the system, a methodological error I alluded to at the outset (section 1.3.2).

66. By "liberal" I mean people and groups who are more open to new ways of thinking and living and less wedded to the traditions of the past than those whom I have termed "conservative."

67. This is not something completely new. The Buddhists, for example, established a more radical redefinition of *dharma* by using that term to designate their doctrine and value system.

68. The *Mahābhārata* records the story of the two Asura brothers Sunda and Upasunda who attempted to kill all those who offer sacrifice because they strengthen the gods: "The royal seers and the brahmins feed the might, strength, and glory of the gods with their great sacrifices and oblations. All these prosperous enemies of the Asuras we must attack and annihilate today" (MBh 1.202.10–11).

procreate. It is his major reason for rejecting the system (BDh 2.11.27). Most of the vedic texts he cites in opposition to the system also declare the obligation to procreate. From Baudhāyana's argument we can safely conclude that his opponents, that is, the supporters and possibly the authors of the *āśrama* system, also supported the legitimacy and even the superiority of celibate and non-ritual modes of life. They certainly were not conservative upholders of the old order.

Even though Āpastamba and Vasiṣṭha accept the *āśrama* system, it appears that they were not representative of the opponents against whom Baudhāyana and Gautama argued. Āpastamba and Vasiṣṭha clearly belong to the Brāhmaṇical mainstream but probably lived during a time when the system had gained widespread acceptance within that mainstream.[69] Āpastamba's arguments (section 3.2.2.1), however, in one sense parallel Baudhāyana's. The opponents of both appear to share similar views regarding the *āśramas*. Those whom Āpastamba argues against because they preach the superiority of the celibate *āśramas* appear to have views very close to those whom Baudhāyana combats as the originators of the *āśrama* system.

The views ascribed by Baudhāyana and Āpastamba to these partisans of the *āśrama* system are very similar to the anti-ritualist and pro-celibacy views we have discussed in chapter 2 (sections 2.3.1–2). We may not be far wrong in assigning the authorship of the system to this anti-ritualist Brāhmaṇical tradition that finds expression in some of the early Upaniṣads. Indeed, the text which, according to Baudhāyana (BDh 2.11.30), proponents of the *āśrama* system cite in support of the celibate states is also found in the *Bṛhadāraṇyaka Upaniṣad* (4.4.23). Āpastamba's statement that according to the proponents of the system one attains final bliss by mere knowledge also agrees with the upaniṣadic views on knowledge.[70] A clue buried in the *Baudhāyana Dharmasūtra*, moreover, points in the direction of renouncers. As we have seen in section 3.2.1.2, this text underwent extensive additions during a later period. One of these additions (BDh 2.17–18) describes the rules of renunciation and cites a text in praise of renunciation. This is the same text (TB 3.12.9.6–7) that Baudhāyana ascribes to the proponents of the *āśrama* system (BDh 2.11.30). This evidence, however, is insufficient to conclude that the system was created by Brahmin renouncers. The preponderance of the evidence, nevertheless, points in the direction of Brahmins who, if they were not actually renouncers, were at the very least sympathetic to the ideals of celibacy and renunciation.

The authors of the *āśrama* system were without doubt Brahmins. It is true that the arguments we have examined were written by learned Brahmins. This fact may be responsible for the Brāhmaṇical slant contained in their presentation of the opponents'

69. Vasiṣṭha clearly belongs to a later period. The relative date of Āpastamba vis-à-vis Gautama and Baudhāyana, as we shall see, is far less clear. The consideration of this issue is complicated by our ignorance of the regions in which these texts were composed. Theoretically it may well be possible that the system may have been accepted in one region and not in another, and the writers may represent this regional variance rather than a temporal sequence.

70. Altekar (1955, 186) proposes a similar view: "The new school undoubtedly regarded Renunciation as superior to vedic sacrifices, presupposing matrimony, but could not openly say so, owing to the great hold of the vedic religion over the popular mind. It, therefore, followed the strategy of provoking the least possible opposition and began to plead for Renunciation the status of an alternative 'mārga' or path for salvation." It is unclear whether their strategy in devising the *āśrama* system was one "of provoking the least possible opposition," but I agree with his view regarding its authorship.

viewpoints. But the substance of that viewpoint also shows all the marks of the Brāhmaṇical way of thinking and arguing. The proponents base the system on vedic texts and cite vedic and smṛti passages in support of their position. The theory of option (*vikalpa*), moreover, comes from the Mīmāṃsā tradition. The structure of the original formulation also shows a Brāhmaṇical mind at work. The system attempts to fit itself into the pre-existing framework of life-cycle rituals (*saṃskāra*), giving a new significance to the period of initiatory studentship as a preparatory school for all the adult modes of life.[71]

In the light of what we have said about the socio-economic conditions of this time (section 2.2), moreover, I am inclined to believe that the *āśrama* system is an urban invention, or at least reflects the openness of an urban mentality. It is certainly more likely that Brahmins living in urban centers were influenced by and open to new ideas and institutions than their village counterparts. The most persuasive argument, however, is the very nature of the original *āśrama* system. It envisages the *āśramas* as voluntary institutions. People are free to choose what they want to be as adults. The same principle was the basis of other voluntary organizations, such as Buddhist and Jain monastic orders. It is difficult to see how the assertion of individual freedom that is at the heart of this bold theological innovation could have arisen within a village context.

3.3.3 Kapila, Sāṃkhya, and the Āśramas

The only instance in which an individual is mentioned as the author of the *āśrama* system occurs in the text cited by Baudhāyana (BDh 2.11.28; see section 3.2.1.2), where an Asura named Kapila is said to have invented the system in his struggle against the gods. The story is presented within the mythical framework of the battle between Asuras (demons) and gods. Is there, however, a kernel of history in the myth?[72]

Kapila is the reputed founder of the Sāṃkhya system of philosophy,[73] which is connected in the epic literature and especially in the *Bhagavad Gītā* with the life style of renunciation. It appears that one of the earliest forms of Brāhmaṇical renunciation was associated with Sāṃkhya; however, we have very little information about this form of renunciation (Renou and Filliozat 1947, n. 1238). In the *Mahābhārata* Kapila is often depicted as a defender of the renunciatory point of view.[74]

71. An interesting question for which the available evidence does not permit an adequate answer relates to the vedic schools (*śākhā*) and the specialized traditions of learning to which these innovators may have belonged. The early Śrautasūtras and Gṛhyasūtras do not mention the *āśramas*. This may, of course, be due either to their subject matter or to the time they were composed. The former is likely at least in the case of the Śrauta- and Gṛhyasūtras of Āpastamba, which, although composed by the same individual as the Dharmasūtra (see Bühler's introduction to his translation of ĀpDh, p. xiii), do not mention the system. It appears likely that the system originated within the specialized tradition of Dharmaśāstra, or at least it was this tradition that felt the need to deal with this novel doctrine regarding *dharma*.

72. On this passage and the relation between it and the MBh (12.260–62) passage containing the dialogue between Kapila and the cow, see Winternitz 1926, 225–26.

73. Some, such as Garbe (1917), accept the historicity of Kapila as the founder of the Sāṃkhya system. Others recognize him as a purely legendary figure. For a survey of scholarly opinion, see Larson 1969, 16–76.

74. On references to Kapila in the *Mahābhārata* see Hall 1982, pp. 18f; Hopkins 1969, p. 97. On the relation between Kapila, the Sāṃkhya system, and asceticism, see MBh 3.211.21; 12.211.17–18, 52;

Kapila, for example, is said to be considered the highest seer (*paramarṣi*) by renouncers (MBh 3.211.21). Pañcaśikha, another ancient Sāṃkhya teacher and traditionally the pupil Āsuri, who was Kapila's pupil, is also said to have been a renouncer and a proponent of the value of renunciation.[75]

The association of Kapila with renunciatory values in general and with the *āśrama*s in particular is expressed most dramatically in the dialogue between Kapila and a cow led for sacrifice (MBh 12.260–62). Kapila, who is called an ascetic (*yati*), seeing the cow exclaims "Oh Vedas!" A seer named Syūmaraśmi enters the cow and engages Kapila in a debate regarding the relative merits of renunciation and the ritual religion of the householder. The significant part of this long dialogue for our purpose is Kapila's reference to the *āśrama* system. The actions of those who belong to all *āśrama*s have the same goal. Renouncers, hermits, students, and householders proceed along "the four eternal paths leading to the gods." Their relative superiority, however, is determined by their respective fruits. Since ascetics attain the highest goal, Kapila asks, what is the use of the householder's life? So, according to Kapila, even though all *āśrama*s lead to the gods, only ascetics attain the highest goal. Later in the dialogue (MBh 12.262.19, 21) Kapila calls *āśrama* the fourfold or four-footed *dharma* (*dharmam catuṣpādam*), an expression which parallels Baudhāyana's "fourfold division of *dharma*." Kapila's argument, moreover, is reminiscent of the views ascribed in the Dharmasūtras to the proponents of the *āśrama* system, and his description of the system is very similar to its original formulation. The reference to the four paths leading to the gods clearly refers to the vedic text (TS 5.7.2.3) given by Baudhāyana as the basis of the system. It appears likely that Kapila in this passage also looks upon this vedic text as a justification for the fourfold division of *dharma* in terms of the *āśrama*s.

Syūmaraśmi's reply, likewise, echoes the arguments of the authors of the Dharmasūtras. The householder is the best because he supports all others, because he procreates offspring, and because he sacrifices. How can men attain freedom (*mokṣa*), he asks, when they are burdened with debts to ancestors, gods, and men?

All this is very suggestive, but we cannot be sure that the Asura Kapila of Baudhāyana is the same as the Kapila of the epic literature. If that connection is established, however, we can conclude that there may have been at least one tradition that associated the *āśrama* system with Kapila and the followers of the Sāṃkhya system of philosophy. The probable date of the *āśrama* system, moreover, coincides with the period during which Saṃkhya rose to prominence as a major philosophical tradition.

The only other reference to an author of the *āśrama*s occurs in a prose passage of the *Mahābhārata* (MBh 12.184–85) that appears to be a fragment of an old Dharmasūtra (Deussen 1909, 131). Twice in this passage the *āśrama*s are said to have been created by Brahmarṣi (MBh 12.184.7; 12.185.2), who is referred to at 12.184.8 as *bhagavat* ("lord"). It would be pure conjecture to see here a reference to Kapila, even though he is frequently referred to as a *ṛṣi*.

12.231–32; 12.289–303; 12.290.3, 71, 78; 12.294.36; 12.306; 12.326.64; 12.327.64–66; 12.330.30; 13.14.159; 13.135.70. The *Bhagavad Gītā* closely associates renunciation (*saṃnyāsa*) with Sāṃkhya, especially in chapters 3, 5, and 6. Significantly, a procedure of becoming a renouncer given in the *Baudhāyana Gṛhyaśeṣasūtra* (ed. in BG) 4.17 is ascribed to Kapila (*kapilasaṃnyāsavidhi*; see n. 44).

75. See MBh 12.211–12; 12.308.24. For the *Bhikṣusūtra* of Pārāśarya, sometimes identified with Pañcaśikha, and the type of ascetics called "Pārāśarin," see Olivelle 1992, 13–14, and Shastri 1975.

3.3.4 The Purpose of the Āśrama System

From the above discussion it becomes clear that the purpose[76] of the *āśrama* system was not to defend "orthodoxy" against external assaults, principally from renunciatory institutions and ideologies. Its purpose was rather to create a scheme within which the pivotal category of *dharma* could be extended to include religious modes of life different from that of the Brāhmaṇical householder. Its architects were—if I be permitted the use of modern political terminology—not the reactionary defenders of orthodoxy but liberal reformers bent on leading the vedic tradition in new directions.

It is a common phenomenon in religions that new ideas and institutions are hardly ever presented as something new. One way of effacing their novelty is to relate them to central concepts of the old order through the hermeneutical labor of theologians and exegetes. Even when entirely new symbolic worlds emerge, they maintain significant continuities with symbols and ideas of the ones they replace. Perhaps the most central concept of the ancient Indian religious world was *dharma.* Even Buddhism and Jainism adopted the term as a pivotal idea of their symbolic worlds. It comes as no surprise, therefore, that Brāhmaṇical groups favoring new ideas and institutions should attempt to relate them to this central concept.

Baudhāyana (BDh 2.11.9) states explicitly that the authors of the system presented it as a classification of *dharma.*[77] It is possible, though not altogether certain, that they intended the division of *dharma* in terms of the four *āśrama*s to parallel its older division into the four *varṇa*s ("social classes"). The connection between the two, however, was soon established within the dharmaśāstric tradition.[78] We have seen (section 1.1.4) that originally the term *āśrama* probably indicated the ideal life style of a Brahmin. The choice of this term for the new classification of *dharma* extended the meaning of both these significant concepts of the old world, relating them to alternate modes of life.

Allowing a choice among the *āśrama*s clearly placed these modes of life on at least an equal footing with that of the householder. Choice also opened the door to debates regarding the relative merits of the different *āśrama*s. It was now possible to argue about which *dharma* was better, an uncertainty revealed in the *Mahābhārata* passage I cited at the end of chapter 2 and, indeed, throughout the great epic.[79] The authors of the system presented the celibate *āśrama*s not only as equal but even as superior to the life of a householder, provoking strong rebuttals from the champions of the ritual religion.

One significant feature of the original formulation is that the choice, which is limited to a specific period of a man's life, is irrevocable, the *āśrama*s being permanent and lifelong vocations. This is a rather artificial scheme. Other sources, including Buddhist, depict married men as adopting celibate modes of life. What then was the purpose of this scheme? We can, of course, only speculate here, but one possible reason may have been

76. I am, of course, not talking about the motives of its creators, which we will never know, but about what we can glean regarding the functions it served or was seen as serving during the early period of its history.

77. The *Chāndogya* passage (ChU 2.23.1) that we will examine later (section 3.5) also sees a division of *dharma* in terms of legitimate religious activities that a person may pursue.

78. See section 7.2. For the significance of the number four and the relationship between the four *āśrama*s and other sets of four within the Brāhmaṇical tradition, see sections 7.6 and 8.3.

79. For some recent attempts to deal with these moral ambiguities, see Matilal 1989.

to eliminate the socially disruptive practice of people with families abandoning their responsibilities. Affirming the permanence of family responsibilities may have made the system more acceptable to the Brāhmaṇical mainstream, and it may indeed have facilitated the endorsement it gradually received from that mainstream. The significance of this position may be seen in the fact that most later debates regarding *āśramas* centered on the time when a person is permitted to become a renouncer.

The *āśrama* system can thus be seen as a structure for inclusion. In this sense the ideology of the *āśrama* system is similar to that of the *varṇa* and caste systems. They both aim at managing diversity not by eliminating it but by recognizing and including the diversities within an overarching system. The creators of the *āśrama* system intended to do to the diversity of religious life styles what the creators of the *varṇa* system did to the diversity of social and ethnic groups.[80] In this sense it was a forward-looking and reformist scheme rather than a defensive wall put up by beleaguered conservatives.

3.4 Date

The primary evidence for dating the creation of the *āśrama* system comes from the Dharmasūtras, which are the earliest documents to record it. The task of dating the system would be considerably easier were it possible to date these documents with some accuracy and certitude. Unfortunately there is no scholarly consensus regarding their relative or absolute chronology.[81]

We can safely ignore Vasiṣṭha because there is general agreement that he is later than at least Āpastamba and Baudhāyana. The major controversy concerns the relative antiquity of Gautama and Āpastamba. Bühler and Kane take Gautama to be the oldest, whereas Meyer, Kangle, and Ghosh favor Āpastamba. The text of Baudhāyana, as we have seen in section 3.2.1.2, poses serious problems because it was subjected to major additions and interpolations. The dates proposed for Baudhāyana refer only to the original section and not to Deutero-Baudhāyana.

The best one can say regarding this scholarly controversy is that the evidence provided by both sides is inconclusive. Almost all the arguments are based on internal evidence which is subject to diverse interpretations. The probability of interpolations in most of these texts makes arguments from internal evidence even more hazardous. Even the positions of the Dharmasūtras with regard to the *āśrama* system do not provide any

80. The two are different in that no explicit hierarchy is established in the *āśrama* system, even though, as we have seen, different groups attempted to place either the householder or the renouncer at the top of the heap.

81. It is beyond the scope of this study to examine in detail the scholarly controversies regarding the dates of the Dharmasūtras. For discussions of the issues surrounding their dates, see Bühler's introductions to his translations of these texts, SBE 2, xviii–xlvi, liii–lx; SBE 14, xvii–xxlii; Kane 1968, I.1, 12–111; Meyer 1927, 253–326; Kangle 1968; Skurzak 1948, 7; 1958, 6; Ghosh 1927; Banerjee 1962, 13–50. We must, of course, dismiss the wild speculations regarding the date of the *āśrama* system, such as that proposed by Kakar (1968, 128), by assigning Manu to 600–300 B.C.E. Other broad dates proposed by scholars are mere guesswork. T. W. Rhys Davids (1903, 249–50): "Some time after the rise of Buddhism." Ghurye (1964, 2): "Sometime before Buddha and Mahāvīra." Sharma (1939): "Most probably . . . before the rise of Buddhism." See also Winternitz 1926, 224–26.

secure evidence for their relative dates. We saw that the formulation of the system given by all four is substantially the same. Āpastamba and Vasiṣṭha accept the system, however, while Gautama and Baudhāyana reject it. It is tempting to consider the rejection as an earlier position of the dharmaśāstric tradition vis-à-vis the *āśrama* system, its acceptance and integration into the *dharma* framework coming at a later date. However, it is equally possible that, as I have already noted, the two positions are related to different geographical regions. The only firm conclusion that can be drawn is that the authors who reject the validity of the system must have belonged to an early period. The *āśrama* system became a powerful theological model, and, with the spread of urbanism during the Maurya empire, it was inevitable that the Brāhmaṇical mainstream would come to adopt it as its own. Given their total rejection of the system, therefore, it is highly unlikely that Gautama and Baudhāyana could have belonged to a later period.

For dating the *āśrama* system I will focus on Āpastamba and Baudhāyana, regarding whose dates there is less controversy. Kane sets their upper and lower limits: Baudhāyaṇa 500–200 B.C.E. and Āpastamba 450–350 B.C.E.[82] These are clearly tentative dates. Proceeding very conservatively, however, we shall not be far wrong in concluding that at least one of these documents must have been composed by the beginning of the fourth century B.C.E.

By the time of these documents, however, the system must have become sufficiently known and gained a degree of acceptance within the Brāhmaṇical schools for it to have been taken seriously by their authors. This process of dissemination and acceptance must have taken a considerable period of time. The fact that it is not noticed by any of the early Upaniṣads, however, provides an upper limit and shows that it could not have been in existence too long before the composition of the earliest Dharmasūtras. If my argument for the urban background of the system is accepted, moreover, it could not have arisen before the sixth century B.C.E. A later date is also suggested by the persistence of the original meaning of the term *āśrama* in documents belonging roughly to this period and by its use with that meaning in the Dharmasūtras themselves in their discussion of the *pariṣad*.[83]

As we have seen, moreover, the system was not yet integrated into the general structure of these early Dharmasūtras. Āpastamba, Baudhāyana, and Gautama deal with the *āśramas* either parenthetically or in a section that appears to be an appendix to the main body of the text. Only Vasiṣṭha, admittedly several centuries later than the others, incorporates the system into the main body of his work. The *āśrama* system as presented by the earlier authors has the appearance of a new doctrine. We shall not be far wrong, therefore, in assuming in the most tentative way that the *āśrama* system must have been created sometime during the fifth century B.C.E. In any case, the system was known within the dharmaśāstric tradition in the fourth century B.C.E.

This tentative date for the creation of the original *āśrama* system and the date I will propose[84] for the development of its classical formulation are supported, I believe, by

82. In the first edition of the his work Kane (see 1968, I.1, 36, 52, 70, 105) had given slightly earlier dates: Āpastamba 600–300 B.C.E. and Baudhāyana 500–200 B.C.E. His date for Gautama is 600–400 B.C.E., and for Vasiṣṭha 300–100 B.C.E.

83. We have examined above the use of *āśrama* in the *Āruṇi Upaniṣad* and the *Śvetāśvatara Upaniṣad* (section 1.1.4). For a discussion of *pariṣad* see section 7.4.

84. The beginning of the common era: see the introduction to Part 3 in this volume.

the absence of any reference to the system in two important texts, the *Rāmāyaṇa* and the *Bhagavad Gītā*.

3.4.1 The Silence of the Rāmāyaṇa

The *Rāmāyaṇa* poses an intriguing historical problem of silence. After a careful reading of both epics, I have counted 160 occurrences of the term *āśrama* in the *Mahābhārata* (see section 5.3.5, n. 54), and I could well have missed some. In the *Rāmāyaṇa*, on the contrary, I have encountered the term in only a single verse in praise of the householder.[85] Such praise is a cliché in the *dharma* literature, and one may question the authenticity of this verse in light of the fact that the rest of the poem either ignores or is ignorant of the *āśrama* system. Arguments from silence are always weak, and Goldman's point regarding the nature of the *Rāmāyaṇa* as opposed to the *Mahābhārata* is well taken:

> The *Mahābhārata* is encyclopedic and became a sort of compendium of traditional law and custom. As a result, it accumulated episodes illustrating virtually every social custom known to the epic bards and redactors. . . . Under these circumstances, the exclusion of a practice or convention from the *Mahābhārata* constitutes fairly good evidence that it was not known to the compilers and expanders of the text. This is not the case with the *Rāmāyaṇa*, which was never intended to be so inclusive. Therefore, the omission of a traditional practice from the *Rāmāyaṇa* does not, to our way of thinking, conclusively demonstrate that its authors were ignorant of the practice. It may be that they simply had no occasion to mention it. (Goldman 1984: 19–20)

The silence with regard to the *āśrama* system is, in my opinion, quite different. The author of the *Rāmāyaṇa* had plenty of occasions to refer to it during the course of his long poem, which contains frequent and lengthy accounts of forest hermits and itinerant mendicants. The author never relates these institutions to the *āśrama* system. Hermits and renouncers are never introduced as belonging to a particular *āśrama*. Their duties and practices are never presented as *āśramadharma*.

From his silence, therefore, we can at least tentatively claim that the author of the *Rāmāyaṇa* was either ignorant of the *āśrama* system or could choose to ignore it because it had not gained the prominence that it did in later times. If we accept that the *Rāmāyaṇa* was composed before the fifth century B.C.E., as suggested by Goldman (1984: 22–23) or even a century or so later, the author's silence with regard to the *āśrama*s can well be explained, because during that time, as I have demonstrated (section 3.4), the *āśrama* system was either not invented or at the most limited to a group of thinkers outside the mainstream of the *dharma* tradition represented by Gautama and Baudhāyana. Bards and poets certainly would have little reason to engage in theological disputes and could have naturally ignored such an unconventional institution.

3.4.2 The Silence of the Bhagavad Gītā

In sharp contrast to the rest of the *Mahābhārata* (section 5.3.5), the very term *āśrama* does not occur at all in the *Bhagavad Gītā*. In a relatively short text such as the *Gītā*,

85. Rām 2.98.58: *caturṇām āśramāṇāṃ hi gārhasthyaṃ śreṣṭham āśramam / āhur dharmajña dharmajñās taṃ kathaṃ tyaktum arhasi //*—"Those who know the *dharma*, O knower of the *dharma*, proclaim the householder's *āśrama* to be the best among the four *āśramas*. How can you abandon it?"

however, an argument from silence is even more precarious than in the case of the voluminous *Rāmāyaṇa.* Yet the central problem of the *Gītā*, the question that is raised at the very beginning and serves as the frame of reference for the entire dialogue, relates to the controversy regarding the relative values of work (*karma*) and the renunciation of work. The book opens with Arjuna's decision not to fight (BhG 2.9), a decision the author interprets within the broader set of questions posed by that controversy (BhG 3.3–4). Arjuna's abandonment of war is tantamount to the abandonment (*saṃnyāsa*) of action (*karma*) and, implicitly, to the abandonment of one's duties (*svadharma*). It is clear that the author's intent goes beyond Arjuna's dilemma; he sees in it the dilemma confronting all people faced with the two contradictory value systems of *dharma* (interpreted as the obligation to perform ritual and social activities) and *saṃnyāsa* (abandonment of rites as a precondition for achieving liberation). This conflict within the tradition is recapitulated in the opening verse of the fifth chapter:

saṃnyāsaṃ karmaṇāṃ kṛṣṇa punar yogaṃ ca śaṃsasi /
yac chreya etayor ekaṃ tam me brūhi suniścitam //

You praise the renunciation of actions, Kṛṣṇa, and then also their performance. Tell me for certain which is the better of them.

Now, the same dilemma appears in many other passages of the *Mahābhārata*, and in each of them the *āśrama* system is presented at least as one possible solution. The clearest occurs in the dialogue between Vyāsa and Śuka (MBh 12.233–37). Referring to conflicting vedic statements, some enjoining action and others its abandonment, Śuka asks Vyāsa bluntly to explain the contradiction.[86] After several attempts that do not satisfy Śuka, Vyāsa resorts to the classical *āśrama* system to resolve the apparent conflict within the Veda. This dilemma, as we shall see in section 5.3.5, is also raised when, after winning the war, Yudhiṣṭhira decides to renounce, a decision that clearly parallels Arjuna's decision at the beginning of the same war. Yudhiṣṭhira's decision opens the voluminous *Śāntiparvan*, as Arjuna's does the *Gītā*. Unlike the *Gītā*, however, the *Śāntiparvan* uses, among others, the *āśrama* system as an argument for Yudhiṣṭhira's acceptance of royal responsibilities.[87] Other instances are the dialogues between Kapila and the cow[88] and between Janaka and Sulabhā.[89]

The problems and issues dealt with in the *Gītā* are thus not unique; they occur throughout the great epic.[90] Why is it then that the *Gītā* totally ignores the *āśrama* system as a possible solution to the dilemma? Now, I agree with van Buitenen's (1981, 5) assessment that

> the *Bhagavadgītā* was conceived and created in the context of the *Mahābhārata.* It was not an independent text that somehow wandered into the epic. On the contrary, it

86. The recurrent phrase is *kuru karma tyajeti ca*—"perform action and abandon it": MBh 12.233.1; 12.234.3, 10. The same phrase occurs in the section on Yudhiṣṭhira's decision to renounce: MBh 12.19.1.

87. See, for example, MBh 12.11.15; 12.21.15; 12.23.2, 5; 12.25.6.

88. See especially MBh 12.260.12–17; 12.261.5–15; 12.262.19–30.

89. See MBh 12.308.44, 60, 177, 180.

90. Besides the passages we have indicated above, earlier in the epic at MBh 5.151 the same dilemma is voiced not by Arjuna but by Yudhiṣṭhira himself.

> was conceived and developed to bring to a climax and solution the dharmic dilemma of a war which was both just and pernicious.[91]

It is, therefore, difficult to argue that the author of the *Gītā* was ignorant of the *āśrama* system. His intellectual world could not have been radically different from that of the authors of the rest of the didactic portions of the *Mahābhārata*, unless we are willing to date the *Gītā* as early as the fifth century B.C.E. Indeed, he shows familiarity with most of the other central institutions and ideas of the classical Brāhmaṇical world. If he was aware of the *āśrama* system, why did he choose to completely ignore it, without even mentioning it in passing?

One can, of course, only guess, and I would venture to offer the following, hopefully educated, guess. We need to note, first of all, a couple of points regarding the *Gītā's* argument. In almost all other discussions, the dilemma is finally viewed in terms of an institutional opposition principally between the householder and the renouncer. There the relevance of the *āśrama* system is obvious. The *Gītā*, however, does not see the dilemma in institutional terms; indeed, the very term householder (*gṛhastha*) is absent in it. The *Gītā* never makes clear what sort of a life its ideal human who participates in devotional and ritual activities (*bhaktiyoga* and *karmayoga*) leads. It is never said that he is in fact a householder. The argument of the *Gītā* takes place at a more abstract level. It seeks to show that true renunciation does not consist in the physical abstention from activity but in the proper mental attitude toward action. Abandonment of desire for the results of one's actions is true renunciation, which the *Gītā* sees as an inner virtue rather than an external life style. In other words, the *Gītā* is proposing a more radical solution to the dilemma—the very elimination of the dilemma by a new interpretation of the two horns—than that offered by either formulation of the *āśrama* system.

Another reason for the reluctance to drag the *āśrama* system into the debate may hinge on the formulation familiar to the author. Given his strong inclusivist tendency evident throughout the text, it seems to me very likely that he would have at least mentioned the *āśrama* system as at least one solution to the dilemma if he had been familiar with its classical formulation. Based on the classical system, the author could have made a strong case against Arjuna's decision: because he was in the householder's *āśrama*, it was incumbent on Arjuna to perform the duties of that state. Renunciation was the exclusive preserve of the fourth *āśrama*.

If we accept the conventional wisdom that the *Gītā* was composed sometime during the last few centuries before the common era,[92] however, it is likely that the author would not have known the classical system, which, as we shall see, did not arise until the beginning of the common era. If the author was familiar only with the original formulation, we can better understand his reluctance to mention it. One of its principal features, as we have seen, is the admission of individual choice. It is just such choice in matters of *dharma*—the very choice that Arjuna had decided to exercise in deciding not to fight—that Kṛṣṇa is attempting to combat. Halbfass (1988, 336) captures well the mind of our author:

91. Zaehner (1969, 7) makes a similar assessment: "Hence, it is fair to conclude that the Gītā was originally conceived of as an integral part of the Epic."

92. van Buitenen (1981, 6) suggests circa 200 B.C.E. as a likely date, which seems reasonable to me.

> The karmic result which is manifested as caste membership and hereditary social role must be accepted and upheld against all temptations posed by the inclinations and dispositions of the individual. This is the core of the doctrine of *svadharma*.[93]

It could have hardly helped his cause to invoke the original *āśrama* system.

The total absence of the term *āśrama* in the *Gītā*, however, remains a riddle, and no scholar, to my knowledge, has until now even recognized the existence of this riddle, let alone attempted to solve it. The hypothesis I have tentatively presented both explains the *Gītā*'s silence and supports the broad chronology of the early development of the *āśrama* system that I have presented in this study, as well as the date of this document proposed by van Buitenen.

3.5 The Pre-History of the Āśrama System and the Question of the Three Āśramas

A significant formulation of doctrine in the history of religions frequently signals the conclusion of a long process of theological reflection. It is often only one, albeit historically the most successful, among many attempts at addressing similar theological issues. Can we discover in the early Brāhmaṇical literature a theological process that culminated in the creation of the *āśrama* system?

Tracing such a pre-history, we have already seen (section 1.3.1), should not be confused with uncovering the origins of the institutions comprehended by the *āśrama* system. Its pre-history consists rather of the theological attempts at legitimizing those institutions within the framework of *dharma*. These attempts, moreover, cannot be simply equated with the *āśrama* system; they give us, nevertheless, an insight into the intellectual milieu and the theological disputations that were the context of its creation.[94]

The creators of the system, as we have seen, placed themselves explicitly within an existing theological tradition. They cited vedic texts that they believed contained in essence the *āśrama* system. This, of course, does not mean that the composers of those vedic texts had the *āśrama* system in mind, but it means that the creators of the system worked within a tradition of textual interpretation and theological evolution. Given the meager evidence, however, it is extremely difficult to trace the history of the intellectual

93. Halbfass (1988, 335), however, ignores the total absence of any reference to *āśrama*s when he says that verse 3.35 of the *Gītā* "leaves no doubt whatsoever that the *svadharma* is linked completely to the *varṇāśramadharma*, the hereditary order of castes and stages of life.". Larson and Bhattacharya (1987, 8) likewise make the erroneous claim that the *Gītā* presents "*varṇāśramadharma* as *karmayoga*." Even van Buitenen (181, 13) claims that Kṛṣṇa of the *Bhagavad Gītā* was "the upholder of the *dharma* of class and life stage." This common error is repeated by Thapar (1982, 290), who contrasts the Brāhmaṇical concept of *svadharma* to the Buddhist conception of a universal *dharma* and cites the *Gītā* as an example: "The contrast can perhaps best be seen in the discourse on the duty of the Kshatriya in the *Bhagavadgītā* where the protection and the unholding [upholding?] of the varṇāśrama dharma in its specificity is his concern." The *Gītā*, in fact, never defines *svadharma* in terms of one's *āśrama*.

94. Sprockhoff (1979, 1981) has dealt at length with the anachronism involved in interpreting vedic texts in the light of the *āśrama* system. Even though such texts do not teach the *āśrama* system, however, they can provide valuable information regarding the theological milieu of its authors. This is an aspect to which Sprockhoff has not paid adequate attention.

tradition that gave birth to the *āśrama* system. Most previous attempts, as we shall see, have been historically naive and have not thrown much light on that history.

Some scholars argue that the system of four *āśrama*s evolved from an original threefold scheme. Such a claim fits the ancient Indian pattern of classification where a fourth is added to a primordial threefold division. Three constitute a complete whole; and so do four, especially within the image of the four feet of an animal. The expression "four-footed *dharma*," for example, is used frequently to indicate the fullness and perfection of *dharma*. The classificatory system of "three-plus-one," therefore, takes the totality to a new completeness (Gonda 1976; Malamoud 1982).

The classical examples of this process are the triple Veda plus the fourth, the Atharva, and the three twice-born classes plus the fourth, the Śūdra. Gonda (1976, 123), for example, sees that pattern repeated in the classification of the *āśrama*s: "To the original triad of chaste Veda student, householder, forest-dweller, a fourth stage, asceticism was in course of time added, ultimately replacing the forest-dweller stage in function, although this was maintained in theory."

Deussen (1906, 60–61, 367–68; 1909, 129–30) and Winternitz (1926, 216–18) find the evidence for an original system of three *āśrama*s principally in the older Upaniṣads.[95] "All these passages," says Deussen (1906, 368; 1909, 129), "assume only three stages of Brahman-student, householder, and anchorite, and contrast with them the men who know the *ātman*. This very position, however, of exaltation above the *āśramas* became in course of time a fourth and highest *āśrama*."

Deussen and Winternitz, as well as others who posit an original system of three *āśrama*s, do not make a sufficiently clear distinction between the system and the institutions. I want to discuss here, nevertheless, some of the major vedic passages used by these scholars as well as other texts that may be interpreted as evidence of such an original system.[96]

We have already examined the compound words *atyāśramin* and *āśramapāra* (section 1.1.4). In all likelihood *āśrama* in these compounds is used in its primitive meaning with reference to an ideal type of Brahmin householder and does not imply the existence of the *āśrama* system. Deussen's (1909, 129) rendering of *atyāśramin* as one "exalted above the (three) *āśramas*," an interpretation followed by Winternitz (1926, 217), is therefore not warranted by the text or the context.

Deussen (1906, 60, 368) also cites the *Bṛhadāraṇyaka Upaniṣad*, 4.4.22, as evidence of the three *āśrama*s which "are contrasted with the man who has learnt to know the ātman [self]," who is the renouncer. Interestingly, however, neither the word *āśrama* nor the name of any institution besides religious mendicancy is mentioned in this passage. Deussen resorts to the practice we have noted earlier (section 1.3.1) of considering certain terms such as study, sacrifice, and austerity as code words for the *āśrama*s. The *Bṛhadāraṇyaka* passage reads:

95. See also McKenzie 1922, 82; O'Flaherty 1973, 79; Modi 1935; Sharma 1939, 15, 20; Skurzak 1948, 37–39; 1958, 7–8. Sources also refer to three *āśrama*s within the context of the Brāhmaṇical council of experts known as *pariṣad*. I shall examine this question later (7.4).

96. Sprockhoff (1981, 67–83) has examined in detail many of the upaniṣadic passages presented as evidence of a primitive *āśrama* system.

> Brahmins seek to know this very (self) by the study of the Veda, by sacrifice, by giving, by austerity, by fasting. Having come to know that very (self) one becomes a sage (*muni*). Desiring that very (self) as their world wanderers go forth.

Deussen (1906, 60) takes the study of the Veda as a code for the *āśrama* of a student,[97] sacrifice and gift giving for that of a householder, and austerity and fasting for that of a hermit. It is highly unlikely, however, that in this passage they are meant to be code words. They are common religious practices of a Brahmin that are contrasted with the life of religious mendicancy and celibacy, a contrast that is made frequently in the Upaniṣads. The contrast here as elsewhere is not between the first three *āśramas* and the last, but between the ritual life of a householder and the celibate non-ritual life of mendicancy.

The text that is cited most frequently by scholars as evidence of a primitive system of three *āśramas* is the *Chāndogya Upaniṣad*, 2.23.1:[98]

> There are three divisions of *dharma*. Sacrifice, study, and giving are the first. Austerity indeed is the second. A vedic student living at his teacher's house is the third—he settles himself permanently in his teacher's house. All these will take possession of worlds earned by merit.[99] He who is steadfast in Brahman attains immortality.[100]

We have here a clear reference to the vedic student who lives with his teacher until death, the institution that constitutes the first *āśrama* in the original formulation. The first and the second divisions of *dharma*, unfortunately, do not refer directly to any modes of life but contain four types of religious acts. Are we justified here in taking these to be code words for two modes of life?[101]

Sprockhoff (1981, 80–82) answers firmly in the negative. Given that the third division refers to a permanent mode of life, that of the permanent student, however, I think that there is some justification in taking the other two divisions as constituting similar lifelong pursuits. The identity of these pursuits is less clear. The first division, which includes sacrifice and giving, can only refer to the householder, because a student cannot perform these duties. Whether "austerity" of the second division refers to a hermit is not at all clear, that term being associated with a variety of life styles, including the householder and the student. It is clear, however, that the man who is "steadfast in Brah-

97. The hazard of interpreting code words is demonstrated by Deussen's interpretation of study. Here he takes it as a code for the student. At ChU 2.23.1, however, he takes the same term together with sacrifice and giving as a code for the householder.

98. There seems to be near unanimity among scholars (with the notable exception of Sprockhoff) in seeing in this passage a clear reference to the *āśramas*: Deussen 1906, 60–61; 1909, 129; Winternitz 1926, 217; Kane, 1974, II.1, 420–21; Apte 1951, 493–94; McKenzie 1922, 81–82; Modi 1935, 315; Ranade 1926, 61; Belvalkar and Ranade 1927, 214–16; Das 1962, 103. Skurzak (1948, 35–36) attempts, I think mistakenly, to find a progression from a system of two *āśramas* to one of three and finally to one of four.

99. The term *puṇyaloka* may also mean holy or auspicious worlds.

100. *trayo dharmaskandhā yajño 'dhyayanaṃ dānam iti prathamas tapa eva dvitīyo brahmacāry ācāryakulavāsī tṛtīyo 'tyantam ātmānam ācāryakule 'vasādayan. sarva ete puṇyalokā bhavanti. brahmasaṃstho 'mṛtatvam eti.* For the history of interpretation of this text see Sprockhoff 1981, 80–82. In an earlier work (1974, 33–34) I considered this text as a precursor of the *āśrama* system. I have now modified this view somewhat.

101. MBh 12.72.30 gives a similar division based on sacrifice (*iṣṭi*), study (*adhīti*), and austerity (*tapas*).

man" and attains immortality stands outside the threefold division of *dharma*. One can only assume that such a man is in some way related to renunciation.

Whatever may be said regarding the identity of the three divisions, it is certain that this threefold division of *dharma* is not an early version of the *āśrama* system. As we have seen, the purpose behind the *āśrama* system was to include several celibate life styles within the context of *dharma*. The threefold division of the *Chāndogya*, on the contrary, draws a sharp distinction between the three major aspects of *dharma* and those who seek immortality, possibly through renunciation. In this regard the passage stands squarely in the tradition of the other upaniṣadic texts we have examined that contrast life at home to wandering mendicancy.

There is, however, one aspect of the threefold division that is significant: it presents different duties that a person can follow, at least one of which is a permanent mode of life, as divisions or branches of *dharma*. This is precisely the kind of thing that the *āśrama* system does, a system that also presents itself, according to Baudhāyana (see section 3.2.1.2), as a division of *dharma*. Whether or to what extent the *āśrama* system was influenced by the theology that finds expression in the *Chāndogya* text, we will probably never know. It is interesting, however, to find another ancient example besides the system where *dharma* is divided, not merely according to the group one is born into (the *varṇa* ideology) but also according to the way an individual lives after birth. In this sense we can see the *Chāndogya* text as a theological precursor of the *āśrama* system.

The literature of a much later period also contains references to three *āśramas*. Manu, for example, equates the father, the mother, and the teacher to the three *āśramas*.[102] These references provide no evidence for an original system of three *āśramas*; they can be quite satisfactorily explained within their own literary contexts. In the case of Manu, the individual addressed is the student, who in the classical formulation of the system is a member of the first *āśrama*. The three *āśramas* in that context refer to those *āśramas* that a student aspires to enter after he has completed his own *āśrama* and not to some early system of just three *āśramas*.[103]

Ludwik Skurzak in several of his writings has made a concerted effort to demonstrate the existence of a system of five *āśramas*. His basic text is the *Āpastamba Dharmasūtra*, which he considers to be the oldest of the Dharmasūtras (Skurzak 1948, 7).

> According to *Āpastamba Dharma S.*, II.9.21–2: 'There are four orders [*āśramas*], namely that of the householder, the student, the ascetic and the hermit in the woods.' Then rules are given successively for *parivrājaka*, *vānaprastha*, and again for *vānaprastha*. These two *vānaprastha-s*, however, are quite different. The first one (II.9.21.18–21 and II.9.22.1–5) is a *muni* and as such he appears in further *sūtra-s*; he lives in the same way as the *muni* of the Epic and Upaniṣad-s. The other *vānaprastha* is a hermit living in the forest; he lives all the time in a hut and is devoted to liturgic duties and ascetic training.

102. MDh 2.230: "For they, indeed, are the three worlds; they, indeed, are the three *āśramas*; they, indeed, are the three Vedas; and they, indeed, are said to be the three fires." The same verse occurs also in the ViDh 31.7, where *surāḥ* ("gods") replaces *āśramas*. See also MBh 12.109.6; *Dakṣasmṛti* 1.12; Rhys Davids, trans. of DN, I, pp. 216, 219.

103. Gauḍapāda's *Kārikā* on the *Maṇḍūkya Upaniṣad* (3.16) also has a reference to three *āśramas* associated with low, medium, and superior views. Although the passage is brief and elliptic, it probably refers to three types of people living in *āśramas* and not to an original system of three *āśramas*.

In his study of the epic Skurzak also affirms the existence of five *āśramas*: student, householder, *muni*, forest hermit, and itinerant mendicant.[104] His major point is to establish a clear distinction between two types of ascetics living in the forest, the *muni* and the hermit. The former lives in the forest as an itinerant mendicant, whereas the latter lives a settled life in a hut.

There are several problems with Skurzak's analysis. First, I think his distinction between the itinerant and sedentary types of forest dwellers, at least as far as Āpastamba is concerned, is incorrect. It is true that Āpastamba has two sections devoted to the hermit. The distinction between the sections, however, is not based on their dealing with two types of hermits. Rather, as we shall see (section 4.1.1), in the second section Āpastamba records an opinion that permits a person to become a hermit after he has become a householder, accompanied by his wife and children (ĀpDh 2.22.6–8). This provision is a departure from the norms of the original *āśrama* system, and Āpastamba presents it as an exception permissible only the the case of a hermit. Contrary to Skurzak, Āpastamba does not reserve the term *muni* for the hermit described in the first section. Indeed, he introduces that section, saying: "Next, the hermit" (*atha vānaprasthaḥ:* ĀpDh 2.21.18). The term *muni* appears only in a verse (2.21.21) that Āpastamba quotes, a verse that is cited almost verbatim with reference also to the renouncer. It is only in this verse that the hermit is said not to possess a house (*aniketaḥ*). The point that Āpastamba wants to make in both sections, however, is that hermits can proceed gradually to assume practices and modes of life that are more austere. They reduce their food, for example, until they live on just air. It is in this context that wandering appears as a feature of a hermit's life, and this feature is mentioned in both sections and with reference to both types of hermits, those who went to the forest as celibate young adults and those who live in the forest with their families.

The major problem with Skurzak's analysis, however, is that he confuses the institutions with the *āśramas*, an error of method to which I have already drawn attention (section 1.3.1). Even if we grant that there were two types of hermits in the woods, there is still no justification to conclude that there were also five *āśramas*. Indeed, as I have already mentioned, the four *āśramas* need not, and in all likelihood did not, correspond to four socio–religious institutions. Several similar institutions were collapsed into a single theological entity, and it is these theologically defined entities that bear the name *āśrama*.

There is clearly no evidence, therefore, for the existence of a primitive system of three—and much less five—*āśramas* to which a fourth, that of the renouncer, was subsequently added.[105] The earliest and the only evidence we possess indicates that the system

104. "En reconstruisant le développement des āśramas on peut constater qu'l y en avait de suivantes: (a) celle de l'élève (brahmacārin), (b) celle du père de famille (gṛhastha), (c) celle du muni, (d) celle de l'eremite (vānaprastha) et (e) celle de l'ascète errant (parivrājaka ou bhikṣu). Il y a donc cinq āśramas et non pas quatre." Skurzak 1958, 6.

105. Even though the "three-plus-one" was not the way the *āśrama* system originated historically, that does not mean that that model was not applied to the *āśrama* scheme by later theologians, the three being the inferior set to which a superior one is added. Sometimes, as in Manu (see section 5.3.1), the one is the householder from whom others receive their support. Most often, though, the one is the renouncer who aspires to liberation, whereas the others are content with lower goals.

originally included all four institutions. The system did not form through a process of aggregation. It was a theological scheme of four invented by one or more bold theologians and not something that simply came into being through an unconscious historical process. The intellectual history that gave rise to the system, moreover, should be searched for not in the number of *āśrama*s but in the disputes and discussions regarding *dharma*, such as that found in the *Chāndogya* passage. Unfortunately we do not have records of many such disputes in texts that we can assign to this period with some confidence. Disputes regarding what is the "true" *dharma* abound in the epic literature, but these, in all likelihood, belong to a later period.

4

Ingredients of Change

The original *āśrama* system that we have just examined was subjected to radical changes when it was converted into what I have called its classical formulation. In this chapter I want to examine the historical circumstances that may have brought about or at least paved the way for those changes, including the disparity between the original *āśrama* theology and the institutions that it sought to regulate, and the increasing links between that theology and other aspects of Brāhmaṇical ideology and institutions, especially the rites of passage.

Two central features of the original system—the permanence of the *āśrama*s and limiting the opportunity to choose one to the brief period between studentship and marriage—appear to reflect more the exigencies of theology than historical reality. The literature of the period, both within and outside the Brāhmaṇical tradition, show that married people also left their homes and families to become wandering mendicants.

It is also likely, as I have already pointed out, that the *āśrama*s of hermit and renouncer did not correspond directly to a single social institution and that each of them may have comprehended several related or similar institutions. At some point the theologians would have had to take into account the actual differences existing among these institutions, differences that were not recognized within the framework of the original *āśrama* system.

Finally, the system of *saṃskāra*s—which for convenience I shall call the sacramentary system—especially initiation and marriage, the two central rites of passage, exerted a direct influence on the development of the *āśrama* theology.

4.1 The Third Āśrama *and the Problem of the Hermit*

It appears that in ancient India there were several socio-religious institutions that were associated with withdrawal from human culture and with living in the wilderness or the woods.[1] At least some of these were associated with old age and retirement. The original formulation of the *āśrama* system ignores this multiplicity and, following its own theological scheme, depicts a hermit's life in the woods as a celibate and permanent mode suitable for a young adult. The earliest recorded challenge to the provisions of the original formulation, in fact, took place with reference to the hermit.

1. On the distinction between the wilderness (*araṇya*) and the woods or forest (*vana*), and on the history of the hermit's (*vānaprastha*) institution, see Sprockhoff 1981, 1984, and 1991.

4.1.1 The Special Provisions of Āpastamba

In his discussion of the *āśramas* Āpastamba devotes more space to the hermit than to any other institution. The reason for such a lengthy treatment appears to be a then-current dispute regarding the rules governing the entry into and the proper conduct of a hermit. Some of Āpastamba's contemporaries appear to have disagreed with the provision of the *āśrama* system according to which only a young unmarried man who had completed his studies could choose to become a hermit. Indeed, this provision contradicts much of what we know about this institution from other sources which record the presence of hermit families and often associate this mode of life with retirement in old age and political exile.

Āpastamba says that "some prescribe solely in the case of a hermit an orderly sequence."[2] He goes on to specify the "orderly sequence" (*ānupūrvya*): "After completing his studies, a man should marry a wife, kindle the sacred fires, and commence the prescribed rites that end with the Soma sacrifice. Then he should build a house and live outside the village either with his wife, children, and fires, or alone" (ĀpDh 2.22.7–9). The "orderly sequence," therefore, refers to the fulfillment of the major obligations of a man enunciated in the theology of debts (see section 2.1.3)—study, sacrifice, and procreation—prior to assuming the life of a hermit.

Providing for an "orderly sequence" in the case of a hermit implies several major modifications in the *āśrama* system. The choice of the hermit's *āśrama*, for example, may be exercised not only after completing one's studies as enjoined in the original system, but also after one has got married and become a householder. The householder's *āśrama*, consequently, is not necessarily a permanent state, and the hermit's *āśrama* is not necessarily a celibate state. A hermit has the option of taking his family with him, and, since nothing is said about his being celibate, we must assume that even after becoming a hermit he may have continued normal sexual relations with his wife.[3] That wives could accompany their husbands in this mode of life appears, also according to other sources, to be a distinctive mark of this *āśrama*. When Pāṇḍu is cursed to die during sexual intercourse and decides to become a mendicant ascetic, for example, his two wives, Mādrī and Kuntī argue against it and entreat him to enter an *āśrama* to which they can accompany him: "For there are also other *āśramas*, O hero of the Bharatas, in which you can perform great austerities in the company of us, your two lawful wives" (MBh 1.110.26).

Āpastamba's discussion reveals, moreover, that hermits did not have a uniform life style. A man who becomes a hermit immediately after completing his studies, according to Āpastamba, remains celibate, does not live in a house (ĀpDh 2.21.21),[4] and wanders about (ĀpDh 2.22.2), whereas a man who becomes a hermit after marriage lives initially

2. ĀpDh 2.22.6: *atha vānaprasthasyaivānupūrvyam eka upadiśanti.*

3. Skurzak (1948, 37f; 1958, 6; 1967–68, 206) sees in the celibate and the married hermits two different types of ascetical institutions, the former being the oldest known type of Indian ascetic. I have already dealt with his argument for five *āśramas* (section 3.5). On Skurzak's analysis of the ĀpDh, see Sprockhoff 1979, 413–20, and 1991, 5–29.

4. Although, as I have already pointed out (section 3.5), this provision is found only in a verse he cites here and in his discussion of the renouncer, and it is unclear whether Āpastamba intended to prescribe it.

in a house. Another feature that distinguishes hermits, both the celibate and the married, are that they undertake increasingly difficult austerities.[5] With reference to a celibate hermit, Āpastamba says: "Then he shall wander about, subsisting on roots, fruits, and leaves, and finally on what has fallen down.[6] Thereafter he shall live on water, on air, and finally on ether.[7] Of these, each succeeding mode is more excellent in its reward" (ĀpDh 2.22.2–5). The same prescriptions are given later also with regard to a married hermit (ĀpDh 2.23.2).

The exception to the general provisions of the *āśrama* system made in the case of the hermit does not constitute a new formulation of the system. We are still far from the classical formulation. The "orderly sequence" of Āpastamba does not refer to the *āśramas* but to ritual obligations.[8] The temporary period of studentship following initiation is not called an *āśrama*, and there is no provision for a passage from the hermit's to the renouncer's *āśrama*. The concern appears to be not with the *āśrama* system as such, but with the proper time for becoming a hermit, a concern we will encounter also with regard to the renouncer (section 4.2). Nevertheless, at least in the case of a hermit we find here both a substantial departure from the scheme of the original formulation and a firm step in the direction of considering the *āśramas* as modes of life that are not mutually exclusive. There is also the assumption that a religious life can lead a person progressively to more and more difficult forms of austerity especially in the way he obtains his food.[9] This will offer a model for later theorists who will present the *āśramas* themselves as constituting a similar ladder leading to increasingly arduous and progressively holier modes of life.

4.1.2 The Institutions of Old Age

Āpastamba does not associate old age with a man's decision to become a hermit after marriage. Indeed, the statement that he may leave the village with his children implies that he is not an old man, for married children are unlikely to follow their father into the wilderness.

There is, however, a tradition that considers a man's departure from home and village as a form of retirement in old age. Such retired people were expected to lead an ascetic life away from home and village, although it is unclear whether a uniform way of life was expected of them. Their association with the hermit and the third *āśrama*, how-

5. At MBh 14.46.12 the term *ānupūrvya* ("orderly sequence") is used with regard to this gradual progress in austerity.

6. The meaning is that he should not pick fruits and leaves but eat only what he finds fallen on the ground.

7. This amounts to a total fast leading ultimately to death. Death by starvation is often prescribed as the final ascetic exercise for hermits, a practice also found in Jainism. See Settar 1986.

8. On this point I disagree with Sprockhoff (1991, 27), who criticizes me for not noting this divergence from the original formulation in an article I wrote 18 years ago (Olivelle 1974a). Contrary to Sprockhoff, Āpastamba here provides at best an exception to the provisions of the original formulation with reference only to a hermit; there is no mention of passing from one *āśrama* to another.

9. On the food habits of Indian ascetics and the relation between these habits and the ascetic ideologies, see Olivelle 1991.

ever, took place in all likelihood at a later time and within the context of the classical formulation of the *āśrama* system. The significant point for our study is that institutions of old age had a profound impact both on the ascetical traditions and on the *āśrama* system.

In a little noticed work, Haberlandt (1885) proposed the theory that the third *āśrama*, which requires the old to retire to the woods, was a Brāhmaṇical modification of the ancient custom of killing or exiling old people, a custom that was once common among many Indo-European peoples.[10] The modification gave the custom and the life of exile a religious and ascetical dimension. More recently Skurzak (1948 and 1958), Lingat (1973, 50), and Sprockhoff (1979 and 1981) have dealt with the economic basis of ascetic retirement of the aged and specifically with the relationship between the custom of exiling old people and the ascetic institutions comprehended by the *āśrama* system.

It is debatable whether the practice of killing old people or of forcibly sending them into exile was a widespread custom or even whether it ever existed in ancient India.[11] Nevertheless, even voluntary retirement, when it is expected by society and becomes an ethical norm, can have many features of exile. The most significant aspect of this hypothesis is that, given the association of old age with the assumption of an ascetic mode of life, economic factors may have played an important role both in the development of Indian ascetical institutions and in the history of the *āśrama* system.

The economic benefit from the exile of the aged to societies existing at marginal subsistence was simply that it would mean having fewer mouths to feed. Northern Indian society since about the sixth century, however, was at a more advanced stage of economic development. It was not a time of scarcity but of relative abundance. The possibility exists, however, that a custom that originated in an earlier time may have survived and may have been given a different significance during later and more affluent times.

From a legal, economic, and domestic point of view, however, the retirement of aged parents was related in all probability more to the partition of the paternal estate (see section 7.3.2) than to the direct economic benefit of not having to feed the parents. Sons would normally have to wait until their father's death to divide the estate. In the joint family system that existed in ancient India the partition of the estate was also the time when the brothers could establish their own separate households. It was also the time when they became independent ritual actors and established an identity separate from their father's. Waiting for the father's death would certainly have created domestic tensions and strife.

Ancient Indian sources clearly demonstrate that sons did divide the paternal estate during the lifetime of their father and sometimes even against their father's will.[12] The *Ṛgveda* (1.70.5) already hints at such a practice. In the version of the Nābhānediṣṭha story given in the *Aitareya Brāhmaṇa* (5.14), the brothers of Nābhānediṣṭha deprived

10. Haberlandt's thesis is presented with approval by Liebich 1936, 14–24. See also Sprockhoff 1979, 411–12.

11. Keith (1925, 263, 282) dismisses Hillebrandt's interpretation of the Śunaḥśepa legend as implying the ritual killing of the old king.

12. For a full treatment of partition in the Indian legal tradition, see Kane 1973, III, 542–641. On the time of partition, see Ibid., III, 563–72.

him of his share, the partition having taken place while he was away studying. It is unclear whether the brothers did the partitioning themselves, but the *Aitareya* version appears to give the brothers a larger role than the version in the *Taittirīya Saṃhitā* (3.1.9.4). There the father, Manu, is said to have divided his property among his sons. In either case, however, this ancient story is based on the division of the paternal estate during the lifetime of the father, although these sources do not tell us what the father did after the partition. The Pāli Canon records the story of one Poṭaliya who partitioned his wealth among his sons before assuming an ascetic life style (DN I, 359–60). The later Indian legal tradition also recognizes the legitimacy of that practice.[13]

Retirement in old age is more specifically associated with royalty. The voluntary abdication of the old king is directly related to succession. The restlessness of ordinary sons as they waited for their father's death to divide his estate pales in comparison with that of the heir to the throne. Buddhist sources contain stories of heirs murdering their fathers to assume the throne.[14] The rules of succession were also not entirely clear in ancient India, especially as the kings had numerous children from a variety of wives. Abdication would have made the succession smoother and within the control of the father.

Abdication in old age and the consequent retirement of the old king to the wilderness are considered central features of the royal ethic. The *Rāmāyaṇa* (2.20.21) states that the custom of a king abdicating in his old age in favor of his son and retiring to the wilderness was established by ancient royal seers. The *Mahābhārata* (3.186.2–3) likewise says that Kalki Viṣṇuyaśas, the first king of the Kṛta age, started this practice, which has been followed ever since. The epics contain numerous accounts of famous kings who followed that custom.[15] The only death suitable for a royal person is death either in the battlefield or in the forest (MBh 15.8.12).

The Pāli Canon also records a similar tradition. The universal emperor Daḷhanemi installed his son and retired in his old age, a practice continued by his successors (DN III, 60–64). Elsewhere (MN II, 75–82) the practice is said to have been started by King Makhādeva of Mithilā, who asked his barber to inform him when the barber noticed any gray hair. When he was so informed, he summoned his eldest son and told him: "The messengers of the gods, dear boy, have come to me; gray hairs have appeared on my head. I have enjoyed human pleasures. It is now time for me to seek divine pleasures. Come, dear boy, you rule this realm, and I shall shave my hair and beard, put on the yellow robes, and go forth from home to the homeless state." He then instructed his son to do likewise in his old age. Makhādeva, it is said, was in fact the Buddha himself in a former life, lending thereby a special significance to the custom within the Buddhist tradition.

13. Such a partition is recognized by the authors of Dharmasūtras: "While he is still alive, he should divide his property equally among his sons" (ĀpDh 2.14.1). See also BDh 2.3.2–5, 8; GDh 28.2; NSm 13.3; 13.25; Kane 1973, III, 567; Lingat 1973, 58; Olivelle 1984, 142–43.

14. On parricide in Indian history and culture, see Obeyesekere 1990, 75–88, 143–214. On the presence of parricide and the Oedipus complex in India, see Ramanujan 1983; Godman 1978.

15. Rām 1.41.3; 7.69.7; MBh 1.81.1–2; 1.92.23; 1.94.18; 1.154.8–9; 2.17.22–23; 3.106.40; 3.190.43; 3.193.6–7; 12.29.91; 12.280.22; 15.5.20–21.

In the case of both kings and ordinary people, retirement in old age is associated with the assumption of an ascetic mode of life. It appears that an ascetic life was required of any person exiled from society and not just of those who retire in old age. The clearest examples are found in the heroes of the two major epics. Rāma's exile involved the assumption of a hermit's dress and life style. Indeed, the verb *pra* √*vraj* ("to go forth"), which normally indicates an ascetic's departure from home, is used frequently also in the case of Rāma's exile.[16] The exile of the Pāṇḍavas is referred to as "forest dwelling" (*vanavāsa:* MBh 2.67.19–20).

We do not know, of course, the historical basis of such retirement in old age or of its connection with ascetical life styles. Our information comes from legends and normative literature. The practice, however, is presented as a norm and an ideal, and as such clearly influenced the thinking of theologians about asceticism and the *āśrama*s and strengthened the association of ascetical life styles in general and of the third *āśrama* in particular with old age and retirement.

4.2 The Fourth Āśrama *and the Time of Renunciation*

The original formulation of the *āśrama* system, as we saw, posits a single specific time—immediately after completing the initiatory studentship—for becoming a renouncer. Both Brāhmaṇical and non-Brāhmaṇical sources of this period, however, depict people of all ages, even householders with families, as choosing to become renouncers. The system clearly did not reflect social reality.

The proper time for renunciation became a major point of controversy within the Brāhmaṇical tradition, although it is unclear whether that controversy was a response to the severe restriction imposed by the original *āśrama* system. What is clear, however, is that the controversy had a profound impact on the development of that system.

4.2.1 The Time of Renunciation in the Saṃnyāsa Upaniṣads

The question of the time when a person is allowed to renounce occupies a central position in the group of texts commonly referred to as the Saṃnyāsa Upaniṣads.[17] Five Upaniṣads of this group belong roughly to the centuries immediately preceding and following the beginning of the common era: *Āruṇi, Laghu-Saṃnyāsa, Kaṭhaśruti, Paramahaṃsa,* and *Jābāla.*[18] All these Upaniṣads directly or indirectly deal with the question of the proper time for renunciation.

16. Rām 2.11.6; 2.23.18; 2.71.6; 2.73.2; 2.84.11; 3.35.10; 3.37.14; 3.45.13, 17; 5.20.5; 5.29.7; 6.107.14; 6.114.5. The *Mahābhārata* also uses the term to refer to forced exile of the Pāṇḍavas: MBh 2.72.3; 5.53.10; 5.53.10

17. These were critically edited by Schrader (cf. SUS) and subjected to a detailed study by Sprockhoff 1976. For my translation and study of these Upaniṣads, see Olivelle 1992. The references are to the page numbers of Schrader's edition.

18. Sprockhoff (1976, 32, 47, 72f, 106f) assigns them to the last three or four centuries before the common era. I would push them closer to the beginning of the common era, and assign some of them to the first few centuries of the common era (see Olivelle 1992, 8–11).

Speaking about the rite of renunciation, the *Āruṇi Upaniṣad* (5) says: "A householder or a vedic student or a forest hermit should discard his sacrificial string on the ground or in water." There is no mention here of *āśramas*, much less of any passage from one *āśrama* to another. The statement, however, indicates that a man in any one of those three modes of life is permitted to renounce. Later on, the same Upaniṣad (ĀrU 9) makes an even more radical statement: "In truth, a man who knows the import of the Veda may abandon these either before or after his vedic initiation: father, son, fire, sacrificial string, rites, wife and everything else here below." The *Āruṇi* thus permits a man who knows the meaning of the Veda to renounce even before his vedic initiation.

The list of items that a person abandons is also instructive. Wife, son, and fire can be abandoned only by a married man. A similar list is given also in the *Paramahaṃsa Upaniṣad* (46): "That man should renounce his sons, friends, wife, relatives, and so forth, as well as the topknot, the sacrificial string, vedic recitation, and all rites." The *Kaṭhaśruti Upaniṣad* (31) also mentions wife and sons among the items a renouncer has to give up. Indeed, in the rite of renunciation given in the *Kaṭhaśruti* (32, 36-37) the son of the prospective renouncer plays a significant role.

The *Kaṭhaśruti* contains, moreover, a passage regarding the course a man should follow before he takes to renunciation:

> After a vedic student has studied one, two, or all the Vedas and completed his studentship, he should marry a wife, beget sons, place them in suitable occupations, and offer sacrifices according to his ability. It is proper for such a man to renounce with the consent of his elders and relatives. (KśU 37)

This passage is remarkably similar to Āpastamba's statement with reference to the hermit, the major difference being that, unlike a hermit, a renouncer is required to leave behind his wife and children. The *Kaṭhaśruti*, just like Āpastamba, neither mentions the term *āśrama* nor prescribes the passage from one *āśrama* to another. What it does say is that a person can choose to become a renouncer after completing his family duties.

The statements regarding the proper time for renunciation in both the *Āruṇi* and the *Kaṭhaśruti* stand in sharp contrast to the provisions of the original *āśrama* system. The *Jābāla Upaniṣad* goes a step further in prescribing an orderly sequence prior to renunciation: "After he has completed his vedic studentship, a man should become a householder. After he has been a householder, he should become a forest hermit. After he has been a forest hermit, he should renounce" (JU 64). The *Laghu-Saṃnyāsa Upaniṣad* (18–19) also appears to prescribe a similar sequence. Even though the term *āśrama* is not used in either document with reference to the stages one must pass through, it is clear that these provisions are identical to those of the classical formulation of the *āśrama* system.[19]

After giving the above sequence, the *Jābāla* offers an alternative: "Or rather,[20] he may renounce directly from vedic studentship, or from home, or from the forest" (JU

19. It appears to me that at least the author of the *Jābāla* was familiar with the classical formulation of the system. His formulation is too close to that of Manu for it to be independent of the *āśrama* system. Although in an earlier work (1976, 99) Sprockhoff states that the *Jābāla* presents the classical *āśrama* theory, in a later publication (1981, 83) he says—I believe wrongly—that the *Jābāla* knows nothing about *āśramas*.

20. The Sanskrit *atha punar* in this context may also mean "besides," "nevertheless," or "on the other hand."

64). It offers a further alternative to those who are detached from worldly things: "Let him, moreover, renounce on the very day that he becomes detached, regardless of whether he has taken the vow or not, whether he has graduated or not, and whether he has kindled the sacred fire or is without a fire" (JU 64).[21] These two alternatives are very similar to those of the *Āruṇi Upaniṣad.* Medieval authors and modern scholars often refer to these provisions of the *Jābāla* as the *locus classicus* of the view that upholds the choice (*vikalpa*) of *āśramas*. Such a view is clearly unwarranted (see section 6.2.2). The *Jābāla* does not speak about *āśramas*, much less of the *āśrama* system. It does not provide a choice of *āśramas*, but only a choice regarding the time when one can become a renouncer. This position should not be confused with the theory of choice found in the original formulation of the *āśrama* system.

Even though there are specific requirements for each alternative method given in these Upaniṣads, the fact remains that according to these documents a person could renounce at any time during his life. Renunciation at an early age, however, is presented as somewhat extraordinary and limited to those individuals who have acquired a high degree of knowledge (*Āruṇi*) or detachment (*Jābāla*). The statements regarding the major objects that a man renounces—namely wife, son, and fires—as well as the major role the son and ritual fires play in the rite of renunciation described in these documents, demonstrate that the normal candidate for renunciation was a married man.

These positions regarding the proper time for renunciation stand in sharp contrast to the original *āśrama* system according to which one can renounce only after completing one's studies but before one gets married.

4.2.2 The Time of Renunciation in Deutero-Baudhāyana

We have already seen (section 3.2.1.2) that the sections of the *Baudhāyana Dharmasūtra* dealing with the rite of renunciation (BDh 2.17–18) do not belong to the original Sūtra. They, along with the last two books, were later additions, which, for convenience, I have called "Deutero-Baudhāyana." In discussing the proper time for renunciation, Deutero-Baudhāyana, like the Saṃnyāsa Upaniṣads, does not present explicitly the classical formulation of the *āśrama* system. Even though its date is probably later than the Upaniṣads we have examined and may even be after the creation of the classical *āśrama* system,[22] Deutero-Baudhāyana provides useful information regarding the controversies surrounding the proper time for renunciation.

Prior to his description of the rite of entry into renunciation, Deutero-Baudhāyana (BDh 2.17.2–6) presents six divergent views on the time in life when a man may renounce: (1) a student immediately upon completing his vedic studies; (2) Śālīna or

21. "Vow" refers to vedic initiation. One who has "graduated" is a young adult who has performed the ceremonial bath that concludes the period of vedic studies. Such a man, technically called *snātaka* ("bathed"), is the one entitled to choose an *āśrama* in the original system. Kindling the sacred fire is an indirect reference to marriage, because only a married man can have a sacred fire.

22. Deutero-Baudhāyana (2.17.15, 16) cites two verses which contain the identical expression: "proceeding from *āśrama* to *āśrama*"—*āśramād āśramam upanīya* (15) and *āśramād āśramaṃ gatvā* (16). This is a clear reference to the central feature of the classical formulation which requires a man to proceed from one *āśrama* to the next at prescribed times.

Yāyāvara householders[23] who are childless; (3) widowers; (4) a man who has settled his children in their own duties; (5) people who are 70 years or older;[24] (6) a hermit.

Regarding the first category, Deutero-Baudhāyana's statement agrees verbatim with and appears to be a citation of Āpastamba.[25] It is clearly a reference to the provision of the original *āśrama* system. All the other options refer to people who have completed their ritual obligations or who are unable to perform them. The association with old age is unmistakable. Even though Deutero-Baudhāyana does not express his own preference, the dominant view that emerges from his enumeration is that renunciation is normally reserved for a time of life when a person has completed his customary family and ritual obligations, an assumption that underlies the classical formulation of the *āśrama* system.

4.2.3 Renunciation and Old Age

Other sources also point to the increasingly widespread association of renunciation with old age and retirement. The *Mānava Śrautasūtra* (8.25) contains a description of the procedure of *saṃnyāsa.* Both the translator, Van Gelder, and Sprockhoff (1987) take *saṃnyāsa* in this context to be a resignation or retirement rather than ascetic renunciation. They are probably right, but in time such institutions of old age coalesced with renunciation proper. This is evident both in the later literature on renunciation and in the classical rite of entry into renunciation, which has borrowed several elements from the rites associated with retirement. The *Mānava Śrautasūtra* (8.25.1) states clearly that the procedure it is about to describe is intended for a householder who is approaching the age of retirement:

> Now we shall describe the procedure of retirement (*saṃnyāsa*). It applies to a householder. After he has produced children, seen them and even[26] his children's children, provided a livelihood for them, and entrusted his family to a virtuous son, there takes places his separation from his fires.[27]

The candidate for this ritual of retirement is a man whose children are grown and established in their own occupations, and who may even be a grandfather.

The *Baudhāyana Śrautasūtra* (29.5, p. 375–76) likewise says that an old man who is

23. On these types of holy householders, see sections 6.1.1-2.

24. The fourth and fifth are two separate opinions, and Buhler is mistaken, I think, in presenting them as a single provision in his translation.

25. Baudhāyana's (2.17.2) statement reads: *so 'ta eva brahmacaryavāṇ pravrajatīty ekeṣām.* Compare this with ĀpDh 2.21.8 cited in section 3.1.1, n. 3.

26. Both van Gelder in her translation and Sprockhoff (1987, 237) take the particle *vā* as the disjunctive "or," which makes little sense, because one cannot see one's grandchildren without first seeing one's own children. I have preferred to take it as an emphatic particle, because the text clearly has in mind a time when the father's children are settled down on their own. See the remarkable similarity between this statement and that of the MDh with reference to the time when a person should become a hermit (section 5.3.1).

27. *athātaḥ saṃnyāsavidhiṃ vyākhyāsyāmaḥ. gṛhasthe prayogo 'patyam utpādya dṛṣṭvāpatye 'patyāni vā teṣāṃ vṛttiṃ kalpayitvā guṇavati putre kuṭumbam āveśyāthāgniviniyogaḥ*. The separation from the fires is done through a ritual known as depositing the fires in one's self: see Olivelle 1992, 86–89.

unable to perform the daily fire ritual should deposit his sacred fires within himself, lead a celibate life, and give up normal household duties.

A similar retirement, called *saṃnyāsa* (MDh 1.114) and *vedasaṃnyāsa* (MDh 6.86),[28] is referred to by Manu. Before retirement, according to Manu (MDh 6.94), a man should have followed the tenfold Law and paid his three debts. After retirement he lives at ease under the protection of his son (MDh 6.95). Both the Śrauta and the Dharma texts of the Mānava tradition, therefore, appear to recognize the retirement of an old man. The very juxtaposition of this retirement with ascetic renunciation in the Dharmaśātra, however, indicates the increasingly close associations between the two institutions within Brāhmaṇical theology.

I have already referred to the story of Poṭaliya, recorded in the Pāli Canon, who partitioned his property among his sons and abandoned all worldly activities. He wants to be regarded as a genuine ascetic and is offended when the Buddha addresses him as a householder.

The view that ascetic renunciation itself is more appropriate for persons of an advanced age, moreover, was becoming widespread. Aśvaghoṣa, the Brahmin poet turned Buddhist monk, who probably lived in the first century C.E., puts into the mouth of Śuddhodana, the father of the future Buddha, the prevalent view regarding the proper time for leaving the world as a renouncer.[29] When the future Buddha informs his father of his intention to leave the world, Śuddhodana tells him:

> Abandon this plan, dear child; it is not yet time for you to resort to religion (*dharma*). For practicing religion in the first period of life, when the mind is subject to vacillation, they say, is beset with dangers.
>
> The mind of a young man, with his senses prone to excitement by pleasures and unable to remain resolute in bearing the hardships of ascetic vows, shrinks from the wilderness, especially when he is not used to solitude.
>
> But for me, lover of religion, the time for religion has come, after I hand over the kingdom to you, who are prosperity incarnate. If you leave your father in violation of the proper order, you who are firm in courage,[30] your religion (*dharma*) will become irreligious (*adharma*).
>
> So give up this resolve now and devote yourself to the religion (*dharma*) of a householder, for it is a delightful thing when a man enters the penance grove after he has enjoyed the pleasure of youth. (Aśvaghoṣa, *Buddhacarita*, 5.30–33)

After the future Buddha had left home, Śuddhodana sends his counselor and domestic priest to persuade him to return. They tell him (*Buddhacarita*, 9.14, 17) that he had left "at the improper time" (*akāle*) and request him to go to the forest "at the time prescribed

28. Manu makes a clear distinction between this type of retirement and ascetic renunciation, which he calls *mokṣa* (MDh 1.114) and with reference to which he uses the verb *pari* √*vraj*, "to wander around." This distinction has not always been recognized by scholars: Olivelle 1984, 132–36, and section 5.3.1.

29. For the date and the Brāhmaṇical background of Aśvaghoṣa, see Johnston's introduction to his translation of the *Buddhacarita*, pp. xiii–xxiv.

30. Aśvaghoṣa plays on the word *vikrama*, which can mean both "violation of the proper order or sequence" and "courage." Johnston misses the point when he translates the first meaning as "forcibly" and explains it as "the wrong course of action" (note to verse 32). The term *krama* clearly refers to the sequence of duties that precedes renunciation.

in the scriptures" (*kāle śāstradṛṣṭe*). Elsewhere also Aśvaghoṣa alludes to the duty to bear a son before a person, even a Bodhisattva, takes to renunciation (*Buddhacarita*, 1.79; 2.56).

Apart from stating that old age is the proper or the prescribed time for renunciation, Aśvaghoṣa introduces another reason why young people should not renounce: they are insufficiently mature and too affected by sensual pleasures to withstand the rigors of asceticism.

4.3 Ritual Appropriations of Renunciation

Brāhmaṇism was essentially a ritual religion. Ritual categories were at the heart of Brāhmaṇical theology and its understanding of reality. The logical, if somewhat paradoxical, result of this ritualism was that Brāhmaṇism more than either Buddhism or Jainism, both of which had strong anti-ritualistic tendencies, defined renunciation as consisting of the abandonment of ritual activities. Renunciation, for Brāhmaṇism, is essentially a non-ritual state.[31]

Significant practical and theological conclusions, moreover, derive from that premise, conclusions that have a direct impact on the *āśrama* system. The non-ritual state of renunciation, on the one hand, determines who is entitled to assume that state and, on the other, relates it to other non-ritual states that at first may not have been regarded as ascetic modes of life.

4.3.1 Renunciation as the Abandonment of Ritual

The definition of renunciation as a non-ritual state was given ritual expression within Brāhmaṇism in the rite whereby a person became a renouncer. It is a measure of the importance of this definition that other central aspects of renunciatory asceticism, such as celibacy, mendicancy, homelessness, and abandonment of the family, recede totally into the background within the rite of renunciation. The rite's complete focus is on the abandonment of ritual.

This abandonment is expressed in the rite of renunciation through several steps, at each of which a prominent symbol of a Brahmin's ritual life is discarded. The most important of these symbols are the ritual fires and implements, the sacrificial cord, and ritual formulae.[32] There are variants of the rite for people who do not possess the ritual fires and the like, but the abandonment of these constitutes the typical rite of renunciation within Brāhmaṇism.

The person who is able and qualified to perform this rite and, consequently, to become a renouncer, therefore, is a married householder, for, as we have seen (section 2.1.1), only he is entitled to possess the ritual fires and perform sacrifices. The conclusion is simple: to abandon the ritual one must possess the ritual or the ability to perform the ritual. Abandoning what one does not possess or is not entitled to is an empty gesture

31. See Olivelle 1975; 1992, 60–67.
32. For a description of the rite see my translation of Ypra, and Kane 1974, II.2, 953–62.

without meaning or significance. Thus before a person is able to renounce the ritual religion he must become part of it, as before renouncing wealth one must acquire it. Only a married householder, therefore, is able to perform meaningfully the act of renunciation.

The rite and theology of renunciation that developed within Brāhmaṇism, therefore, contradict the central provision of the original *āśrama* system—namely, that a person should choose an *āśrama*, in this case renunciation, before marriage.

The Brāhmaṇical understanding of renunciation as a non-ritual state also led to its being homologized with other non-ritual states existing within Brāhmaṇism. Old age was the most common of such states. We have already seen that retirement in old age was called *saṃnyāsa*, a word that at a later time becomes the most common term within the Brāhmaṇical tradition for ascetical renunciation (Olivelle 1981). It was a common Brāhmaṇical view that old age absolves a person from the obligation to perform rites.[33] The partition of the property among the sons while the father is still alive also creates a similar non-ritual state for the father.[34] Ownership of property is closely related to the obligation to offer sacrifices; the economic head of a family is the same as its ritual head. Once the property is partitioned, the obligation to offer sacrifices transfers to the sons together with the wealth. The father goes into economic and ritual retirement.

A similar non-ritual state based on the non-ownership of property arises after the performance of several types of vedic sacrifices which involve the donation of all one's property to the priests. The non-ritual period appears to be temporary after the Viśvajit and Abhijit sacrifices, while it is permanent after the Puruṣamedha and the Sarvamedha.[35] Unlike retirement in old age, it is not clear whether these ritually created non-ritual states were homologized with ascetical renunciation, but their influence on the Brāhmaṇical theology of renunciation is unmistakable. The rite of renunciation, after all, also creates ritually the non-ritual state of ascetical renunciation. That rite, furthermore, calls for the donation of all one's property as a sacrificial fee to the priests (*sarvavedasadakṣiṇā*) who officiate at one's renunciation.[36]

The influence of these homologies no doubt strengthened the position of the renunciatory theology according to which only a ritual actor can properly abandon ritual activities. These homologies are also conducive to considering renunciation as a state that is ritually established to signal either the end of a man's ritual life or his transcendence of the ritual religion. In any case, renunciation is properly performed not by a young unmarried man who has yet to enter the ritual path but by an older adult who has reached the end of that path.

4.3.2 Renunciation and the Rite In Extremis

One of the oldest and most significant of such non-ritual states is created after a rite which is performed by a dying man. Several ancient Brāhmaṇical sources record the

33. See JB 1.51 (section 2.1.1, n. 27), where the daily fire sacrifice (*agnihotra*) is said to end only in old age.

34. See n. 13

35. See ŚB 13.6.2.19–20; 13.7.1.1–15; ĀpŚ 20.24.16; ŚāṅŚ 16.15.20f. On the relationship between these non-ritual states occasioned by sacrifices and ascetical renunciation, see Heesterman 1964, 26.

36. See MDh 6.36; Ypra 12.12.

custom according to which a man who is approaching death performs a rite called *saṃpratti* or *saṃpradāna* ("transmission").[37] The earliest evidence of it is found in the *Bṛhadāraṇyaka Upaniṣad* (1.5.17–20). Its description of the rite is brief:

> When a man thinks that he is about to die, he addresses his son: "You are Brahman! You are the sacrifice! You are the world!" The son replies: "I am Brahman! I am the sacrifice! I am the world!" The sum of all that has been learnt is expressed by the term "Brahman." The sum of all the sacrifices that have been offered is expressed by the term "sacrifice." The sum of all the worlds gained is expressed by the term "world." (BāU 1.5.17)

The rite of transmission transfers all that the father has and is to his son; the father enters the son and becomes the son. The son becomes the father's support in procuring a world and assures the continued life of the father by nourishing him with food offerings: "'Being thus the all, may he provide me nourishment from here.' Therefore they call a son who is instructed 'world-procuring'" (BāU 1.5.17)

The transfer of the father's powers and faculties to the son and the resulting identity between the father and the son are brought into sharper focus in the longer description of the rite contained in the *Kauṣītaki Upaniṣad* (2.15):

> Now the father-son ceremony which they call the "transmission." A father, when he is about to die, calls his son. After spreading new grass on the floor of the house, kindling the sacred fire, and placing near it a pot of water with a dish, the father remains lying down dressed in a fresh garment.[38] The son comes and lies on top, touching his father's organs with his own organs; or he may transmit while he is seated face to face. Then he delivers to him:
>
> Father: "I will place my speech in you."
> Son: "I place your speech in me."
> Father: "I will place my breath in you."
> Son: "I place your breath in me."
> Father: "I will place my eye in you."
> Son: "I place your eye in me"
>
> [This dialogue is repeated with regard to ear, tastes, rites, pleasure and pain, bliss, delight, procreation, movement, mind, and intelligence.]
>
> If, however, he is unable to speak much, the father may say briefly: "I will place my breath in you." The son: "I place your breath in me." Then, turning to the right, the son goes out toward the east. The father calls after him: "May you enjoy glory, sacred luster, and fame!" The other looks back over his left shoulder and, hiding his face with his hand or covering it with the hem of his garment, he says: "May you obtain heavenly worlds and their delights."

The significant aspect of the rite of transmission for our study is what happens if

37. This entire subject has been studied in detail by Sprockhoff 1976, 52–66; 1979, 386–98; 1987. Ancient and medieval sources also list signs by which a person may recognize the approach of death: see VaiG 5.1; *Caraka Saṃhitā*, Indriyasthāna, 5; Kane 1973, IV, 181.

38. Kane (1973, IV, 182–84) gives a detailed account of various procedures for preparing a dying man.

after performing this ceremony the father does not die but recovers his health. The *Bṛhadāraṇyaka* is silent on that point. The *Kauṣītaki*, however, after describing the rite, continues: "If he should recover, the father should live under the authority of his son or wander about. If he should die, they should perform the obsequies that befit him." The expression "wander about" (*parivrajet*) is probably used here in its technical meaning of ascetic wandering.

The transmission rite transfers the father's position as paterfamilias to his son. It must have also involved handing over the paternal estate. The transfer is irrevocable, and hence the father who does not die has only two options. He may live under the authority and with the support of his son. Alternatively, he may leave home and become a religious mendicant. Thus, the ascetical institution of religious mendicancy becomes associated with another institution of old age, this time with a rite performed *in extremis*.

The *Laghu-Saṃnyāsa Upaniṣad*, in fact, opens its discussion of the rite of renunciation with what appears to be an implied reference to the rite of transmission: "Now, when a man who had maintained the sacred fires dies, his funerary rite is performed with mantras. If he happens to recover, however, he should resolve:[39] 'I wish to go beyond the *āśrama*'."[40] It then goes on to describe the rite through which a man renouncers rites, ritual implements, and the sacred fire,[41] and whereby he becomes a wandering mendicant. The *Laghu-Saṃnyāsa* thus establishes a close association between the rite of renunciation and assumption of a mendicant life on the one hand and the recovery of a person who had been on the point of death and who had performed rituals *in extremis* on the other.

Another influence on the Brāhmaṇical association of renunciation with extreme old age and the time of death may have come from the general belief that one's thoughts and state of mind at the moment of death determine one's state after death.[42] The belief extended from the state of mind to the condition, time, and place of death. It was a common belief, for example, that dying or even killing oneself at a holy place assured heaven and even liberation (Kane 1973, IV, 186–89). To be a renouncer at the time of death came to be considered similarly significant. The concluding statement of the *Jābāla Upaniṣad* (71), for example, refers to the abandonment of the body through renunciation. The belief in the importance of the dying moment also gave rise to the practice of renouncing when one is in danger of death due to a sickness or some other reason. This practice, already referred to in the *Jābāla Upaniṣad* (68), is technically referred to as *āturasaṃnyāsa* ("renunciation of those in mortal danger"). The dying man merely has to say orally or mentally the formula of renunciation: "I have renounced."

39. The statement that he wishes to go beyond the *āśrama* is the public declaration of intent (*saṃkalpa*) that precedes any ritual act. Such an act is prescribed even in medieval accounts of the rite of renunciation (Ypra 21.37). Sprockhoff (1976, 52) misses this point when he takes this declaration as a mere expression of a personal wish. The text appears to require that a person who recovers must make this declaration of intent and perform the rite of renunciation.

40. LSU 15. For the expression "beyond the *āśrama*" (*āśramapāra*), see section 1.1.4, n. 65.

41. The text uses the verb *saṃnyasya* ("having renounced") with reference to the abandonment of the sacred fire.

42. See ChU 3.14.1; PraśU 3.10; BhG 8.5–6; VaiG 5.1; Kane 1973, IV, 185–86; Edgerton 1927.

The same belief may be at the root of the custom of permitting those who have become renouncers to commit suicide.[43]

In the *Kaṭhaśruti Upaniṣad* (31–32) the rite of transmission is presented outside the context of dying as an integral part of the rite of renunciation. The transmission and the consequent renunciation is performed by an adult man who has a son. During the rite of renunciation he addresses his son:[44] "You are Brahman! You are the sacrifice! You are all!" A more elaborate version of this greeting is given later (KśU 36).

The rite of transmission performed *in extremis* required a man who recovers to go into retirement either within his son's household or as a religious mendicant. This association of the rite of transmission, undoubtedly an institution of old age, with the adoption of religious mendicancy greatly influenced both the rite and the theology of renunciation. Renunciation itself becomes associated with old men, even though they may not be all in imminent danger of death.

4.4 The Āśramas *and the Rites of Passage*

The final ingredient of change I want to discuss is the association between the *āśrama*s and the rites of passage.[45] The Brāhmaṇical tradition employs the term *saṃskāra,* which for convenience I shall translate as "sacrament," with reference to a variety of purificatory rites, including sacrifices and the consecration of sacrificial utensils.[46] The central sacraments, however, are the rites that signal significant moments in an individual's life. Most of these take place either during pregnancy or during the early years of a child's life; they are intended to ritually purify and strengthen the fetus or the child during those critical years when the child's life is in greatest danger. Only two sacraments, vedic initiation and marriage, prepare an individual for assuming a new way of life and are true rites of passage.

The early Brāhmaṇical literature displays two strikingly different ways of presenting the sacramentary system. Most Gṛhyasūtras—texts that describe the domestic ritual—begin with marriage. This makes sense from both a literary and a theological

43. Five methods of suicide are given: dying as a hero in battle, starving, entering a fire, drowning, and undertaking the Great Journey, that is, walking toward the north until one drops dead (JU 68; KśU 39; *Mānava Śrautasūtra,* 8.25.15; Ypra 17.32; cf. Olivelle 1978b). I cannot follow Sprockhoff's (1979, 395; 1987, 257) argument against calling such a death suicide. Suicide is defined as the act of bringing death upon oneself intentionally. The fact that one accepts that death freely does not make such a death less a suicide. Although in starvation, heroic death, and the Great Journey one does not positively bring about death, yet entering fire and drowning constitute positive acts of suicide. For studies of religious suicide in India, see Kane 1974, II.2, 924–28; 1973, IV, 604–14; Thakur 1963. For Buddhist suicide, see Wiltshire 1983; and for Jain, see Settar 1986.

44. The text gives a modified version for a man who has no son. He thinks of his own self with the words that are normally addressed to the son. The rite of transmission has remained a part of the rite of renunciation even in medieval times: cf. Rudradeva, *Saṃnyāsapaddhati,* 12.4–9. On the relationship of the description in the *Kaṭhaśruti Upaniṣad* to the rite of *saṃnyāsa* described in the *Mānava Śrautasūtra* (section 4.2.3), see Sprockhoff 1987.

45. For a theoretical discussion of the rites of passage, see van Gennep 1960.

46. Gautama (GDh 8.14–22), for example, enumerates 40 sacraments, including 21 types of sacrifices. For a detailed discussion, see Kane 1974, II.1, 188–98.

standpoint: the description of the home ritual directed at a householder begins with the rite that establishes a home and creates a householder. With the exception of the funeral, all other sacramentary rites are, in fact, performed by the householder for his children.

A few Gṛhyasūtras[47] and all the works on *dharma* describe first the vedic initiation and the duties of a student. The intent here appears to be to present the vedic studentship as a period that prepares an adolescent for marriage and household responsibilities. This scheme follows the individual as he grows from childhood into adulthood and offers ritual and educational guidance so that this important transition could be made smoothly and successfully. It is this sacramentary scheme which is followed by the original *āśrama* system and which probably influenced the development of its classical formulation.

We have seen above that in the original formulation of the system the initiatory studentship was conceived as a period of preparation for assuming the adult responsibilities of the *āśrama*s and for making a wise choice among the four alternate ways of life that are open to an individual. This is only an extension of the idea that the life of a student is a preparation for marriage. As marriage is a permanent way of life within the sacramentary system, so all *āśrama*s are permanent in the original system. Further, the rites of entry into the hermit's and renouncer's *āśrama*s may have been viewed as rites of passage paralleling marriage. Instead of marriage being the only rite of passage into adulthood open to a student who has graduated, the *āśrama* system offered him four alternate rites of passage. So far the two systems appear to dovetail perfectly.

There is, however, a crucial ideological difference between the two systems. The sacramentary system is based on the hermeneutical principle of *samuccaya* ("totality"), which I will discuss later (section 5.2). Briefly, according to this principle all the various rites of the sacramentary system are obligatory on an individual; but, since they cannot be performed together, they are to be performed at different moments in an individual's life. This principle is the very opposite of the hermeneutical principle of *vikalpa* ("option"), on which, as we saw (section 3.1.1.), the original *āśrama* system is based. This principle assumes that the various rites prescribed contradict each other in such a way that it is impossible for them to be performed by the same individual. The reason for that impossibility in the case of the *āśrama*s is the assumption that they are permanent modes of life.

The transition from the original to the classical formulation of the *āśrama* system entailed a shift from the hermeneutical principle of "choice" to that of "totality." There is no literary evidence that would demonstrate the influence of the sacramental model on this hermeneutical shift, but I believe that such an influence is plausible and probable. Besides that influence, two other factors, which we have already discussed, were necessary for that shift to occur: the conception of the *āśrama*s as temporary or at least not necessarily permanent states and of the last two *āśrama*s as institutions of old age. Under this scheme, the entry into the *āśrama*s could be viewed as sacramentary rites of passage, all of which are to be performed at specific times in an individual's life.

This view was probably facilitated by the fact that the rites associated with the *āśra-*

47. For example, the Sūtras of Hiranyakeśin, Bhāradvāja, Manu, Jaimini, and Laugākṣi. See Kane 1974, II.1, 195.

mas of a student and a householder, namely initiation and marriage, were indeed rites of passage within the sacramentary framework. The only change required was to identify the student's *āśrama* with the period of initiatory studentship. The identity of their respective names (*brahmacarya*) and duties would have made this change easy and almost unnoticeable. The *āśramas* of a student and a householder, therefore, could be seen as identical with the periods of life into which the passage was marked by initiation and marriage within the sacramentary system. The same principle of "totality" could then be applied to the other two *āśramas*, even though the sacramentary system did not provide ready parallels for them. As marriage (the rite of passage into the householder's *āśrama*) is preceded by vedic initiation (the rite of passage into studentship), so the rites that make a man a hermit and a renouncer are rites of passage that are preceded by marriage and performed at the conclusion of household life. The stage is thus set for the classical formulation of the *āśrama* system.

III

THE CLASSICAL PERIOD

The division of history into neat periods is always artificial and often misleading. Such periodizations are categories created by historians as tools for organizing their data for specific scholarly purposes. Although historical periods most often are based on actual historical processes and changes, yet they are not themselves data or entities of history and often project the priorities and prejudices of the historians. The division into historical periods is especially difficult in India where it is almost impossible to determine with any precision or certitude the dates of most major historical events, whether they be the reign of kings, the birth of leaders, or the writing of texts.[1]

The category "classical period" as used here has no significance outside the context of the history of the *āśrama* system; I use it to indicate the period that begins with the creation of what I have called the classical formulation of the system. I use "classical," moreover, in contradistinction to the ancient or the early and not to the modern. Indeed, there is no modern version, and hence no "modern period," of the system.

The earliest evidence of the classical system is found in the metrical law book ascribed to Manu, which may be placed in the first couple of centuries of the common era.[2] We may thus not be far wrong in placing the upper limit of the classical period around the beginning of the common era. It is much more difficult to set its lower limit, because acting, thinking, and writing in accordance with the classical *āśrama* system has continued in India until modern times. For the purposes of this study, however, I will take as its lower limit the end of the fifteenth century C.E., by which time the major commentaries on the law books and the independent legal treatises (*nibandha*) had been composed.

In chapter 4 I discussed the changes that took place during the centuries following the creation of the *āśrama* system, changes both in the practice and in the ideology of the institutions that comprised the system. The social and theological context that gave birth to the *āśrama* system had changed radically by the beginning of the classical period. These institutions were now considered as thoroughly Brāhmaṇical. A structure for inclusion, such as that envisaged in the original formulation of the system, was unnecessary and superfluous. Instead, the four *āśrama*s came to be regarded as constituting four

1. On modern historiography and the problem of periodization, see Thapar 1978, 1-25, who points out the European biases that gave rise to the early periodization of Indian history into Hindu, Muslim, and British, which persists in the more common division into ancient, medieval, and modern periods.

2. See section 5.3.1, n. 13.

ideals of the Brāhmaṇical ethic, ideals that can and as far as possible should be realized by each individual. The new theological definition of the system put it at the very heart of the Brāhmaṇical self-definition as the *varṇāśramadharma*, the *dharma* of social classes and *āśrama*s. It is this new theology of the *āśrama* system and its increasing ties to other Brāhmaṇical institutions that I examine here in the final part of this volume.

5

The Classical *Āśrama* System

5.1 Description of the Classical System

In contrast to the original system, the classical formulation considers the *āśrama*s not as alternative paths open to an adult male but as obligatory modes of life suitable for different periods of a man's life. Choice, which was a central element in the original formulation, is eliminated, and the *āśrama*s are transformed from permanent and lifelong vocations to temporary periods, the only exception being renunciation, which in the new formulation occupies the final days of a man's life. The strictly ascetical modes of life—those of the hermit and the renouncer—are recast as institutions of old age. At least ideally, an individual is expected to pass from one *āśrama* to the next in an orderly manner and at specific periods in his life. We can see here clearly the influence of the sacramentary model discussed in the previous chapter. The *āśrama*s accompany an individual as he grows old and assumes new and different duties and responsibilities. The entry into each *āśrama* is a rite of passage that signals the closing of one period of life and the beginning of another.

The journey through the *āśrama*s, according to the new system, begins at a boy's vedic initiation, which is now considered the rite of entry into the first *āśrama*. The initiatory studentship, thus, constitutes the first *āśrama*. The fusing of the initiatory studentship and the first *āśrama* converted the latter from an adult into an adolescent mode of life and converted the former from a period of preparation for all *āśrama*s into one that prepares a youth to assume the responsibilities of marriage, representing a return to the conception of initiatory studentship as envisaged within the sacramentary system.

The period of initiatory studentship concludes with the ritual bath of the student and his return (*samāvartana*) from the teacher's to his parents' home. We saw that in the original formulation this was the critical time of a young adult's life when he had to make a decision regarding how he would live his adult life by choosing one of the four *āśrama*s. In the classical formulation, however, the return of the student signals the completion of his first *āśrama* and the immediate preparation for assuming the second.

After he returns home, his parents set about finding him a suitable partner. The rite of marriage initiates the young man into his second *āśrama*, the life of a married householder. The productive years of an adult's life are thus spent in activities that contribute to the welfare of family and society. He raises a family, engages in economically productive activities as required by his caste affiliation, acts as the leader of the ritual life of his family, and lives as a responsible member of society.

According to the classical system, this mode of life is also temporary. When a householder has produced children, educated them, given them in marriage, settled them in their occupations, and seen his children's children—when, in other words, he has completed his household obligations and, as Manu (MDh 6.2) puts it, sees wrinkles on his skin and his hair turn grey—he is ready to assume the third *āśrama*, that of a forest hermit. Passage into the third *āśrama* is clearly related to old age and retirement. Here a man is able to set aside the worries of everyday life and dedicate himself to penance, mortification, and meditation in preparation for what awaits him after death.

The entry into the first *āśrama*, as well as the passage from it to the second *āśrama* and from the second to the third, signals an important transition in an individual's life. The symmetry of this scheme, however, breaks down when it deals with the passage from the third to the fourth *āśrama*, namely renunciation. Both are related to old age, retirement, and preparation for death. The reason one must pass from the third to the fourth and the time in life one must do it are left unexplained and vague. The sources merely say that one should spend some time in the third *āśrama* and afterward, during the final years of one's life, become a renouncer. The anomaly of having two *āśrama*s relating to old age and the centrality of the ideal of liberation (*mokṣa*) with which renunciation was closely connected may have contributed to the third *āśrama*'s eventually becoming obsolete (section 6.2.1).

With the formulation of the classical system we see a parallel change in the image used to illustrate the *āśrama*s. We saw that in the literature dealing with the original system the dominant image was that of a path: the four *āśrama*s are four parallel paths leading to the same goal. Within the classical system, however, the path is replaced by the ladder. The four *āśrama*s form a ladder of four rungs, and climbing this ladder lets one gradually reach the highest goal. A medieval text, in fact, cites one passage which depicts even the gods and the forefathers (*pitaraḥ*) as attaining immortality by climbing the ladder of the *āśrama*s.[1]

The division of an individual's life into different stages with corresponding duties was not created by the authors of the classical system. We find similar divisions in very early sources. The *Chāndogya Upaniṣad* (3.16.1–7), for example, employs a threefold division that corresponds to elements of the vedic ritual. The three parts consist of 24, 44, and 48 years, corresponding to the number of syllables in the three major vedic meters, Gāyatrī, Triṣṭubh, and Jagatī, respectively. These three divisions of a man's life are compared to the morning, midday, and evening offerings of Soma. Even though the division is ritualistic and artificial—the full life span being considered to be 116 years—it points to a conception of human life in terms of youth, adulthood, and old age. A similar division is also implied in the terse comment of the *Aitareya Āraṇyaka* (5.3.3) that forbids the teaching of the *Mahāvrata* rite "to a child or to one in the third (period of life)."[2]

Ancient Indian medical texts also follow a similar threefold division. The *Caraka Saṃhitā* (Vimānasthāna, 8.122), a medical text belonging to the second century C.E.,

1. *saiṣāśramaniḥśreṇir yayā devāḥ sapitaraś cāmṛtatvam agacchan.* Hārīta's Dharmasūtra cited in KKT, Brahmacārikāṇḍa, p. 268. The same image is found also in the MBh 12.20.4.

2. *na vatse ca na tṛtīya iti.* It is clearly anachronistic to see in these divisions the existence of the classical *āśrama* system, as suggested, for example, by Altekar 1955, 188.

takes the human life span to be 100 years, consisting of (1) youth (*bāla*), with an immature stage (1–16 years) and a mature stage (17–30 years); (2) adulthood (*madhyama*): 31–60 years; and (3) old age (*jīrṇa*): 60–100 years. Another medical treatise, the *Śuśruta Saṃhitā* (Sūtrasthāna, ch. 35), gives a similar division, where youth is ages 1–16, adulthood 16–70, and old age over 70.[3]

Vātsyāyana's *Kāmasūtra* (1.2.1–6), the treatise on eroticism belonging probably to the second century C.E., prescribes different goals for the three periods based on the three or four aims of human life (*trivarga*: see 7.6):

> The life span of a man is one hundred years. Dividing that time, he should attend to the three aims of life in such a way that they support rather than hinder each other. In his youth he should attend to profitable aims such as learning, in his prime to pleasure, and in his old age to righteousness (*dharma*) and liberation (*mokṣa*).

What is original in the classical formulation is that it fitted the *āśrama*s into the framework of the periods of human life, even though, as I have noted, it was difficult to fit four *āśrama*s into this threefold division.

A significant question that emerged from the classical formulation of the system relates to the number of years one must pass in a given *āśrama*. The early sources for the classical system leave this issue somewhat vague. Manu, for example, speaks of spending the "first quarter or portion" of life in the first *āśrama* and so forth without specifying the number of years. Medieval sources give more precise numbers, although they too appear to reflect more the mathematical mind of a taxonomist than actual practice. The *Nāradaparivrājaka Upaniṣad* (131 and 133–34), for example, enjoins a person to live for 12 years as a student and for 25 years each as a householder and a hermit. According to this scheme, a man can become a renouncer sometime after he is 70 years old, depending on his age at his vedic initiation. Another prevalent view divided the life span of a man, normally assumed to be 100 years,[4] into four equal parts, assigning 25 years to each *āśrama*. Nīlakaṇṭha (*Saṃskāramayūkha*, p. 64) regards this as the common view of the medieval legal experts. Others, such as Medhātithi, Govindarāja, and Kullūka, consider such a mathematical division to be unrealistic, given the uncertainty of life, and regard the fourfold division to refer to broad divisions of youth, adulthood, and old age.[5]

The association of the *āśrama*s with distinct periods of life produced another consequence: as one is unable to return to an earlier age, so one is not permitted to assume an earlier *āśrama*. The image of the ladder illustrates that there is an order and a direction to the *āśrama*s; in contrast to the original system, it is now possible to talk meaningfully about the first or the second *āśrama*. The sources speak of *ānulomya*, literally "rubbing

3. Later astronomical treatises speak of the planets that influence the different stages of a person's life: Moon—age 1, Mars—ages 2–3, Mercury—ages 4–12, Venus—13–32, Jupiter—33–50, Sun—51–70, Saturn—71–120. Varāhamihira's *Bṛhajjātaka*, VIII. 9; *Bṛhatsaṃhitā*, XCVI. 17 (p. 859). See Wayman 1963.

4. See section 2.1.1, n. 28.

5. See their commentaries on MDh 4.1. Other commentators, such as Rāghavānanda, Nandana, and Rāmacandra, follow the division into 25 years.

in the direction in which the hair grows," with reference to the *āśramas*; one can proceed legitimately only in one direction. The opposite—*prātilomya* ("going against the grain")—is not permitted. A verse ascribed to Dakṣa states this principle clearly: "In the case of the three (*āśramas*), it is possible to proceed only with and never against the grain. A man who goes against the grain becomes thereby the vilest of sinners."[6]

5.2 The Hermeneutics of the Classical System

We saw earlier that both the "option" (*vikalpa*) theory of the original formulation (section 3.1.1) and its repudiation by Gautama and Baudhāyana (sections 3.2.1.1–2) were based on accepted rules of textual interpretation developed within the tradition of vedic hermeneutics known as Mīmāṃsā. A major aim of these rules was to resolve conflicts between vedic injunctions. A close examination of the classical system likewise shows that its creators also followed them, even though these rules of interpretation are not always referred to explicitly in the descriptions of the system.

The hermeneutical tradition developed three ways of resolving conflicts arising from vedic injunctions that appear to contradict each other. First, one may choose (*vikalpa*) one or the other of the alternatives if the contradictory injunctions have the same power or authority. With regard to the *āśramas*, as we have seen, this view is represented by the supporters of the original formulation. Second, if it can be demonstrated that one injunction is more authoritative than the other—if one, for example, is found in the Veda, while the other is found only in Smṛtis—then the injunction of lesser authority is annulled (*bādha*). In this case there is no real conflict, for the latter is not a true injunction and therefore unable to contradict the former. Gautama and Baudhāyana represent this point of view with regard to the *āśramas*. The third view is called *samuccaya* or "aggregation," according to which all the items enjoined by conflicting injunctions are considered equally obligatory, the conflict being resolved by referring them to different times, individuals, or activities.[7] The classical formulation of the *āśrama* system favors this hermeneutical principle: there are injunctions prescribing all four *āśramas*, and a way must be found for all of them to be followed. This formulation, patterned after the sacramentary model, provides a scheme within which it is possible for an individual to follow the modes of life of all four *āśramas*.

The Brāhmaṇical tradition manifests a growing distaste for permitting choice in matters of *dharma*. This distaste was influenced by the development of the doctrine of *karma* and found expression in the concept of *svadharma*, "the *dharma* proper to a specific individual."[8] An individual's essence (*svabhāva*) is defined by his or her actions performed in previous existences. This essence is defined primarily not by one's indi-

6. Cited in PāM I, p. 531: *trayāṇām ānulomyaṃ syāt prātilomyaṃ na vidyate / prātilomyena yo yāti sa pāpakṛttamaḥ //* The VeS (3.4.40) also declares that one who has assumed a state of lifelong celibacy is not permitted to abandon that state. In a different context, Āpastamba (1.13.19–21) records the opinion of one Śvetaketu who recommended that a householder spend two months each year as a student at his teacher's house in order to master a larger part of the Veda. Āpastamba rejects such a return to studentship as going against the scriptures.

7. For a discussion of *samuccaya* in Mīmāṃsā, see PMS 12.3.9–17; Kane, 1962, V.2, 1326–30.

8. See Halbfass 1988, 310–33.

viduality but by the social context one is born into, that is by, one's sex and caste, to which was added one's *āśrama* when the system became an integral part of the Brāhmaṇical world. This core of one's human existence, in turn, defines one's *svadharma*, which, as the *Bhagavad Gītā* clearly enunciates, stands above personal inclinations, ambitions, and preferences as a sort of categorical imperative:

> It must always be remembered that all human existence and experience is conditioned by past actions, is karmic result or even "metaphysically congealed act," and that there is no purely factual, empirically ascertainable human "reality" from which an "ought," an obligation, could be derived. The karmic result which is manifested as caste membership and hereditary social role must be accepted and upheld against all temptations posed by the inclinations and dispositions of the individual. This is the core of the doctrine of *svadharma*. (Halbfass 1988, 335–36)

The hermeneutical tradition developed the theory of the eight faults of an option or choice to demonstrate the danger of adopting that strategy to resolve conflicts between injunctions.[9] All these faults boil down to a single problem: selecting one injunction over another results in voiding the authority of a vedic or smṛti text, compromising the very foundation of the entire theological edifice of *dharma* based on the absolute authority of the Vedas. The clear implication of this hermeneutical principle is that choice or option in matters relating to *dharma* should be avoided almost at any cost.

Within Brāhmaṇical hermeneutics choice or following one's own inclination in matters of *dharma* was permitted only when injunctions of equal authority contradicted each other or when a choice was explicitly permitted within an injunction.[10] As more and more texts came to be included within the broad category of Smṛti, the corpus of traditionally authoritative literature, and as changing customs made many ancient regulations obsolete or even seemingly immoral, such contradictions became increasingly numerous and commonplace. The distaste for choice, however, prompted the exegetes to adopt various strategies to eliminate choice as far as possible even when vedic or smṛti injunctions provided for divergent courses of action. The division of time into four ages (*yuga*), for example, provided one hermeneutical device for resolving contradictions.[11] As each age has its own proper *dharma*, some of the obsolete rules were referred to past ages and, therefore, made inapplicable to current practice (see section 8.4).

The more common hermeneutical strategy, however, was the use of a principle

9. The eight faults result from two basic flaws in every option that an individual exercises. In the classical example of contradictory injunctions (see section 3.1.1), a man may choose rice or barley as the grain for making the sacrificial cake. If he chooses rice, it would mean that (1) he has to abandon the authority of the injunction prescribing barley, an authority that had already been ascertained and whose ascertainment gave rise to the conflict, and (2) he has to accept its unauthoritativeness, which cannot be ascertained. Now, if he opts in a subsequent sacrifice to use barley, then it would mean that (3) he has to accept again the authority of the injunction prescribing barley that one had earlier abandoned, and (4) he has to abandon its unauthoritativeness that he had earlier accepted. The same four faults would ensue with respect to the injunction of rice, if a man chooses barley first and then rice.

10. The latter is indicated by the use of the term *vā* ("or") within an injunction. Thus Manu (4.95) says: "Having duly performed the rite for commencing vedic study on the full moon of Śrāvaṇa or [*vā*] Prauṣṭapada."

11. For an examination of these strategies, see Kane, 1962, V.2, 1265f.

known as *vyavasthā*, which may be translated as "limited reference." According to this principle, the alternatives provided by an option resulting from either an injunction that explicitly permits a choice or a conflict between injunctions are not open to everyone; rather, they are restricted to definite groups of people. Such an option, technically called *vyavasthitavikalpa* ("restricted option"), is really not an option at all. For example, when Manu (MDh 4.95) says that a person may perform the rite that opens the period of vedic study on the full moon of Śrāvaṇa (July–August) or Bhādrapada (August–September), commentators explain it as a restricted option. Those who belong to the *Sāmaveda* tradition should perform the rite on the full moon of Bhādrapada, whereas those belong to the *Ṛgveda* should do so on the full moon of Śrāvaṇa. The seeming option merely indicates that one group of people should follow one course while another should follow a different course. Likewise, when Baudhāyana (BDh 2.17.45) says that a renouncer may carry a single or a triple staff, many commentators interpret the statement to mean that lower types of renouncers should carry triple staffs, while the higher types, such as Paramahaṃsas, should carry single staffs.[12]

The proponents of the classical formulation of the *āśrama* system follow this principle in eliminating the conflict between injunctions used by the creators of the original system as the hermeneutical justification for their creation. The argument would run something like this: We agree that there are valid injunctions of equal authority prescribing all four *āśrama*s. There is, however, no conflict between these injunctions, because they refer to different age groups. Thus we protect the authority and authenticity of all these injunctions. As a man passes from one of these groups to another, he is obliged to enter the *āśrama* appropriate to that group.

5.3 The Classical System in the Smṛtis

So far I have sketched the theology of the classical *āśrama* system as it is ideally conceived. This is the description of the system that we usually find in late medieval sources and in modern studies. When we examine the early sources that record this formulation, however, the picture becomes less clear. We note the practical difficulties that the authors encountered in combining it with the variety of customs and provisions that governed the four institutions comprehended by the system.

Whereas in the four early Dharmasūtras, the discussion of the *āśrama* system centers on its original formulation, in the classical Smṛtis that belong roughly to the first five centuries of the common era, the *āśrama* system is presented by and large in its classical formulation. The texts that I have chosen to examine here are the Dharmaśāstras ascribed to Manu and Yājñavalkya, along with the *Viṣṇu Dharmasūtra*, the *Vaikhānasa Smārtasūtra* , and the *Mahābhārata*. These texts are the earliest sources we possess that record the classical *āśrama* system. A careful examination of them will permit us to reconstruct the early history—no doubt sketchy and tentative—of the classical system.

12. On the frequent use of this principle in medieval works, see Olivelle 1986, 57–65.

Manu &
classical
system

5.3.1 Manu

The law book of Manu, the *Mānava Dharmaśāstra* (MDh), generally assigned to around the first couple of centuries of the common era,[13] is commonly regarded as the locus classicus of the *āśrama* system. It is certainly the earliest text to present the classical system. A closer reading of the book, however, shows that, contrary to the common scholarly assumption, Manu does not assign to the system the central and preeminent position that it assumes in later Brāhmaṇical thought. The system occupies a significant but not a central position within the structure and theology of Manu's work, and it is presented as one among several competing schemes for living a religious life.

The book opens (MDh 1.2) with a request addressed to Manu by the great seers: "Lord, please tell us in an exact and orderly manner the laws (*dharmān*) of all the main and intermediate classes (*varṇān*)." Similar introductions to the subject occur in most classical Dharmaśāstras and later in the Purāṇas, but the significant point in this opening verse is what it leaves out: the *āśramas* are not mentioned. In similar contexts, as we shall see in the following sections, other works on *dharma* of a slightly later period invariably use the expression *varṇāśramadharma* ("the *dharma* of classes and orders"), shorthand for the totality of *dharma*. The absence of this expression here is noteworthy. It is missing also at MDh 1.107, where Manu restates the subject of his work only in terms of the *varṇas*. Indeed, the term *āśrama* is not used at all by Manu in the lengthy (MDh 1.111–18) table of contents.

Another place where one would expect to find the *āśrama* system introduced is a boy's vedic initiation. According to the classical system, this is also his first rung in the ladder of *āśramas*. Manu, however, ignores the system completely in his long description of initiation and the duties of a student (MDh 2.36–249). Indeed, unlike the four Dharmasūtras, Manu nowhere gives a formal list of the four *āśramas*.[14]

Manu mentions the system for the first time at the beginning of his discussion of the householder and within the context of a student who, after he has completed his studies, returns home to get married and establish a household (MDh 3.2). When we compare this verse with Vasiṣṭha's (VaDh 7.3) statement that a student who has completed his studies may choose any *āśrama* he likes, it becomes clear that Manu's is a deliberate modification of Vasiṣṭha's prose, converting it, on the one hand, into verse and changing it, on the other hand, to suite the requirements of the classical system.

Vasiṣṭha (7.3)	Manu (3.2)
teṣāṃ vedam adhītya vedau vedān vāviśīrṇabrahmacaryo yam icchet tam āvaset.	*vedān adhītya vedau vā vedaṃ vāpi yathākramam / aviplutabrahma-caryo gṛhasthāśramam āvaset //*
After studying one, two, or	After studying one, two, or (all) the

13. For detailed discussions on the date of Manu, see Bühler's introduction to his translation of Manu, especially p. cxiv, and Kane, 1968, I.1, 327–45.

14. Neither Viṣṇu nor Yājñavalkya lists the four *āśramas*. Manu's omission is, therefore, not significant in itself. One may assume that the system had become so commonplace at this time that the authors did not think it necessary to present a formal list of the *āśramas*. Of the later *dharma* texts, only the *Vaikhānasa* provides an explicit list.

(all) the Vedas, a person who has not violated his vow of celibacy may enter whichever of these (*āśramas*) he prefers.	Vedas in the proper order, a person who has not violated his vow of celibacy may (or should) enter the householder's *āśrama*.

Manu eliminates choice, the hallmark of the original system, and converts the qualification (*adhikāra*) for exercising such a choice to the eligibility for marriage.

At the beginning of chapter 4, Manu returns to the theme of passing from the stage of a student to that of a householder: "Having spent the first quarter of his life at his teacher's, a twice-born man should get married and spend the second quarter at home."[15] After concluding the section on household duties, Manu reiterates: "During the second quarter of his life, he should get married and live at home."[16] At the beginning of chapter 6, which deals with the ascetic modes of life, Manu likewise introduces the duties of a forest hermit with a verse dealing with the passage from life at home to the life in a forest: "Having thus dwelt in the householder's *āśrama* according to the law, a twice-born *snātaka* should duly live in the forest, steadfast and with his senses subdued."[17] A similar statement concludes the section on the forest hermit and introduces the discussion of renunciation: "And having thus spent the third quarter of his life in the forest, he should give up attachments and live as a wandering ascetic during the fourth quarter."[18]

Even though Manu does not mention the *āśrama*s in presenting the plan of his work or structure his discussion around the *āśrama*s, it is clear that he considers the passage through the *āśrama*s as important an aspect of a Brahmin's life as the performance of the sacramentary rites.[19] The only place where Manu appears to present the *āśrama*s as a significant classification of *dharma*, however, is at the end of chapter 6, which also concludes his discussion of proper conduct (*ācāra*): "I have thus declared to you the fourfold *dharma* of Brahmins."[20] Although he does not say so explicitly, the context makes it clear that the fourfold division consists of the four *āśrama*s.

A significant aspect of Manu's discussion of the *āśrama*s is that he relates them to the four quarters (*bhāga*) of a man's life. Even though, as we have seen, many later authors take a quarter to consist of 25 years based on the theoretical human life span of 100 years, it is unlikely that Manu had such a precise division in mind.[21] The term *bhāga* here probably means "period" or "portion" rather than an exact quarter. There were

15. MDh 4.1: *caturtham āyuṣo bhāgam uṣitvādyaṃ gurau dvijaḥ / dvitīyam āyuṣo bhāgaṃ kṛtadāro gṛhe vaset //*

16. MDh 5.169: *dvitīyam āyuṣo bhāgaṃ kṛtadāro gṛhe vaset //*

17. MDh 6.1: *evṃ gṛhāśrame sthitvā vidhivat snātako dvijaḥ / vane vaset tu niyato yathāvad vijitendriyaḥ //* A *snātaka*, literally "one who has taken a bath," is a person who has completed his statutory studentship and taken the ritual bath that signals its completion.

18. MDh 6.33: *vaneṣu ca vihṛtyaivaṃ tṛtīyaṃ bhāgam āyuṣaḥ / caturtham āyuṣo bhāgaṃ tyaktvā saṅgān parivrajet //*

19. This passage is emphasized in MDh 6.34 in the expression also found elsewhere: *āśramād āśramaṃ gatvā*—"Having passed from *āśrama* to *āśrama*." See also BDh 2.17.16.

20. MDh 6.97: *eṣa vo'bhihito dharmo brāhmaṇasya caturvidhaḥ /*

21. Indeed, Manu (3.1) prescribes 36, 18, or 9 years for studentship, or even just the time required to master the Vedas completely.

established customs with regard to the age at initiation and marriage, and it seems unlikely that the *āśrama* system would have changed them substantially. The time when one should undertake the last two *āśrama*s, on the other hand, was much less specific. Neither Manu nor the other authors we are about to discuss give any specific instructions, except that both are related to old age. According to Manu (MDh 6.2) the time for going to the forest to become a hermit is when a man's skin has become wrinkled, his hair has turned gray, and he has become a grandfather. The proper time to leave home, therefore, is not just when one has become old but also when one has completed one's duties as a father by seeing to it that his children are settled down.

With regard to a man's entry into the fourth *āśrama*, Manu's main concern appears to be less with the proper time for renunciation than with the obligations that one must fulfill before one is permitted to renounce. Here once again we come across the theology of debts. We have seen (section 3.2.1.2) that Baudhāyana uses it as an argument against the original *āśrama* system. Manu, on the other hand, uses the theology of debts in support of the classical *āśrama* system and, more specifically, as a powerful argument for the position that a person should not become a renouncer before he has fulfilled the obligations of studentship and marriage. He asserts this position firmly in three verses at the very beginning of his discussion of renunciation:

> A man should pay the three debts before he sets his mind on renunciation.[22] If he devotes himself to renunciation before he has paid them, he will fall.
>
> A man should set his mind on renunciation only after he has studied the Vedas in accordance with the rules, fathered sons in keeping with the Law, and offered sacrifices according to his ability.
>
> If a twice-born man chooses renunciation before he has studied the Vedas, fathered sons, and offered sacrifices, he will fall. (MDh 6.35–37)

The payment of the three debts, then, is for Manu the necessary and sufficient prerequisite for entering the fourth *āśrama*. Later authors, as we shall see, interpret this to mean that it is unnecessary to pass through the third *āśrama*, because the payment of debts is completed in the first two. Manu himself does not address the question of the necessity of the hermit's *āśrama*, but the prominence given to the theology of debts may have contributed to the theological (the historical reality is less certain) obsolescence of the hermit (see section 6.2.1).

I said that the classical *āśrama* system does not occupy as central a place within Manu's own thinking as commonly assumed. My contention is further supported by the presence in Manu's work of programs for leading a religious life that are opposed to the central provisions of the *āśrama* system. The most important of these, I believe, is the provision for living as a householder until death.

As for the authors of the Dharmasūtras, so for Manu marriage and family life constitute the central religious institution. Within the classical *āśrama* system this centrality is evident in the fact that the second *āśrama* spans the productive adult years of a person's

22. The Sanskrit term *mokṣa* literally means liberation, but, as we shall presently see, Manu attaches a technical meaning to the term, using it as a synonym of renunciation, a life dedicated to the search after personal liberation.

life. The other three *āśramas* occupy the marginal years of youth and old age. Manu praises the householder's as the most excellent of the *āśramas*:

> As all living beings depend on air for their survival, so all the *āśramas* depend on the householder for their survival.
>
> The householder constitutes the most excellent *āśrama*, because it is the householder who daily supports everyone belonging to the other three *āśramas* with knowledge and food.[23]

The influence of celibate and renunciatory values is evident in Manu's attempt to find equivalences in the duties of a householder. Thus, a man who does not engage in sexual activity with his wife during the forbidden days is said to practice celibacy (MDh 3.50). Only the first-born is a son conceived according to *dharma*, for he alone is fathered in fulfillment of a debt, whereas subsequent sons are the result of passion (MDh 9.107). The householder in this manner can appropriate to himself the values of other *āśramas* without abandoning home and family.

Manu returns to this theme towards the end of the sixth chapter (6.87–90), which he devotes to the ascetic institutions. After concluding his treatment of the hermit (6.1–32) and the renouncer (6.33–85), he states: "There, I have explained to you the law (*dharma*) of self-controlled renouncers; listen now to the ritual discipline (*karmayoga*) of Vedasaṃnyāsikas."[24] I believe that this verse signals the passage to a different topic. Throughout his work Manu uses similar verses to signal the transition from one topic to another.[25] According to the table of contents given in the first chapter, moreover, Manu clearly indicates that he has two separate topics in mind here; the sequence of topics at 1.114 is *tāpasyaṃ mokṣaṃ saṃnyāsam eva ca. Tāpasya* ("life of austerity") refers to the hermit. *Mokṣa* is a clear reference to the life of a renouncer, that is, the fourth *āśrama;* Manu uses the term with that technical meaning throughout his work.[26] *Saṃnyāsa* is undoubtedly a topic different from *mokṣa;* nowhere else in the list of contents does Manu use two terms to refer to a single topic. The term *saṃnyāsa* must refer to the life of

23. MDh 3.77–78. Similar statements are found in other texts: VaDh 8.14–16; ViDh 26–28. The dependence of others on the householder often refers to the fact that students and renouncers obtain their food from householders, the hermit being tacitly ignored in most such statements. In his commentary on the MDh, Medhātithi hints at a more radical meaning when he says that verse 77 reaffirms the necessity of performing the five great sacrifices. Indeed, in verse 76 Manu affirms the traditional doctrine that sacrifices produce rain, rain food, and food creatures. Thus, the dependence of others on the householder may finally rest on the fact that householders offer sacrifices that sustain the entire ecology of the universe.

24. MDh 6.86: *eṣa dharmo 'nuśiṣṭo vo yatīnāṃ niyatātmanām / vedasaṃnyāsikānāṃ tu karmayogaṃ nibodhata //*

25. See 2.25; 5.146; 6.97; 9.103, 220, 325, 336; 10.131; 12.82, 107. Here is just one example: *eṣa vo 'bhihito dharmo brāhmaṇasya caturvidhaḥ / puṇyo 'kṣayaphalaḥ pretya rājñāṃ dharmaṃ nibodhata //*—"There, I have explained to you the fourfold law of Brahmins which is holy and yields unending rewards after death; listen now to the law of kings" (6.97).

26. See 6.35, 36, 37, 44. For a more detailed discussion of Manu's use of the term *mokṣa* and its distinction from *saṃnyāsa*, see Olivelle 1984, 132–36. Bühler in his translation of MDh 1.114 takes the term in its literal sense as "liberation," thus missing totally the technical meaning given to it by Manu and failing to note that two separate topics are listed here. He follows the commentators who also fail to note this meaning. See Olivelle 1984, 132, n. 89.

Vedasaṃnyāsikas, which is the subject of the last section of chapter 6, a section that opens with the verse cited here.

Now, who were the Vedasaṃnyāsikas? Many commentators of Manu, such as Kullūka, consider them to be a lower type of renouncer. I believe that commentators, such as Govindarāja and Bhāruci, who take them to be a type of householder are right. We have already noted that Manu indicates here a transition to a new topic. His discussion, furthermore, confirms that he considers Vedasaṃnyāsikas to be retired householders who aspire to holiness without resorting to the two types of asceticism that he had described earlier. Immediately after introducing the topic, Manu eulogizes the householder:

> Student, householder, hermit, and renouncer: these four distinct *āśramas* are rooted in the householder.
>
> Now, when a Brahmin acts as prescribed and undertakes these in the proper sequence as spelled out in the sacred texts, each and every one of them[27] leads him to the highest state.
>
> Yet, as the Veda and the Smṛtis state, the householder is the best of all these, for he supports the other three.
>
> As all rivers and rivulets ultimately end up in the ocean, so people of all *āśramas* ultimately end up with the householder.[28] (MDh 6.87–90)

Manu appears to be saying something like this: "I grant that all these four *āśramas* can lead a person to the highest state. Nevertheless, the householder is the best and chief among them, and as such it is unnecessary to leave the household life in old age. I give now this alternative way of leading a holy life in old age in one's own house."

Manu reserves the term *saṃnyāsa* for this institution;[29] within this context the term means retirement rather than renunciation.[30] Immediately after the eulogy of the householder cited above, Manu introduces the tenfold law (*daśalakṣaṇaka dharma*) consisting of ten primary virtues (6.91–92). A person (a householder is clearly intended) who practices these ten virtues also "reaches the highest state" (6.93). Such a householder, who is

27. The Sanskrit term *api* appear to have a concessive force here. As several commentators point out, the intention is not to assert that a person must undertake all the four *āśramas* in succession in order to attain the highest state, but that each and every one of these four (this appears to be the sense of *sarve 'pi*—"all") can lead one to the highest state.

28. The meaning of "end up in" (*yānti saṃsthitim*) appears to be as follows. The existence of rivers depends on their connection with the ocean: it provides them initially with their water and into it they finally merge. Similarly, the existence of people in other *āśramas* depends on the householder in a variety of ways: they obtain food from householders, and new recruits are either householders or their children (see MDh 3.77–78). In a more pregnant sense, however, they end up with the householder, because in the rebirth process they end up as the semen of the householder through whom they receive their new birth. Bühler's translation of the expression as "find a resting-place" with reference to the ocean and as "find protection" with reference to the householder fails to capture the analogy.

29. The term *vedasaṃnyāsin* also occurs at BDh 2.18.24, where its meaning is far from clear. The *Āśrama Upaniṣad* (97) employs the term *ghorasaṃnyāsika* as one class of holy householders, whereas the *Kūrma Purāṇa* (1.2.79) uses *saṃnyāsika* and the *Garuḍa* (1.49.13) *saṃnyāsin* with reference to a class of hermits. See section 6.1.2.

30. I have discussed earlier (section 4.2.3) a similar use of the term with reference to retirement of an aged Brahmin in the *Mānava Śrautasūtra* 8.25. See Sprockhoff 1987.

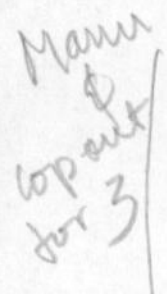

freed from his three debts, may enter this old-age institution. Manu (6.94–96) uses the verb *saṃnyaset* with reference to this entry. The Vedasaṃnyāsika hands over his position as the head of the household to his son and thus abandons the normal ritual life associated with that position. But he neither becomes a wandering mendicant nor retires to the forest. He continues to live at home under the authority of his son (*putraiśvarye*). Manu implicitly refers to this institution also earlier at the end of chapter 4 (4.257) when he concludes his discussion of the householder: "After he has duly freed himself from his debts to the great seers, to his forefathers, and to gods, he should hand over everything to his son and live free from all concerns."

The institution of Vedasaṃnyāsika, therefore, permits a person to remain a householder all his life. Indeed, Manu envisages similar provisions for students and forest hermits. The institution of perpetual studentship was known to Manu, and he gives it at the conclusion of his discussion of studentship as an acceptable alternative to becoming a householder (2.243–49). A person who passes his entire life at his teacher's house is also assured the highest state; he will not be born again in this world. Similarly, at the conclusion of the section on the forest hermit, Manu says that a hermit may increase his austerities and finally walk without food until he drops dead (6.31–32). Such a hermit is assured the world of Brahman.

It is clear, therefore, that for Manu the passage through the four *āśrama*s was one among several paradigms for leading a religious life. Although Manu presents the classical system, it is neither as central nor as normative in his law book as it is in later Brāhmaṇical literature.

5.3.2 Yājñavalkya

There is no consensus regarding the date of the *Yājñavalkya Dharmaśāstra* (YDh). This work is heavily dependent on Manu, and it is evident that a considerable interval of time separates the two works. We would not be far off the mark to assign it to the third or fourth century C.E.[31]

The work begins with the following verse: "The sages paid homage to Yājñavalkya, the chief of yogins, and asked him: 'Tell us all the laws pertaining to the classes, *āśrama*s, and others.'"[32] Here we encounter for the first time the compound word *varṇāśrama*, which becomes in later literature a shorthand term for the totality of *dharma*. The term *itara* ("others" or "the rest") probably refers to areas of *dharma* not covered by either *varṇa* or *āśrama*. The fact that Yājñavalkya thought it necessary to append that word to *varṇāśrama* reveals that he used this compound with a more literal meaning than later authors. Clearly he was not using it purely as a code word for the totality of *dharma*.

This opening statement should lead one to expect that the *āśrama* system would provide an organizational framework for the text. That, however, is not the case. The sys-

31. Kane (1968, I.1, 447) disagrees with Jolly's date of the fourth century and assigns it to "the first two centuries of the Christian era or even a little earlier." That would put Manu too far back into the pre-Christian era. Regarding the dates of these texts, see Lariviere's translation of the *Nāradasmṛti*, pp. xix–xxiii.

32. YDh 1.1: *yogīśvaraṃ yājñavakyaṃ saṃpūjya munayo 'bruvan / varṇāśrametarāṇāṃ no brūhi dharmān aśeṣataḥ //*

tem occupies at best a marginal position within the text. The discussion of duties of students and householders, the first two *āśramas*, is conducted without any explicit reference to the *āśrama* system. Yājñavalkya uses the term *āśrama* just three times in the body of his text. In all three instances the term is used not in a discussion of the *āśrama* system but while dealing with some other topic.[33]

The only reference to the classical system is found at the beginning of Yājñavalkya's discussion of the forest hermit and the renouncer. A hermit should go to the forest either with his wife or after entrusting her to his son (YDh 3.45). The implication is that one becomes a hermit after one's children are settled. The two opening verses of the section on the renouncer, likewise, imply that one should renounce only after fulfilling the duties of a householder:

> No one but a man who has studied the Vedas, muttered prayers (*japa*), fathered sons, given food, maintained the sacred fires, and offered sacrifices according to his ability, may set his mind on renunciation.[34] He may do so either from the forest or from home, after offering the sacrifice to Prajāpati at which all his possessions are given as a gift to the priests and, at its conclusion, depositing the fires in his self. (YDh 3.56–57)

Unlike Manu, Yājñavalkya does not refer explicitly to the theology of debts; the fulfillment of the duties underlying the debts—study, sacrifice, and procreation—is, however, required prior to renunciation. A point worthy of note is that Yājñavalkya permits a man to renounce either as a householder or as a hermit. The release from debts can be achieved as a householder. The intermediary stage of a hermit may, therefore, be dispensed with. This passage is one of the earliest indications that the institution of the forest hermit comprehended by the third *āśrama* had become or was in the process of becoming obsolete (see section 6.2.1).

Yājñavalkya, just like Manu, indicates a variety of religious life styles that are at variance with the central provision of the classical *āśrama* system requiring a person to pass through all the *āśramas*. He concludes the section on studentship, for example, with a reference to the perpetual student (*naiṣṭhika brahmacārin*) who lives with his teacher all his life (1.49). At the end of his discussion of the householder, likewise, he mentions several holy modes of life suitable for a householder: "He may become one who lives on grain that fills a granary or a pot, or on grain sufficient for three days or for just a single day; or he may live on what he gleans. Each following mode is superior to the one preceding it."[35] Although Yājñavalkya does not state explicitly that a householder may live in this manner until death, it appears to be strongly implied. The section on hermits also concludes with the option of committing suicide by fasting (YDH 3.55).

Yājñavalkya divides his treatise into three broad sections dealing with legal procedure (*vyavahāra*), proper conduct (*ācāra*), and penance (*prāyaścitta*). It is significant that

33. At 3.65 Yājñavalkya says that the mere fact that one belongs to an *āśrama*, especially renunciation, does not make one virtuous. At 3.191 he says that the self is to be known by all the *āśramas*, and at 3.241 he counts the fault of not belonging to an *āśrama* among the secondary sins (*upapātaka*).

34. Here too, as in Manu, *mokṣa* is used with reference to the last *āśrama*, renunciation.

35. YDh 1.128. Vijñāneśvara in his commentary, *Mitākṣarā*, says that a "granary-full" means one who has grain sufficient for 12 days, while a "pot-full" means one who has grain sufficient for six days. The different livelihoods became the basis for the later subclassification of the *āśramas*: see section 6.1.2.

he discusses the last two *āśramas* not within the context of proper conduct, as one would have expected, but under penance. It appears that Brāhmaṇical theology increasingly looked upon ascetic modes of life not just as institutions of old age but as consisting of a prolonged period of penance. This was another way in which asceticism was integrated into the broader theological schemes of Brāhmaṇism. Ascetic modes of life, according to such reasoning, are special instances of the broader category of penances. They are assumed in order to expiate the sins one commits during one's younger years.

5.3.3 Viṣṇu

The text bearing the name Viṣṇu—the *Viṣṇu Dharmasūtra* (ViDh)—is written partly in the aphoristic *sūtra* style. It is clear, however, that, although it may contain some older material, much of the extant text is later than Manu and Yājñavalkya.[36] The text begins with the myth of the creation of the universe by Viṣṇu. The goddess Earth, who had earlier been rescued by the tusks of Viṣṇu incarnate as a boar, recalls that episode and asks Viṣṇu who would support her now (1.45–46). Viṣṇu replies that she has been entrusted to the care of "those who take delight in the duties pertaining to classes and *āśramas*" (*varṇāśramācāraratāḥ*—1.47). Earth then asks Viṣṇu to tell her "the laws of classes and *āśramas*" (*varṇānām āśramāṇāṃ ca dharmān*—1.48). In the introduction, therefore, the author of Viṣṇu, just like Yājñavalkya, refers to the totality of *dharma* to be dealt with in his work as the *dharma* of *varṇas* and *āśramas*. Unlike Yājñavalkya, however, Viṣṇu does not see the need to qualify this expression in any way.[37]

Viṣṇu, just like other dharmaśāstric authors, does not refer to the *āśrama* system in his discussion of initiation or marriage. More than any other author we have dealt with so far, however, Viṣṇu likes to use the term *āśramin* ("one who belongs to an *āśrama*") with reference to students and householders. He refers to a student as *brahmacaryāśramin* once (51.43), to a householder as *gṛhāśramin*—considered by Viṣṇu to be the highest and best of the *āśramas*—a total of six times,[38] and to a renouncer as *pravrajāśramin* (96.1). The frequent use of this term even in contexts without any connection to the *āśrama* system is an indication of its centrality for Viṣṇu.

He assumes that a person who decides to become a hermit is an old householder: "A householder should resort to the forest when he sees his skin wrinkled and his hair turned gray, or when he sees the son of his son" (94.1–2). It is significant, however, that Viṣṇu omits any reference to either a householder or a hermit living out his days in those *āśramas*. The only such reference is to perpetual studentship (28.43–46), possibly because it was too entrenched an institution within the *dharma* tradition to be passed off in silence. The opening statement in his section on renunciation further confirms that Viṣṇu is more wedded to the classical *āśrama* system requiring a person to pass through all the *āśramas* than any of his predecessors: "Then, having extinguished his passions (by living) in the (first) three *āśramas*, he should enter the *āśrama* of renunciation."[39]

36. See Kane 1968, I.1, 118–27, and Jolly's introduction to his translation of the ViDh.

37. In the introduction, Viṣṇu repeatedly connects *varṇa* and *āśrama* with reference to *dharma:* 1.62, 63.

38. ViDh 33.2; 58.1; 59.1; three times in Viṣṇu's eulogy of the householder: 59.27, 28, 29.

39. ViDh 96.1: *atha triṣv āśrameṣu pakvakaṣāyaḥ prājāpatyām iṣṭiṃ kṛtvā sarvavedasaṃ dakṣiṇāṃ dattvā pravrajyāśramī syāt.*

Unlike Manu and Yājñavalkya, Viṣṇu does not speak about the payment of debts or fulfilling the duties of a householder; the only requirement according to him is the passage through the first three *āśrama*s.

5.3.4 Vaikhānasa Smārtasūtra

The Gṛhyasūtras, which deal with domestic rites, by and large either ignore or are ignorant of the *āśrama* system. One of the few exceptions is the *Vaikhānasa Smārtasūtra* (VaiSm) that comprises both the Gṛhya and the Dharmasūtras.[40] It appears that the Gṛhya and the Dharma were written by the same author probably as late as the fifth century C.E.[41]

The Gṛhya section does not directly enunciate the *āśrama* system but references to it within the context of diverse topics show that the system was not only a major institution in the eyes of the author but also a category around which he organized his material in the Gṛhya as well as the Dharmasūtra. Thus, he opens the section on bathing with the words: "Next, the procedure of bathing for people belonging to the four *āśramas*."[42] Under initiation, likewise, he states that the teacher "should explain to him [student] the rules of his *āśrama*."[43]

The Dharmasūtra begins: "Next, the law of *varṇa*s and *āśrama*s" (VaiDh 1.1) and, departing from the practice of the Dharmaśāstras, which never list the *āśrama*s, goes on to enumerate the four *āśrama*s in imitation of the early Dharmasūtras. The use of the expression *varṇāśramadharma* that was to become a cliché in the dharmaśāstric tradition clearly shows the central position given to the *āśrama* system in the *Vaikhānasa*. Unlike the other texts we have examined, the *Vaikhānasa Dharmasūtra* is organized around the categories and institutions of *varṇa* and *āśrama*. It is the first text, for example, to relate the *āśrama*s to the *varṇa*s: all four *āśrama*s are open to Brahmins, the first three to

40. The only other Gṛhyasūtra that alludes to the *āśrama* system is the rather late *Āgniveśya Gṛhyasūtra*. Even though it does not use the term *āśrama*, it contains clear allusions to the classical system in the context of describing the rites for becoming a hermit and a renouncer. One becomes a hermit after completing the *dharma* of a householder (2.7.10). It also states that a person may spend the third quarter of his life as a hermit and become a renouncer during the fourth quarter (2.7.10), which appears to be a citation from Manu (6.33). Regarding the date of the *Āgniveśya*, Ram Gopal (1959, 30) states: "Judged from the point of view of matter, style and language, this Gṛihya is far removed from the other Gṛihyas. Its style is diffuse and discursive and is marked with a stamp of recentness. Some of the topics treated of in the Agni. G. S. are absolutely foreign to the tenor of the other Gṛihyasūtras and bear the stamp of later religious ideas." The *Āgniveśya* and the *Vaikhānasa* are also the only Gṛhyasūtras to deal with the rites for becoming hermits and renouncers and to use the technical term *saṃnyāsa*.

41. On the authorship and date of the *Vaikhānasa*, see Caland's introduction to his translation of the VaiSm, p. x, xv; Bloch 1989; Kane, 1968, I.1, 259–60; Eggers 1929, 9–10; Lingat 1973, 25.

42. VaiG 1.2: *atha cāturāśramiṇāṃ snānavidhiḥ*.

43. VaiG 2.8: *tasmā āśramadharmāṇy ācakṣīta*. It is unclear whether *āśramadharmāṇi* refers to the *dharma*s of all *āśrama*s or those of his—i.e., the student's—*āśrama*. Caland assumes the latter, which is supported by the statement later on (VaiG 2.12) that a perpetual student should perform *āśrama-dharmāṇi* until death (*naiṣṭhiko yāvajjīvam āśramadharmāṇy anutiṣṭheta*), where the expression clearly refers only to the duties of a student. A similar reference is found in the description of the marriage rite (VaiG 3.4): the newly married man performs the householder's *dharma* (*tataḥ prabhṛti gārhasthyaṃ dharmam anutiṣṭhatīti vijñāyate*), where *gārharthyaṃ dharmam* parallels *āśramadharmāṇi* of the earlier passages.

Kṣatriyas, and the first two to Vaiśyas (VaiDh 1.1,9; section 7.2). The very absence of the Śūdra clearly shows that the *āśrama* system was limited to the twice-born Āryas. The *Vaikhānasa* is also the first text to propose subdivisions of each *āśrama* (see section 6.1.2). Indeed, it appears more like a text that expounds the four *āśramas* within the context of the *varṇas* than a traditional Dharmasūtra (or Śāstra).[44] It does not deal at all with many of the common topics of *dharma*, such as inheritance, the judicial process, and the duties of a king.

Although the *Vaikhānasa* does not explicitly state that a person should assume each *āśrama* successively, it is clear that its author takes the classical scheme for granted. A householder who fulfills his duties of sacrifice and procreation becomes "freed from the triple debt and debtless" (VaiDh 1.4). The author also assumes that the man who becomes a hermit is married (VaiDh 1.6). One should become a hermit only after he has seen his son's son (VaiDh 2.1). The proper time for becoming a renouncer also clearly reflects the classical scheme:

> A man may perform the rite of renunciation when he is past seventy, old, childless, or a widower, when he thinks of birth, death, old age, and the like, and when he desires (to perform) yoga; or else, from the forest [i.e. from the hermit's *āśrama*], after entrusting his wife to his son and directing his mind on the Highest Self. (VaiDh 2.6)

There is a significant passage in the *Vaikhānasa Gṛhyasūtra* (2.18) that appears to be a ritual expression of the classical *āśrama* system and an implicit rejection of the original system that permitted a young adult who had completed his studentship to choose any *āśrama*. The passage occurs at the conclusion of the description of the ritual return (*samāvartana*) of the student after graduation from his teacher's house to his parental home and just before the beginning of the section on marriage. At the conclusion of the rite of return, the young graduate (*snātaka*) performs the *prāṇāgnihotra*, the ritual offering of food in his own breaths, which are now considered equal to the sacred fires. Then the text states:

> As he goes away after eating it in that manner,[45] his mother, father, or teacher should restrain him gently with the words: "Only a debtless man will reach Brahman's abode," and tell him: "A Brahmin at his very birth is born with the three debts to the fathers and so forth." So is it prescribed.[46]

Caland follows the commentator, Nṛsiṃha, in interpreting the "going away" as going to Benares on a pilgrimage.[47] I believe that this interpretation is incorrect. What would be the purpose of preventing the young man from going on a pilgrimage, and why would that prevention be incorporated into the ritual? Further, what is the point of refer-

44. Except for the later addition to the BDh (that is, the Deutero-Baudhāyana), the *Vaikhānasa* is also the only text to provide detailed descriptions of the rites for becoming a hermit (VaiDh 2.1–4) and a renouncer (VaiDh 2.6–8).

45. That is, after performing the rite of *prāṇāgnihotra*.

46. *tad evaṃ bhuktvā gacchantam anṛṇo brahmapadam abhyetīti sāmapūrvaṃ mātā pitā gurur vā paitṛkādikam ṛṇatrayaṃ jāyamānasya brāhmaṇasya sahajātam ity uktvā vārayed iti vijñāyate.* Some manuscripts read *iti vikhanāḥ* ("so states Vikhanas," i.e., the founder of the Vaikhānasa order) in place of *iti vijñāyate*.

47. The commentator glosses *gacchantam* with *tīrthayātrayārthaṃ vrajantam* ("leaving for the purpose of going on a pilgrimage"). See Caland's trans., p. 66, n. 10.

ring to the obligation to pay the debts—which amounts to the obligation to get married—if the young man is only going on a temporary pilgrimage? The ritual context appears to be the decision of the young man to go away from home to undertake a celibate mode of life. Under the original *āśrama* system this was precisely the time when he was expected to decide on an *āśrama* for his adult life. The departure from home and the life style he intends to adopt are permanent. The parents oppose such a decision. This scenario is taken away from the concrete to the ritual context, and the whole question of whether it is permissible for a man to become an ascetic before marriage is resolved ritually.

The *Vaikhānasa* is the only Gṛhyasūtra to record this element in the rite of return. It is, therefore, impossible to determine how widespread the custom was. What it does indicate is that the impact of the original system was significant enough for at least some ritual experts to modify a well-known rite in their attempt to minimize that impact. It also supports my contention (section 5.2) that the major aim of the classical system was to eliminate choice, the central feature of the original system, and thereby to make marriage and household duties obligatory to all.

The *Vaikhānasa* is also the only text to present a ritualized expression of the classical *āśrama* system with reference to two significant articles used in Brāhmaṇical rites of passage: sacrificial string and staff. Although the term *yajñopavīta* initially meant the manner in which the upper garment was worn during ritual proceedings, around the beginning of the common era the garment was replaced by a string and the term was used exclusively with reference to that sacred string which every Brahmin was expected to wear continuously from the day of his initiation.[48]

Vasiṣṭha, in a discussion unrelated to the *āśramas*, records a practice according to which a student wears a single sacrificial string, while a *snātaka* and by implication a householder wear two sacrificial strings.[49] Within the context of these rites of passage, the number of sacrificial strings appears to signify the progress from adolescence to adulthood. The *Vaikhānasa*, however, applies this progressive increase in the number of sacrificial strings also to hermits and renouncers, giving the strong impression that the increase is used to ritually express a man's progress along the ladder of *āśramas*.[50] Although the text does not explicitly enjoin a single string on a student, the use of the singular *yajñopavītam* (VaiG 2.5) indicates that the student wears only one string. It explicitly prescribes two sacrificial strings for a householder (VaiDh 3.1), three for a hermit (VaiDh 2.2), and four for a renouncer (VaiDh 2.7). The increase in the number from one for a student to four for a renouncer is unmistakably a ritual expression of the classical system. The presence of four strings indicates that a person has undertaken all four *āśramas*, that he truly has accumulated (*samuccaya*) all the *āśramas*.[51]

The ritual expression of the classical system is even more evident in the number and

48. For further details, see Kane, 1974, II.1, 287–300; Olivelle 1986, 29–35.

49. See VaDh 12.14; Kane, 1974, II.1, 292–93. A single sacrificial string is made by twisting three strands of thread.

50. There is evidence that the increase in the number of strings was used for a variety of ritual purposes. Thus Medhātithi (on MDh 2.44), for example, prescribes one string for some types of vedic sacrifices, three for those requiring three fires, and five or seven for yet others.

51. The *Vaikhānasa*, however, permits the renouncer the option of wearing either four or just one sacrificial string (VaiDh 2.7). This appears to be a concession to those renouncers who renounced before marriage, who are here likened to perpetual students, an identification that is common also in later literature.

kind of staffs prescribed for the different *āśramas*. At vedic initiation a boy is given a single staff made from the wood of different trees depending on the boy's *varṇa*. During the ceremony that concludes the period of vedic study the young adult is presented with *one* staff made of *bamboo.*[52] One gets the strong impression that within the context of the rites of passage, bamboo symbolizes adult life. The *Vaikhānasa* contains the only description we possess of the rite by which a man becomes a forest hermit. At the end of that rite the new hermit takes a *double bamboo* staff (*vaiṇavaṃ dvidaṇḍam*), that is two bamboos tied together (VaiDh 2.3). The *Vaikhānasa*, likewise, prescribes a *triple bamboo* staff for the renouncer (VaiDh 2.8).

The view that the increase in the number of bamboo staffs is a ritual expression of the *āśramas* is supported by the fact that the number of ritual formulae recited at the taking of a staff also shows a parallel increase. When a single bamboo staff is taken by a *snātaka*, one ritual formula is recited: "On the impulse of god Savitṛ" (TS 1.1.4.2).[53] A hermit, when he takes a double staff, recites this formula plus a second: "My staff which fell down to the ground" (VaiDh 2.3), while a renouncer, taking a triple staff, recites these two plus a third: "Friend, protect me" (VaiDh 2.8). One is thus left with the strong impression that each bamboo staff is addressed with a special formula, the number of formulae increasing with the number of staffs taken and creating a cumulative effect. The hermit does not merely take two staffs; he takes one staff in addition to the *snātaka*'s staff. The renouncer, likewise, takes a staff in addition to those of the *snātaka* and the hermit. This appears to be a ritual expression of the classical *āśrama* system that posits three adult modes of life. Bamboo symbolizes the adult nature of these modes, and the number indicates the *āśrama* to which one belongs.

5.3.5 The Mahābhārata

In sharp contrast to the *Rāmāyaṇa* (see section 3.4.1), the *Mahābhārata* contains an enormous amount of material relating to the *āśramas*. The problems inherent in using that information for historical purposes become clear in van Buitenen's (1973, xxv) assessment of the date and composition of the *Mahābhārata*:

> Such a dating, from 400 B.C. till A.D. 400, is of course absurd from the point of view of a single literary work. It makes sense when we look upon the text not so much as one opus but as a library of opera. Then we can say that 400 B.C. was the founding date of that library, and that A.D. 400 was the approximate date after which no more substantial additions were made to the text.

"What is the *Mahābhārata*'s view regarding the *āśramas*?" is, therefore, a question that is both improper and impossible to answer. The best we can do is to note the variety of opinions and views recorded there and attempt to relate them in some way to the broad history of the system.

52. Cf. BDh 1.5.2; 2.6.7; VaDh 12.37; MDh 4.36; ViDh 71.13; YDh 1.133. The Gṛhyasūtras of Manu (1.2.15), Āśvalāyana (3.8.1) and Āpastamba (5.12.11) state simply that a *snātaka* takes a staff, without specifying that it should be bamboo, while those of Śāṅkhāyana (3.1.11), Pāraskara (2.6.31), Khadira (3.1.26), Gobhila (3.4.27), Hiraṇyakeśin (1.3.11.7), and the VaiG (2.15) specify a bamboo staff. On the history of the staff of a renouncer, see Olivelle 1986, 35-54.

53. VaiG 2.15. The same formula is given in the *Hiraṇyakeśi Gṛhyasūtra*, 1.3.11.7.

A careful reading of the entire epic yields 160 occurrences of the term *āśrama.*[54] Many of them are, of course, stray references to a well-known institution. It is, nevertheless, clear that as far as the authors of the didactic portions are concerned the *āśrama* system was a recognized and well-established institution. This is confirmed, for example, by the numerous occasions when they assess the value of another institution or activity in terms of the *āśramas*. It is a common practice in Indian religious writings to use a well-known religious practice as almost a currency to estimate the value of another, and possibly lesser known, religious activity. Thus it may be said that a person who performs a particular vow will acquire the merits of a hundred horse sacrifices or a thousand Soma sacrifices. A king who rules his kingdom justly, for example, receives the same rewards as if he had lived in all the *āśramas* (MBh 12.66.5–37). A man killed in battle likewise obtains the rewards of all four *āśramas* (MBh 12.99.46).

In other contexts also the authors indicate that the *āśramas* were so well known that they could be used as examples. Thus in the verbal battle between Aṣṭāvakra and Bandin at which each has to list classes containing progressively larger number of items, when they reach four Bandin refers to the four *āśramas*.[55] Similarly, in the panegyric of Śiva where he is called the best of each class, he is called "the householder among the *āśramas*" (*āśramāṇāṃ gṛhasthaḥ:* MBh 13.14.155). So also Nārāyaṇa is worshipped by all four *āśramas* (MBh 12.321.25), Ātman is worshipped by Vedas and *āśramas* (MBh 12.321.41), and Gaṅgā is served by all four *āśramas* (MBh 13.27.68).

Besides such passing references, there are many passages in the *Mahābhārata* that deal extensively with the classical *āśrama* system.[56] These fall into two categories. Some present the topic in the manner of a Purāṇa or a Dharmaśāstra with a formal request by someone for instruction in the *āśramadharma*, as when Krisṇa asks Bhīṣma, telling him that he, Bhīṣma, knows, among other aspects of *dharma*, the duties of *varṇas* and *āśramas* (MBh 12.50.31).

Others introduce the discussion of the system by way of resolving a dilemma or a problem, as when Śuka presents Vyāsa with the dilemma that vedic texts enjoin us both to perform rites and to abandon them (*kuru karma tyajeti ca*), a dilemma similar to that of the *Bhagavad Gītā*. Vyāsa replies by showing that both those injunctions can be carried out by following the ladder of the *āśramas* (MBh 12.233–37). A similar instruction is given by Janaka to Śuka (MBh 12.313.10–19).

54. In such a large work it is likely that I may have missed some occurrences. My work in the *Mahābhārata* and the *Rāmāyaṇa* made me acutely aware of the urgent need for a reliable word index to the two epics. Following is a list of the *Mahābhārata* passages in which *āśrama* (or a derivative such as *āśramin*) occurs: **1**—3.83; 110.26, 32; **3**—2.50, 59; 148.18, 20; **5**—71.3; **7**—55.25; **12**—11.15; 12.6, 11, 21; 15.40; 23.2, 5, 6; 46.22; 50.31; 59.81; 60.2; 61.1, 2, 4, 9, 12, 15, 21; 62.2, 6; 63.7, 10, 11, 13, 21, 23, 28; 64.1, 3, 6, 8, 24; 65.4, 6, 7, 8, 9, 17, 23, 25; 66.1, 4, 5, 6, 7, 8, 9, 10, 11, 12, 18, 19, 20, 21, 22, 23, 24, 25, 29, 35, 37; 67.1; 92.7, 46; 99.46; 109.6; 111.2; 112.13; 139.3; 154.14; 155.9; 158.6; 168.1; 184.7, 8, 10, 15, 17; 185.6; 189.1; 213.8; 226.4; 230.14, 17; 234.14, 27; 235.27; 236.2, 5, 22, 26, 30; 237.1, 2, 8; 245.13; 260.12; 261.5, 6, 44; 262.21, 34; 269.6; 276.8, 12, 14; 279.7; 292.20; 308.44, 60, 177, 180; 311.27; 313.18, 19, 20, 21, 26, 27; 321.25, 41; 340.1; 342.10; **13**—2.39, 49, 53, 56, 90; 14.155; 24.71; 27.34; 128.36; 135.104; **14**—33.6; 35.27, 30; 45.13; 53.6. In some of these passages the term occurs more than once.

55. MBh 3.134.10: *catuṣṭayaṃ brāhmaṇānāṃ niketanam.* The latter term here clearly refers to the *āśramas*. Likewise, Viṣṇu is called "*āśramaḥ śramaṇaḥ*" (MBh 13.135.104).

56. The *Mahābhārata* passages containing the original system are given in section 5.4.2.

With reference to the *āśramas*, perhaps the most significant episode of the *Mahābhārata* is Yudhiṣṭhira's despondency, which also provides the setting for the great *Śāntiparvan.* Yudhiṣṭhira, dejected after the carnage of the war, decides to renounce the kingdom that he had won at so great a cost. He laments the death of relatives, friends, and loved ones caused by his lust for the kingdom. Just like Arjuna's decision not to fight in the *Gītā,* this decision of Yudhiṣṭhira is placed within a broader context and presented as a choice between action and non-action, social responsibility and renunciation. One after the other his brothers and his wife scold, plead with, and cajole him to abandon the foolish path he has chosen. Many of the central elements of the classical *āśrama* system, such as the proper sequence of *āśramas*, the superiority of the householder, and the obligation to fulfil the *dharma* of one's state, are prominent in their arguments.

Arjuna (MBh 12.11), for example, admonishes Yudhiṣṭhira by narrating a legend (*purāṇa*). Once some young men of noble birth became renouncers even before they had grown beards, thinking that it was the *dharma.* Indra then became a bird to instruct them in the true *dharma.* Indra begins by praising the difficult path of those who "eat left-overs" (*vighasāśin*).[57] The young renouncers think that Indra is praising their way of life, whereas his praise is, in fact, directed at householders, who are the "true eaters of left-overs." The householder's *āśrama* is praised as the "only great *āśrama*" (MBh 12.11.15). It is also the most difficult; as gods attained the highest state by doing what is difficult (*duṣkara*), so will householders.

This and other passages of the *Mahābhārata* show the central theological feature of the classical system that I have already noted. Whenever the opposition between life in the world and its renunciation is presented as either a theological issue or an existential problem in the life of a person—as in the cases of Arjuna in the *Gītā* and Yudhiṣṭhira in the *Śāntiparvan*—the classical system permitted their resolution both by presenting renunciation as suitable only for the old and the retired and by upholding the householder's life as the best *āśrama*—the most altruistic, the most difficult, and the most virtuous.

As we shall see in the rest of this study, this attempt to blunt the opposition between domesticity and renunciation was at most only partially successful. The rejection of the compromise proposed in the classical system is presented most vividly in the conversation between a father, the guardian of the old order, and his son, representing the troubled and anguished spirit of the new religious world.[58] To the son's question regarding how a person should lead a virtuous life, the father replies: "First, learn the Vedas, son, by living as a vedic student. Then you should desire sons to purify your forefathers, establish the sacred fires, and offer sacrifices. Thereafter, you may enter the forest and seek to become an ascetic." The son retorts that death does not respect human intentions; it may steal our life away at any moment. There is an urgency to the quest for salvation: evening's duties we must perform in the morning, tomorrow's tasks we must complete

57. For a discussion of those who "eat left-overs," see Wezler 1977.

58. MBh 12.169. A version of the story appears also in the *Markaṇḍeya Purāṇa,* ch. 10. As Winternitz (1923, 5–8) has pointed out, this story, appearing as it does in Jain (*Uttarādhyayana,* 14, in *Jaina Sūtra,* II, 61–69) and Buddhist (*Jātaka,* 509) texts as well, probably belonged to the generic ascetic folklore before it was incorporated into the MBh. It thus points to the ascetic rejection of societal attempts to convert asceticism into an institution of old age.

today. Sacrifices are empty rites, and sons cannot redeem their dead fathers. We alone are the architects of our own future. As this story illustrates, and as we may well have expected, the proponents of ascetic ideals rejected the compromise of the classical system. This set the stage for further elaborations of and disputes about the *āśrama* system, disputes and developments that I examine in the final three chapters of this book.

5.4 The Original System in the Classical Period

Before turning to those developments, however, I want to look at what happened to the original *āśrama* system after the creation of its classical counterpart. The classical *āśrama* system together with its several modifications we are about to examine so dominated the theological discourse from the early medieval period that it all but eclipsed the original system. With a few notable exceptions, the very existence of the original system is overlooked in the medieval theological literature.

The orignal system, nevertheless, did not totally disappear, and in this section I want to examine some survivals of that system during the classical period. Given the difficulty of dating Indian texts, it is impossible to assert with certainty that the documents which contain these survivals belong to that period. Some, such as the Purāṇas, were certainly composed several centuries after the beginning of the common era. The originals of other passages are lost; they are found only in later citations, and it is difficult to assess the dates of the originals. On the dates of others, such as Kauṭilya's *Arthaśāstra*, scholarly opinion is sharply divided. I bring all these sources together here, because they cannot be shown with even a modicum of certainty to have been composed before the common era. By and large, therefore, they can be assumed to bear witness to the survival of the original *āśrama* system during the classical period.

5.4.1 The Arthaśāstra

The first and possibly the earliest of these sources is the *Arthaśāstra* ascribed to Kauṭilya. Trautmann (1971) has demonstrated convincingly, I believe, that the *Arthaśāstra* is a composite work, sections of which may belong to different periods. For our purposes the significant point is Trautmann's (1971, 118–19) conclusion, tentative though it may be, that books 1 and 2 belong together. His date of 150 C.E. for book 2, and by extension possibly for book 1, is as probable as we can get without new evidence (Trautmann 1971, 184). It is in the first book that the discussion of major religious topics, including the *āśramas*, takes place. If we accept Trautmann's date, then the evidence of the *Arthaśāstra* does not constitute a late survival but confirmation that the original system was still an accepted doctrine early in the common era, during a time when the classical system was taking shape.

That *āśrama* was a well-known and central category for the author of the first book is evidenced by his repeated use of the twofold classification of *dharma* into *varṇa* and *āśrama*, which defines for him the essence of *svadharma* ("the *dharma* proper to each"). The king is advised, for example, to ensure that people follow their *svadharma*:

> The king, therefore, should not permit people to transgress their *svadharma*, for by safeguarding the *svadharma* he finds joy both in this life and after death. Those people prosper and do not perish, among whom the bounds of the Aryas are fixed and the *varṇas* and *āśramas* are established, and who are governed by the triple Veda. (1.3.16–17)

Likewise, at the end of the very next chapter the author says: "People of the four *varṇas* and *āśramas* become devoted to activities of their *svadharma* and follow their respective paths when they are governed sternly[59] by the king" (1.4.16). It is significant that for the author of the first book the major division of both the *svadharma* and of the people of a kingdom is according to *varṇa* and *āśrama*,[60] supporting Trautmann's conclusion that it could not have been written prior to the second century C.E. and certainly not in the fourth century B.C.E.

The third chapter of book 1 is devoted to the discussion of authoritative texts and the *dharma* of *varṇas* and *āśramas*. After listing the texts, including the triple Veda, the author says: "The *dharma* laid down in the triple Veda is beneficial, because it establishes the *svadharma* of the four *varṇas* and *āśramas*" (1.3.4). He goes on to describe the *svadharma* first of the four *varṇas* and then of the four *āśramas* (1.3.9–12). The author, however, merely gives the *dharma* associated with each *āśrama* and does not deal with the question of how and when a person enters any of these *āśramas*. It is not immediately evident, therefore, whether the system presented is the original or the classical.

A closer examination, however, reveals that his conception of the *āśramas* was at the very least closer to that of the original system than that of the classical. It is clear, for example, that for him the *āśramas* are permanent and lifelong undertakings, as he states explicitly with reference to the student: "residing with his teacher until death" (*ācārye prāṇāntikī vṛttiḥ*). He appears to take for granted that the others are lifelong, and the explicit statement with regard to a student, as we saw also in the Dharmasūtras (section 3.1.2), is obviously intended to distinguish such studentship from the temporary period of study following a person's vedic initiation. This conception of the permanent student as the subject of the first *āśrama* is identical with that of the original system. Another clue is the very order in which the author lists the *āśramas*. He places the householder first giving him the pride of place. As we have seen (section 3.1.6), the order is of little significance in the original system, whereas in the classical system the *āśramas* are uniformly listed according to the order in which they are adopted.

I believe it is safe to conclude that the author of the first book of the *Arthaśāstra* conceived of the *āśramas* as permanent modes of life. He does not tell us, however, whether or how a person chooses one of them. Although his statement about adopting an *āśrama* "according to one's aptitude and bent of mind" may be an overstatement, I think Kangle (Kangle 1965, III, 151) is right in his assessment of the *āśrama* system in the *Arthaśāstra*: "It would, in fact, appear that the four *āśramas* are represented as four dif-

59. *Daṇḍena* (lit. "with the rod") here probably means with the threat of severe punishment.

60. That this division was ingrained in the author's mind is borne out by another statement. Talking of the king's power of punishment (*daṇḍa*), he says: "When unjustly inflicted out of love, hatred, or contempt, it angers even hermits and wandering ascetics—how much more the householders" (Artha 1.4.12).

ferent ways of life to be adopted according to one's aptitude and bent of mind, rather than as successive stages in the life of the same individual."

5.4.2 The Mahābhārata

As we have seen, discussions of the *āśramas* in the *Mahābhārata*, especially within the *Śāntiparvan,* which contains most of the didactic and dharmaśāstric passages, usually follow the pattern of the classical system. There are, however, a few passages in which either the original system or something approximating it is presented.

First, there are several texts that make no mention of a passage from one *āśrama* to another and, judging from the context, appear to regard the *āśramas* as permanent states of life. Thus in the story of Yayāti, Aṣṭaka asks Yayāti:[61] "By what conduct does a householder attain the gods, by what a mendicant and he who serves a teacher, by what a forest hermit set on the path of the virtuous? Nowadays people hold many opinions on this" (MBh 1.86.1). Yayāti responds by giving a brief description of the duties of each. Note that the term *āśrama* is not mentioned in the entire episode, yet the enumeration of the four institutions leaves the strong impression that the author is, in fact, speaking of the *āśramas*. Even though Yayāti in his response follows the usual order and places the student first, it is noteworthy that in the question that order is not followed. The assumption, furthermore, that by following the *dharma* proper to each people of all four *āśramas* attain the gods suggests that the *āśramas* are conceived of as permanent states of life.

Nakula, in advising his older brother Yudhiṣṭhira not to renounce his throne, praises the householder's as the best *āśrama*, better than the three others combined. Once, when the four *āśramas* were weighed in a balance, the householder was found to be heavier than the other three combined (MBh 12.12.11). Nakula's brief comments on the four *āśramas* (MBh 12.12.7–10) make no mention of passage and appear to assume that the *āśramas* are permanent states.

My third text comes from Bhīṣma's long discourse on *dharma*. Yudhiṣṭhira (MBh 12.60.2) asks him to teach the *dharmas* of the four *varṇas*, the four *āśramas*, and the king. The discussion of the *āśramas* opens the next chapter:

> Listen, O long-armed and mighty Yudhiṣṭhira, to the duties in this world of the four *āśramas* and *varṇas*: the life of a forest hermit, mendicancy, and the great *āśrama* of a householder; the fourth is said to be the *āśrama* of a student, beloved of Brahmins. (MBh 12.61.1–2)

In the description of the duties also the author follows this random order of enumeration. He states explicitly that one enters the hermit's *āśrama* only after one has completed the following: initiation, vedic study, marriage, and offering sacrifices. A man may enter it with or without his wife (MBh 12.61.3-6). In the case of a mendicant, however, a different provision is given: "A Brahmin who aspires to liberation is deemed here to be qualified for mendicancy after he has completed his vedic studentship" (MBh 12.61.7). Then he praises the householder's as the best and the most difficult of the *āśramas* (12.61.10–17). A householder who performs his duties is assured of heaven and eternal happiness after death. These final remarks leave no doubt that this state was considered

61. The same story is given also in the fortieth chapter of the *Matsya Purāṇa*.

as permanent and lifelong. The final section (12.61.18–21) deals with the duties of a student, and here too no mention is made of this being a temporary period.

In this passage the only *āśrama* that requires a passage through another is the hermit's, and we have already seen that even Āpastamba takes the hermit to be an exception to the rules of the original *āśrama* system (section 4.1.1). Initiation and vedic study are made requirements for hermits, householders, and mendicants, but this period of study is not mentioned as an *āśrama* or equated with the *āśrama* of a student. The probability, therefore, is that here too the *āśrama*s are considered permanent ways of life.

An interesting passage on the *āśrama*s (MBh 12.184–85) is found in the dialogue between Bhṛgu and Bharadvāja in the *Mokṣadharma* section of the *Śāntiparvan.*[62] Bharadvāja asks Bhṛgu to teach him the practices specific to each of the four *āśrama*s (12.184.7). Bhṛgu's discourse on the *āśrama*s that follows is in the *sūtra* style of prose, and it is especially significant because it is undoubtedly a remnant of an old Dharmasūtra.[63] It describes the duties of the four *āśrama*s, but does not address the issue of when and how one enters them. The order of enumeration is the usual one, although the use of the expression *gurukulavāsa* ("living at the teacher's house") for the first *āśrama* is reminiscent of Āpastamba's *ācāryakula* (ĀpDh 2.21.1). The passage does not mention any pre-requisites for entering an *āśrama.* The significant point is that the description of each *āśrama* concludes with the rewards that a person who performs its duties attains after death. Here also the probable conclusion is that the *āśrama*s are regarded as permanent states rather than temporary stages.

The text that contains the most forthright presentation of the original system, however, occurs in the dialogue between Vyāsa and Śuka.[64] After completing his discourse on the *yuga*s and the creation of the visible universe, Vyāsa opens his discussion of the duties of a Brahmin with a description of the *āśrama* system:

> Having studied all the Vedas and gained the knowledge of the sacrifice while he found delight in the service of his teacher, he should pay his debt to his teacher and, returning home with his teacher's permission,[65] follow one of the four *āśrama*s according to the rule until he is freed from his body: begetting offspring with a wife, practicing chastity in the forest or in the presence of a teacher, or following the *dharma* of ascetics.
>
> Of all these four, however, the householder alone is said to be the root, for extinguishing the passions there a subdued man achieves success everywhere.
>
> Then, freed from the three divine debts by having children, becoming learned, and performing sacrifices, and purified by rites, he goes thereafter to the other *āśrama*s. (MBh 12.226.3–7)

Several of the central elements of the original system are expressly mentioned here. One

62. For an examination of this dialogue, see Frauwallner 1973, I, 98–105.

63. The prose passage is quite out of place here, lying as it does in the middle of a long dialogue in verse. That this is probably a remnant of an ancient *sūtra* is also noted by Deussen 1909, 131.

64. On the philosophical issues discussed in this dialogue, see Frauwallner 1973, I, 89–98.

65. It could also be translated as "returning home, follow one of the four *āśrama*s with the permission of his teacher."

of the four *āśrama*s is to be chosen after the young adult has completed his period of temporary studentship. Once chosen, the *āśrama* is to be pursued until death. In the final verse, however, an exception appears to be made in the case of a householder, who is permitted to proceed to the other *āśrama*s after he has paid his three debts. This is an interesting integration of the original and the classical systems. That the original formulation appears here as a remnant from the past is confirmed by the fact that a little later in the same discourse the author devotes four chapters (12.234–37) to the description of the classical system.

My final example comes from the dialogue between the ascetic Kapila and the seer Syūmaraśmi in the form of a cow being led to be sacrificed (12.260–62; see section 3.3.3). In reply to Syūmaraśmi's objection that Kapila's denunciation of animal sacrifice amounts to insulting the Veda, Kapila says:

> I am not insulting the Vedas and I never wish to engage in disputes. We have learnt from the Vedas that the different duties of those who belong to different *āśrama*s have the same goal.
>
> A renouncer does indeed go, and so does a forest hermit. A householder and a student, both these also go.[66]
>
> For there are believed to be four eternal paths leading to the gods. One speaks of their relative superiority and inferiority, their strength and weakness, with reference to their fruits. (MBh 12.260.12–14)

Elsewhere also in the same dialogue the author affirms "the unity of all the *āśrama*s with respect to their end" (12.262.34) and calls the *āśrama*s the four feet of *dharma* (12.262.19, 21).

Here too, I believe, we have a conception of the *āśrama*s as four permanent and alternate modes of religious living. The mention of the "four paths leading to the gods" is suggestive and reminds us of the argument used by the proponent of the original system according to Baudhāyana (section 3.1.1).

5.4.3 The Purāṇas

The Purāṇas are documents composed well after the classical *āśrama* system had become entrenched within the Brāhmaṇical tradition. In general they present the classical system in all its details. It is, therefore, significant to find even in this class of literature survivals of the original system.

In the *Viṣṇu Purāṇa* the main discussion of *āśramadharma* takes place in the ninth chapter of the third book. There the classical system with its orderly progression from *āśrama* to *āśrama* is given. In the very next chapter the author describes the sacramentary rites of passage (*saṃskāra*), beginning with the birth ceremonies. In presenting the conclusion of the period of vedic study following initiation, however, the author returns to the *āśrama* system and this time presents the original formulation:

66. The expression "go" probably refers to the paths leading to the gods mentioned in the next verse. All these go to the gods through the performance of their respective duties. Note also the order in which the *āśrama*s are enumerated.

Having completed his studies and given the teacher's fee, O king, if he wishes to undertake the life of a householder he should marry a wife.

Or else, he may end his days[67] as a student after making a formal declaration of intent. He should serve his teacher or a person such as his teacher's son.

Or, if he wishes, he may become a hermit or a wandering ascetic. He should follow the course, O king, that he had earlier decided.[68]

The context and the wording leave little doubt that the decision is irrevocable and that these adult vocations are permanent. Note also that a clear distinction is made here between the temporary period of study following initiation and the permanent *āśrama* of a student.

The *Vāmana Purāṇa* (14.7–9) contains the following passage right at the beginning of its discussion of the *āśramas*.[69] After stating the duties of a student, it continues:

Having learnt from the teacher's mouth one, two, or all the Vedas, he should give the teacher a gift and the fee. Then, with his permission, a person who desires the householder's *āśrama* should enter the householder's *āśrama*. Or else he may according to his own wish enter the forest hermit's or the fourth *āśrama*. Or a twice-born man may remain permanently there in the very house of his teacher, and in the absence of the teacher with his son, and, if there is no son, with his pupil.

This is as clear a presentation of the original system as possible. The interesting point is that, immediately after this presentation, the *Vāmana* (14.11; 15.1–61) gives the classical system of passage from one *āśrama* to another. One gets the impression that the author is not bothered by the fact that the system presented in these verses contradicts what is said later on. He appears to be presenting an anthology rather than a single doctrine.

The *Bhāgavata*, one of the most recent Purāṇas, presents the major elements of the original *āśrama* system on two occasions, but, just like the *Vāmana*, it does so within discussions that also present the classical system of passage. The first is found in the seventh book (*skandha*). Yudhiṣṭhira asks Nārada to teach him the *dharma* relating to *varṇāśrama* (7.11.2). At the conclusion of his discussion of the duties of a student (7.12.1–13), Nārada states what a student should do after he completes his studies:

Having given, if he is able, a desired gift to his teacher, and, with his teacher's permission, he should enter a house or the forest, go forth as a wandering ascetic, or continue to live there. (BhāgP 7.12.14)

Such a student, forest hermit, ascetic, or householder, who practices (his *dharma*) and acquires wisdom, attains the highest Brahman. (BhāgP 7.12.16)

67. The expression *kālaṃ karoti* here probably is a double entendre: "he spends his time" and "dies" as a student.

68. ViP 3.10.13–15. Parts of this passage are ascribed by Nīlakaṇṭha (*Saṃskāramayūkha* , p. 64) to a *Bhaviṣyat Purāṇa*, and by Vaidyanātha Dīkṣita (*Smṛtimuktāphala*, Varṇāśramadharmakāṇḍa, pp. 121 and 172) to Vyāsa and to the *Viṣṇu Purāṇa* and the *Bhaviṣyat Purāṇa*.

69. A similar statement is found in the *Nṛsiṃha Purāṇa* (58.34–36), although there it is not altogether clear whether the reference is to the original system or to a modification of the classical system we are about to discuss (6.2.2).

This passage clearly states both that the *āśramas* are permanent and that they are to be chosen by a young adult after he has completed his studies. Entering a house or the forest is a technical expression for becoming a householder or a forest hermit common in these texts. "Continue to live there" refers to a student who decides to remain with his teacher until death. The descriptions of forest hermits (7.11.17–31), wandering ascetics (7.12.1–46), and householders (7.14.1–42) that follow contain only one suggestion that there is a passage between the *āśramas*. With reference to a hermit, it is said that if he is unable to perform his duties because of sickness or old age he should undertake a fast unto death (7.12.23). One who is able, however, should become a wandering ascetic (7.13.1).

The second discussion of the *āśramas* in the *Bhāgavata Purāṇa* takes place in the eleventh book. In an extraordinary juxtaposition, the *Bhāgavata* alludes to the Ṛgvedic myth of the origin of the four *varṇas* from the mouth, arms, loins, and feet of the cosmic man, here identified with the Lord himself, and goes on to place the following words in his mouth: "The *āśrama* of the householder was born from my loins, vedic studentship from my heart, and forest life from my chest, while renunciation rests on my head" (11.17.14). The higher the place of origin the higher the *varṇa* and the *āśrama* (11.17.15). The implication, especially in the light of the subsequent description of the *āśramas*, is that the *āśramas* are as permanent modes of life as are the *varṇas*.

The Lord himself describes the duties of a student following his vedic initiation (11.17.22–30). If the student desires to attain the world of Brahmā, he should live with his teacher until death (11.17.31). After a brief account of such lifelong students, the text turns to what one should do if one does not desire to remain a student:

> Now, when one intends to enter the (way of life) that immediately follows in keeping with the sacred texts he has investigated, he should give the fee to the teacher and, with the teacher's cheerful approval, take the bath.
>
> A Brahmin should then enter a house or the forest, or go forth as a wandering ascetic. He should go from *āśrama* to *āśrama;* a man devoted to me should not act otherwise. (BhāgP 11.17.37–38)

Only three *āśramas* are mentioned here as the subject of choice, since the option of becoming a lifelong student was given earlier. The meaning of going "from *āśrama* to *āśrama*" is not altogether clear. If it refers to a passage—that is "going from one *āśrama* to another *āśrama*"—then it may mean that the classical system is an option to those who do not want to stick to one *āśrama* all their life. It may mean also that one should go from "the *āśrama*," that is the student's state, to another *āśrama*, in which case it restates what was said earlier.[70]

In the descriptions of the different *āśramas* that follow, however, the author clearly admits the possibility of passing from one *āśrama* to another. At the conclusion of the discussion of householders, the author permits a householder either to continue living at home or to become a hermit or a renouncer (11.17.55). He opens his section on the forest hermit, moreover, with the statement that "he who desires to enter the forest should live

70. The absence of definite or indefinite articles ("the" or "a") in Sanskrit makes it difficult to decipher the meaning of these pithy statements.

tranquil in the forest during the third quarter of his life, either entrusting his wife to his sons or accompanied by her" (BhāgP 11.18.1). Likewise, a forest hermit is permitted to renounce when he achieves total detachment from all the heavenly worlds won by good works (BhāgP 11.18.12).

5.4.4 Miscellaneous Sources

The *Ahirbudhnya* is one of a series of sacred texts with the title "*saṃhitā*" belonging to the Pāñcarātra tradition. The earliest of these cannot be dated prior to the fifth century C.E., while most of the major Saṃhitās, including the *Ahirbudhnya*, were probably composed prior to the ninth century C.E.[71]

Of all the Pāñcarātra texts that I have been able to examine, only the *Ahirbudhnya* presents the *āśrama* system according to its original formulation. After describing the duties specific to each *varṇa* (15.28–33), it turns to the description of the *āśramas*. Significantly, that description begins with the initiation into vedic studentship and a brief account of a student's duties (15.39–42). At the conclusion of his studentship he takes the ceremonial bath and gives the fee to his teacher (15.43). At this point the *Ahirbudhnya* (15.44–45) introduces the selection of an *āśrama* by the young adult who has duly completed his studentship: "Obtaining the assent of his teacher, let him desire [or choose][72] one of the four *āśramas*. If that student desires studentship as his *āśrama*, self-controlled, he should serve his teacher alone until death." The *Ahirbudhnya* clearly states both that the young adult should choose one of the *āśramas* and that the first *āśrama* is distinct from the temporary studentship that follows vedic initiation.

In medieval literature also we encounter citations from earlier sources that are no longer extant, citations that record formulations which approximate that of the original *āśrama* system. A *sūtra* cited in several texts, for example, appears to present the original system: "After studying the Veda, four *āśramas* are open to the three *varṇas*."[73] If there are four *āśramas* after studying the Veda, that is after the initiatory period of studentship, then that period is not considered here as an *āśrama*. This brief text does not explicitly state that there is a choice among the *āśramas* or that the *āśramas* are permanent. There is, on the other hand, no suggestion that a man passes from one *āśrama* to another. The likelihood is strong, however, that the system presented here is closer to the original than to the classical.

A clearer statement of the original system is found in a verse ascribed to Uśanas by Vaidyanātha Dīkṣita: "With the permission of his teacher let him duly follow one of the four *āśramas* until death."[74]

71. For the dates of the Pāñcarātra literature, see Schrader 1916, 18–22, 110–114; Krishnamacharya's edition of the *Jayākhyasaṃhitā*, pp. 26–35. On the literature of the Pāñcarātra, see Smith 1975.

72. The Sanskrit term *icchet* literally means "to desire." In this context it may well mean "he should choose."

73. *trayāṇāṃ varṇānāṃ vedam adhītya catvāra āśramāḥ.* It is cited by Vijñāneśvara (YMtā 3.56–57) as *sūtrakāravacana.* Devaṇṇabhaṭṭa (*Smṛticandrikā*, I, p. 65) identifies the *sūtrakāra* as Kātyāyana, while Vāsudevāśrama (Ypra 3.56–57) ascribes it to the *Chandogasūtra*, and Nīlakaṇṭha (*Saṃskāramayūka*, p. 65) to the *Kāṭhakasūtra.*

74. Vaidyanātha Dīkṣita, *Smṛtimuktāphala*, Varṇāśramadharmakāṇḍa, p. 172: *ācāryeṇābhyanujñātaś caturṇām ekam āśramam / ā vimokṣāc charīrasya so' nutiṣṭhed yathāvidhi //*

An equally clear presentation is found in a couple of verses ascribed to Vyāsa by Yādavaprakāśa:

> After duly completing his learning through the service of his teacher, a twice-born should give the gift of a cow to his teacher and, with his permission, bathe. Whatever *āśrama* the Brahmin likes—that of perpetual student, sage, or wandering ascetic—in that very *āśrama* let him live, self-controlled.[75]

All the main elements of the original system are presented here unambiguously: the choice of *āśramas*, the time for the exercise of that choice, and perpetual studentship as the first *āśrama*. The enumeration of the *āśramas*, however, is somewhat ambiguous. Only three are mentioned and it is unclear whether "sage" (*muni*) refers to a hermit, as it often does in similar contexts, or to a householder.

5.4.5 Medieval Theologians

I have already noted that the original *āśrama* system all but disappeared from the theological discourse of medieval Brāhmaṇism. As I will point out later (section 6.2.2), whenever theologians of this period refer to the "option theory" (*vikalpa*) they refer not to the original system but to the modification of the classical system in the case of renunciation.

Even when these theologians cite the original formulation of the system as found in the Dharmasūtras, they appear to be oblivious to its import. Vaidyanātha Dīkṣita,[76] for example, cites Gautama and Vasiṣṭha together with texts that permit a person to renounce at any time during his life, assuming all of them to reflect the *vikalpa* view.

There are, however, a couple of refreshing exceptions, the earliest and the most prominent of whom is Yādavaprakāśa. After presenting the classical system and the modified version of it permitting a man to renounce at any time, Yādava gives a third opinion: "For a temporary vedic student there is a free choice among the four *āśramas*: so state the teachers."[77] He goes on to cite relevant passages from the Dharmasūtras of Vasiṣṭha, Āpastamba, and Gautama that we discussed earlier (sections 3.1.1–3). In stating that all four *āśramas* are open to a temporary student, Yādava implicitly acknowledges that the temporary studentship is not an *āśrama*. The phrase *icchayā vikalpaḥ*, which I have translated "free choice," is significant.[78] It is clearly meant to exclude the other type of choice known as *vyavasthitavikalpa* that we discussed earlier (section 5.2) where the choice is restricted to a particular group. The free choice attaches no condition for its exercise. The total freedom of choice distinguishes this theory of the *āśramas* from the view that a detached person may renounce immediately after his temporary stu-

75. Yādavaprakāśa, *Yatidharmasamuccaya*, p. 10: *guruśuśrūṣayā vidyāṃ saṃprāpya vidhivad dvijaḥ / snāyīta gurvanujñāto datvāsmai dakṣiṇāṃ hi gām // naiṣṭhikaṃ vā muner vāpi pārivrājyakam eva vā / yam icched āśramaṃ vipro vaset tatraiva saṃyataḥ //*

76. *Smṛtimuktāphala*, Varṇāśramadharmakāṇḍa, p. 172.

77. *Yatidharmasamuccaya*, p. 10: *upakurvāṇasya brahmacāriṇaś caturṣv āśrameṣv icchayā vikalpa ity ācāryāḥ*. Some manuscripts of this work have the variant reading *icchāvikalpaḥ*.

78. The same technical phrase is used by Vijñāneśvara (YMtā 3.56–57, p. 443) in declaring that a person may freely choose to follow any one of the three views on the *āśramas*, viz. *samuccaya*, *vikalpa*, and *bādha*, because all three are supported by authoritative texts.

dentship (see section 6.2.2). The latter is a case of *vyavasthitavikalpa*, the choice being restricted to those who are detached. Yādava clearly understood this difference, which has escaped the notice of most other medieval theologians.[79]

Nīlakaṇṭha in his *Saṃskāramayūkha* (pp. 64–65)[80] also presents the original system, although it is unclear whether he drew as sharp a distinction between it and the modified classical system as Yādavaprakāśa. After citing several authorities, Nīlakaṇṭha concludes:

> What they state, therefore, is this: "vedic studentship is the initial prerequisite. Thereafter, if a person is fond of that life, then he should live all his life as just a student. If that is not to his liking, then he should become a householder, a forest hermit, or an ascetic." Consequently, he should live out his days in just the householder's state, or in the hermit's *āśrama*, or in the ascetic's *āśrama*.[81]

Nīlakaṇṭha's intent appears to be twofold. First, by using the word *ruci* ("fondness" or "liking") he shows that the student may exercise his choice freely according to his own liking. Second, in the concluding sentence Nīlakaṇṭha appears to draw the conclusion that just as the choice to become a perpetual student requires one to remain in that state until death, so also do the other three choices. This is as clear a statement of the original system as one is ever likely to find in medieval theology.

These two examples—and there are bound to be others I may be unaware of—show that the original system did not altogether disappear from the collective memory of Brāhmaṇical theology. That memory became very faint after the classical system eclipsed the original, but, as we have seen, its traces are detectable both in the sacred texts and in theological discourse at as late a period as the seventeenth century.

79. Aparāditya's commentary, *Aparārka*, on the YDh also contain hints. He says, for example, that according to Vasiṣṭha one may become a hermit immediately after studentship (on YDh 3.44, p. 940). See also his comments on pp. 946 and 950.

80. Kane (1975, I.2, 938–941) places the literary activity of Nīlakaṇṭha between 1610 and 1645 C.E.

81. *Saṃskāramayūkha*, p. 65: *tataś caivam uktam. prathamaṃ brahmacaryam āvaśyakam. tato yadi tatraiva rucis tato brahmacaryeṇaiva yāvajjīvaṃ tiṣṭhet. yadi na rucis tato gṛhī vanī yatī [yatir ?] vā bhaved iti. tato gārhasthyenaivāyuḥ kṣapayed vanāśrameṇa vā yatyāśrameṇa.*

6

Development of the Classical System

The *āśrama* system, we have seen, was primarily a theological construct. On the one hand, the system imposed its own tidy fourfold scheme on a variety of behavior patterns. The classical system, on the other hand, imposed a somewhat artificial sequence for the assumption of the four *āśrama*s, a sequence that did not totally correspond to actual practice, especially in the case of renunciation. In this chapter I examine some further elaborations of the classical system that were intended to address these issues.

6.1 Classifications of the Āśrama

The *āśrama* system itself, we have seen, was a theological classification that reduced numerous religious ways of life to four basic categories. The early literature on the *āśramas*, including the Dharmasūtras and the Dharmaśāstras, make no mention of any further classifications of the *āśrama*s. Even the admittedly late didactic sections of the *Mahābhārata* do not contain an explicit classification of the *āśrama*s. The earliest documents to present such subclassifications are the *Vaikhānasa Dharmasūtra* and the *Āśrama Upaniṣad*. Both these documents belong roughly to the middle of the first millennium C.E.,[1] and both provide a fourfold classification of each *āśrama*.

A point that we need to bear in mind as we explore these classifications is that, even though they are not totally unrelated to reality, the numbers we encounter in them are for the most part artificial and contrived. Unlike modern taxonomy, the numbers of these classifications are not derived from a careful analysis of actual patterns. Rather they follow accepted numerological schemes.[2] Further, as we see clearly in the case of the classification of renouncers (section 6.1.3), within the context of medieval theology these classifications were not simple taxonomies but hermeneutical tools.

1. Both Caland (VaiDh, pp. xv–xix) and Kane (1968, I.1, 260) place the *Vaikhānasa* between 300 and 400 C.E. Sprockhoff (1976, 136) assigns the *Āśrama Upaniṣad* to the fourth century C.E. The latter document existed as a *smṛti* text before it was eventually converted into an "Upaniṣad." It is cited in medieval literature as *Kāṇvāyanasmṛti* and *Kātyāyanasmṛti*. See Sprockhoff 1976, 120–24.

2. For the significance of different numbers, especially four, in ancient India, see Gonda 1976; 1984, 50–53; sections 7.6 and 8.3.

6.1.1 Early Classifications of the Four Institutions

In the early literature we find classifications of students, householders, hermits, and renouncers without a direct and explicit reference to the *āśrama* system. These were the precursors of the formal classifications of the *āśramas*.

One of the earliest such classifications relates to two types of holy householders known as Śālīna and Yāyāvara. These terms are found in very early texts and outside any taxonomic context.[3] Heesterman (1982) has demonstrated, I believe convincingly, that Śālīna and Yāyāvara were originally two types of vedic sacrificers. As their names suggest, the former maintained a stable residence (*śālā*) whereas the latter was given to wandering. In the early literature these two are not opposed to each other; together they constitute the category of vedic sacrificer who is distinguished from the ordinary householder.

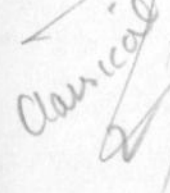

In later literature their connection to the sacrifice is by and large lost sight of, and they are seen as subtypes of the general category of householder. An early taxonomy of holy householders that includes these two classes is found in the later addition to Baudhāyana's Dharmasūtra (BDh 3.1) that I have called "Deutero-Baudhāyana."[4] It lists three: Śālīna, Yāyāvara, and Cakracara. Even though Baudhāyana does not state here explicitly that these are householders, it is clear both from the Black Yajurveda tradition to which he belongs and from their descriptions here and elsewhere in the text that they are indeed householders and not ascetics.[5] The *Mahābhārata*, for example, says that Jaratkāru was born in the lineage of Yāyāvaras (*yāyāvarakule:* MBh 1.34.12) and calls his forefathers Yāyāvara seers (1.41.16).

These three types of householders, according to Baudhāyana, employ nine means of livelihood (BDh 3.1.7; 3.2.1–17):

1. Ṣaṇṇivartinī: cultivating a small plot of land lent by its owner.[6]
2. Kauddālī: plowing near a place of water and cultivating bulbs, roots, fruits, and vegetables.
3. Dhruvā: obtaining food by presenting oneself with a yoke in front of houses in a village.
4. Saṃprakṣālanī: living on what one obtains daily.
5. Samūhā: living on the grains one can sweep up from places where grain is grown.[7]
6. Pālanī: also called Ahiṃsakā ("not hurting"), living on husked rice or seed one obtains from virtuous people.

3. TS 5.2.1.7; KS 19.12: 14.10; MS 3.2.2: 16.14; ĀpŚ 5.3.22.

4. See section 3.2.1.2. For a detailed examination of this passage of Baudhāyana and for a discussion of Śālīna and Yāyāvara, see Sprockhoff 1984, 20–29. Sprockhoff (1984, 21) is right in assuming that these two types are connected with the tradition of the Black Yajurveda, given that they are mentioned primarily in the texts of that tradition. The two words also occur in BDh 2.12.1; 2.17.3; 2.18.4.

5. See Sprockhoff 1984, 22 (n. 61 for further bibliography) and Heesterman 1982. Varenne (in MNU II, 81–82) is off the mark when he identifies them with hermits or renouncers.

6. The name is derived from the extent of the land: six *nivartanas*. Each *nivartana* is approximately 110 sq. yards.

7. Although the text is not altogether clear, the meaning probably is that he sweeps up the grains left over after threshing.

7. Śiloñchā: living on what one obtains by gleaning.
8. Kāpota: living like a pigeon (*kapota*), picking up single grains with just two fingers.
9. Siddhecchā:[8] obtaining cooked food from virtuous people when one becomes old or sick. The last method requires the householder to deposit the fires in himself and to behave like a renouncer (*saṃnyāsin*).

A tenth mode is also given according to which one subsists on the produce of the forest, just like a forest hermit.

It is clear that Śālīna, Yāyāvara, and Cakracara represent a classification not of all but of just three very special and holy types of householders. Thus the text (BDh 3.1.9–25) requires people to undergo a special initiatory rite before undertaking any of these modes of life. They leave their homes and live in a hut (*kuṭī* or *maṭha*) at the edge of the village. The statement that they may remain chaste or approach their wives during the proper season[9] implies that these holy householders were married and lived with their wives. The nine means of livelihood, moreover, do not form the basis of a taxonomy in Baudhāyana; any one of them may be followed by holy householders. Some of these means, as we shall see, become the basis for later classifications of the *āśrama*s.

Manu also gives different means of subsistence for holy householders without providing a taxonomy based on those means. He first lists six such means (MDh 4.4–6) which are given palpably artificial names:

1. Ṛta ("truth"): gleaning.
2. Amṛta ("immortal" or "ambrosia"): what is given unasked.
3. Mṛta ("death"): begged food.
4. Pramṛta ("extreme death"): agriculture.
5. Satyānṛta ("truth and falsehood"): trade.
6. Śvavṛtti ("dog's life"): servitude.

Next, Manu (MDh 4.8) lists four types of householders according to the amount of food or grain they hoard: a Kusūladhānyaka possesses enough grain to fill a granary and a Kumbhīdhānyaka enough to fill a jar; a Trihaihika has enough for three days and an Aśvastanika lives from day to day without making any provisions for the morrow. Of these four, each following mode is considered superior to each that precedes. These four names may merely be descriptive;[10] I think, however, that they may in addition be proper names designating the people who follow these modes. Yājñavalkya (YDh 1.128) in addition to these four lists Śiloñcha, or gleaning. Manu's category of Vedasaṃnyāsika, which we have already discussed (section 5.3.1), is probably also a type of holy householder.

We have already seen that Āpastamba (2.22.6–8; section 4.1.1) recognized divergent modes of life falling under the broad rubric of forest hermit. Some, following the model of the original *āśrama* system, become hermits immediately after completing

8. Bühler's translation, following the commentator Govinda, gives the name as "Siddhoñchā," but the critical edition of Hultzsch published subsequently shows that the name is in fact "Siddhecchā."

9. BDh 3.1.24: *brahmacaryam ṛtau vā gacchati.* The "season" immediately follows her monthly period.

10. This is how Bühler understands them when he translates the meanings of the terms.

their vedic studentship, remain celibate, and have neither a fire nor a house. Others become hermits later in life and live a retired life in a hut outside the village either alone or in the company of their wives and children.

Deutero-Baudhāyana (BDh 3.3.1–15), however, is the first to provide an explicit classification of forest hermits. He divides hermits into two broad classes: those who cook their food and those who do not. Each is divided into five further classes, some of which are further subdivided:

A. Those who cook (*pacamānaka*)
  1. Those who subsist on all kinds of wild produce (*sarvāraṇyaka*)
    a. Vegetarians (*indrāvasikta*)
    b. Non-vegetarians (*retovasikta*)
  2. Those who subsist on unhusked grain (*vaituṣika*)
  3. Those who subsist on bulbs and roots (*kandamūlabhakṣa*)
  4. Those who subsist on fruits (*phalabhakṣa*)
  5. Those who subsist on potherbs (*śākabhakṣa*)

B. Those who do not cook (*apacamānaka*)
  1. Those who do not use iron or stone implements (*unmajjaka*)
  2. Those who take food with their hands (*pravṛttāśin*)
  3. Those who take food with their mouths (*mukhenādāyin*)
  4. Those who subsist on water (*toyāhāra*)
  5. Those who subsist on air (*vāyubhakṣa*)

Deutero-Baudhāyana concludes the list with the statement: "These are the ten observances ordained for Vaikhānasas."[11] The use of the technical term *dīkṣā*, which means "initiation," for these modes of life indicates that a person was initiated into them through a religious ceremony. The noteworthy point in this classification, as in most classifications of holy people in ancient India that we encounter, is that it is based almost exclusively on food, on what and how the hermits eat.[12]

Manu (MDh 6.17–18) also gives various food practices that a hermit may follow, but it is unclear whether these are given as alternate ways in which a hermit may live or as practices that differentiate hermits into distinct types. These practices include (1) eating cooked food, (2) eating food cooked by time, that is, ripe or mature fruits and the like, (3) using stones for grinding, (4) using the teeth to grind, (5) living from day to day

11. BDh 3.3.15: *iti vaikhānasānāṃ vihitā daśa dīkṣāḥ*. I think Bühler is reading too much into the term *vaikhānasa* when he translates it as "hermits who follow the rule of Vikhanas." Even though a relationship to the institutes of Vikhanas may be in the background, the term probably refers to hermits in general and not to a particular class of hermits as in later classifications (section 6.1.2).

12. All these classes of hermits appear to be food gatherers, for cultivation or culturally mediated production of food is forbidden to them. See GDh 3.33; BDh 2.11.15; VaDh 9.3; MDh 6.16. The non-vegetarians among the first class of cooking hermits are in fact scavengers, eating carrion left over by carnivores of the forest. Cultural mediation is further reduced in the non-cooking classes; some do not use implements, while others use only their hands or mouths to obtain food in imitation of animals. One must assume that the last two types, who are anorexic, aim at withering their bodies away until death finally overtakes them. For a more detailed discussion of ascetic food and its relationship to ascetic ideologies, see Olivelle 1991.

without storing food, (6) storing food sufficient for a month, (7) storing food sufficient for six months, and (8) storing food sufficient for a year.[13]

We do not encounter any classification of renouncers in the early *dharma* literature. The older Saṃnyāsa Upaniṣads use the term "Paramahaṃsa," literally "highest swan or gander," with reference to an exalted type of renouncer (ĀrU 11; JU 69, 71). The *Paramahaṃsa Upaniṣad*, as its name indicates, is devoted to an exposition of the state of a Paramahaṃsa renouncer. The *Āruṇi Upaniṣad* refers to a "celibate Kuṭīcara" (*kuṭīcaro brahmacārī:* ĀrU 6) and appears to distinguish him from a Paramahaṃsa, although there is no indication that the author has a classification of renouncers in mind. Both Paramahaṃsa and Kuṭīcara, more commonly called Kuṭīcaka, however, appear in later classifications of renouncers.

With regard to vedic students, the only division we find in the early sources is that between temporary students who return home after completing their course of study and permanent students who live a celibate life in the house of their teachers until death. The latter, we saw, constituted the first *āśrama* within the original system. These two types became the basis for later classifications of this *āśrama*.

6.1.2 Formal Classifications of the Āśramas

The earliest extant classification of the four *āśramas* is found in the *Āśrama Upaniṣad* (95–103)[14] and the *Vaikhānasa Dharmasūtra* (1.3–9). Their classifications agree closely, often verbatim, with each other; it is likely that either the one is based on the other or both derive from a common source. Each of the four *āśramas* is subjected to a fourfold division, giving rise to 16 subclasses of *āśramas*:

A. Vedic Student

1. *Gāyatra:* after his vedic initiation studies the *gāyatrī* verse for three nights, during which he abstains from salt.
2. *Brāhma:* lives as a student for 48 years, or for 12 years per Veda, or for as long as it takes to master the Veda.
3. *Prājāpatya:* is devoted to his wife, approaches her during the proper season, and avoids the wives of others.[15]
4. *Bṛhan:*[16] is a perpetual student who does not leave his teacher until death.

B. Householder

5. *Vārttāvṛtti:* engages in agriculture, cattle rearing, and trade; offers sacrifices lasting a hundred years; and thus seeks the self.
6. *Śālīnavṛtti:* offers sacrifices but does not officiate at them; studies but does not teach; gives but does not receive; offers sacrifices lasting a hundred years; and thus seeks the self.

13. Similar divisions are found in YDh 3.47, 49; ViDh 94.11–12; 95.13–14; MBh 12.236.8–14.

14. For detailed explanatory notes on this text, see Sprockhoff 1976, 117–38, and my annotated translation: Olivelle 1992.

15. Alternatively, according to the *Āśrama Upaniṣad*, a Brāhma is one who lives at his teacher's for 24 years, while a Prājāpatya is a person who lives with his teacher for 48 years.

16. The VaiDh calls him Naiṣṭhika ("perpetual student"), a term used to describe the Bṛhan in the *Āśrama Upaniṣad*.

7. *Yāyāvara:* offers sacrifices and officiates at them; studies and teaches; gives and receives; offers sacrifices lasting a hundred years; and thus seeks the self.
8. *Ghorasaṃnyāsika:*[17] performs rites with water that is drawn out and purified; lives on gleanings gathered each day; offers sacrifices lasting a hundred years; and thus seeks the self.

C. HERMIT

9. *Vaikhānasa:* tends the sacred fires using plants and trees that grow on unplowed land outside the village; performs the five great sacrifices; and thus seeks the self.
10. *Audumbara:* tends the sacred fires with figs, jujubes, wild rice, and millet fetched from the direction which he faces when he gets up in the morning; performs the five great sacrifices; and thus seeks the self.
11. *Vālakhilya:* has matted hair; wears rags, skin, or bark; throws away flowers and fruits on the full moon of Kārttika[18] and follows the regular livelihood during the remaining eight months; tends the sacred fires; performs the five great sacrifices; and thus seeks the self.
12. *Phenapa:* feigning insanity, eats withered leaves and rotten fruits; dwells here and there; tends the sacred fires; performs the five great sacrifices; and thus seeks the self.

D. RENOUNCER

13. *Kuṭīcara:* begs food from the houses of his sons, and thus seeks the self.
14. *Bahūdaka:* carries a triple staff, a water pot, a sling, a shoulder yoke, a water strainer, a bowl, shoes, and a seat; wears a topknot, a sacrificial string, a loincloth, and an ochre garment; begs food from virtuous Brahmin households; and thus seeks the self.
15. *Haṃsa:* carries a single staff; wears a sacrificial string but not a topknot; carries a sling and a water pot; spends only one night in a village and five nights in a town or a sacred bathing place; performs penances such as the one- and two-day fasts, the kṛcchra, and the lunar fast (section 8.1, nn. 8–9); and thus seeks the self.
16. *Paramahaṃsa:* carries no staff; is shaven-headed; wears a loincloth and a patched garment; keeps his emblem and conduct concealed; although sane, acts like a madman; abandons the triple staff, the water pot, the sling, the shoulder yoke, the water strainer, the bowl, the shoes, the seat, the topknot, and the sacrificial string; lives in deserted houses and temples; is beyond right and wrong and even falsehood; endures everything; is the same toward everyone; regards a clod, a stone, and gold as the same; begs his food from any of the four classes that he happens to come across; and thus liberates himself.[19]

17. Called Ghorācārika in the VaiDh.

18. October–November, the end of the four months of the rainy season.

19. The *Bhikṣuka Upaniṣad* (SUS, 233–36) gives only the classification of renouncers and its description differs somewhat from that of the *Āśrama*.

According to the *Vaikhānasa,*[20] the Brāhma student spends 12 or 20 years at his teacher's. Both texts are somewhat ambiguous with regard to the Prājāpatya student. The *Āśrama Upaniṣad* itself, as we saw, gives an alternate meaning based on the number of years spent at the teacher's. The *Vaikhānasa* states that, on the one hand, such a student takes a wife after he has concluded the period of studentship with the ceremonial bath and, on the other, he is devoted to *brahmacarya,* which in all likelihood means here "celibacy" rather than "studentship." It goes on to state: "The seers declare that one should not live in the Prājāpatya state beyond three years." From this I would venture to conclude that according to the *Vaikhānasa* a Prājāpatya student is a married man who remains celibate while he lives with his wife; this explains why he is required to put a time limit to this practice. The *Āśrama Upaniṣad,* on the other hand, sees him as a normal householder who engages in sexual intercourse solely during his wife's fertile period immediately following her menses. The assumption here is that he does so not for pleasure but for duty, and thus can be recognized as a celibate, an assumption common in later literature.

The *Vaikhānasa* makes a generic classification of hermits into those who live with their wives (*sapatnīka*) and those who do not (*apatnīka*), in keeping with the general prescription that a person who becomes a hermit may either leave his wife with his son or take her with him into the forest.[21] The four subclasses of hermits with wives correspond to the general classification of hermits given in the *Āśrama Upaniṣad.* They are: Audumbara, Vairiñca, Vālakhilya, and Phenapa. Although the descriptions in the two texts differ somewhat, broadly Audumbara and Vairiñca of the *Vaikhānasa* parallel Vaikhānasa and Audumbara of the *Āśrama Upaniṣad,* respectively. With regard to hermits without wives, the *Vaikhānasa* (1.8) states:

> There are numerous types of hermits without wives. It is stated that they observe diverse practices: those who eat at specific times; those who go about with upraised staffs; those who use stones for grinding; those who use strong arrow-heads;[22] those who use their teeth as a mortar; those who live by gleaning; those who live on what they happen to see;[23] those who live like pigeons; those who live like deer; those who receive (food) in their hands; those who live on stony fruits; those who live on sun-dried (fruits); those who live on wood-apples; those who live on flowers; those who live on pale [i.e., non-green] leaves; those who skip meal times—those who eat once a day and those who eat every other day; those who lie on thorns; those who sit in the Vīra posture;[24] those who lie between five fires; those who inhale smoke; those

20. VaiDh 1.3–9. The classification of householders is referred to also in the VaiG 4.2.

21. See ĀpDh 2.22.8–9; MDh 6.3; YDh 3.45; ViDh 94.3.

22. The term *udagraphalinaḥ* is obscure. Caland admits its obscurity and translates: "those who live upon elevated fruits." The commentary cited by Caland is of little help and Caland's translation makes no sense. I take *phalin* to refer to some type of iron tool rather than to fruits, especially because this phrase is preceded and followed by others referring to ways in which hermits cut or grind their food.

23. The reading is obscure and possibly corrupt. Caland, calling "the reading and translation equally uncertain," translates: "those who live by pressing together," relying on the reading *saṃdaṃśanavṛttikāḥ.* Given the context, I feel the reference may be to how the hermit gathers his food. The *saṃdarśana* may refer to the rule recorded elsewhere that some hermits gather food only from the direction they happen to face when they get up in the morning.

24. Sitting on one's haunches with the legs beneath crossed over each other.

> who lie on stones; those who plunge into water;[25] those who live in jars filled with water; those who remain silent; those who hang with their heads down; those who gaze at the sun; those who keep their hands raised; those who stand on one foot.

In the Sanskrit each practice is referred to by a single compound word. It is unclear, however, whether these terms represent a taxonomy or merely refer to diverse vows that hermits without wives keep.

Both documents give the identical fourfold classification of renouncers, a classification that will remain the standard throughout later history, even though the descriptions of each category vary somewhat from source to source. The sources generally agree that the Kuṭīcara, or Kuṭīcaka as he is more commonly known, lives a sedentary life in a hut and receives his food from his relatives. The *Vaikhānasa,* however, appears to place him outside society and in the forest, for he is expected to beg his food from forest hermitages.

The *Mahābhārata* does not give a formal classification of the *āśrama*s. In one extended discussion (MBh 12.234–36), however, the text gives a fourfold classification of just householders and hermits. It divides householders into Kusūladhānya, Kumbhīdhānya, Aśvastana, and Kāpotī (MBh 12.235.2–3). The first three are also found in Manu (MDh 4.8) in the passage we discussed in section 6.1.1. The last is a category we have encountered under hermit and refers to those who live on gleanings in imitation of pigeons. The four classes of hermits are divided according to their food storage: those who store food sufficient for one month, or for one year, or for 12 years, or those who live from day to day.[26] Immediately after these four classes, however, the text goes on to enumerate numerous penances and vows, such as using the teeth as a mortar, that appear as classifications in other texts, confirming the doubt I expressed earlier regarding the nature of many of these taxonomies.

The Purāṇa literature by and large ignores the classification of *āśrama*s. Two exceptions are the *Kūrma Purāṇa* (1.2.74–84) and the *Garuḍa Purāṇa* (1.49.6–19). They contain a nearly identical passage presenting a twofold division of the *āśrama*s. The two classes of students are the temporary (*upakurvāṇa*) and the permanent (*naiṣṭhika*). Householders are divided into *sādhaka* ("efficient") and *udāsīna* ("indifferent"). The former are busy looking after the affairs of their families, whereas the latter leave their wives and wealth after paying the three debts and live alone intent on liberation. The two types of hermits are called *tāpasa* ("one engaged in mortifications") and *saṃnyāsika.*[27] The former perform austerities, worship gods, and study, whereas the latter are given to meditation. Finally, there are two classes of mendicants: *pārameṣṭhika* and *yogin.* The former practice yoga, control their senses, and seek knowledge, whereas the latter always find delight and satisfaction in themselves and possess true insight. The

25. The preceding two phrases are left out in Caland's translation, no doubt through an oversight. The latter may refer to the practice of some ascetics remaining for long periods of time in water: cf. MBh 13.50.3–19; 13.57.18; Aśvaghoṣa, *Buddhacarita,* 7.17.

26. MBh 12.236.8–9. The last, *sadhyaḥprakṣālaka,* literally means "those who clean their bowl immediately after their meal." The implication is that they do not keep any food for the morrow.

27. The *Garuḍa* reads *saṃnyāsī.* We saw earlier that the term is used by Manu with reference to a holy householder (section 5.3.1).

Pārameṣṭhikas are further divided into Jñānasaṃnyāsin, Vedasaṃnyāsin, and Karmasaṃnyāsin, while the Yogins are divided into Bhautika, Sāṃkhya, and Atyāśramin.[28]

In the medieval legal literature also we find citations of earlier Smṛtis presenting twofold divisions of the *āśrama*s. Maskarin, commenting on the GDh 3.2, cites a prose passage ascribed to Uśanas:

> There are two types of students: temporary and permanent; two types of hermits: with wives and without wives; two types of renouncers: Bhikṣusaṃnyāsin and Vedasaṃnyāsin. There are numerous types of householders, classified as Śālīna, Yāyāvara, and so forth.[29]

There are two noteworthy points in this classification. First, as in the *Vaikhānasa*, hermits are here broadly classified in terms of their relation to their wives. Second, the text makes no attempt to classify householders, recognizing the large variety in their modes of life.

Yādava cites four verses ascribed to Śaunaka that present a twofold division identical to that of Uśanas. After listing the divisions, this passage goes on to ascribe the twofold classification to Manu: "Manu has proclaimed only this twofold division of people belonging to the *āśrama*s."[30] Śaunaka describes a Bhikṣusaṃnyāsin as a wise man who is detached from all the pleasures of this life and the next and who becomes a renouncer after performing the Vaiśvānarī oblation at which he gives all his possessions as the sacrificial fee. Yādava identifies the Vedasaṃnyāsin of Śaunaka with Manu's Vedasaṃnyāsika, who, as we have seen, is a special type of householder (section 5.3.1), and goes on to say that some consider the *dharma* of the Vedasaṃnyāsika to be identical with that of the Kuṭīcaka. The holy householder of Manu is thus transformed into the lowest category of renouncer. This is an example of the broader tendency within Brāhmaṇical theology to collapse all forms of holy living, whether they be connected with householders or hermits, into the general category of renunciation or *saṃnyāsa*.

After giving the twofold classification of all the *āśrama*s, Yādava records the fourfold classification of renouncers into Kuṭīcaka, Bahūdaka, Haṃsa, and Paramahaṃsa. He goes on to state, however, that some reject this division, because it is based only on the Pāñcarātra[31] and Sāṃkhya treatises and not on the Veda, a clear indication of contin-

28. The *Garuḍa* calls the last two *kṣatra* and *antyāśramin*. The texts provide no description of the three classes of Pārameṣṭhika, although literally the terms mean "one who renounces on account of knowledge," "one who renounces the Veda (or 'in accordance with the Veda')" and "one who renounces rites or works." We shall encounter some of these categories later in classifications of renouncers. The Bhautika is said to be engaged in "initial meditation" (*prathamā bhāvanā*), the Sāṃkhyas in the meditation on the imperishable (*akṣarabhāvanā*), and the Atyāśramins in the meditation on the Supreme Lord (*pārameśvarī bhāvanā*). The last category, which literally means "one beyond the *āśramas*" (or "one in the final *āśrama*" if we read Antyāśramin), we will discuss in section 8.2.

29. Nīlakaṇṭha in his *Saṃskāramayūkha* (pp. 62, 131–33) also gives twofold classifications of students (temporary and permanent) and householders (Śālīna and Yāyāvara). He does not classify hermits, but gives the traditional fourfold classification of renouncers.

30. Yādavaprakāśa, *Yatidharmasamuccaya*, Ch. 5 (p. 20): *dvidhaivāśramiṇāṃ bhedaś caturṇāṃ manur abravīt //*

31. Even though Yādava mentions that the fourfold division of each *āśrama* is given in Pāñcarātra texts, I have been able to locate such a passage only in the *Sanatkumāra Saṃhitā* (5.5–42). Later the *Sanatkumāra* (5.118–25) classifies people into four classes irrespective of the *āśrama* to which they may belong.

uing debate regarding the validity both of these subclassifications and, as we shall see below (section 8.5), of the *āśrama* system itself.

6.1.3 Hermeneutics and the Classification of Renouncers

In most Hindu sects the renouncer was considered the paradigmatic holy man. These sects were for the most part founded and led by renouncers. The highest levels of holiness within each sect were thus related to the renunciatory mode of life. It should come as no surprise then, that of all the classifications of *āśrama*s it is those relating to renunciation that command the attention of medieval theologians and perform significant functions within the theologies of holiness in medieval sects.

These classifications are not mere taxonomies; they perform two hermeneutical functions. On the one hand, they reflect the sectarian theologies of holiness which provide the criteria for classification. The hierarchy of renouncers established by the various classificatory schemes points out the path toward holiness and the distinct steps it involves. On the other hand, they provide frameworks for interpreting the theologies of other sects; it is a common hermeneutical strategy in India to assign lower positions within one's own scale to the highest level of holiness posited by other sects, thus eliminating their threat by this stifling theological embrace.

An early example of the first is found in the *Vaikhānasa Dharmasūtra.* In its formal classification of the four *āśrama*s, it first presents the common fourfold classification of mendicants (*bhikṣu*) that I have given above. Later in the same passage (VDh 1.10–11), however, it divides *yogin*s into three classes—Sāraṅga, Ekārṣya, and Visaraga—subdivides the first into four and the second into five, and states that the Visaragas are numberless. The author does not state explicitly that there is a difference between a *bhikṣu* and a *yogin* or what that difference might be. Under the rubric of *yogin,* however, the *Vaikhānasa* appears to be giving a classification of ascetics in terms of the theology of its own tradition or sect. This is clearly evident in its denunciation of the Visaragas, whose path it advises its readers not to follow.[32]

The several classifications given in the *Nāradaparivrājaka Upaniṣad* also appear to be based on its Advaita theological position according to which the highest type of holiness (and therefore the highest form of renunciation) results in the total withdrawal from activity and the complete freedom from rules. Thus it presents the hierarchy of renunciation as a gradual withdrawal from activities and rules, culminating in the antinomian state of the highest renouncer. The *Nāradaparivrājaka* (174–75) gives a sixfold classification, adding the Turīyātīta and the Avadhūta to the traditional four:

> A Turīyātīta uses his mouth in the manner of a cow.[33] He eats fruits, and, if he eats cooked food, he obtains it from three houses. He is left with nothing but his body. He is naked, and the activity of his body is like that of a corpse.

32. A theological criterion is also used in the classification of the *āśrama*s of the *Sanatkumāra Saṃhitā* referred to in the previous note.

33. A renouncer who follows this practice does not use his hands to accept food. The donor throws the food on the ground and the renouncer picks it up with his mouth in imitation of a cow. One who follows this practice is also referred to as *udarapātrin* ("one who uses his stomach as a begging bowl"), and is distinguished from the *pāṇipātrin* ("one who uses his hands as a begging bowl"); both give up the use of a begging bowl to collect alms food.

> An Avadhūta, however, is subject to no restrictions. He is given to obtaining food in the manner of a python,[34] receiving it from all classes except outcastes and the infamous. He is devoted to meditating deeply on his own true nature.

The Avadhūta in this classification represents the highest renouncer. He is often viewed as possessing the knowledge that liberates a man while he is still alive (*jīvanmukta*). Such a man is beyond any rule of ritual or morality; no restriction can be imposed on him. Other texts, such as the *Turīyātītāvadhūta Upaniṣad* (241–45) and the *Bṛhadavadhūta Upaniṣad* (303–10), make a single category of the Turīyātīta and the Avadhūta, placing it above that of the Paramahaṃsa, who represents the highest class in the traditional fourfold classification. Basically such a man gives up everything normally considered distinctive of a renouncer, such as begging bowl, staff, ochre garment, and shaving. The *Paramahaṃsa Upaniṣad* (45–55), on the contrary, presents the Paramahaṃsa as the highest class but divides it into two. The highest Paramahaṃsa is described in terms closely resembling the Avadhūta.

The theological basis is even more evident in another classification given by the *Nāradaparivrājaka* (171–73). The author shows how renunciation, which is essentially one, came to be divided into four on the basis of the factors that motivate a person to renounce. Thus a person may renounce because he is detached from the world, because he knows the transient nature of the world, because he has attained knowledge and detachment, or because he has completed the duties of the first three *āśrama*s and now wishes to enter the fourth. These motives are thus the basis for this fourfold division of renunciation.

The most comprehensive statement of this theological basis from an Advaita standpoint is made by Vidyāraṇya in the introduction to his *Jīvanmuktiviveka:*

> Detachment is the reason for renunciation, according to the vedic statement: "One should wander forth on the very day that one becomes detached" [JU 64]. Its[35] division, however, is given in the Purāṇas. Detachment is said to be twofold: intense and very intense. When there is intense detachment, a yogin should renounce into the Kuṭīcaka state or, if he is able, into the Bahūdaka. When there is very intense detachment, one should renounce into the Haṃsa or, if one desires liberation, into the Paramahaṃsa state, which is the means of direct knowledge.
>
> "To heck with *saṃsāra*!" Such fleeting resolve at the loss of one's sons, wife, wealth, and the like constitutes the feeble level of detachment. "May I not have sons, wife, and the like in this life!" Such a firm resolve constitutes the intense level of detachment. "May I not obtain any world subject to rebirth!" Such is its very intense level.
>
> At the feeble level there is no room for any type of renunciation. At the intense level there are two types of renunciation, the Kuṭīcaka and the Bahūdaka, depending on whether one is or is not able to undertake pilgrimages and other such activities; both these carry triple staffs. At the very intense level there are two types distinguished in terms of Brahmā's world and liberation. A Haṃsa acquires the knowledge of the

34. Such a renouncer does not actively seek food. He remains in one place and waits for someone to give him food without being asked, just as a python does not hunt but waits for its prey (food) to come to it.

35. In the Sanskrit text also the referent of the pronoun "its" (*tadbhedaḥ*) is unclear. It may refer to either renunciation or detachment. In what follows the division of the former is related to and dependent on the division of the latter.

> truth in that world, whereas a Paramahaṃsa does so in this world. . . . There are said to be two types of Paramahaṃsas: one who seeks after knowledge and one who possesses knowledge.

Vidyāraṇya here makes two significant theological statements regarding renunciation. First, he grounds renunciation solidly on the internal disposition of the renouncer: the only legitimate motive for renunciation is detachment. The levels of detachment, furthermore, determine the classes of renouncers. A very mild type of detachment may be occasioned by a variety of circumstances and does not entitle one to renounce. The two classes of renouncers at the intense level of detachment are distinguished by their relative physical strength, because Bahūdakas are expected to visit places of pilgrimage. Second, Vidyāraṇya bases the classification of the higher types of renouncers on their objectives. Haṃsas aspire to attain the highest heaven, the world of Brahmā, whereas Paramahaṃsas seek liberation in this very life. Paramahaṃsas themselves are divided on the basis of their relationship to the liberating knowledge. As he elaborates later on, the seeker after knowledge is still bound by rules and restrictions of his state, whereas the enlightened Paramahaṃsa is subject to neither injunctions nor prohibitions. This is the Advaita stand with regard to the *jīvanmukta*, the man liberated while still on earth, who is also the highest type of renouncer.

The second hermeneutical function of the classification of renouncers, namely the interpretation of sectarian theologies, is evident both in the very classifications and especially in polemical contexts. Thus, in the classification of the Vaiṣṇava text, *Sanatkumāra Saṃhitā* (5.34–38), Haṃsa and Paramahaṃsa are the first two, and inferior, classes. These are described according to the Advaita model: both carry single staffs, and the Paramahaṃsa discards the topknot and the sacrificial string. Above them, however, stand the Bhagavān and the Prabhu. They are clearly Vaiṣṇava ascetics carrying triple staffs and other Vaiṣṇava insignia. Thus the triple-staffed Vaiṣṇava ascetics are presented as hierarchically superior to the single-staffed Haṃsas and Paramahaṃsas. Although the text does not explicitly say so, no one in the medieval theological milieu could have failed to detect the last two as the highest types of renouncers according to the Advaita tradition.

Within the Advaita tradition the triple-staffed ascetics are Kuṭīcakas and Bahūdakas, the two lower classes, whereas the highest types of ascetics carry either single staffs or no staff at all.[36] Here the Vaiṣṇava ascetic practice of carrying triple staffs is relegated to lower levels of asceticism.

Polemical works bring out a different hermeneutical potential of the classification of renouncers. All sides to the Hindu theological debates on renunciation subscribe to the authority of an identical body of sacred texts, the Vedas and the Smṛtis. This body, however, was only vaguely demarcated and many new Smṛtis, both purāṇic and dharmaśāstric, continued to be composed often under the influence of sectarian practice and ideology. Vedic and especially *smṛti* passages, therefore, could be cited in support of sundry and mutually contradictory positions. Such is the scriptural context of the medieval theological debates whose heart consisted of exegesis. To illustrate this point I

36. On the controversy between the Advaita and the Śrī-Vaiṣṇava traditions concerning the emblems of a renouncer, see Olivelle 1986–87.

will use the example of the controversy regarding the staff, topknot, and sacrificial string between the Advaita and Śrī-Vaiṣṇava traditions, a controversy that I have dealt with more fully elsewhere (Olivelle 1986, 57–76).

There are numerous scriptural passages cited by the Vaiṣṇavas that prescribe the carrying of a triple staff—that is, three bamboos tied together—by renouncers. Other texts similarly enjoin the wearing of a topknot and a sacrificial string. Such passages, of course, contradict the Advaita practice. Advaitins, in turn, cite passages that prescribe a single staff and the abandonment of the topknot and sacrificial string. The Advaita strategy is simple and uses the hermeneutical principle of *vyavasthā*, or restricted option. When two scriptural passages are in conflict, we have already seen, there arises an option. But as we have also seen (section 5.2), Brāhmaṇical theology attempted whenever possible to eliminate options by interpreting the conflicting injunctions as referring to different situations or people. Thus the Advaita theologians interpret the passages cited by the Vaiṣṇavas as referring to Kuṭīcakas and/or Bahūdakas, the two lower classes in their classification of renouncers. Ānandānubhava in his *Nyāyaratnadīpāvali* enunciates this principle clearly:

> The prescription of a triple staff, just like the rule regarding the offering before sunrise,[37] does not contradict the rule about a single staff, because the authority of both is maintained by restricting them to specific classes of people with different qualifications. (In Olivelle 1986, 109)

Thus any text proposing anything contrary to the Advaita position about Paramahaṃsas can be dismissed as referring to lower classes of renouncers. In the hands of medieval theologians, therefore, the classification of renouncers was not a simple taxonomy but also a hermeneutical tool.

6.2 Modifications of the Classical System

We have already seen that the classical *āśrama* system is rarely encountered in its pure form; the early sources provide a variety of alternatives and modifications. Here I explore in greater detail two major modifications and the historical circumstances and theological reasonings that underlie them.

6.2.1 Skipping the Third Āśrama

Even though in the classical system the *āśramas* appear to be modeled after and in many ways resemble the Brāhmaṇical rites of passage, there remained important differences, especially in the case of the ascetic institutions comprehended by the last two *āśramas*. People continued to become ascetics not just because their advancing age called for it but also because of personal decisions based on a variety of factors; many indeed chose

37. This is a maxim used in Mīmāṃsā. An injunction to perform the morning oblation before sunrise does not invalidate other injunctions requiring the offering to be made after the sun has risen. Cf. MK II, p. 1117; MDh 2.15.

to become ascetics not only in old age but also at other times in their life. That there were personal reasons for and an element of choice in adopting at least some of the *āśrama*s sets the *āśrama* system apart from the normal sequence of life-cycle rituals.

This point is nicely illustrated in an episode recorded in the *Mahābhārata* (1.110). While out hunting in a forest, King Pāṇḍu shot a buck and a doe as they were mating. The buck happened to be a hermit of great power called Kiṃdama, who cursed Pāṇḍu to die in a similar manner during sexual intercourse. Pāṇḍu, overcome by grief, decides to become a renouncer. His wives, Kuntī and Mādrī, plead with him not to become a renouncer but to resort to another *āśrama* into which they can accompany him, and he follows their advice. There are two significant points in this story. First, Pāṇḍu's decision was based not on any preestablished pattern but on an incident in his life that changed his outlook. Second, taking everything into consideration he chose one *āśrama* (probably that of a hermit, even though this is not directly stated) over another.

The first significant modification of the system we detect in the classical sources, in fact, concerns the last two *āśrama*s. We have already noted the anomaly of having two *āśrama*s, the hermit and the renouncer, for old age. The question was: is it necessary to go through them both sequentially? The answer increasingly was negative: we have seen that Yājñavalkya (YDh 3.56) explicitly permits a person to renounce "either from the forest [third *āśrama*] or from home [second *āśrama*]." A passage ascribed to Śaṅkha-Likhita states explicitly: "Renunciation is permitted for a tranquil person of advanced age even prior to becoming a forest hermit."[38]

Vijñāneśvara, the great medieval commentator of Yājñavalkya, remarks that the provision permitting renunciation directly from the householder's *āśrama* shows that the *samuccaya* view, that is the classical system ideally conceived requiring a person to pass through all four *āśrama*s sequentially, is optional.[39] Mādhava in his commentary on Parāśara (PāM I, 530) calls this modified system *āśramatrayasamuccaya* ("the three-*āśrama* aggregate") and the pristine classical system *āśramacatuṣṭayasamuccaya* ("the four-*āśrama* aggregate"). Significantly, however, the optional *āśrama* is not the last, that is renunciation, but the third. Indeed, the debate is whether one can renounce directly as a householder or whether one has to pass some time as a hermit.

There are two possible reasons for this modification to the classical system making the third *āśrama* optional—one historical, and the other theological. It appears that by the first few centuries of the common era the institution of forest hermits had become obsolete, its memory preserved only in legend, poetry, and drama. The works on *dharma* continued to devote a section to the duties of forest hermits right up to medieval times. That, however, is no evidence for the continued existence of the institution on the ground; these *dharma* works were exegetical treatises intent more on preserving and explaining the ancient rules than on merely presenting matters "relevant" to people of the time. The reasons for its obsolescence are unclear, but the increasing prominence of the renouncer as the ideal holy man may have played a role. Further, as we have seen (section 6.1.2), renunciation itself became further subdivided, providing an umbrella for

38. See Aparāditya on YDh 3.56–57, p. 947; Kullūka on MDh 6.33.

39. YMtā 3.56, p. 442: *anena ca pūrvoktaś caturāśramasamuccayapakṣaḥ pākṣika iti dyotayati.*

absorbing into itself other institutions of holiness. In time, as we shall see in section 8.4, the third *āśrama* came to be viewed not just as obsolete but as something that people should avoid during the current Kali age (*kalivarjya*). Even though some people may have occasionally become hermits, it is safe, I believe, to assume that the institution as such was no longer a live option for people wishing to lead religious lives. The modification to the classical *āśrama* system under review appears to be a recognition of this fact.

The theological reason permitting this modification concerns the age-old controversy between the competing values of celibacy and of procreation and ritual activity. We have already seen how Manu uses the doctrine of three debts to support the classical *āśrama* system. All later writers on *dharma* follow Manu's lead. The main concern of these Brāhmaṇical theologians was not to ensure that everyone followed the *āśrama* system but to support the traditional Brāhmaṇical *dharma* centered on the duties of a householder. Their paramount concern was that all males get married, procreate sons to continue their line, and participate in the ritual religion.

Several episodes found in the *Mahābhārata* illustrate this concern. One day the sage Agastya finds his forefathers hanging upside down in a cave and discovers that they have been reduced to that miserable condition because of his decision to turn celibate without leaving any progeny to continue his line and to provide his forefathers with ritual offerings (MBh 3.94.11–15). A similar story is told even more graphically in the case of the ascetic Jaratkāru.[40] As he was wandering the earth devoted to a life of celibacy and asceticism, he too encounters his ancestors in a cave hanging face down from a single strand of grass that was being gnawed by a rat. His ancestors tell him that they have been reduced to that miserable state because of Jaratkāru's decision to become a celibate ascetic without first begetting a son. Jaratkāru is the single strand of grass on which they hang; time is slowly but surely eating at that strand. When Jaratkāru dies childless all his ancestors will fall.

In another episode (MBh 9.49) Asita Devala is depicted as a sage who was following the *dharma* of a householder. He encounters the wandering mendicant Jaigīṣavya, who convinces him of the superiority of renunciation over the household life. Asita decides to becomes a renouncer and Jaigīṣavya performs the necessary rites. At this point the forefathers of Asita as well as other beings begin to cry, saying: "Who will feed us now?" Asita's decision disrupts the ritual foodcycle that unites all beings, but especially the past and future generations of human beings. At the center of this foodcycle stands the householder, the sole producer of food, who feeds the gods with sacrifices, forefathers with oblations, and humans with hospitality.

That a man must marry and beget a son before renouncing appears to have been the theological bottom line for conservative Brahmins. It is illustrated in a story told in a Digambara Jain work called *Dharmaparīkṣā* by Amitagati.[41] Once an ascetic by the

40. MBh 1.41–42. One encounters similar exhortations to beget sons and to pay one's debts frequently in the *Mahābhārata*: 1.111.11–15; 1.220.9–14; 12.10.22; 12.11.19; 12.25.6; 12.28.54–55; 12.226.1–7; 12.281.9–11; 12.313.14–19. See also O'Flaherty 1973, 68–76.

41. Cited by Bandarkar 1933, 301–3. According to Bhandarkar, the *Dharmaparīkṣā* was written in 1023–24 C.E.

name of Maṇḍapakauśika sat down to dinner with other ascetics. These immediately got up and left, afraid to touch him as if he were an outcaste. Maṇḍapakauśika asked them why they reacted to him as at the sight of a dog. They told him that he had become an ascetic immediately after his vedic studentship, without marrying and seeing the face of a son. A man without a son, they tell him, does not go to heaven, and his austerities are unfruitful.

The centrality of procreation in discussions of the *āśrama*s is demonstrated by the works of the great poet Kālidāsa (circa 400 C.E.), who presents the classical *āśrama* system frequently in his writings. He refers to a student's life as "the first *āśrama*"[42] and speaks of King Duṣyanta as living "in the *āśrama* given to every pleasure," that is, as a householder.[43] In the *Vikramorvaśīya* (5.12–13) Purūravas tells his son Āyus that, since he, Āyus, has completed the first *āśrama*, it is time for him to proceed to the second. An explicit formulation of the classical system is found in the *Raghuvaṃśa* (1.8). Kālidāsa describes the royal line of the Raghus as people "who studied the Vedas in their childhood, indulged in pleasures during their youth, lived as sages in their old age, and in the end gave up their life while practising yoga." Raghu consecrates his son Aja as king and goes to "the last *āśrama*" (8.14).

It is clear, however, that Kālidāsa's major concern is with the duty to have children. Dilīpa's lament at not having a son reflects this concern: his forefathers will be denied food and water after he is gone. The debt to the forefathers is difficult to fulfil (*Raghuvaṃśa*, 1.66–71). At the birth of a son one is freed from this debt (3.20).[44]

Buddhist literature also indicates that "being without debt" was a condition for becoming a monk. The Buddha himself is called "debtless."[45] One of the questions put to the candidate for ordination is "Are you without debt?"[46] A man with debts should not be allowed to become a monk (Vin I, 76). Monks and nuns are frequently said to be "debtless."[47] It is clear the debts referred to in Buddhist literature are for the most part secular debts.[48] One can understand the concern of the Buddhists; they did not want their monasteries to become havens for people trying to dodge debt collectors. It is, nevertheless, interesting that both the Buddhists and the Brāhmaṇical theologians insist that peo-

42. *Prathamāśrama* and *pūrvāśrama* in Kālidāsa, *Kumārasaṃbhava*, 5.30, 50.

43. *āśrame sarvabhoge* in Kālidāsa, *Abhijñānaśākuntala*, 2.14.

44. Elsewhere, Kālidāsa says that a son frees a man from his debt to the fathers (*Raghuvaṃśa*, 10.2) and that Daśaratha became debtless after paying the debts to seers, gods, and forefathers through study, sacrifice, and offspring (8.30).

45. *anaṇa:* Vin I, 6; DN II, 39; MN I, 169; SN I, 137, 233. The Buddha himself, of course, is said to have married and fathered a son before his renunciation. Within the Jaina tradition also there is the story of Nemi, the twenty-second Tīrthaṃkara, who wanted to renounce without getting married. Kriṣṇa, Nemi's cousin, reminds him "that all previous world Saviors had married and raised families before abandoning worldly affairs to follow the quest of religion. He should therefore marry and please his father." Brown 1970, 46. I have already cited a similar story regarding the Buddha recorded by Aśvaghoṣa (section 4.2.3).

46. Vin I, 93; II, 271. The Bodhisattva sends his charioteer back, saying that a man must first pay his debts before becoming an ascetic (Jāt 6, 18). See also SuN 120, 246; MN I, 463; Jāt VI, 193.

47. MN II, 105; *Theragāthā*, 138, 789, 882; *Therīgāthā*, 2, 110, 364.

48. There are, however, instances where the concept of debt is extended to other obligations even in Buddhist literature. For example, supporting old parents is said to be the payment of a debt, whereas supporting young children is likened to giving them a loan (Jāt IV, 280).

ple pay their debts before becoming ascetics. We can see here the theological strategy of the Brahmins when they defined their central obligations as debts. These debts, no less than the secular debts, must be paid before one is permitted to renounce family and society.

The primary concern of Brāhmaṇical theology, therefore, was not that one should faithfully follow the sequence of *āśrama*s but that the obligations of the ritual religion be fulfilled before a person commits himself to a celibate life. A householder who has paid his three debts by studying the Vedas, begetting offspring, and performing sacrifices, is thus permitted to become a renouncer immediately. Whether or not a person becomes a hermit prior to renunciation is not an issue about which these theologians show great concern.

6.2.2 Renunciation as an Exception to the Classical System

The other significant modification to the classical *āśrama* system concerned specifically the fourth *āśrama* and in all probability originated among those who were favorably disposed toward renunciation. They saw the decision to renounce as dependent not merely on external circumstances, such as old age or the payment of the three debts, but on internal dispositions and aspirations. We have seen that Manu uses the term *mokṣa* ("liberation") as a synonym of renunciation and that it is often referred to as *mokṣāśrama.* The goal of renunciation was regarded as liberation.

The personal aspiration for immediate liberation is preceded by a mental disposition and attitude toward *saṃsāra*—that is, the physical and social world one lives in—a disposition that is referred to as *vairāgya.* This term occurs frequently in ascetic literature and has a range of meanings. It refers primarily to indifference to, detachment from, and even disgust and loathing toward everything that constitutes *saṃsāra*, including the most valued objects such as family and heaven. As we saw in the passage from Vidyāraṇya's *Jīvanmuktiviveka* (section 6.1.3), the presence of *vairāgya* or detachment is considered an indispensable condition for renunciation. A couple of verses cited in a medieval work put it as follows:

> Only when indifference (*vaitṛṣṇya*) toward all things has arisen in their minds, do they seek renunciation. Otherwise a man shall become an outcaste.
>
> Let a wise man renounce when he is detached (*virakta*) but live at home so long as he is attached (*sarāga*). For the vile Brahmin who renounces while he is attached will go to hell. (NpU 138)

The classical *āśrama* system places no obstacle to this conception of the necessary precondition for renunciation so long as the detached person aspiring to renunciation and ultimately to liberation is a householder who has paid his triple debt. What happens, however, if a person becomes detached from worldly things before he has paid his debts or even before he has got married? As we have seen in the telling episode of the father and the son (section 5.3.5, n. 58), the answer from the supporters of renunciation is that such a person not only can, but indeed must, renounce without regard to those external circumstances.

In our earlier discussion of the time of renunciation (section 4.2.1) we saw that several Saṃnyāsa Upaniṣads explicitly permit people of all ages and states of life to renounce. The *Āruṇi Upaniṣad* (5), for example, referring to the abandonment of the sacrificial string that accompanies renunciation, states: "A householder or a vedic student or a forest hermit should discard his sacrificial string on the ground or in water." Later the same Upaniṣad (ĀrU 9) permits a person to renounce even before his vedic initiation. Although this document makes no explicit reference to the *āśramas*, nevertheless such provisions directly contravene both the *āśrama* sequence and the obligation to pay the triple debt which are at the heart of the classical system.

The *locus classicus* of the provision that makes renunciation based on *vairāgya* an exception to the classical system, however, is found in the *Jābāla Upaniṣad* (64) that I have already discussed (section 4.2.1). After first presenting the sequence of stages identical to the one found in the classical system, even though it does not use the term *āśrama*, the *Jābāla* gives what appears to be an exception to this general rule in the case of those who possess *vairāgya:*

> Or rather, he may renounce directly from vedic studentship, or from home, or from the forest. Let him even renounce on the very day that he becomes detached, regardless of whether he has taken the vow or not, whether he has graduated or not, and whether he has kindled the sacred fire or is without a fire.

According to the *Jābāla*, therefore, the presence of *vairāgya* renders null all other obligations and eliminates all other preconditions for renunciation. *Vairāgya* alone is not only the necessary but also a sufficient condition for renunciation.[49]

The same point is made in *dharma* texts cited by medieval authors. One passage is found both in the *Nṛsiṃha Purāṇa* and the *Nāradaparivrājaka Upaniṣad*: "If his tongue, sexual organ, stomach, and hands are all under control, a Brahmin may renounce while he is still a student and unmarried."[50] Another frequently quoted verse states: "Seeing that *saṃsāra* is truly without substance,[51] people are imbued with intense detachment (*vairāgya*) and, desirous of seeing the true substance, renounce while they are still unmarried."[52]

The rule of the *Jābāla Upaniṣad* that permits a person to renounce at any time in his life is given the technical term *vikalpa* by medieval theologians.[53] *Vikalpa*, as we have seen (sections 3.1.1 and 5.2), refers to a choice between two or more courses of action, either resulting from a conflict between injunctions or permitted explicitly by a rule.[54]

49. Śaṃkara cites this *Jābāla* passage in asserting that celibate states are open to people who have neither become householders nor paid their debts: see his commentaries on VeS 3.4.17 and BhG 2.54, 72.

50. *Nṛsiṃha Purāṇa* 58.37; NpU 138–39. The verse is cited in PāM I, 531; Aparāditya on YDh 3.55–56 (p. 951); KKT, Mokṣakāṇḍa, p. 32.

51. There is a play on the Sanskrit word *sāra* ("pith" or "substance"). *Saṃsāra*, if one ignores the nasal, can mean "with substance." In reality, however, *saṃsāra* is *niḥsāra* or "without substance." The true *sāra* or substance behind the phenomenal world is Brahman.

52. NpU 139. Many sources ascribe it to Bṛhaspati: cf. Yād, p. 9. It is cited in JMV, p. 8 and YDhS p. 4, and ascribed to Aṅgiras in PāM I, p. 532.

53. Śaṃkara (on VeS 3.4.49) already uses that term together with *samuccaya* to distinguish the two views on the *āśramas*.

54. Vijñāneśvara (YMtā on YDh 4.53–57) and Nīlakaṇṭha (*Saṃskāramayūkha*, p. 64) cite the *Jābāla* passage as a rule that explicitly permits a choice.

Even modern scholars follow the medieval authors in considering the position of the *Jābāla* as the *vikalpa* view of the *āśramas*. Thus Kane (1974, II.2, 424), after stating that "With reference to the four āśramas, there are three different points of view (*pakṣas*) viz. *samuccaya* (orderly co-ordination), *vikalpa* (option) and *bādha* (annulment or contradiction)," explains the *vikalpa* position:

> The second view is that there is an option after brahmacarya, i.e. a man may become a *parivrājaka* ["wandering ascetic"] immediately after he finishes his study or immediately after the householder's way of life. This view is put forward by the Jābālopaniṣad as an alternative to the first view of *samuccaya*. This is the view also of Vasiṣṭha VII.3, Laghu Viṣṇu III.1, and Yāj III.56. Āp. Dh. S. (II.9.21.7–8 and II.9.22.7–8) seems to favour this view.

What the medieval theologians and the modern scholars sharing their view of the *vikalpa* position have failed to note is that the *Jābāla* passage and others like it (see section 4.2.1) deal specifically and only with a single *āśrama*, namely renunciation. The "option" relates only to this *āśrama*. Thus it cannot be construed as a distinct formulation of the system; it is merely a rider to or a modification of the classical system. From the standpoint of Brāhmaṇical hermeneutics, the relationship between these two views can be presented as follows. The classical system requiring a person to go through all the *āśramas* sequentially is the general rule (*utsarga*) applicable in common to all, while the permission—or even the requirement—to renounce whenever a person becomes detached is an exception (*apavāda*) that lays aside the provisions of the general rule with respect to such an individual. It is a common maxim of Mīmāṃsā that an exception has greater force than a general rule.[55] The *Kūrma Purāṇa* (1.3.2–3) states explicitly that the regular sequence of *āśramas* is set aside only for a special reason; one may renounce directly as a student only when one has knowledge, detachment, and a desire to attain liberation.

From a historical point of view what is most disconcerting is that these authors confuse the *Jābāla* position with what I consider to be the true *vikalpa* theory of *āśramas*, namely the original *āśrama* system that we have already examined. In the above passage Kane explicitly equates the *Jābāla* view with that of Vasiṣṭha and Āpastamba, who present the original system. Elsewhere (Kane 1962, V.2, 1251) he says that "this option [i.e. that of the *Jābāla*] is referred to by Gautama [GDh 3.1]." In the original system, as we saw, the choice (*vikalpa*) extends to all the *āśramas*: after completing one's studies a person may choose any one of the four *āśramas*. This is quite different from the provision of the *Jābāla* passage. It is inaccurate, therefore, to lump the former and the latter together merely because there is an element of choice in both.

The modification proposed by the *Jābāla*, however, created a hermeneutical problem for medieval theologians, because it appeared to contradict the obligation to pay the triple debt. The payment of the debts, as we have seen, is explicitly stated by Manu

55. The general rule is also called *apūrvavidhi* or *utpattividhi*. The maxim states *utsargāpavādo balīyān*—"an exception has greater force than the rule." Cf. MK II, 1110. Thus the *vikalpa* with reference to renunciation is a *vyavasthitavikalpa* ("restricted option"), which, as we have seen (section 5.2), is not a true option at all.

(MDh 6.35–37) as a necessary precondition for renunciation. When a person renounces before marriage he fails to pay his debts. Indeed, the *Jābāla* passage explicitly states that it is unnecessary even to be initiated before one renounces.

Yādavaprakāśa[56] deals with this problem in the second chapter of his *Yatidharmasamuccaya*. He gives the two opposing positions, the one allowing renunciation only after one has lived as a hermit, and the other permitting it while one is still a student in the case of a person who is detached. Both positions are supported by authoritative texts. He rejects the attempt of some theologians to resolve the contradiction by interpreting the texts permitting renunciation before marriage as referring to people disqualified from marriage, such as the impotent. Yādava's solution is to interpret the vedic injunction regarding the payment of debts as referring to people who are not detached from this world. Such an obligation does not extend to those who are detached. Detached people, therefore, are permitted to renounce at any time, whereas those who are attached are obliged to pay the debts and spend some time as hermits before renouncing. Thus, according to Yādava, there is no contradiction, because the two injunctions are directed at two different types of people.[57]

Mādhava (PāM I, 532–33) likewise first presents the view of an opponent (*pūrvapakṣin*) who speaks against permitting renunciation before marriage, arguing that it would violate all the injunctions that require the payment of debts by every person. Mādhava's reply is identical to that of Yādava; such injunctions as well as the entire classical system of *āśrama*s are directed only at those who are not detached.[58]

Medhātithi addresses the problem in his commentary on MDh 6.36. His argument is somewhat convoluted, and he appears at a loss to reconcile Manu and the *Jābāla* text. Like Yādava, he first considers the argument that the *Jābāla* provision may refer to ritually handicapped people, such as the impotent, and dismisses it. Medhātithi's solution is to invoke a well-known hermeneutical principle regarding the morning oblation. When a text censures those who offer the morning oblation after sunrise, it merely intends to praise the offering before sunrise; it does not entail a prohibition of that offering after sunrise (see 6.1.3, n. 37). Applying this principle to Manu's requirement to pay the debts, Medhātithi sees it as censuring those who renounce without paying the debts merely to present the *samuccaya* position as the more praiseworthy. Thus the rule does not prohibit one from becoming a renouncer before one pays the debts and does not contradict the *Jābāla* passage.

The most thorough and interesting response, however, is given by the two commentators on Yājñavalkya, Aparāditya and Vijñāneśvara. The reasoning of these two

56. Yādavaprakāśa was an elder contemporary and teacher of the famous Śrī-Vaiṣṇava theologian Rāmānuja (traditional date 1017–1137 C.E.). Tradition has it that Rāmānuja converted his former teacher from a non-dualist form of Vedānta to his Viśiṣṭādvaita philosophy. Yādava's literary activities, therefore, must have taken place in the second half of the eleventh century C.E., since the *Yatidharmasamuccaya* by and large follows the Vaiṣṇava views on renunciation.

57. See my comments on *vyavasthā* ("limited reference") as a hermeneutical device in section 5.2.

58. Mādhava (PāM I, 459–60) offers the same argument against an opponent who says that permitting perpetual studentship amounts to an annulment of the householder's state. The householder's *āśrama* is enjoined, Mādhava says, only for those who entertain desires (*rāgin*).

authors, who were near contemporaries,[59] is identical. Kane (1975, I.2, 719–21) is probably right in concluding that Aparāditya used Vijñāneśvara's commentary, and a careful examination of the two passages indicates that Aparāditya has merely expanded on Vijñāneśvara's terse explanation.[60] I cite Vijñāneśvara, because he is probably older and certainly clearer. After stating that Yājñavalkya's (YDh 3.56–57) and Manu's verses on the debts (MDh 6.35) demonstrate that a householder who has paid his three debts is qualified to renounce, he remarks:

> The restrictive rule that one should beget offspring [before renouncing], however, does not apply when one renounces as a student, both because one who has not married a wife is not qualified to beget offspring and because marriage is prompted by desire. One should not think that the very rule enjoining the payment of the three debts implies a wife, because, just like the restrictive rule on acquiring wealth for the sake of knowledge, this too lacks such an implication since we find that men obtain wives for other reasons.[61]
>
> [OBJECTION] "A Brahmin, at his very birth, is born with a triple debt—of studentship to the seers, of sacrifice to the gods, of offspring to the fathers": does this text not demonstrate that begetting offspring and so forth become obligatory as soon as one is born?
>
> [REPLY] Surely not! For one is not qualified to perform sacrifices and the like as soon as one is born and before one has married a wife and established the sacred fires. The meaning of that text, therefore, is as follows: when a Brahmin and the like has become [lit. "born"][62] qualified he should perform sacrifices and so forth. Therefore, vedic study is indeed obligatory for a person who has undergone vedic initiation, as also the begetting of offspring for one who has married a wife and established the sacred fires. (YMtā 3.56–57)

Vijñāneśvara's explanation undercuts the force of the traditional argument based on the doctrine of debts. His main point is that a debt can accrue only to a person who has the capacity to pay it.[63] Otherwise it would lack any meaning, for then duties can be

59. Kane assigns Aparāditya to the first half of the twelfth century C.E. (1975, I.2, 721–723) and Vijñāneśvara to 1100–1120 C.E. (1975, I.2, 609).

60. Aparāditya's explanation looks clumsy compared to the clear and terse prose of Vijñāneśvara. The following explanations of the TS passage on debts shows how closely the former follows the latter. Vijñāneśvara: *tasmād adhikārī jāyamāno brāhmaṇādir yajñādīn anutiṣthed iti tasyārthaḥ*. Aparārka: *tasmād adhikārī jāyamāno brāhmaṇādis tribhir ṛṇavā jāyata iti vākyārthaḥ*. Vijñāneśvara's explanation is cited also by Vaidyanātha Dīkṣita in his *Smṛtimuktāphala*, Varṇāśramadharmakāṇḍa, pp. 172–73. A similar argument is presented in Maskarin's commentary on GDh 3.1 (p. 59).

61. What Vijñāneśvara wants to point out is that even though there are rules stating that a person should acquire wealth only in order to obtain knowledge—that is, to pay the teacher—people normally want wealth for many common reasons. Similarly, in spite of what the theory of debts may say, people get married for sexual pleasure.

62. Here Vijñāneśvara interprets *jāyamāna* ("being born") as referring not to a person's physical birth but his ritual birth into a condition which is defined by those ritual obligations.

63. Here Vijñāneśvara is following a hermeneutical principle clearly laid down in the PMS 6.2.21–22 that duties enjoined by the Veda are not applicable from the very birth of a person but only after he has undergone vedic initiation. For the Mīmāṃsā view of the three debts, see PMS 6.2.31.

imposed on anyone regardless of one's qualification or ability to fulfil them. Thus, according to Vijñāneśvara, the three debts are not generic obligations incumbent on all but are specific duties of certain people. The obligation to study extends to all who have been initiated, and the duties of procreation and sacrifice belong only to married householders. When a person decides to renounce at an early age, therefore, he does not violate the injunctions implied in the triple debt.[64]

64. Modern Indian law also appears to recognize the distinction between the two classes of people established by Vijñāneśvara: "It is necessary to examine the principles on which the obligatory character of the marriage ceremony rests. There are two paths laid down for the Hındu in the sacred texts. . . . One is the path of work or attachment to the things of this world and the other the path of non-attachment or renunciation. The four *āśrama*s or stages of life are prescribed for the regenerate classes. . . . The journey from stage to stage in regular order of succession is contemplated as progress along the path of worldly work. It is true . . . that if he has conquered his passions and cultivated the feeling of non-attachment he may pass directly . . . to the *āśrama* of the *sannyāsin*. . . . But except for him . . . the stage of householder is practically compulsory." Kameswara Sastri v. Veeracharlu—(1910) 34 Mad. 422, cited in Derrett 1968, 70. Derrett observes: "This distinction between *pravṛtti* and *nivṛtti* is not mere philosophy divorced from law."

7

The *Āśramas* and Other Brāhmaṇical Institutions

Although, as we shall see in the next chapter, debates and disputes continued to surround the *āśrama* system, nevertheless, by at least the middle of the first millennium C.E. the system had become fully integrated into and assumed a central position within the Brāhmaṇical world. Its centrality is evidenced by the increasing use of the expression *varṇāśramadharma* even in epigraphy, drama, and poetry[1] as a shorthand term for the totality of the Brāhmaṇical *dharma.* It was only natural, therefore, that the *āśrama* system came to be related to other aspects and institutions of that *dharma* within the theological discourse of Brāhmaṇism. In this chapter I examine these evolving relationships that permit us to gain further insights into both the history of the *āśrama* system and the development of Brāhmaṇical theology.

7.1 Gender and Āśrama

In spite of repeated attempts throughout Indian history to universalize and to ethicize *dharma*, the mainstream of Brāhmaṇical theology represented by Mīmāṃsā and Dharmaśāstra has continued to regard *dharma* as what Halbfass appropriately calls "positive law."[2] *Dharma* is positive law insofar as these laws are known not through reasoning and inference but through injunctions and prohibitions contained primarily in the authoritative and sacred texts of the Veda and derivatively in the Smṛtis. A central aspect of *dharma*, moreover, takes it further from a universal ethic: most rules of *dharma* are not generic but refer to specific groups or classes of people within society. Here we come to the concept of *svadharma*—that is, the *dharma* proper to a particular individual as defined by his or her group affiliation.

Within theological discourse, three major lines of group affiliation intersect in an individual at any given moment of his or her life: *varṇa*-caste, gender, and age group. *Dharma* in terms of age was at first related to the rites of passage (*saṃskāra*), but, after

1. See section 7.3.1. For evidence from Kālidāsa, see section 6.2.1.

2. Halbfass 1988, 332. Attempts to universalize *dharma* were made in the Buddhist and Jain traditions, but they are evident in Hindu-Brāhmaṇical works, and even in the Dharmaśāstras, as well. The essence of *dharma*, for example, has been reduced to "non-injury" (*ahiṃsā*) or to the "golden rule." For a more extensive study, see Halbfass 1988, 330–33.

the creation of the *āśrama* system, *āśrama*s came to define people's *svadharma* in terms of age. A significant question with respect to *dharma*, consequently, is the ways in which *svadharma* in terms of *āśrama* intersects *svadharma* related to *varṇa*-caste and gender. I shall turn to the question of *varṇa* in the next section and focus here on the relationship between *āśrama* and gender.

Women occupy an ambivalent and often contradictory position within the Brāhmaṇical theology of *dharma*. On the one hand, women play a central and indispensable role in the central acts of the Brāhmaṇical religion: sacrifice and procreation (2.1.1–2). There is also ample evidence that at least in the early period women participated in major Brāhmaṇical institutions, such as vedic initiation. On the other hand, Brāhmaṇical theology considers women never to be independent agents; in many respects their status is similar to that of children and Śūdras.

The history of Brāhmaṇical theology is a constant movement in the direction of an ever increasing restrictive ideology regarding the status and role of women. This movement is illustrated in the manner medieval authors interpret a well-known passage from the Dharmasūtra of Hārīta that permits vedic initiation and study for women:

> There are two types of women: those who become students of the Veda and those who marry immediately. Of these, the students of the Veda undergo initiation, kindle the sacred fire, study the Veda, and beg food in their own houses. In the case of those who marry immediately, however, when the time for marriage comes, their marriage should be performed after initiating them in some manner.[3]

Now the medieval authors who cite this passage uniformly dismiss it as referring to a previous age (*yuga*) and as inapplicable to the present age.[4] Even though there is plenty of evidence that women were initiated into vedic study during the period of the Gṛhyasūtras (roughly the second half of the first millennium B.C.E.), women were excluded from both initiation and vedic study during the classical and medieval periods (Kane 1974, II.1, 293–96).

Uninitiated and barred from studying the Veda, women are only marginally superior to Śūdras. The twice-born status of non-Śūdra women comes merely from their group affiliation, not from their ritual rebirth through vedic initiation. Their low theological status corresponds to the widely shared view that women are by nature prone to evil.[5] Already in the *Ṛgveda* women are said to have uncontrollable minds (RV 8.33.17) and to have the hearts of hyenas (RV 10.95.15). Women are put on a par with Śūdras, dogs, and crows: all embody falsehood, sin, and darkness (ŚB 14.1.1.31).

That women are never independent in regard to *dharma* is the main theological point

3. Cited by Devaṇṇabhaṭṭa (*Smṛticandrikā*, Varṇāśramadharmakāṇḍa, p. 24) and Kamalākarabhaṭṭa (*Nirṇayasindhu*, p. 200): *dvividhā striyo brahmavādinyaḥ sadyovadhvaś ca. tatra brahmavādinīnām upanayanam agnīndhanaṃ vedādhyayanaṃ svagṛhe ca bhikṣācaryeti. sadyovadhūnāṃ tu upasthite vivāhe kathaṃcid upanayanamātraṃ kṛtvā vivāhaḥ kāryaḥ.* For an extensive discussion of the status of women and for further sources, see Kane 1974, II.1, 293–96, 365–70.

4. See, for example, Mādhava (PāM I, 485), who cites a passage of Yama according to which women were initiated and studied the Veda in a former age. For a discussion of *yugadharma*, see section, 8.4.

5. On the changing status of women in Indian history, see Meyer 1930; Marglin 1985. Jaini (1991) brings together an interesting collection of Jaina documents on the debate regarding the ability of women to achieve liberation.

vis-à-vis women within the dharmaśāstric tradition.[6] The following verse has gained well-deserved notoriety, and its importance within the tradition is demonstrated by the fact that it is cited in most of the ancient Dharmaśāstras: "Her father guards her in her childhood; her husband guards her in her youth; and her sons guard her in her old age. A woman is not fit to act on her own."[7]

The Sanskrit term *rakṣati* has the meaning of both protection and guarding: women need to be protected from the outside and guarded against their own natural propensities. This dependence manifests itself at a variety of levels, the most obvious being that women are not independent ritual actors; they participate as co-actors in their husbands' rites (see section 2.1.1). It is evident, however, that the male guardianship of females is directed in a special way at their sexual life. A husband should guard his wife carefully, says an ancient Brāhmaṇa, "lest in my womb, in my world somebody else come into existence."[8] Unrestricted female sexuality has always been regarded as powerful and dangerous, not just to the husband but also to the community at large.

Recent anthropological studies[9] with regard to Hindu goddesses have highlighted interesting aspects of the Indian image of female sexuality. As Babb (1970b, 146–47) puts it: "Divinity appears to be manifest in two separate aspects, feminine and masculine, goddess and god. In general, masculine divinity seems to act as a restraining factor, while feminine divinity is a potentially destructive force which must be restrained." Thus, when a goddess is represented alone or in a position of authority over male divinities, she is a dangerous and often malevolent force.

> When the goddess is shown in her role of consort to her lord, this dangerous and sinister force is transformed into its opposite; the goddess becomes the tender wife, the source of wealth and progeny. When the goddess is placed in the context of a restraining social relationship, that is, in a relationship of marriage, she transforms herself into a benign force. (Marglin 1985, 43)

Marglin argues that it is not merely the single and independent status of the goddess, as Babb maintains, that makes her dangerous but her celibate status. In either case, it is clear that these images of divine female sexuality have sociological implications, for humans create gods and goddesses in their own image.[10] If celibate and independent

6. GDh 18.1: "A woman is not independent with regard to *dharma*"—*asvatantrā dharme strī*. See also VaDh 5.1–2; BDh 2.3.44–47. On the status of women in the dharmaśāstric tradition, see Kane 1974, II.1, 574–82.

7. MDh 9.3: *pitā rakṣati kaumāre bhartā rakṣati yauvane / rakṣanti sthavire putrā na strī svāntantryam arhati //* The verse is also found in VaDh 5.2; BDh 2.3.45; MBh 13.21.19; 13.46.13.

8. JB 1.17 (Bodewitz's translation). See section 2.1.2, n. 39. Āpastamba (ĀpDh 2.13.6) likewise cites a vedic text: "After his death the man who planted the seed carries off his son into Yama's world; fearful of another man's seed, therefore, they guard their wives. Take vigilant care over (the procreation of) your children, lest the seed of others be sown on your soil."

9. See Babb 1970a and 1970b; Marglin 1985.

10. I do recognize that theological discourse and ritual performance with regard to gods and goddesses cannot be simply transferred to the social sphere. The primacy of the goddess may coexist with suppression of women. Nevertheless, the theological and ritual expressions of the relationship between gods and goddesses especially within the context of marriage, I believe, reflect in some way the gender relations within society.

goddesses are dangerous, so are celibate and independent women. It is in this light that we need to understand the centrality that Brāhmaṇical theology gives to the marriage of women.

It is noteworthy that, with the exception of widowhood and pre-pubertal childhood, Brāhmaṇical theology does not recognize any celibate state for women. An adult woman has a single theological identity: she is wife-mother. Her identity and selfhood are thus derived from her relationships to males: husband and sons. Marriage, therefore, is the only institution that adult women are not only entitled but definitely obliged to assume. Women, the theologians assert ceaselessly, were created for procreating children; they are merely the fields in which men sow their seed.[11]

Ideally an adult woman is under the control of her husband, just as a benign Hindu goddess is subject to her divine consort. Her sexuality is placed at his service, resulting in the procreation of sons and the continuity of the family. As she has no sexual role apart from her husband, so she is never an independent religious actor. She is expected to perform all religious acts, even fasting and pilgrimages, with the approval of her husband. As one text puts it: "Women are not entitled to perform independently sacrifices, ancestral oblations, or even fasting, for they attain the worlds they desire solely by the obedient service of their husbands."[12] Serving the husband is thus the highest *dharma* of a woman, a duty that is epitomized in the institution of *satī*, where a woman remains united to her husband even in death. Within this ideology it would indeed be unthinkable that a woman would be allowed to—or, given the cultural context, even want to—reject marriage and the opportunity to have a husband and a family.

Ethnographic and literary evidence indicates that this theology of the woman was internalized by most—though certainly not all—women.[13] The poems of Bahiṇā Bāī studied by Feldhaus (1982) illustrate the plight of a woman who has internalized the Brāhmaṇical standpoint but still wishes to dedicate her life to god:

The Vedas cry, the Purāṇas shout
I was born with a woman's body—
how am I, now, to attain the Goal?
They're foolish, selfish, seductive, deceptive—
any link with a woman brings harm.

. . . .

I haven't the right to hear the Vedas.
I may not say "Om,"
I may not hear *mantras'* names.
I must not speak of these things with another.[14]

Feldhaus (1982, 594) points out that "Bahiṇā identifies service to a husband as the duty

11. See MDh 9.96; NSm 12.19.

12. *Mārkaṇḍeya Purāṇa,* 16.61: *nāsti strīṇāṃ pṛthag yajño na śrāddhaṃ nāpy upoṣitam / bhartṛśuśrūṣayaivaitā lokān iṣṭān vrajanti hi //.* For further references, see Kane 1974, II.1, 563–68, 577. For a detailed account of the duties of women (*strīdharma*), see Leslie 1989.

13. For evidence of women who rejected marriage and carved out independent religious lives, see Ramanujan 1973; Filliozat 1972; Goetz 1966; Ojha 1981. For further bibliography, see Feldhaus 1982.

14. Translation from Feldhaus 1982, 594.

of a woman, adherence to duty as the teaching of the Vedas, and disregard of the Vedas as the surest way to miss the ultimate Goal. Thus she cannot renounce the world; for her to do so would frustrate the very purpose of renouncing it." Bahiṇā thus decides to pursue her spiritual path through her wifely duties toward her husband:

> Keeping my proper duties in mind,
> I'll reach God by listening to the scriptures.
> I'll serve my husband—he's my god.
> My husband is the supreme Brahman itself.
> The holy water that has washed my husband's feet
> combines all holy waters in one.
> Without that water, nothing is of worth.
> The Goal is in serving my husband.
> In my husband alone is all my aim.
> If I have any other god but my husband,
> it will be as bad as killing a Brāhman.
> My husband's my guru; my husband's my way—
> this is my heart's true resolve.
> . . . .
> What beauty has flesh without breath,
> Or moonlight without the night?
> My husband's the soul; I'm the body.
> My husband is all my good.
> My husband's the water; I'm a fish in it.
> How can I survive?
> My husband's the sun; I'm its light.
> How can I be separated from him?[15]

The central duty, therefore, of a father toward his daughters is to get them married at the earliest possible opportunity. Already in the Gṛhyasūtras and the Dharmasūtras we find the injunction that girls should be given in marriage before they reach puberty.[16] A father who failed in this duty committed a sin. In a passage that illustrates the danger of female sexuality uncontrolled by marriage, Gautama (GDh 18.20) goes as far as to state that if her father fails to give her in marriage before three menstrual periods have passed, a girl may give herself in marriage to a man of her choice.

It is within this context of the Brāhmaṇical theology of women that we need to examine the relation between women and the *āśrama* system. The original formulation of the system, as we saw, established four voluntary religious institutions which could be chosen by a young adult male soon after he has completed his vedic education. If, as we saw (section 5.2), choice and voluntarism for men in the area of *dharma* was repugnant to Brāhmaṇical theology, they would have been unthinkable for women. None of the sources that presents the original *āśrama* system makes the slightest reference to women. Indeed, these sources do not consider women as eligible for either vedic initiation or vedic study, whereas the person who is qualified to choose an *āśrama* should

15. Translation from Feldhaus 1982, 597.

16. Such a girl is called by the technical term *nagnikā* or "naked," that is, a girl who could still go about naked. For an extensive discussion of the age of marriage for girls, see Kane 1974, II.1, 438–46.

have undergone initiation and completed his vedic study. The pronouns and adjectives that these sources use with reference to the person making the choice among the *āśramas*, moreover, are always masculine. In the original system all the *āśramas* except that of the householder were celibate, and we have seen how repugnant female celibacy was to Brāhmaṇical theology. We can say without the slightest hesitation that in the original formulation *āśramas* were considered as ways of life meant solely for adult males.

The situation is not much different when we come to the classical *āśrama* system. If anything, the theological status of women became even lower during the classical period, and Brāhmaṇical theologians would have frowned on any institution that affirmed female independence. Vedic studentship and renunciation were clearly celibate states; male students and renouncers were not attached to any woman. The rites of entry into these two institutions as well as that of the hermit also assume that the candidate is a male.

Marriage, on the other hand, is by its very nature an institution in which both the husband and the wife participate. As such one may be able to consider marriage as the entry into the second *āśrama* for a woman just as for a man. But this is a theological reasoning that, however logical it may appear to be, we do not find in the tradition, and it is highly unlikely that the married state of a woman would have been regarded in the Brāhmaṇical tradition as constituting an *āśrama.* At the most, a wife could be regarded as participating in her husband's *āśrama*, just as she participates in other religious actions of her husband.

The same is true in the case of the forest hermit, who in the classical system is permitted either to take his wife with him into the forest or to leave her behind under the protection of her sons. If she accompanies her husband she will participate in her husband's religious duties and imitate his mode of life. The *Mahābhārata,* as we have seen, contains an interesting example of wives insisting on participating in their husbands' religious life. When Pāṇḍu, after he is cursed to die at the time of sexual intercourse, decides to become a renouncer, his two wives, Kuntī and Mādrī, implore him not to do so: "For there are also other *āśramas*, O hero of the Bharatas, in which you can perform great austerities in the company of us, your two lawful wives" (MBh 1.110.26). But a woman's assuming the hermit's mode of life is dependent on her husband's will, and it is uncertain whether Brāhmaṇical theology would have in any case regarded that life of hers as an *āśrama.*

The four *āśramas* are regarded as paths (in the original system) or as a ladder (in the classical system) leading to the gods or to liberation. Especially in the classical system the *āśramas* are presented as a gradual but sure way to advance spiritually and to attain the final goal of human beings. By denying women this ladder of spiritual assent Brāhmaṇical theology clearly asserts the spiritual superiority of men.

So far we have examined the theology, because as I stated at the outset (sections 1.2.1 and 1.3.1) the *āśrama* system is primarily a theological construct. The fact that the system was envisaged exclusively for men does not necessarily mean that women did not participate in the social institutions comprehended by that system. We have seen above evidence of female vedic initiation and study during the ancient period. There is overwhelming evidence, furthermore, for the existence even within the Brāhmaṇical tradition of independent female ascetics.

At a very early period in their history Buddhism and Jainism established monastic orders for women parallel to those for men. Early Sanskrit grammatical literature records several names for female ascetics, although it is unclear whether such references imply a recognition of the legitimacy of female asceticism on the part of the Brāhmaṇical elite.[17] The Dharmaśāstras themselves refer to female ascetics frequently, often without condemnation. Thus Vasiṣṭha (VaDh 19.29–34) says that when a king dies the new king should maintain the wives of the deceased monarch. If, however, the wives do not wish to live under his protection, Vasiṣṭha permits them to become ascetics.[18]

Other legal texts take into account female ascetics in enunciating the criminal law. Sexual intercourse with female ascetics, for example, is considered a crime, even though its severity was judged differently by different writers depending in all likelihood on the contemporary status of female ascetics. Thus Manu (MDh 8.363), Yājñavalkya (YDh 2.293), and even the *Arthaśāstra* (Artha 4.13.36) impose a small fine, whereas Viṣṇu (ViDh 36.7) and Nārada (NSm12.73–74) consider sexual intercourse with a female ascetic as a crime equal to violating the teacher's bed. The evidence of the *Arthaśāstra*, which advises the king to use female ascetics for a variety of political purposes including secret agents and spies, suggests that such ascetics were a common phenomenon in ancient Indian society.[19] One passage (Artha 1.12.4–5) explicitly states that these female ascetics were Brahmins.

The *Mahābhārata* contains several references to both female renouncers and female hermits; the contexts make it clear that these female ascetics were considered to have been broadly within the Brāhmaṇical tradition. The most celebrated of such female renouncers is Sulabhā, who entered into a debate on the superiority of asceticism over home life with the famous king Janaka (MBh 12.308). Sulabhā is clearly recognized in the story as a Brāhmaṇical ascetic carrying a tripod and well-versed in philosophy and yoga. Then there is the story of Ambā, rejected both by her captor, Bhīṣma, and her suitor, Śālva. She decides to become a hermit to perform *tapas* and, going to a hermitage, she asks the hermits to do her a favor: "I want to go forth. I shall practice severe austerities."[20] What is significant here is that Ambā's decision is her own, and she requests to be initiated into asceticism as a single woman and not as the wife of a man who intends to become a hermit. Another female hermit named Śabarī is celebrated in the *Rāmāyaṇa* (1.1.46; 3.69–70) as a great disciple of the sage Mataṅga. The *Mahābhārata* likewise records instances where wives go to the forest and become hermits after the death of their husbands.[21]

17. The *Gaṇapāṭha* (233 on Pāṇini 2.1.70) mentions *śramaṇā, pravrajitā,* and *tāpasī.* Patāñjali (on Pāṇini 3.2.14) uses the term *parivrājakā* to refer to a female renouncer named Śaṃkarā.

18. The Sanskrit reads *anicchantyo vā pravrajeran*—"those who do not wish may depart." In all likelihood the verb *pra√vraj* is used here in its technical meaning of "going forth from home as a wandering ascetic."

19. For further information on ascetics and asceticism in the *Arthaśāstra*, see Olivelle 1987.

20. MBh 5.173.14: *pravārjitum ihecchāmi tapas tapsyāmi duścaram /* Here again the technical term for ascetic initiation—*pra√vraj*—is used, making it clear that she desired formal initiation into the hermit's way of life.

21. Thus, after the death of King Pāṇḍu, his wife, Satyavatī, and her two daughters-in-law became hermits (MBh 1.119.11). After Kṛṣṇa's death, likewise, his wives departed to the forest (MBh 16.8.72). See also Kālidāsa, *Kumārasaṃbhava*, 5.20, 42, 44.

Now, these literary references do not necessarily demonstrate the historical reality of such female ascetics. What they do demonstrate is that at least within some segments of the Brāhmaṇical tradition female asceticism was recognized as both legitimate and praiseworthy and that such women could choose to become ascetics on their own and not at the behest of their husbands.

Such independent and celibate modes of life for women, however, never came to be integrated into the *āśrama* system. The one instance in which a Brāhmaṇical authority appears to suggest that the renunciation of women constitutes an *āśrama* is in Vijñāneśvara's commentary on Yājñavalkya (YDh 3.58). Vijñāneśvara interprets the expression "delighting in solitude" (*ekārāma*) to mean that a renouncer should not have female renouncers or other women as companions. He goes on to cite the following *sūtra* from Baudhāyana that permits even women to renounce: "Some (teachers permit renunciation) also for women."[22] This statement is made within the context of the discussion of the fourth *āśrama*, and it may well be that Vijñāneśvara recognized female renunciation as an *āśrama*. Yet, even here there is no explicit statement of that recognition.

Sarvajñanārāyaṇa, however, in his commentary on MDh 6.97 records an interesting opinion of some according to whom the entire *āśrama* system is open also to women. They also cite the above *sūtra* of Baudhāyana as the scriptural basis for their position and interpret the masculine *brāhmaṇasya* ("for a Brahmin") in Manu's verse as a synecdoche meant to include also the feminine.

The medieval theologian Vidyāraṇya attempts a compromise by distinguishing between renunciation preceded by the appropriate ritual which alone constitutes the corresponding *āśrama* and the abandonment of activities prompted by desire. According to Vidyāraṇya, all scriptural references to female renouncers should be interpreted as pertaining to the latter type of informal asceticism (JMV, p. 4).

7.2 *Varṇa* and *Āśrama*

Given that the very essence of the Brāhmaṇical *dharma* came to be defined as *varṇāśramadharma*, it is no surprise that the theological relationship between these two central institutions became a point of discussion and controversy. The controversy centers on the qualification or eligibility (*adhikāra*) for assuming the modes of life considered *āśramas*. Are all people qualified to enter the *āśramas* or only those belonging to particular *varṇas*? Are people of a particular *varṇa* qualified to enter all the *āśramas* or only some? In other words, are the four *āśramas* distributed in some way among the four *varṇas*? These are the questions that Brāhmaṇical theology wrestled with, and there was no unanimity either in the way the questions were framed or in the way they were resolved.

The issue of the relation between the *āśrama* and *varṇa* systems is not addressed explicitly in the Dharmasūtras. These documents, however, present the original formu-

22. Vijñāneśvara on YDh 3.58: *ekārāmaḥ pravrajitāntareṇāsahāyaḥ saṃnyāsinībhiḥ strībhiś ca*, "*strīṇāṃ caike*" *iti baudhāyanena strīṇām api pravrajyāsmaraṇāt*. This *sūtra* is not found in the extant version of the BDh. Nandapaṇḍita (on ViDh 25.14) also cites this *sūtra* but restricts its application to widows.

lation of the *āśrama* system, within which, as we have seen, the *āśramas* are regarded as adult vocations chosen by a young adult male soon after he has completed his vedic education. Now, the same documents restrict vedic initiation and study to males belonging to the first three *varṇas*, namely Brahmins, Kṣatriyas, and Vaiśyas. It is fair to assume, therefore, that the proponents of the original *āśrama* system presented it as a scheme for the three twice-born *varṇas*. A question that looms large in later discussions, namely whether all twice-born males are entitled to enter all the *āśramas*, is not raised in the documents of the early period. It is clear, however, that Śūdras and other lower social classes were at least implicitly excluded from the system.

The picture does not change radically in the classical period when the *āśramas* came to be regarded as stages of an individual's life. The Dharmaśāstras of Manu, the earliest representative of this period, Yājñavalkya, and Viṣṇu, just like their predecessors of the earlier period, do not address the question explicitly. The classical system, however, envisages an orderly passage from one *āśrama* to the next. Now, the first stage in this process is vedic studentship preceded by the rite of initiation, restricting that stage to males of the twice-born *varṇas*. As an individual should be in the first stage prior to entering the second, all the *āśramas* would be necessarily restricted to twice-born men. There is nothing in Manu or the treatises of Yājñavalkya and Viṣṇu to contradict such a conclusion.[23]

The relationship between *āśramas* and *varṇas* is addressed explicitly for the first time in the *Vaikhānasa Dharmasūtra*. In the very opening section, after enumerating the four *varṇas* and describing the duties and occupations of each, the author declares: "(All) four *āśramas* are meant for a Brahmin, the first three for a Kṣatriya, and just two for a Vaiśya."[24] Two important points are made here: the rule, on the one hand, restricts renunciation to Brahmins (see section 7.2.2) and, on the other, excludes Vaiśyas from both the ascetical institutions comprehended by the final two *āśramas*. Śūdras, significantly, are completely left out of the enumeration. Both Farquhar (1925, 480–81) and Winternitz (1926, 224) have overlooked this omission and ascribed to the *Vaikhānasa* the theory found in later literature that there is just one *āśrama* for Śūdras, namely that of the householder. The *Vaikhānasa* itself makes no such claim. It appears that the author of the *Vaikhānasa*, just like the authors of the other Dharmaśāstras, is making a clear distinction between the *āśrama* of a householder and the social institution of marriage.[25] Śūdras, no doubt, got married and led family lives. Yet that household life of theirs was not considered an *āśrama* by these authors.

The relation between *varṇa* and *āśrama* is made even closer in some of the Purāṇas according to which both institutions were established at the beginning of creation as part

23. I shall discuss later the problem created by the occasional use of *brāhmaṇa* and *dvijottama* ("highest of the twice-born") with reference to the last *āśrama*, renunciation: see section 7.2.2.

24. VaiDh 1.1: *brāhmaṇasyāśramāś catvāraḥ kṣatriyasyādyās trayo vaiśyasya dvāv eva*. In all likelihood the two *āśramas* of a Vaiśya are the first two. The *Mahābhārata* (12.61.1–2; 12.62.2) also asserts that the four *āśramas* are meant only for Brahmins.

25. This implicit recognition by native theologians of the distinction between the *āśramas* and the corresponding social institutions reinforces my claim that *āśramas* should be viewed primarily as theological constructs (see section 1.2.1). This distinction, as we shall see, will become gradually eroded in medieval theology.

of the creative act. Thus the *Kūrma Purāṇa* (1.2.39) states: "Then, after he had instituted the *varṇas*, he established the *āśramas*: householder, forest hermit, mendicant, and student." The clearest statement regarding the common origin of the *āśrama* and *varṇa* systems is found in the *Bhāgavata Purāṇa* (11.17.13–15):

> From the mouth, arms, thighs, and feet of Virāṭ-Puruṣa were born the Brahmin, the Kṣatriya, the Vaiśya, and the Śūdra, respectively, each with his own special conduct. From my loins was born the householder's *āśrama*, from my heart the state of a student, and from my chest the forest life; renunciation abides in my head. The natural propensities of people are in accord with the place from which their respective *varṇas* and *āśramas* originated.

This statement harks back to the Puruṣa hymn of the *Ṛgveda* (10.90), which describes the origin of the *varṇas* from the dismembered body of Puruṣa, the primordial sacrificial victim. If the *varṇas* and the *āśramas* originate from different parts of the creator's body, it is easy to see that there could be a stricter connection between a *varṇa* and an *āśrama* that originate from the same or similar parts.

The symmetrical relationship between the *varṇas* and the *āśramas* is most clearly established in the *Vāmana Purāṇa*. It states that "undertaking the four *āśramas* is enjoined *only* on Brahmins."[26] The expression *brāhmaṇasyāpi* may also mean "also for Brahmins," but in the light of what the *Vāmana* says in the next chapter it is clear that the term *api* in the present context is used in an exclusive sense to mean "only." Indeed, in the very next chapter the *Vāmana* (15.62–63) distributes the *āśramas* among the other three *varṇas*: three for Kṣatriyas, two for Vaiśyas, and one for Śūdras. We thus have the following symmetrical distribution of the four *āśramas* among the four *varṇas*:

Brahmin:	Householder, Hermit, Student, Renouncer.
Kṣatriya:	Householder, Hermit, Student.
Vaiśya:	Householder, Hermit.
Śūdra:	Householder.

It is interesting and somewhat anomalous that this scheme does not permit Vaiśyas to become vedic students.[27] This prohibition contradicts the provisions of all the treatises on *dharma* as well as what the *Vāmana* itself states in other parts of the text. Even more significant, however, is the provision that recognizes the married status of a Śūdra as an *āśrama.*[28] Here we have the final identification of the social institution, namely married life, with its theological appropriation as *āśrama.*

7.2.1 Status of the Śūdras

Mādhava, the fourteenth-century theologian, cites the above passage of the *Vāmana* and a verse ascribed to Yogi-Yājñavalkya that distributes the *āśramas* among the *varṇas* in a

26. VāmP 14.2: *brāhmaṇasyāpi vihitā cāturāśramyakalpanā.* The very next verse also speaks of "the four *āśramas* of Brahmins" (*viprāṇāṃ cāturāśramyam*).

27. For possible economic reasons why Vaiśyas and Śūdras may have been forbidden to become ascetics in the early middle ages, see section 7.2.2.

28. A similar statement is made by Sarvajñanārāyaṇa in his commentary on MDh 6.97.

manner similar to the *Vāmana:* "The Veda has enjoined four *āśramas* on Brahmins, three on Kṣatriyas, two on Vaiśyas, and one on Śūdras," even though here the *āśramas* belonging to the latter three are not specified. Mādhava then undertakes a discussion about the legitimacy of assigning an *āśrama* to Śūdras by first presenting a possible objection:

> "For Śūdras, surely, there is no *āśrama* at all, because of the prohibition: 'There are four *āśramas*, my dear, but Śūdras are not entitled to them.' So how can they assume the state of a householder?"
>
> I respond: only that form of marriage is forbidden to them which uses mantras, not the form that is performed without mantras. Otherwise, the statements referring to Śūdras that have been cited in the section on marriage[29] as well as the statements that acknowledge the qualification of Śūdras for performing the duties incumbent on householders, such as the five great sacrifices, would stand contradicted. Therefore, Śudras are indeed entitled to the householder's life.

If we examine this passage carefully, it becomes evident that both Mādhava and his putative opponent take one thing for granted: both assume that married life coincides with the householder's *āśrama.* The opponent works under the assumption that the exclusion of Śūdras from the *āśrama* system results in their inability to get married. Mādhava, on the other hand, deduces their inclusion within the system by the fact they are permitted to get married. We see here the unmistakable identification of the social institution of marriage with the corresponding *āśrama.*

Even though Brāhmaṇical theology generally accepted the legitimacy of Śūdra marriage either within or outside the *āśrama* structure, Śūdras were clearly excluded from the first *āśrama,* while there was a deep controversy with regard to the legitimacy of Śūdras' becoming hermits or renouncers.[30] Even outside the context of the *āśrama* system, however, there was a widespread abhorrence among Brāhmaṇical theologians at the very thought of Śūdras even hearing the Vedas by accident, let alone learning them deliberately. It is forbidden to recite the Vedas in the vicinity of Śūdras.[31] Gautama (GDh 12.4) goes as far as to state that molten lead should be poured into the ears of a Śūdra who listens to the Veda! It comes as no surprise, therefore, that there is unanimity among Brāhmaṇical authors in excluding Śūdras from vedic initiation and vedic study, that is, from the *āśrama* of a student.

The widespread belief that Śūdras should not assume any sort of ascetic life style is echoed in an episode of the *Rāmāyaṇa* (7.64–67). When the young son of a Brahmin dies in his kingdom, Nārada informs Rāma of the cause of that unfortunate event. There is a Śūdra practicing penance in Rāma's kingdom. Rāma sets out to find that evil Śūdra and finds an ascetic named Śambūka practicing austerities and hanging upside down from a tree. He tells Rāma that he is a Śūdra aspiring to become a god through penance. While he is still speaking Rāma beheads him![32] Sources repeatedly state that the practicing of

29. See, for example, PāM I, 485–87.

30. On the position of Śūdra within Brāhmaṇical *dharma* and their disabilities, see Kane 1974, II.1, 154–64.

31. See GDh 16.19; ĀpDh 1.9.9; VaDh 18.11–15; MDh 4.99; YDh 1.148; Śabara on PMS 6.1.38.

32. Rām 7.67.2–4. See also Kālidāsa, *Raghuvaṃśa,* 15.49–50; Bhavabhūti, *Uttararāmacarita,* 2.8.

austerities by Śūdras is a sure sign of the Kali age.[33] Practicing austerities and becoming renouncers are listed among the six practices that cause the downfall of Śūdras and women.[34] In the *Mahābhārata* (13.150.*692) a Śūdra confesses: "I am a Śūdra, and I am not entitled to follow the four *āśramas*."

A more liberal attitude toward Śūdra asceticism is taken in another passage of the *Mahābhārata*:

> All the *āśramas*, O king, except the one entailing indifference [i.e., renunciation], are prescribed for a Śūdra who has completed his duty of service, who has produced offspring, and who has only a few years to live or has reached the tenth decade [i.e., 90th year], after he has received the permission of the king.

Likewise, it is stated that the body of Vidura, a Śūdra, should not be cremated because he was a renouncer (MBh 15.33.31–32).

Two medieval commentators take diametrically opposite views in interpreting these two texts, indicating the disagreements on this question that persisted even in the medieval period. Medhātithi (ninth to tenth centuries C.E.), commenting on Manu (MDh 6.97) interprets the first passage to mean that Śūdras do not actually assume the *āśramas* but only obtain their fruits by their lifelong service:

> All the *āśramas*, nevertheless, are not to be assumed (actually by a Śūdra). On the contrary, by service and by begetting offspring he obtains the fruits of all the *āśramas*. By living as a householder while serving twice-born people he obtains the fruits of all the *āśramas*, with the exception of liberation, which is the fruit of renunciation.

Nīlakaṇṭha, the seventeenth-century commentator of the *Mahābhārata*, on the other hand, interprets the episode of Vidura forthrightly, saying: "This shows that the renouncer's *dharma* is open even to those who are born from a Śūdra womb."[35]

In the case of Śūdras, as with women, we must distinguish the issue of legitimacy in the eyes of theology from legality and historical fact.[36] Most, if not all, Brāhmaṇical authorities consider the asceticism of Śūdras as illegitimate and, as exemplified in the episode of Rāma's beheading of Śambūka, attempt to co-opt the civil authority to enforce that rule.[37] There is ample historical evidence, however, to show that Śūdras and low-caste people in general did become ascetics and that their ascetic status was recognized by the civil authority.[38]

33. See *Brahmāṇḍa Purāṇa*, 1.31.60.

34. See *Atri Smṛti*, 136–37.

35. Nīlakaṇṭha on MBh 15.33.31–32: *śūdrayonau jātānām api yatidharmo 'stīti darśitam.* Kane (1974, II.1, 163) fails to note these dissenting voices of the tradition when he asserts that only the householder's *āśrama* was open to Śūdras.

36. The inability or unwillingness to distinguish these issues has led to much confusion. See, for example, Kane 1974, II.2, 942–46; Chakraborti 1973, 90–99; Sharma 1939, 63–64.

37. A passage ascribed to Kātyāyana, for example, advises the king to punish a Śūdra who takes to renunciation (*Kātyāyanasmṛti*, 486). For a discussion of this passage, see Olivelle 1984, 114.

38. Buddhist sources (e.g., DN II, 35–36) record that low-caste people were permitted to become monks. Rhys Davids (tr. of DN, II, p. 103) observes: "We have seen how in the *Sāmaññaphala Sutta*, it is taken for granted that a slave could join an Order (that is any Order, not only the Buddhist). And in the *Aggañña Sutta* of the Dīgha and the *Madhurā Sutta* of the Majjhima, there is express mention of the

Evidence of Śūdra asceticism is found in the Dharmaśāstras themselves. Viṣṇu (5.115) and Yājñavalkya (2.235) impose a fine on anyone who feeds a Śūdra renouncer (*śūdrapravrajita*) at a feast for gods or manes. The *Arthaśāstra* (3.20.16) likewise imposes a fine for feeding a *vṛṣalapravrajita* ("Śūdra or outcaste renouncer"), as well as Buddhist and Ājīvika ascetics, at such functions. While the *Arthaśāstra* here distinguishes Śūdra renouncers from ascetics belonging to Buddhist and other heretical sects, there is a tendency in the Dharmaśāstras to group together all these ascetics, because their position within *dharma* is similar. This general class of renouncers may be intended by Āpastamba (1.18.31) when he lists "one who has improperly renounced" (*avidhinā ca pravrajitaḥ*) among people whose food is not to be eaten. This rule implies that people did become ascetics without keeping to the śāstric provisions and that such ascetics were generally tolerated by the civil authority.[39]

7.2.2 Varṇa *and Renunciation*

In medieval theology the debate regarding the relationship between *āśramas* and *varṇas* focused principally on the question whether people of all three upper *varṇas* or only Brahmins were permitted to renounce, that is, to enter the last *āśrama*. Theologians on both sides of the issue could cite vedic and smṛti texts in support of both positions and invoke Mīmāṃsā rules of interpretation to explain away the texts apparently supporting the opponents' position.

We have seen that both the *Vaikhānasa Smārtasūtra* and several passages in didactic portions of the *Mahābhārata* explicitly restrict renunciation to Brahmins.[40] Earlier dharmaśāstric texts, however, do not address this issue explicitly. They use both the generic term *dvija* ("twice-born") as well as *brāhmaṇa* and *dvijottama* ("highest of the twice-born") that refer specifically to Brahmins when they talk about renouncers. Later writers will find this a fertile ground for the exercise of their hermeneutical skills. Historically, however, it is unlikely that these authors would not have been more explicit if this had been a question of significance to them. My own view is that in the earlier period (at least up to Manu and Yājñavalkya) the central institutions of *dharma*, such as sacrifice, sacraments, and *āśramas*, were considered open at least theoretically to all twice-born *varṇas*. This is supported by the writings of Kālidāsa, who, without attempting to prove a point, accepts without argument that renunciation is open to kings. He characterizes the lineage of Raghus as devoted to following the four *āśramas* during the

---

Śūdras becoming Samaṇas as if it were a recognized and common occurrence, long before the time of the rise of Buddhism. So in the Jātakas (iii, 381) we hear of a potter, and at iv, 392, of a Caṇḍāla, who became Samaṇas (not Buddhist Samaṇas)." The Buddhist monastic law (Vin I, 76), however, forbids entry of slaves and debtors into the order. Jaina sources also state that a low-caste person who becomes a renouncer is honored by the king: Uttarādhyanana, ch. 12 (in Jaina Sūtras, II, 50–56).

39. On the legality of a Śūdra's renunciation in modern Indian law, see Kane 1974, II.2, 952.

40. Besides the passages already cited, there are numerous texts in the *Mahābhārata* that declare religious mendicancy to be the special *dharma* of Brahmins: 3.34.49–50; 5.71.3. One of the central arguments of the Pāṇḍava brothers and others in their attempt to convince Yudhiṣṭhira that he should not take to renunciation after his victory in battle is that renunciation and mendicancy are for Brahmins, while the duty of Kṣatriyas is to rule justly and to die in battle: MBh 12.10–25.

four stages of life (*Raghuvaṃśa*, 1.8). After abandoning his kingdom, Raghu "resorted to the last *āśrama*," and he is referred to as *yati* ("renouncer": *Raghuvaṃśa*, 8.14, 16).[41]

Even though asceticism may have been open to all twice-born males, the impression one gets from the ancient documents is that it was increasingly associated with Brahmins. Thus when Sītā sees Rāvaṇa dressed as a mendicant ascetic she immediately assumes that he is a Brahmin.[42] The rite of renunciation also, in prescribing the abandonment of the sacrificial string and the top knot, assumes that the candidate is a Brahmin. We may not be far wrong in concluding, therefore, that at least by the fourth or fifth century C.E. within some segments of the Brāhmaṇical tradition an opinion arose that favored limiting access to the final *āśrama* to Brahmins.

Evidence indicates that the latter view gained increasing acceptance over time. The vast majority of prominent medieval writers, beginning at least with the Advaita theologian Śaṃkara (eithth to ninth century C.E.), support the position restricting renunciation to Brahmin males. Śaṃkara, commenting on the use of the word *brāhmaṇa* in the *Bṛhadāraṇyaka Upaniṣad* with reference to religious mendicancy, enunciates this position in the clearest possible terms: "The word 'Brahmins' is used because Brahmins alone possess the qualification for abandonment."[43] Later in the same commentary, Śaṃkara restates this position. In an extended argument aimed at demonstrating that vedic and smṛti statements enjoining lifelong performance of rites and, consequently, the life of a householder, are not intended to forbid renunciation[44] he claims that such statements refer to Kṣatriyas and Vaiśyas who are not entitled to renounce:

> Or, the vedic statement on the lifelong (performance of rites) is made with reference to other *varṇas*, for renunciation is not acknowledged for Kṣatriyas and Vaiśyas; likewise, passages such as, "[Know that no person other than one for whom the sacramentary rites beginning with impregnation and ending with the funeral] are prescribed to be performed with the recitation of mantras [is entitled to study this treatise]" (MDh 2.16), and "But the Venerable Teacher (prescribes) a single *āśrama*,"[45] refer to Kṣatriyas and Vaiśyas.[46]

Now, it does seem rather strange that Śaṃkara, of all people, should espouse such a view. After all, his entire argument for the legitimacy of the celibate *āśramas* in general

41. Medieval authors cite Kālidāsa as an authority in asserting the right of all twice-born people to become renouncers: see Mallinātha's commentary on *Raghuvaṃśa*, 8.14, and Vāsudevāśrama, *Yatidharmaprakāśa*, 3.36–45.

42. Rām 3.44.2–33; 3.45.1–2. Here we see that the author uses the term *dvijāti* ("twice-born") as a synonym for a Brahmin, a practice that becomes common in the *dharma* literature. See also Bhāsa, *Pratimānāṭaka*, 5.6–9, where Rāvaṇa reminds himself that he should adopt the etiquette of a Brahmin.

43. Śaṃkara's commentary on BāU 3.5.1, p. 454: *brāhmaṇānām evādhikāro vyutthāne 'to brāhmaṇagrahaṇam*. Śaṃkara takes *vyutthāna* ("rising above" or "abandoning") as a technical term for the renunciation of a person who has recognized his identity with Brahman: see his commentary on BāU 4.5.15 (pp. 716–17).

44. For an analysis of this and other arguments of Śaṃkara against those who denied the legitimacy of celibate *āśramas*, see section 8.5.

45. GDh 3.36: see section 3.2.1.1.

46. Śaṃkara on BāU 4.5.15 (p. 725): *itaravarṇāpekṣayā vā yāvajjīvaśrutiḥ. na hi kṣatriyavaiśyayoḥ pārivrājyapratipattir asti. tathā mantrair yasyodito vidhiḥ, aikāśramyaṃ tv ācāryā ityevamādīnāṃ kṣatriyavaiśyāpekṣatvam.*

and the renouncer's *āśrama* in particular is based on the neat division of people into those who are either enlightened or aspire to enlightenment and those who are ignorant. By limiting renunciation to Brahmins, Śaṃkara has in effect restricted enlightenment and even the aspiration to enlightenment to Brahmins. Commenting on the *Bṛhadāraṇyaka* 4.4.22, furthermore, Śaṃkara acknowledges that people of all three *varṇas* do indeed desire to know Brahman and interprets the term "Brahmins" occurring in that passage as a synecdoche encompassing all three *varṇas*.[47]

Śaṃkara's pro-Brahmin stand comes out clearly in his commentary on the *Bhagavad Gītā*. In his introductory remarks, Śaṃkara observes that the Lord became incarnate in order to protect "the Brahmin state," because only by protecting it can one guard the vedic *dharma*. He reiterates this position in commenting on BhG 4.1: the Kṣatriyas are made strong so as to protect the Brahmins. He explains that Arjuna's decision not to fight was wrong because he gave up war, which is the *dharma* proper to him (*svadharma*) as a Kṣatriya, and desired to undertake a *dharma* of someone else (*paradharma*) consisting of mendicancy and the like (on BhG 2.10). Here it is clear that Śaṃkara interprets the episode to mean that Arjuna wants to give up war and become a renouncer and that Śaṃkara finds this reprehensible because Arjuna was attempting to adopt the *dharma* of Brahmins. Again in his introductory remarks on chapter three, Śaṃkara asserts that the reason Krisṇa enjoins the path of action on Arjuna is because as a Kṣatriya he is not entitled to embark on the path of knowledge that entails renunciation.

It is also somewhat surprising that Śaṃkara takes this stand only in the commentary on the *Bṛhadāraṇyaka* and the *Gītā*. As far as I can tell, he does not broach the subject in the relevant sections of his commentaries on the *Brahmasūtras* or the *Chāndogya Upaniṣad*.[48]

That this was the view of Śaṃkara, however, is confirmed by the fact that his pupil, Sureśvara, in his subcommentary on Śaṃkara's commentary on the *Bṛhadāraṇyaka*, clearly ascribes this position to his teacher. Sureśvara himself disagrees with Śaṃkara and attempts to demonstrate that his teacher is wrong:

> Since renunciation is mentioned in the Vedas for all three *varṇas*, the statement of the commentary that renunciation is only for Brahmins stands contradicted.[49]
>
> As the Vedas prescribe renunciation equally for the three *varṇas*, the term "Brahmin" should be taken as a synecdoche. If it be admitted that knowledge annihilates a person's qualification for rites, on what authority does one forcibly restrict the qualifica-

47. The root text reads: "Brahmins seek to know him by the study of the Veda, by sacrifices, by gifts, by austerities, and by fasting." Śaṃkara comments (p. 688): "The term 'Brahmins' is meant as a synecdoche, for all three *varṇas* have equal qualification." For a more detailed study of Śaṃkara's contradictory positions, see section 8.2.

48. These works are generally assumed to have been authored by Śaṃkara: see Potter 1982, 111–13. The commentary on the *Chāndogya*, however, has not been subjected to the same scrutiny as the rest (see section 8.2, n. 17). In the *Upadeśasāhasrī* (I.2, 10, 13, 15), another probably authentic work of Śaṃkara, it is assumed that the qualified pupil is both a Paramahaṃsa renouncer and a Brahmin, but renunciation or the acquisition of knowledge is not explicitly denied to members of other *varṇas*.

49. Sureśvara, *Bṛhadāraṇyakopaniṣadbhāṣyavārtika*, p. 758, v. 1651: *trayāṇām api varṇānāṃ śrutau saṃnyāsadarśanāt / brāhmaṇasaiva saṃnyāsa iti bhāṣyaṃ virudhyate //*

> tion to renounce? If one is able to renounce when one acquires the knowledge of one's true identity, then whoever has that knowledge should be entitled to renounce.[50]

The fundamental principle of Śaṃkara's theology is that rites are within the province of ignorance and that it is as impossible for rites and knowledge to coexist as it is for knowledge and ignorance, or light and darkness. Sureśvara has taken this teaching of his guru to its logical conclusion by acknowledging that any person who has the knowledge of Brahman has the capacity and qualification to renounce, for otherwise such a person would find himself in the anomalous situation of being in an *āśrama* which requires him to perform rites while his qualification to perform them has been cancelled by his knowledge of Brahman. Logical conclusions, however, are not always the norm in theological discourse, and Sureśvara himself would hardly have defended the capacity of Śūdras and women to attain knowledge and to become renouncers.

Among medieval theologians Sureśvara is in the minority. Of the commentators of Manu, for example, all except four[51] interpret Manu as restricting renunciation to Brahmins. Medhātithi dismisses the opinion that Manu's occasional use of "Brahmin" should be taken as a synecdoche, especially in the light of his use of the generic "twice-born" in the opening verse of his chapter on renunciation (MDh 6.1). Instead, he argues that the generic "twice-born" should be understood in the light of the meaning of the entire chapter:

> The meaning we settle upon is that derived from a thorough examination of the entire passage. The term "twice-born," therefore, should be taken in a restrictive sense as referring to a Brahmin, for every Brahmin is a twice-born whereas not all twice-born are Brahmins. Given that even in this sentence the literal meaning of "twice-born" is applicable, it is improper to resort to an indirect meaning with regard to their syntactical connection.[52]

Although Medhātithi's argument for taking "twice-born" as referring only to Brahmins is somewhat farfetched—indeed, it is more usual to interpret "Brahmin" as referring to all twice-born—nevertheless, his position highlights the fact the dharmaśāstric works were written by and for Brahmins. As Biardeau (Biardeau and Malamoud 1976, 32) has observed: "Une lecture attentive des premiers chapitres de la *Manu-smṛti*, par

50. Ibid, on II.5.1: *trayāṇām aviśeṣeṇa saṃnyāsaḥ śrūyate śrutau / yadopalakṣaṇārthaṃ syād brāhmaṇagrahaṇaṃ tadā // karmādhikāravicchedi jñānaṃ ced abhyupeyate / kuto 'dhikāraniyamo vyutthāne kriyate balāt // pratyagyāthātmyavijñānasvabhāvaś cet samarthyate / vyutthānaṃ yasya yasya syāt sa sa vyutthātum arhati //*

51. These four—Bhāruci, Rāghavānanda, Nandana, and Maṇirāma—do not take up this issue. Medhātithi (on 6.97), Govindarāja (on 6.97), Kullūka (on 6.97), Sarvajñanārāyaṇa (on 6.38, 97), and Rāmacandra (on 6.38) understand Manu as permitting renunciation only for Brahmins.

52. "In this sentence" refers to MDh 6.97 where the term Brahmin is used. The argument presupposes that the entire chapter forms a single syntactical unit with a single meaning. The opponent wants to interpret "Brahmin" in the last sentence to mean the same as "twice-born" in the first, whereas Medhātithi wants to do the opposite. It is a common interpretive rule that an indirect or metaphorical meaning of a word should be resorted to only if it is impossible to accept the direct meaning. The Sanskrit of Medhātithi is pithy: *kṛtsnavākyaparyālocanayā yo 'rthaḥ sa niścīyate. ato dvijagrahaṇaṃ brāhmaṇaparatayopasaṃhartavyam. asti brāhmaṇasya dvijātitvam na tu sarveṣu dvijātiṣu brāhmaṇyam. atrāpi dvijaśabdārthe saṃbhavati nānvayani lakṣaṇā nyāyyā.*

example, ... révèle que le 'deux-fois-né' auquel s'addressent les prescriptions est en fait le brāhmane."[53]

Most other medieval authorities agree with Śaṃkara and the commentators of Manu. Viśvarūpa, an early commentator of Yājñavalkya,[54] like Medhātithi, states that "the term 'twice-born' (YDh 3.61) refers to Brahmins, because renunciation is prescribed only for them." Vijñāneśvara (twelfth century), the influential author of the *Mitākṣarā* commentary on Yājñavalkya (YDh 3.56–57), also appears to favor the position that only Brahmins should be permitted to renounce. After stating that renunciation is meant only for Brahmins and not for those who are "simply twice-born" (*dvijamātra*), Vijñāneśvara goes on to give the opinion of some who permit renunciation for all three twice-born *varṇas* without rejecting it outright.[55] A significant text cited here in support of the latter position is the *sūtra* "after studying the Veda, four *āśramas* are open to the three *varṇas*," discussed in section 5.3.4.[56]

Mādhava, the fourteenth-century commentator of Parāśara, is even more circumspect and refuses to take a stand.[57] He has one of the longest discussions of the issue (PāM I, 534–36), presenting first the argument of "some" (*kecit*) for restricting renunciation to Brahmins and then that of "others" (*apare*) for opening it to all three twice-born *varṇas*. Mādhava, however, introduces an interesting twist in the argument of the supporters of the latter position. They find it necessary to deal seriously with texts cited by their opponents which clearly state that only Brahmins may renounce. They interpret

53. With specific reference to the renouncer, Biardeau (Biardeau and Malamoud1976, 35) states: "Quoiqu'en principe tous les deux-fois-nés doivent pouvoir devenir *sannyāsin*, puisqu'ils ont à renoncer à leur statut et à leurs devoirs sacrificiels, il se produit pour le renonçant le même phénomène que pour le *gṛhastha*. Le seul qui ait droit au nom de *sannyāsin* est en fait l'ancien maître de maison brāhmane. Aux autres (qui pourront être parfois issus de basses castes), on donnera d'autres noms: *yogin, yati,* (ascète), *parivrājaka* (l'errant)." Biardeau here glosses over the deep controversy within Brāhmaṇical theology itself over this issue. The question was never as neatly resolved as Biardeau presents it. Further, I have not found any source that would restrict the term *saṃnyāsin* to Brahmins, while the other terms are used for ascetics of other castes. Although *saṃnyāsin* has a rather restrictive use (Olivelle 1981), it is nowhere reserved for Brahmins, and the other terms are regularly used for both Brahmin and non-Brahmin ascetics. See also Biardeau 1982, 77–78. Meyer (1927, 347–48, n.1) also agrees that the four *āśramas* are especially meant for Brahmins.

54. The date of Viśvarūpa is uncertain. Kane (1968, I.1, 562–64) and others accept his identity with Sureśvara, the pupil of Śaṃkara, and on that basis date him around 800–825 C.E. This identity, however, is quite uncertain. On the question we are examining, for example, Viśvarūpa's opinion is contrary to Sureśvara's, who, as we have seen, disagrees with his teacher Śaṃkara and opens renunciation to all twice-born people. The problem this contradiction creates for the assumed identity of the two authors is recognized also by Kane (1974, II.2, 944). Viśvarūpa, however, flourished before the 11th century C.E., since he is cited by Vijñāneśvara. Other works that restrict renunciation to Brahmins include Vaidyanātha Dīkṣita's *Smṛtimuktāphala*, I: 176; Nārāyaṇa and Śaṃkarānanda in their commentaries on the *Āruṇi Upaniṣad*, 5 (*Upaniṣadāṃ Samuccayaḥ*, p. 98); *Śāṇḍilya Saṃhitā*, Bhaktikāṇḍa, 4.14.62–63.

55. Kamalākarabhaṭṭa (*Nirṇayasindhu*, p. 441), however, reads Vijñāneśvara as supporting the former position.

56. See also note 73 there. This *sūtra* is cited also by Mallinātha in his commentary on Kālidāsa's *Raghuvaṃśa*, 8.14, in support of permitting all twice-born people to become renouncers.

57. Another significant author of this period who does not deal with this issue is Yādavaprakāśa, the author of the *Yatidharmasamuccaya*. See section 8.5 for Yādava's discussion on the legitimacy of the *āśramas*.

these texts not as outright prohibitions but as forbidding to non-Brahmins only the carrying of the triple staff, regarded as the emblem of Viṣṇu and of the renunciatory state. Thus, even though people of all three *varṇas* can become renouncers, only Brahmins are permitted to carry the triple staff.[58]

Aparāditya (early twelfth century C.E.), the author of the commentary *Aparārka* on Yājñavalkya, however, supports unequivocally the right of all twice-born men to become renouncers. Aparāditya says that "here the term 'twice-born' has the literal meaning and not a synecdochical meaning referring to a Brahmin,"[59] and cites the following Smṛti in support: "After paying the triple debt, free from egotism and selfishness, a Brahmin, a Kṣatriya, or a Vaiśya may wander forth from home." Devaṇṇabhaṭṭa (twelfth to thirteenth century C.E.?), the author of the legal digest *Smṛticandrikā* (I, 176), likewise supports the right of all twice-born men to become renouncers and interprets Manu's use of "Brahmin" as a synecdoche of all twice-born *varṇas*.

Two more recent authors, Kamalākarabhaṭṭa, the author of the *Nirṇayasindhu* (composed 1612 C.E.), and Kāśīnātha Upādhāya, the author of *Dharmasindhu* (composed 1790–91 C.E.), also support this position and follow Mādhava's lead in interpreting those authoritative texts that appear to restrict renunciation to Brahmins. Kamalākara, after presenting the argument restricting only the use of a triple staff as recorded by Mādhava, states: "In truth, however, those texts refer only to Kuṭīcakas and so forth" (*Nirṇayasindhu*, p. 441). Here we note another hermeneutical use of the fourfold classification of renouncers that I noted earlier (section 6.1.3). Thus, non-Brahmins are barred from becoming Kuṭīcakas and the like, but not from becoming Paramahaṃsas.[60] Kāśīnātha's position is very similar, although he uses the distinction between the renunciation of those who seek knowledge (*vividiṣāsaṃnyāsa*) and the renunciation of the enlightened (*vidvatsaṃnyāsa*):

> Only Brahmins are qualified with respect to renunciation which is characterized by such things as the taking of a staff and bears the name "renunciation of seekers after knowledge," whereas Kṣatriyas and Vaiśyas also are qualified with respect to the renunciation of the enlightened.[61]

A significant question to which I can only allude here is the socio-economic reasons for the increasing tendency in medieval Brāhmaṇical theology to limit asceticism to the Brahmin community. Given the current state of our knowledge regarding the social, economic, and political situations in various parts of India during the early and late medieval periods, this question cannot be adequately resolved. Nandi (1986), however, has suggested some interesting avenues of inquiry applicable to our question, even if we

58. For the texts that forbid all but Brahmins from carrying triple staffs, see PāM I, 535–36; Mallinātha on *Raghuvaṃśa*, 8.14. The Ypra (3.9–10, 27–28) also records this interpretation.

59. *atra ca dvijagrahaṇaṃ vivakṣitārthaṃ na brāhmaṇopalakṣaṇārtham. Aparārka* on YDh 3.60 (p. 966).

60. Since, according to Kamalākara, the Kuṭīcaka type of renunciation is forbidden in the Kali age (see section 8.4), the issue becomes moot! The *Mahānirvāṇatantra* goes a step further. According to it, there are only two *āśramas* in the Kali age—those of the householder and the renouncer—and all *varṇas*, not just the twice-born, are permitted to enter both.

61. Kāśīnātha Upādhyāya, *Dharmasindhu*, p. 976: *saṃnyāse daṇḍagrahaṇādirūpe vividiśākhye viprasyaivādhikāraḥ. vidvatsaṃnyāse tu kṣatriyavaiśyayor api.*

may not accept completely his strict and somewhat simplistic correlation between economic realities and religious customs and doctrines. Archaeological and other evidence suggests a decline and decay of cities in both the north and the south beginning toward the middle of the first millennium C.E., accompanied by the demise of the urban market economy. The resultant dispersal of Brahmin families into the countryside and the emergence of a feudal economy, according to Nandi, are at the root of several developments in Brāhmaṇical religious practice and ideology, including the temple complexes associated with the *bhakti* cults as well as the monastic establishments. Both these institutions were dominated by Brahmins and controlled vast agricultural lands. These Brāhmaṇical institutions, furthermore, were patronized by political authorities because they provided the rulers with religious legitimacy.

Now, even though the writers on *dharma* speak only about renunciation, the social reality was that Brāhmaṇical renunciation had become by at least the eighth century C.E. de facto monasticism. When a man became a Brāhmaṇical renouncer he did not just become a lonely wanderer but entered a monastery (*maṭha*) with a hierarchical organization. If we look at the question of who is entitled to become a renouncer in this light, it becomes apparent that what is at issue is the right to become a member of a monastic community with land and a clientele. In spite of what Sureśvara says, the major Śaṃkarite *maṭha*s that became so powerful during the middle ages were exclusively Brāhmaṇical. For Brahmins, who so vigorously argued for Brāhmaṇical privileges in the Dharmaśāstras, it would have been a natural step to limit entry into these rich and powerful institutions to members of their own community.

Some writers go a step further, asserting that in this Kali age there are no true Kṣatriyas or Vaiśyas, leaving only Brahmins and Śūdras.[62] If all the castes that pretend to belong to the Kṣatriya or Vaiśya *varṇa*s are in fact Śūdras, then in practice the question can be seen as moot. Only Brahmins can renounce, because there are only Brahmins, all others being Śūdras and thus clearly excluded from that state.

7.3 The Āśramas *and Civil Authority*

From about the middle of the first millennium C.E., as we have seen, the expression *varṇāśramadharma* begins to be employed with increasing frequency as almost a shorthand term to designate the totality of the Brāhmaṇical *dharma*, thus placing the *āśrama* system, theoretically at least, at the very heart of *dharma*. Since the safeguarding of *dharma* was the principal duty of kings, the protection and regulation of *āśrama*s came to be regarded as one of the duties of the civil authority and a special province of law.

7.3.1 The King as Guardian of the Āśramas

At the root of the ideology of kingship in India was the notion that, but for the strong hand of the king, society would dissolve into a state of anarchic chaos in which stronger individuals would prey on the weak.[63] This natural appetite of humans to prey on the

62. See Kane 1974, II.1, 380–82 for a detailed examination of this issue.

63. See, for example, MBh 12.59.13f.

weak is referred to as the "law of the fish," the big fish eating the little fish. The opening verses of the *Nāradasmṛti* (1.1–2), a text devoted solely to civil and criminal law, attempt to demonstrate why the need for the strong arm of the law and the king arose with the disappearance of the golden age:

> When people were totally devoted to *dharma* and spoke the truth there was no legal procedure; neither was there enmity or jealousy. When *dharma* disappeared among men, legal procedure came into being, and the king was appointed to preside over legal procedures and to wield the rod.

It is the rod (*daṇḍa*) of the king that keeps people in check and on the right path. This central activity of the king is regarded as an act of protection, and the terms *pāla, pati, pa* (all having the meaning of guarding and protection) used in the numerous Sanskrit epithets for a king highlight this aspect of kingship. "The chief duty of a Kṣatriya," say both Manu (MDh 7.147) and Yājñavalkya (YDh 1.119), "is the protection of his subjects."

The protective activity of the king was directed in a special way at safeguarding the *varṇa*s, which encompass castes (*jāti*) within the dharmaśāstric ideology, for the maintenance of this structure was the foundation of social stability. As Nārada (NSm 18.14–16) puts it:

> If the king were not to punish every *varṇa* that deviates from its proper path, the people will perish: Brahmins will neglect their priestly functions, Kṣatriyas will give up governing, Vaiśyas will abandon their work, and Śūdras will excel them all. If there were no kings to wield the rod on earth, the strong will roast the weak, like fish on a spit.

When *āśrama* is coupled with *varṇa* to represent the totality of *dharma*, the essence of royal duty came to be encapsulated in "the protection of *varṇa*s and *āśrama*s," an expression that became a cliché when poets and panegyrists sang the virtues of a king. The earliest recorded use of a similar expression—although there is some doubt about its authenticity—is found in the Dharmasūtra of Gautama: "Let him [the king] protect the *varṇa*s and *āśrama*s according to the law."[64] Its use, however, becomes common in later literature. According to Manu (7.35), kingship was created for the protection of the *varṇa*s and *āśrama*s: "The king was created as the protector of all the *varṇa*s and *āśrama*s, each of which in due order is intent on its own *dharma*." Likewise, at the very outset of his discussion, Viṣṇu (ViDh 3.2–3) defines the *dharma* of a king as "protection of the people and the establishment of the *varṇa*s and the *āśrama*s in their respective *dharma*."

Even the *Arthaśāstra*, a text Machiavellian in its concern for enhancing the power of the king and protecting the security of the state, considers it important for the king to see

64. GDh 11.9: *varṇāśramāṃś ca nyāyato 'bhirakset.* There is some doubt, as I have already pointed out (section 3.2.1.1), about the authenticity of this and other passages (GDh 11.29; 19.1) in GDh that speaks of *varṇa*s and *āśrama*s in the same breath. On the one hand, if we are to accept at face value Gautama's rejection of the *āśrama* system in chapter 3, it is unlikely that he would have given this central place to the system in dealing with the duties of the king. It is also unlikely, on the other hand, that the system would have been so thoroughly integrated into the discourse on *dharma* at such an early age when the very legitimacy of the system was the subject of intense debate. None of the other Dharmasūtras, furthermore, record this expression in its treatment of the duties of a king.

that his subjects follow the duties of their respective *varṇas* and *āśramas*:

> A king, therefore, should not permit his subjects to transgress the *dharma* proper to them, for by ensuring fidelity to their proper *dharma* he will find joy both here and hereafter.
>
> People who keep to the bounds of Aryan propriety, who are steadfast in their *varṇas* and *āśramas*, and who are governed by the Veda, prosper and do not perish. (Artha 1.3.16–17)
>
> People of the four *varṇas* and *āśramas* become attached to the duties of their respective *dharma* and keep to their respective paths when they are ruled by the king with his rod. (Artha 1.4.16)

Sanskrit drama and belles lettres (*kāvya*), as well as inscriptional data, provide further evidence that the primary duty of a king to protect the *varṇas* and *āśramas* had become a cliché outside the technical traditions of *dharma* and *artha* by the fifth century C.E., the tentative date of Kālidāsa.

Kālidāsa, as we have seen (section 6.2.1), uses the *āśrama* scheme of life stages in his works more frequently than other Sanskrit poets. He calls Raghu "the teacher (or father) of the *varṇas* and *āśramas*"[65] and Duṣyanta "the protector of the *varṇas* and *āśramas*."[66] Rāma was ever "watchful in looking after the *varṇas* and *āśramas*."[67] The duty of a king to "protect the *varṇas* and *āśramas*," says Kālidāsa, was proclaimed by Manu himself.[68]

Bāṇa,[69] comparing his royal patron Harṣavardhana to Manu, says that Harṣa, "like Manu, established the laws of *varṇas* and *āśramas*."[70] We find similar statements in later texts such as Somadeva's *Kathāsaritsāgara* (9.2.114) and Kalhaṇa's *Rājataraṅginī* (6.108).

In the voluminous corpus of inscriptions from ancient and medieval times, I have been unable to discover any reference to the *āśrama* system outside the context of a king's duties. As in the belles lettres, here too the label "protector of *varṇas* and *āśramas*" is clearly a laudatory epithet. The fact that kings used that epithet in public documents, however, is significant. The expression *varṇāśrama* in these inscriptions appears to be a shorthand way of referring to both the totality of *dharma* and the spectrum of groups inhabiting a kingdom. The inscriptional use of this expression appears to have begun at least by the beginning of the sixth century C.E.

The earliest inscriptional record of the term *āśrama* that I have been able to locate is the copperplate inscription of Mahārāja Saṃkṣobha dated 528–29 C.E., in which

65. Kālidāsa, *Raghuvaṃśa*, 5.19: *varṇāśramāṇāṃ guruḥ*.

66. Kālidāsa, *Abhijñānaśākuntalam*, 5.11–12: *varṇāśramāṇāṃ rakṣitā*.

67. Kālidāsa, *Raghuvaṃśa*, 14.85: *varṇāśramāvekṣaṇajāgarūkaḥ*.

68. Ibid., 14.67: *nṛpasya varṇāśramapālanaṃ yat sa eva dharmo manunā praṇītaḥ*.

69. Bāṇa was a contemporary of King Harṣavardhana and can be dated with greater precision and certainty as belonging to the first half of the seventh century C.E. Harṣa began his reign in 606 or 607 C.E. See Devahuti 1970.

70. *Harṣacarita*, Ch. 2, p. 79: *manāv iva kartari varṇāśramavyavasthānām*. Bāṇa, in his *Kādambarī* (p. 196), describing Candrāpīḍa's military expedition, says that the king protected the *āśramas* (*pālayann āśramān*), but here it is unclear whether *āśrama* stands for the orders of life (preferred by the translator Kale) or for forest hermitages.

Saṃkṣobha describes his father, Hastin, as "intent on enforcing the *dharmas* of the *varṇas* and *āśramas*."[71] In the Asirgadh copper-seal inscription Sarvavarman describes his great great-grandfather, Harivarman, as "employing sovereignty [lit., turning the wheel] only to regulate the *varṇas* and *āśramas*."[72] Similar expressions are used to describe King Harṣavardhana's father, Prabhākaravardhana, in the Sonpat copper-seal inscription[73] and Kharagraha in the extremely long Alina copperplate inscription of Śīlāditya VII.[74]

Similar expressions are used to describe the piety of kings also in South Indian inscriptions. In a copperplate grant from Andhra ascribed to the sixth century C.E., Pṛthivī-Śrī-Mūlarāja, a Buddhist king, is said to have "guarded the *dharmas* of all the *varṇas* and *āśramas*."[75] Likewise, the Viṣṇukuṇḍi king Govindavarman, also a Buddhist, was loved by *varṇas* and *āśramas*, as well as by his kinsmen and servants.[76]

Although the statements regarding the king's duty to protect the *varṇas* and *āśramas* both in texts and in inscriptions appear to be stock expressions concerning the ideal typical king, nevertheless the necessities of government must also have made it imperative that the social institutions comprehended by the four *āśramas* be taken into account in the practice of law. Since the householders were the central focus of law even outside the *āśrama* framework, the special provisions concerning the *āśramas* focused primarily on the ascetic institutions. The power and social position of ascetic groups and monasteries and the dictates of Realpolitik advocated by political theorists like Kauṭilya, moreover, compelled Indian kings to take a personal interest in ascetic institutions.

7.3.2 The Āśramas, *Ascetics, and the Law*

In defining the components and objectives of legal procedure (*vyavahāra*), Nārada (NSm 1.12) states that "it has four beneficiaries because it protects the four *āśramas*."[77] If people of all four *āśramas* benefit from legal procedure, then Nārada must have considered that procedure to take into account their specific rights, obligations, and modes of life.

It is a common principle of Indian law that the king, as the judicial authority, should not commence a legal procedure in court. Such procedures are considered private litiga-

71. CI, III, 112–16 (Gupta Inscriptions, No. 25): *varṇāśramadharmasthāpanāniratena*. Saṃkśobha and his father, Hastin, ruled Ḍabhālā (modern Bundelkhand) in central India under the patronage of the Gupta kings.

72. CI, III, 219–21 (Gupta Inscriptions, No. 47): *varṇāśramavyavasthāpanapravṛttacakraḥ*.

73. CI, III, 231–32 (Gupta Inscription No. 52). This is the same Harṣa whom we saw praised in an identical manner by Bāṇa.

74. CI, III, 171–91 (Gupta Inscriptions, No. 39, dated 766–67 C.E.): [*samyag vya*] *vasthāpitavarṇāśramācāraḥ*.

75. *anupālitāśeṣavarṇāśramadharmaḥ*. *Epigraphica Indica*, Vol. 38 (1969), pp. 192–95.

76. *anuraktavarṇāśramasvajanaparijanena*. *Epigraphia Āndhrica*, Vol. 2 (1974), pp. 1–14. The editor Sankaranarayanan (p. 8) ascribes this inscription to around 566 C.E.

77. *caturṇām āśramāṇāṃ ca raksaṇāt sa caturhitaḥ*. Asahāya, possibly basing his interpretation on the use of *ca* ("and"), comments that here *āśrama* includes *varṇa*. The text, however, refers only to the four *āśramas*, and the *ca* may be used to connect the two clauses of the verse.

tion.[78] Manu (MDh 8.43) states this principle clearly: "Neither the king nor an officer of his should initiate a lawsuit." There are exceptions, however, and the matters of law that should be investigated and dealt with by the king himself are put into a separate category called *prakīrṇaka* ("miscellaneous") or *kanṭhakaśodhana* ("suppression of criminals"). After listing the subjects falling under "miscellaneous" (NSm 18.1–4), Nārada (NSm 18.5) states: "A king, however, should assiduously regulate [or protect] all the *āśramas* employing the textually prescribed as well as the four basic methods."[79] In this context, I believe, what Nārada wants to convey is that, besides attending to the specific things enumerated in the first four verses, the king has the general duty to look after the four *āśramas*. The *Arthaśāstra* also lists the affairs of ascetics (*tapasvin*) among matters that the judges themselves should investigate. The *Kātyāyanasmṛti* (949–50) likewise lists the duties of *varṇas* and *āśramas* among the miscellaneous topics and goes on to advise the king to investigate them by using spies.[80]

Because it is the householder who is the subject of all the general laws, I limit myself here to discussing the legal position of the other three *āśramas*, especially that of the ascetics.

The rules governing the life of a vedic student are given in the Dharmaśāstras immediately following the description of the initiatory rite. These rules belong to the section of *dharma* called right conduct (*ācāra*) and not strictly to law. The obligations of a student toward his teacher, however, are considered by Nārada (NSm 5.8–14) to be part of contractual law. A student's duty to perform the traditional services for his teacher is put on a par with other forms of contractual labor, such as that of an apprentice or a hired laborer.

In general, students are not independent and, therefore, cannot enter into contracts,[81] and, at least according to some authorities, they are also ineligible to be witnesses in a court of law.[82] The student's ambivalent legal position results both from his ritually liminal status[83] and from the existence of two types of students, the temporary and the permanent. The latter, the subject of the original *āśrama* system, is placed clearly outside of

78. These procedures are classified in the *dharma* literature under *vyavahārapada* ("titles of law"). See Lingat 1973, 243–56; Kane 1973, III, 242f.

79. *rājā tv avahitaḥ sarvān āśramān paripālayet / upāyaiḥ śāstravihitaiś caturbhiḥ prakṛtais tathā //* The four basic strategies are conciliation (*sāma*), giving gifts (*upapradāna*, bribes?), creating dissension (*bheda*), and employing force (*daṇḍa*). The term *paripālayet*, just as other terms employed to indicate the protective function of kings, implies both protection and regulation/supervision.

80. An interesting application of the principle that the king should look after the *āśramas* is found in Kālidāsa's *Raghuvaṃśa* (14.67). Seeing that King Duṣyanta has repudiated her, Śakuntalā decides to become an ascetic. Since it is a king's duty to protect the *varṇas* and *āśramas*, she tells him, he is obliged to look after her in common with other ascetics. If he will not be her husband (*pati*), then he as king will have to be her protector (*pati*).

81. See NSm 1.29–32; Artha 3.1.12. Nārada (1.10), however, upholds the validity of a debt entered into by a student, if it is done for the sake of the family and, presumably, with the consent of the head of the family.

82. See MDh 8.65; NSm, Vyavahāra, 1.164.

83. That the period between initiation and return home is liminal is indicated by numerous practices, such as begging, shaving the head, sleeping on the ground, staying away from home, prohibition of ornaments, and the like. See van Gennep 1960.

society and occupies a status similar to that of an ascetic. Within this context we can better understand the legend of Nābhānediṣṭha, the youngest son of Manu.[84] The older sons divided the ancestral property among themselves—or, according to the version of the *Taittirīya Saṃhitā*, Manu himself so divided it—without giving a share to Nābhānediṣṭha. The reason for his exclusion appears to be the fact that at the time of partition Nābhānediṣṭha was a vedic student and away from home. Later legal texts would not permit such a practice, because studentship was recognized as a temporary period unless a formal commitment to perpetual studentship had been made. At a time when such a demarcation was not clearly established, one can understand how an absent brother could be excluded from the paternal estate.

Even later law recognizes the special status of a student, but in this case of a perpetual student. Thus, Vasiṣṭha's (VaDh 17.52) list of those who are excluded from a share of the paternal estate includes "those who have gone to another *āśrama*." This statement, made from a householder's perspective, clearly refers to anyone who has gone to an *āśrama* different from the householder's (see section 1.1.4), which would theoretically include a student. Kane (1973, III, 608), therefore, is forced to explain that it refers only to hermits and renouncers. Within the context of the original *āśrama* system operative during Vasiṣṭha's time, however, the statement makes perfect sense, for "other *āśramas*" are those of a perpetual student, hermit, and renouncer.[85]

Special provisions also apply to the division of the property, small though it may be, of students, hermits, and renouncers: "The heirs of a hermit, a renouncer, and a student are one's teacher, a pious pupil, one's spiritual brother, and a person living at the same holy place, in that order."[86] Most medieval commentators, including Vijñāneśvara and Mādhava, interpret the term *krameṇa* ("in order") to mean its opposite, namely *pratilomakrameṇa* ("in inverse order").[87] Thus, the heir of a hermit is his spiritual brother or a person who shares his hermitage, the heir of a renouncer is a pious pupil of his, and the heir of a student is his teacher. This interpretation is rather farfetched. Indeed, the *Arthaśāstra* gives the identical rule.[88] Even if one may argue that Yājñavalkya used *krameṇa* for *pratilomakrameṇa* due to the exigencies of meter, Kauṭilya, writing in prose, had no such restriction. It appears more likely, therefore, that the persons mentioned are common heirs of hermits, renouncers, and students, and that the expression "in order" is intended to show that each subsequent person becomes the heir only in the absence of each preceding.[89] This accords with Viṣṇu's (ViDh 17.15–16) statement that the property of a hermit is inherited by his teacher or pupil.

84. See AitB 22.9; TS 3.1.9.4–5.

85. *Vṛddha Hārītasmṛti* (7.259) also excludes, among others, hermits, renouncers, and students.

86. YDh 2.137: *vānaprasthayatibrahmacāriṇāṃ rikthabhāginaḥ / krameṇācāryasacchiṣyadharmabhrātrekatīrthinaḥ //* Here, as in the passages of *Vṛddha Hārītasmṛti* and the *Arthaśāstra* referred to in the previous and following notes, the student is mentioned generically. However, Vijñāneśvara and other commentators are probably right in restricting these provisions to perpetual students. The term *ekatīrthin* (lit., "those who live at one *tīrtha*") probably means a person who lives in the same hermitage or house.

87. See Setlur 1911, 185–86; Olivelle 1984, 144–45.

88. Artha 3.16.37: *vānaprasthayatibrahmacāriṇām ācāryaśiṣyadharmabhrātṛsamānatīrthyā rikthabhājaḥ krameṇa.*

89. This is also the interpretation of Devaṇṇabhaṭṭa in his *Smṛticandrikā*, Vyavahārakāṇḍa, p. 302.

The legal position of renouncers is much clearer than that of students or hermits and is derived principally from the theological premise that renunciation constitutes the ritual and therefore the civil death of the renouncer. Two significant legal consequences follow: on the one hand, renouncers are unable to participate in legal transactions, and, on the other, they are released from all contracts previously entered into.

Kauṭilya (Artha 3.1.12) explicitly excludes renouncers (*pravrajita*) from all legal transactions. Legal consequences of this include their inability to be witnesses in a court of law or to act as sureties. Several sources exempt renouncers also from ordeals, fines, tolls, and taxes.[90]

The principle of a renouncer's civil death is applied to three important areas: marriage, partition of property, and debt. Renunciation on the part of the husband, along with his death and prolonged absence, are the three recognized causes of the dissolution of a marriage. While renunciation results in civil death, a prolonged absence is probably seen as creating a presumption of death.[91] Early writers generally permit the remarriage of women whose marriages are thus dissolved. Kauṭilya (Artha 3.4.37–38) says:

> The wife of a man who has been away for a long time, who has become a renouncer, or who has died should wait for seven menstrual periods or, if she has children, for one year. Thereafter she may marry a full brother of her husband.

Nārada (NSm 12.97) concurs: "When the husband disappears, dies, or renounces, or when he becomes an eunuch or an outcaste—in these five misfortunes another husband is prescribed for women." Gautama (GDh 18.15–16), makes a distinction between the absence and the renunciation of a husband and permits remarriage only in the case of the former and not the latter.[92]

As at his physical death, so at his civil death the property of the father is subject to partition among his heirs.[93] It has been long recognized in Hindu law that the paternal estate could be divided among the heirs when the father was old.[94] Thus, Gautama (GDh 28.2) allows the father to divide his property when the mother is past the child-bearing age. Nārada (NSm 1.2–4) likewise permits a father who is very old to distribute his prop-

---

also Nandapaṇḍita on ViDh 17.15–16. My interpretation is also supported by the fact that the passage lists four heirs for the three āśramas, thus breaking the symmetry. The proponents of the "inverse order," therefore, are forced to give two heirs for a hermit.

90. For a more detailed discussion of these legal disabilities and privileges, see Olivelle 1984, 146–47, where the relevant primary sources are cited.

91. The length of absence that would create a presumption of death has been a matter of controversy, especially because this presumption was linked to the custom of levirate (*niyoga*) and the remarriage of the wife. Gautama (GDh 18.15) has six years, while others adjust the length according to the caste of the absentee: Cf. VaDh 17.75–78; MDh 9.76; NSm 12.98.

92. Vasiṣṭha (17.75–78) and Manu (9.76) do not mention the renunciation of the husband but permit the wife of a man gone abroad for a long time to remarry. There was increasing hostility, however, to the remarriage of widows. Medieval legal digests, therefore, interpret the above passages as referring to a practice of a previous age that is not permitted in the present Kali age. On the question of remarriage, see Kane 1974, II.1, 608–19.

93. "It is before the stage of hermit or ascetic, i.e. in the lifetime of the father, that family property should be divided among sons, according to the theory of the four *āśramas*." (Lingat 1973, 58).

94. For a discussion of the economic basis of the institutions of old age, see section 4.1.2.

erty at will among his sons and even allows the sons to divide the estate on their own when their mother has reached menopause, their sisters are married, and their father has turned away from sexual desires. Śūlapāṇi (on YDh 2.114) interprets the latter condition as referring to the renunciation of the father. He is probably right, for Nārada (NSm 13.24) likewise states that the property of a man who dies or renounces childless is divided among his brothers.[95]

Following the classical *āśrama* model, these documents assume that a person who renounces is an old man. When such a man renounces, consequently, there are two ways in which his property can be divided. He can divide it himself prior to renouncing. The *Kuṇḍikā Upaniṣad* (18) accordingly instructs the candidate for renunciation to partition his property among his sons. If, however, he renounces without doing so he loses all rights with regard to his property, and his heirs can partition it among themselves, just as if the father were dead.

In Hindu law the heirs inherit not only the property of the deceased but also his debts. This principle remains valid also in the case of civil death resulting from renunciation. Viṣṇu (ViDh 6.27) is explicit on this point: when a debtor dies or renounces or is absent for 20 years his sons or grandsons should settle his debts. The *Kātyāyanasmṛti* (575) also acknowledges that those who inherit the wealth of a person also takes upon themselves his debts.

One of the most important legal provisions regarding renunciation relates to the position of a renouncer who becomes an apostate and returns to society.[96] The ritual death resulting from renunciation makes it impossible for a renouncer to assume again his former ritual and caste position. Apostates and any children they may produce are reduced to the level of untouchable Cāṇḍālas.[97] The *Śāṭyāyanīya Upaniṣad* (329–330) says that the sin of apostasy is greater than all the most grievous sins combined and that no expiation is possible for it.[98] The legal consequences of apostasy were no less severe. All the dharmaśāstric writers from Viṣṇu (ViDh 5.152) onward agree that an apostate renouncer should be made a slave of the king. Yājñavalkya (YDh 2.183) specifies that his slavery lasts until death. This position is reaffirmed by *Kātyāyanasmṛti* (731), and Nārada (NSm 5.33) states: "An apostate from renunciation, indeed, becomes the slave of the king. He can never be freed and there is no purification at all for him."[99]

Medieval theologians were divided on whether even a Brahmin, who was generally exempt from slavery, should be made a slave if he becomes an apostate from renunciation. Śūlapāṇi, Aparāditya, and Mitra Miśra (commenting on YDh 2.183) exclude a

95. Manu's (9.104) statement that the brothers should divide the paternal estate after the passing of father and mother (*ūrdhvaṃ pituś ca mātuś ca*) is likewise interpreted by Rāghavānanda to imply also the renunciation of the parents.

96. For an extensive discussion of this issue, see Krishnan 1969.

97. See Vaidyanātha Dīkṣita, *Smṛtimuktāphala*, I, 207–8.

98. Other sources, however, prescribe appropriate penances for apostasy: see Śrīdhara, *Smṛtyarthasāra*, p. 126; VeS 3.4.40–43 and Śaṃkara's commentary on it; Yādavaprakāśa, *Yatidharmasamuccaya*, pp. 69–70.

99. According to Nārada (NSm 5.24–35), only two types of slaves can never be freed: an apostate from renunciation and a man who sells himself into slavery. Some authors, however, acknowledge the possibility of an appropriate penance for an apostate. Vijñāneśvara (on YDh 2.183), for example, says that only an apostate who has not performed the appropriate penance become the king's slave.

Brahmin from this provision on the basis of the legal maxim that slavery is in the direct order of *varṇa*s and not in the inverse order.[100] Accordingly, a Śūdra can be a slave of the three upper *varṇas*, a Vaiśya of a Brahmin or a Kṣatriya, and a Kṣatriya of a Brahmin. The *Kātyāyanasmṛti* (715) explicitly states that slavery is permissible only in the case of the last three *varṇa*s; Brahmins can never be slaves. Consequently, these authors recommend that a Brahmin apostate should be branded on the forehead with the mark of a dog's foot and banished from the kingdom.[101]

Vijñāneśvara and Viśvarūpa (on YDh 2.183), however, disagree. They consider apostasy an exception to the general rule against reducing Brahmins to slavery. Nārada (NSm 5.37), in fact, excludes "those who give up the *dharma* proper to them" from the general rule that slavery is in the direct order of *varṇa*s, and Vijñāneśvara understands this exclusion as referring to apostasy.

From ancient times the legal tradition recognized the power of properly constituted groups to formulate their own laws.[102] These groups included merchant guilds, trade associations, castes, and, more importantly for our study, ascetic communities. One title of law deals with violations of corporate law, and it was the king's duty to respect those special laws and to enforce them on the members of the respective groups.[103] The references to ascetic communities within this context, however, use the term *pāṣaṇḍa*, a term that usually refers to the so-called heretical sects, such as the Buddhist and the Jain.[104] It is unclear whether Brāhmaṇical monastic communities also enjoyed such corporate privileges, but it seems likely that they did.[105] One problem in incorporating those groups into dharmaśāstric rules is that the legal fiction of the itinerant lifestyle of renouncers was maintained within the dharmaśāstric tradition. The existence of monasteries (*maṭha*) is never recognized within Brāhmaṇical *dharma*, and references to *maṭha*s are extremely rare even in texts dealing specifically with the renouncer's *dharma*. The laws of Brāhmaṇical renouncers, furthermore, were part of *dharma* and were theoretically located in the Vedas and Smṛtis and not in private corporations. The fact, however, was that different Brāhmaṇical monastic groups, such as the Śrī-Vaiṣṇavas and the Śaṃkara *maṭhas*, had distinctive rules and practices.[106] The enforcement of these rules, in all likelihood, fell within the same title of law as other corporate bodies.

Indeed, in modern times heads of some of the leading monasteries, especially the Śaṃkarācāryas, "have been in the habit of assuming to themselves jurisdiction over per-

100. See YDh 1.183; NSm 5.37; *Kātyāyanasmṛti*, 716.

101. Aparāditya on YDh 2.183 (II, 787) cites a passage from the *Kātyāyanasmṛti* (721) in support of this view: "When persons belonging to the three twice-born *varṇas* revert from renunciation, the king should banish the Brahmins and make Kṣatriyas and Vaiśyas slaves."

102. For a detailed study of corporate law, called *samaya* or *saṃvid*, see Kane 1974, II.1, 66–69; 1973, III, 158–60, 486–89.

103. See YDh 2.185–92; NSm 10.1–7.

104. Thus, Vijñāneśvara (on YDh 2.192) explains the term as referring to those who do not accept the authority of the Veda.

105. The term *naigama* is used in YDh 2.192 and NSm 10.1 for one type of association. Vijñāneśvara explains it as people who accept the authority of the Vedas and contrasts it to *pākhaṇḍa*. It may thus cover Brahmin monastic groups. But *naigama* has been interpreted in different ways by authors and is too general a term to permit a firm conclusion.

106. See, for example, Olivelle 1986–87.

sons professing to follow their dogmas in ecclesiastical matters such as prescribing penances for lapses, settling disputes between castes, and deciding upon questions of outcasting" (Kane 1974, II.2, 965–66). It is likely, as Kane has shown (1974, II.2, 965–74), that monastic leaders may have played a similar, although more restricted, role even in medieval times.[107]

7.4 Pariṣad *and* Āśrama

Several Dharmaśāstras state that points of law not found in those treatises must be decided by a *pariṣad*, namely an assembly of pious and learned Brahmins.[108] The institution of *pariṣad* is very ancient, and evidence of its existence is found in the older Upaniṣads. Śvetaketu Āruṇeya, for example, went to the *pariṣad* of the Pañcālas and was questioned there by their chief Pravāhaṇa Jaivali.[109] It appears from the legal literature that the special province of a *pariṣad* was to decide the appropriate penance/punishment for a serious sin/crime. Thus, according to Baudhāyana (BDh 2.1.44–45), a vedic student who breaks his vow of chastity should be brought before a *pariṣad*, which decides the penance.[110]

There is no unanimity in the sources regarding the constitution of a *pariṣad*.[111] The standard number, however, appears to have been a minimum of ten (*daśāvara*). In the whole of the *dharma* literature there are only four texts that specify the ten types of individuals forming a *pariṣad*, and two of these are citations of an identical verse. These four texts relate three of these individuals to the *āśrama*s, thereby establishing an apparent connection between the institutions of *pariṣad* and *āśrama*. This connection has been accepted as a fact by most medieval commentators and, following them, by modern scholars. Lingat (1973, 15), for example, describing the constitution of a *pariṣad*, states without reservation that it includes "three individuals, each of them representing the first three stages of life, namely one *brahmacārin*, one householder, and one hermit or ascetic."[112] A careful examination of the four texts, I believe, raises serious doubts regarding the association of these two institutions so readily accepted by many.

The earliest of these texts is found in the *Gautama Dharmasūtra* (GDh 28.49) and comes at the very conclusion of the work. Gautama says that matters that are not dealt with in his work should be decided by a *pariṣad* of at least ten learned Brahmins (GDh 28.48). He goes on to define the constitution of such a *pariṣad*. It should consist of four individuals who have mastered the four Vedas,[113] three who know three different *dharma* traditions, and three that are described in this unclear and ambiguous expres-

107. See also Lingat 1973, 17, and Sadasivaiah 1967, 158f.

108. See ĀpDh 1.3.11.38; GDh 28.48–50; MDh 12.108–14; YDh 1.9.

109. BāU 6.2.1. The *Chāndogya Upaniṣad* (5.3.1) calls the assembly *samiti*.

110. Lingat 1973, 17. See also YDh 3.300.

111. For an extensive treatment of the subject, see Kane 1974, II.2, 966–74; Meyer 1927, 316f.

112. In saying "hermit or ascetic" Lingat adroitly avoids the problem (which I will presently deal with) raised by the texts themselves as to which three *āśrama*s are represented.

113. It is unclear whether each of the four should have mastered all four Vedas or one separate Veda. In translating GDh 28.49 Bühler opts for the first, and in translating BDh 1.1.8 he chooses the latter alternative.

sion: *prāguttamās [-uttamāt] traya āśramiṇaḥ* (GDh 28.49). The commentator Maskarin reads *uttamāḥ* (nominative plural), while Haradatta reads *uttamāt* (ablative singular).[114] Haradatta's reading, I believe, is influenced by his desire to link this passage to an earlier one (GDh 3.2) in which Gautama enumerates the four *āśrama*s and places the mendicant (*bhikṣu*) third and the hermit (*vaikhānasa*) last, an order that Haradatta considered unorthodox (see section 3.1.6). His interpretation is that this artificial sequence permitted Gautama to use the expression *prāguttamāt* ("before the last") in his passage on the constitution of a *pariṣad*, thereby excluding the hermit. Thus, according to Haradatta, the three *āśramin*s are student, householder, and religious mendicant.[115] Even though Maskarin's reading differs from Haradatta's, their interpretations of this passage are identical.

Baudhāyana (BDh 1.1.8) and Vasiṣṭha (VaDh 3.20) cite a common verse. Baudhāyana's introductory remark *athāpy udāharanti* ("Now, they also cite") indicates that this was a verse well known in the tradition. The ten men constituting a *pariṣad* according this verse are as follows: four men who have mastered the four Vedas, an expert in vedic exegesis, one who knows the auxiliary sciences of the Veda,[116] a legal scholar, and three described as *āśramasthās trayo viprāḥ* [*mukhyāḥ*] ("three Brahmins [*or* eminent men] belonging to [*or* living in] an *āśrama*."[117] Even though the text does not specify the *āśrama*s to which they should belong or whether the three should belong to three different *āśrama*s, Govinda (commenting on BDh 1.1.8) follows Haradatta and specifies the student, the householder, and the renouncer, observing that forest hermits are excluded because they live in forests, whereas renouncers do come into villages and towns to beg food.[118]

The final text on the constitution of a *pariṣad* comes from Manu (MDh 12.111), according to whom the ten men are as follows: three who know the triple Veda, a logician, an expert in vedic exegesis, an etymologist, a legal scholar, and three described as *trayaś cāśramiṇaḥ pūrve*, a phrase Bühler translates as "three men belonging to the first three orders." Medhātithi presents two opinions: the first takes the three to be student, householder, and hermit, while the second replaces the hermit with the renouncer. All other commentators of Manu follow the former opinion without reservation, interpreting *pūrve* to mean the "first" or "earlier" three *āśrama*s.

Kane's (1974, II.2, 968) discussion of these passages is uncharacteristically confused and inaccurate. Kane understands Gautama as prescribing a student, a householder, and a renouncer,[119] and Baudhāyana and Vasiṣṭha as prescribing a householder, a hermit, and a renouncer, against the evidence of the texts and the commentaries. Irrespective of their differences, however, all these commentators and modern scholars

114. I deal with these two readings later: see note 123.

115. Haradatta's reading of Gautama and his interpretation of that passage as excluding the hermit are followed by Govinda in his commentary on BDh 1.1.8 and accepted by Kane (1974, II.1, 416).

116. They are pronunciation, meter, grammar, astronomy, and the ritual science (which includes *dharma*).

117. Baudhāyana reads *viprāḥ* ("Brahmins") and Vasiṣṭha *mukhyāḥ* ("eminent").

118. Bühler, in his translations of both Baudhāyana and Vasiṣṭha, accepts the interpretation that the three should belong to three different *āśrama*s.

119. So also Sharma 1939, 68.

assume without question that the terms *āśramin* and *āśramatha* in these texts indeed refer to individuals belonging to one of the four *āśramas*.

It is this assumption that I want to question.[120] Lingat (1973, 17) has rightly observed:

> *Pariṣad* "colleges" disappeared in relatively early times, probably prior to the development of the literature comprised in the *śāstras*. Manu preserves the institution, but the fact that he allows a single qualified Brahmin the function of proclaiming *ācāra* ("custom") is significant. As his commentators Medhātithi and Kullūka see it, that source is involved only where the rules are of secondary interest. All essential rules from then onwards appear in the Smṛtis themselves. The proper functions of *pariṣads*, which are above all to give decisions in particular cases and notably in questions of penance, have been fulfilled at later periods by Brahmins attached to the courts of Indian princes, such as the *paṇḍita* who bears the title *vinaya-sthiti-sthāpaka* ("he who established the lines of good discipline") in Gupta inscriptions. In our own days they are fulfilled by caste meetings or by the heads of religious orders (*matha*). Interpretation in the proper sense of that word, namely that which enables principles or general rules to be singled out, finally passed to commentators and to the authors of independent treatises.

At least by the time of Manu the *pariṣad* with a quorum of ten had ceased to be a practical institution. Manu, as Lingat remarks, pays lip service to the *pariṣad* and goes on to give a variety of "substitutes" that reflect more the actual practice of the time. Indeed, the *pariṣad* of ten members is not mentioned at all in later literature,[121] and significant legal treatises, such as that of Nārada, fail to mention the institution at all.

The early obsolescence of the institution makes the interpretations of medieval commentators unreliable; they were certainly not reflecting contemporary practice in this regard. To examine the early texts afresh, we need to uncouple *pariṣad* from the *āśrama* system.

For the reasons I am about to set forth, moreover, it is extremely unlikely that a connection could have existed between these two institutions. As I have shown in chapter 3, the *āśrama* system first emerged as a theological scheme intended to reevaluate several religious institutions that existed at the margins of the Brāhmaṇical world. We have also seen that the mainstream traditions represented by Gautama and Baudhāyana rejected that novel scheme and strenuously defended the centrality of the householder. It is extremely unlikely, therefore, that the constitution of as practical and as central an institution as the *pariṣad* would be connected to a theological scheme that was new at the time and rejected by the conservative mainstream. Unless we are ready to accept total inconsistency, moreover, it is doubly unlikely that Gautama and Baudhāyana, who

120. Meyer (1927, 136–37) has also questioned the relationship between the *pariṣad* and the *āśramas* and drawn attention to the many problems created by such a connection. Later scholarship has by and large ignored Meyer's rejection of the association between these two institutions.

121. Āpastamba (ĀpDh 1.11.38) mentions the *pariṣad* but is silent on its constitution, while Yājñavalkya (YDh 1.9) merely states that a *pariṣad* is constituted by three or four experts in all the Vedas. Śaṃkara (on BāU 4.3.2) does mention the *pariṣad* with a minimum of ten (*daśāvara*), three, or just one, but it is clearly a somewhat truncated citation of the opening words (*pratīka*) of MDh 12.110–13. The *Mahābhārata* (12.37.15), without mentioning *pariṣad*, says that whatever ten experts of the Veda or four dharmaśāstric scholars declare should be regarded as *dharma*.

rejected the *āśrama* system outright, would have embraced it within the context of the *pariṣad.*

When we examine the other members of the *pariṣad* in the different enumerations, one fact stands out: they are all experts in one or several areas of knowledge. There are vedic scholars and experts in logic, hermeneutics, etymology, and law. Now, simply belonging to one of the *āśramas* does not make an individual an expert in anything. If we accept the traditional interpretation, these three become the odd men out in a *pariṣad.*

A further argument against the traditional interpretation is the inclusion of a student within a *pariṣad.* It may be argued that within the context of the original *āśrama* system a person in the first *āśrama* is an adult perpetual student.[122] For Manu, however, such a person is an adolescent student living temporarily with his teacher. It stretches our credulity to imagine that a mere boy would be allowed to sit in judgment over matters of great importance.

Finally, if we adopt the traditional interpretation, the sources are hopelessly confused regarding the *āśrama* that is excluded. Gautama is understood to exclude the renouncer, while others exclude the hermit. It is hard to imagine how during the early period either could have been thought of as natural candidates to sit in a *pariṣad.* The dharmaśāstric tradition was handed down in vedic schools which were composed of married Brahmin householders deeply suspicious of the renunciatory ideology and life style. If, as Gautama (GDh 3.32) says, hermits were not permitted to step on plowed land, how could he include them in *pariṣads* that convened in villages and towns?

In light of these difficulties I believe we should reject the traditional interpretation. The term *āśrama,* at least in the Dharmasūtras of Gautama, Baudhāyana, and Vasiṣṭha, I propose, is used in its original meaning as the life or place of a very special type of Brahmin householder noted for holiness and learning (see section 1.1.4) and does not relate to the *āśrama* system. *Āśramastha* in the texts of Baudhāyana and Vasiṣṭha, therefore, refers to persons who live in such a place or lead such a life. I prefer Vasiṣṭha's reading of *mukhya* ("eminent"), because to call such people Brahmins would be pleonastic. It also parallels Gautama's adjective *prāguttamāḥ,* which, though no doubt obscure, may mean something like "elderly and eminent."[123]

If my interpretation is right, then during the earliest period a *pariṣad* included, besides seven experts, three people who epitomized the ideal vedic mode of life both in holiness and learning. The author of Manu's verse, on the other hand, may have been operating within the traditional interpretation of the earlier texts. By *āśramiṇaḥ pūrve* he may well have intended three people belonging to the first three *āśramas,* although Manu's connection, if any, between the two institutions had no practical implications because the ten-member *pariṣad* was then obsolete. Manu's verse, however, can also be

122. Kane (1974, II.2, 968) assumes he is a perpetual student. One may question, nevertheless, how widespread and common such students were at any point in Indian history for them to have been considered natural candidates for this institution.

123. I prefer *uttamāḥ* to *uttamāt,* both because the former is the lectio difficilior and because the latter may have been a later emendation to find a reading corresponding to the traditional interpretation. The meaning of *prāg* is not certain, but it may well refer to elderly leaders of people leading the *āśrama* life and parallel *pūrve* of Manu. *Mukhya* is used with references to leaders of guilds and associations (see Majumdar 1922, 29), and may have a similar meaning here. I think Gautama's text can be understood without assuming, as Meyer (1927, 317) does, that he had Manu's text before him when he composed it.

interpreted in line with the older sources if we take *pūrve* to mean something similar to *prāg* of Gautama, namely elderly and eminent people. In either case, the early institution of *pariṣad* with a quorum of ten, I believe, had no connection with the *āśrama* system.

7.5 Āśrama *and Other Aspects of* Dharma

In spite of the lip service paid here and there to the so-called "common *dharma*" that aspired to a universal ethic, Brāhmaṇical *dharma*, as we have seen,[124] was deeply rooted in the hierarchical arrangement of *varṇas*. Every detail from the material of a girdle and the size of a staff to the severity of punishment for crimes was determined by a person's *varṇa*. This tendency to measure everything by the *varṇa* yardstick extended, although to a far lesser degree, also to its companion institution of *āśrama* especially during the medieval period.

People belonging to different *āśramas* are assigned different emblems of identification, which they are required to wear. A verse ascribed to Dakṣa states:

> A vedic student is distinguished by the girdle, antelope skin, staff, and the like; a householder by the staff, the broom of sacred grass, and the like; a forest hermit by the (long) nails and hair; and a renouncer by the triple staff. These are their respective marks.[125]

Common emblems that must be worn by all are similarly enjoined: "By discarding his sacrificial cord a vedic student, a householder, a forest hermit, and even a renouncer will fall. Let no one, therefore, abandon it."[126]

Various religious practices ranging from purification after toilet to bathing and eating are differentiated according to the *āśrama* to which a person belongs. A couple of verses found with slight variations in Vasiṣṭha (VaDh 16.18–19), Manu (MDh 5.136–37), and Viṣṇu (ViDh 60.25–26), and therefore probably belonging to the general gnomic tradition, deals with the purification a man is expected to perform after toilet according to his *āśrama*:

> A man who wants to purify himself should apply earth once on the penis, thrice on the anus, ten times on the (left) hand alone, and seven times on both hands.[127]
>
> This is the purification for householders. Twice that amount is prescribed for vedic students, three times for forest hermits, and four times for renouncers.[128]

124. See section 7.1. Sometimes *ahiṃsā* ("non-injury") or similar central ethical principle is singled out as the essential or the highest *dharma*. On the issue of "universal *dharma*" (*sanātanadharma*), see Halbfass 1988, 310–48.

125. See Yādavaprakāśa, *Yatidharmasamuccaya*, Ch. 3, p. 12 (Olivelle 1987, 15). This verse is found in the *Dakṣasmṛti*, 1.12. The term *veda* here most likely means "broom of sacred grass." In an earlier publication I mistakenly translated it as "Veda" (Olivelle 1987, 15).

126. Uśanas cited in Yādavaprakāśa's *Yatidharmasamuccaya*, Ch. 3, p. 11 (Olivelle 1987, 15).

127. I give the version of Manu. Slightly variant readings occur in the other two texts.

128. See also *Dakṣasmṛti*, 5.8–9. These or similar verses are cited frequently in the medieval literature: Vaidyanātha Dīkṣita, *Smṛtimuktāphala*, I, 196; Devaṇṇabhaṭṭa, *Smṛticandrikā*, Āhnikakāṇḍa, p. 93 (Eng. tr., p. 161); Ypra 26.43; 67.21.

The *Vaikhānasa Dharmasūtra* (VaiDh 2.9) gives a simpler rule. It lays down the basic rules of purification applicable to householders and students and says that hermits and renouncers should perform double the basic purification. Indeed, the *Vaikhānasa* explicitly presents its rules for such common rites as bathing (VaiG 1.2; VaiDh 2.13) with reference to the four *āśramas*.

A significant aspect of these rules is that the householder is taken as the norm. The rules applicable to the others can be gathered by extending with appropriate modifications the basic rule of the householder. We see here the application of a well-known rule of ritual hermeneutics. A detailed description is given only of the rite that is considered the archetype (*prakṛti*) of a class of rites. The others are considered modifications (*vikṛti*) of the archetype and their procedures are obtained by extending to them the procedure of the ideal type with appropriate modifications.[129]

A more general application of the principle of extension involving both the householder and the student is found in Yādavaprakāśa's discussion of the daily practices of a renouncer.[130] He says that whatever practice is not mentioned by him should be gathered from the *dharma* of vedic students, and if a practice is not discussed even there, it should be gathered from the *dharma* of householders. In support of this principle Yādava cites a verse ascribed to Vyāsa: "All the duties of all the *āśramas* that are not in conflict with each other become the duties common to all the *āśramas*."[131]

Vāsudevāśrama (Ypra 69.21–23) cites a passage that extends the above incremental formula 1:2:3:4 to penances. When a person in another *āśrama* commits a sin for which the appropriate penance is mentioned in the texts only with reference to householders, he should multiply that penance accordingly: that is, twice if he is a student, thrice if he is a hermit, and four times if he is a renouncer.

A passage ascribed to Vyāsa specifies the number of times people belonging to different *āśramas* should bathe each day: "Hermits and householders should bathe at dawn and at noon; renouncers should bathe at dawn, noon, and dusk; while vedic students should bathe once a day."[132] A similar text specifying how often one should shave is cited but rejected as unauthoritative by Vāsudevāśrama (Ypra 61.139–142): "(Shaving should be done) every month by householders, every fortnight by sacrificers,[133] every season by renouncers, and at their pleasure by students."

A very ancient text, cited with minor variations already by Āpastamba (ĀpDh 2.9.13), Baudhāyana (BDh 2.13.7; 2.18.13), and Vasiṣṭha (VaDh 6.20) and clearly coming from the ascetic gnomic tradition, specifies the quantity of food a person should eat, depending on the *āśrama* to which he belongs: "Eight mouthfuls constitute the meal of a

129. This principle of extension is called *atideśa*. For an explanation of this principle, see Kane 1962, V.2, 1321–26.

130. *Yatidharmasamuccaya*, Ch. 6, p. 28.

131. This principle is already hinted at by Gautama (GDh 3.10) when he says that the duties prescribed for a vedic student are applicable to other *āśramas* as well if they are not in conflict with the special duties of a particular *āśrama*.

132. Cited in Vaidyanātha Dīkṣita's *Smṛtimuktāphala*, I, 197. It is ascribed to Dakṣa by Devaṇṇabhaṭṭa in his *Smṛticandrikā*, Āhnikakāṇḍa, p. 181 (Eng. tr., p. 301). A similar passage is found in the *Garuḍa Purāṇa*, I.213.59–60.

133. This version of the text has sacrificers and omits hermits. I have been unable to locate other citations of this verse to verify this reading.

renouncer, sixteen that of a hermit, thirty-two that of a householder, and an unlimited quantity that of a student."[134]

The respective goals attained after death by people in the four *āśrama*s also become the subject of discussion. A long passage on the *āśrama*s in the *Mahābhārata* (12.184–85) specifies the goals of the four in a general way: students go to heaven and obtain all desires; householders attain heaven; hermits attain worlds difficult to obtain; and renouncers gain the world of Brahmā. The *Viṣṇu Purāṇa* (1.6.36–39), after listing the worlds attained by people of the four *varṇa*s who perform their respective duties faithfully, states that students attain the world of the 80,000 sages,[135] hermits the world of the seven seers, householders the world of the forefathers, and renouncers the world of Brahmā. The *Kūrma Purāṇa* (1.2.66–71) also connects the worlds of the *varṇa*s and *āśrama*s; the only difference from the *Viṣṇu Purāṇa* is that the world of Prajāpati is assigned to householders and the world of Hiraṇyagarbha to renouncers, while immortality is reserved for yogins. The *Kūrma Purāṇa* (1.21.45) likewise assigns a specific god to each *āśrama:* all gods[136] to householders, Brahmā to students, the sun to hermits, and Śiva to renouncers.

What our discussion here points to is the progressive integration of the *āśrama*s into the central framework, for so long dominated by the *varṇa* ideology, within which Brāhmaṇical theologians understood and explained religious practices, criminal and civil law, and even cosmological and soteriological schemes. A verse ascribed to Yama presents the position of *varṇāśrama*, now considered almost a single category, in Brāhmaṇical theology: "There is none higher than a Brahmin, as there is no one superior to Vāsudeva. There is nothing higher than *varṇāśrama*, and no scripture equals the Veda."[137]

7.6 Sets of Four: The Puruṣārthas and the Āśramas

I have already made reference to the significance of the number four in Indian culture. The centrality of many schemes consisting of sets of four—four Vedas, four *varṇa*s, four *yuga*s, four *āśrama*s, four feet of a typical Indian verse—prove this point beyond doubt.

There is a common tendency, moreover, to relate the various schemes of four to one another. We have already seen such a correlation between the four *āśrama*s and the four *varṇa*s. Another central scheme of ancient Indian religion consists of the aims of human life (*puruṣārtha*). In the most ancient documents these consisted of three: *dharma* ("righteousness"), *artha* ("wealth"), and *kāma* ("pleasure"). These three came to be known by the shorthand term *trivarga* ("triple set"). With the advent of *mokṣa* ("libera-

134. This verse is frequently cited in the later literature: MBh (southern recension) 1.86.*862; Aparāditya on YDh 3.55 (p. 945); KKT, XIV, 59; Devaṇṇabhaṭṭa, *Smṛticandrikā*, Āhnikakāṇḍa, p. 43 (Eng. tr., p. 73); Vaidyanātha Dīkṣita, *Smṛtimuktāphala*, I, 200, 203. For a more detailed examination of this verse, see Sprockhoff 1984, 33–35; 1976, 119.

135. Regarding the 80,000 sages, see section 3.1.3.

136. It is unclear whether all the gods are meant by the term *sarve*, or the class of gods known as "all-gods" (*viśvedeva*).

137. Cited in Yādavaprakāśa's *Yatidharmasamuccaya*, Ch. 6, p. 34.

tion") as the overarching human concern, the scheme of three was expanded into one of four (*caturvarga*).[138] The scheme of *puruṣārtha*s and the *āśrama* system has this much in common: they attempt to classify the different modes and goals of life that human beings pursue. Both presuppose that there is no fundamental contradiction between these various goals and that an individual may legitimately follow all of them either comprehensively or one at a time.

Given that both consist of a set of four and that both deal with the goals humans set for themselves, it is tempting to see them as in some way related to each other within the history and theology of Brāhmaṇism. Many have succumbed to that temptation. Thapar's (1982, 273) opening remarks in her essay on the householder and the renouncer accepting "the four āśramas as theoretical preconditions to the concept of puruṣārthas" show how widespread and how uncritically accepted this assumption is. The theoretical and historical correlation between *āśrama* and *puruṣārtha* underlies Charles Malamoud's (1982) article "On the Rhetoric and Semantics of Puruṣārthas" published in the same Festschrift for Louis Dumont as Thapar's essay.[139]

After discussing the possible correlation between the *varṇa*s and the *puruṣārtha*s, Malamoud (1982, 51–52) observes:

> The correspondence between the puruṣārthas and the āśramas is less involved. On the basis of the entire trivarga, with the hierarchy giving the first place to dharma, being valid for the first three stages of life, a specific blend of puruṣārthas can be assigned to each of the four periods. If mokṣa is the sole preoccupation of the saṁnyāsins, and of them alone, it is clear that kāma and artha are practically forbidden to a Brahman student, who must concentrate on dharma. The same may be said for vānaprastha, with however the rider that this third stage is sometimes considered as the antechamber, as it were, of the fourth. It is thus the householder, gṛhastha, who must learn how to combine and balance the three puruṣārthas of the trivarga, since only at this stage is it dharmic to devote oneself to artha and kāma.

Even though the correlation is not perfect—there is no single *puruṣārtha* for each *āśrama*—Malamoud sees them not just as parallel but as theologically interrelated schemes.

An even closer relationship between the two is envisaged by Klostermaier (1989, 320) in his recent survey of Hinduism:

> The number four serves not only to classify the Veda . . . and to divide humanity into basic sections [i.e., *varṇa*s] but also to structure the life of individuals themselves [i.e., *āśrama*s]. The successive stages of life of a high-caste person was [*sic*] correlated to another tetrad, the *caturvarga* or the "four aims of life" (*puruṣārtha*).

In his recent article on the *puruṣārtha*s, Krishnan (1989, 65–66) attempts to establish a strict correlation:

138. For further details on this history of this theological scheme, see Malamoud 1982; Sharma 1982.

139. The significance of this correlation as a way of approaching the study of Indian culture among the scholars contributing to this volume is also noted by its editor, Madan (1982, 412): "Here sociology, indology and philosophy come together in a collective endeavour to explore the Hindu way of life in terms of puruṣārtha and āśrama."

> Also the importance of a particular *puruṣārtha* varies with the stage of life, the *āśrama*, in which a man is in [*sic*], during the course of his life's journey. In the *brahmacarya āśrama, dharma* is of utmost importance with minimal *artha* and *kāma* essential for bodily maintenance. In the *gṛhastha āśrama, kāma* is of paramount importance, but it must be adequately supported by *artha* and tempered by *dharma.* In the *sannyāsa āśrama, mokṣa* coupled with *dharma* is the *paramapuruṣārtha, artha* and *kāma* playing a minimal role. In fact, one *puruṣārtha* becomes the foundation of either one or two *puruṣārthas* depending upon the stage of life (*āśrama*) of the person concerned.

Perhaps the strictest correlation not merely between the *puruṣārtha*s and the *āśrama*s but between these and the *varṇa*s has been drawn by Sharma (1982). Admitting that everyone is called upon to pursue all four *puruṣārtha*s, Sharma nevertheless posits "a rough correspondence between the four stages of life and the four *puruṣārthas*":

> It is helpful to begin by correlating the *āśramas* (stages of life) with the four *puruṣārthas,* since the correlation is easy to see and conforms well with the order of enumeration. In the first *āśrama* one pursues *dharma*; in the second *artha* and *kāma* as regulated by *dharma*; and in the third and fourth stages one moves towards *mokṣa,* though in the third stage *dharma* is perhaps primary. (Sharma 1982, 16)

He goes on to posit the following correlations between these two schemes and the *varṇa*s (Sharma 1982, 17):

dharma	Brahmin and Kṣatriya	student and hermit
artha	Kṣatriya and Vaiśya	hermit and householder
kāma	Vaiśya and Śūdra	householder
mokṣa	Brahmin	hermit and renouncer

Now, except for the broad connection between the *varṇa*s and the *āśrama*s that we have already noted, there is absolutely no evidence for such neat correlations in the sources themselves. It is interesting that none of these authors cite any primary sources for their conclusions. The reason for the oversight is simple; in all my work on the *āśramas* I have yet to find an ancient or medieval author or text that posits such a correlation. We have already seen (section 5.1) that the *Kāmasūtra* (1.2.1–4) does indeed correlate the *puruṣārtha*s to the three periods of a man's life, but these periods are not identified with any *āśrama.*

> The life span of a man is one hundred years. Dividing that time, he should attend to the three aims of life in such a way that they support rather than hinder each other. In his youth he should attend to profitable aims (*artha*) such as learning, in his prime to pleasure (*kāma*), and in his old age to righteousness (*dharma*) and liberation (*mokṣa*).

Not only does the author of the *Kāmasūtra* not discuss here the *āśrama*s, its distribution of the *puruṣārtha*s among the different periods of life is very different from the one proposed by most scholars. For him the prime years of adult life should be spent in enjoying sensual pleasures!

The only clear historical relationship between a *puruṣārtha* and an *āśrama* is found between renunciation and liberation. The tradition is unanimous that the last *āśrama* is devoted solely to the pursuit of liberation, or at least the world of Brahmā. We have seen that renunciation is often referred to simply as *mokṣa*. Even in passages that establish this relationship, however, *mokṣa* is not presented as one of the *puruṣārtha*s.

The total absence of any primary sources that discuss the *āśrama*s within the context of the *puruṣārtha*s makes it clear that Brāhmaṇical theology did not perceive these schemes in the same way as modern scholars do. This much can be said with certainty: there is no historical connection between the scheme of the four *puruṣārtha*s and the system of the four *āśrama*s. At least in the present case—and, I suspect, frequently elsewhere—the juxtaposition of one set of four with another set of four is purely an act of scholarly imagination.

8

The *Aśrama* System in Medieval Theology

The major developments and changes in the *āśrama* system took place roughly between the fifth century B.C.E. and the fifth century C.E. Medieval theology and law inherited the system so developed. Even though drastic changes in that system did not take place, discussions and debates of interest concerning the *āśrama*s continued during the medieval period. They will be the subject of this last chapter in our investigation of the history of the *āśrama* system.

8.1 Anāśramin: *Obligation to Live in an* Āśrama

For what must have been a variety of historical and theological reasons, which we have not yet fully understood, only four institutions came to be the theologically defined as *āśrama*s, even though each *āśrama* comprehended a cluster of similar religious ways of life. We have seen how these definitions left out women and some social classes, such as the Śūdras. Even when we restrict ourselves to male Brahmins, there are at least two types of individuals significant in other theological schemes who are left out of both the original and the classical *āśrama* system.[1] They are the student who has returned home after graduation (technically called *snātaka*) but has not yet married, and the widower. Such individuals who live outside the *āśrama* scheme are referred to as *anāśramin*, a term that is absent in the early *dharma* literature but is commonly used at least from the time of Śaṃkara.[2]

Within the system of life-cycle rites (*saṃskāra*) the *snātaka* occupies a very important position. Long sections of all the *dharma* treatises are devoted to his duties and privileges. A *snātaka* is one of a handful of guests deemed worthy of receiving the honey-mixture (*madhuparka*).[3] He is considered so sacred and his status so eminent, that

1. The very young child prior to initiation, of course, is also left out, but that would not have caused serious theological problems.

2. The term is used by both Śaṃkara and Bhāskara in their commentaries on VeS 3.4.36–38. Yājñavalkya (YDh 3.241) uses the expression *anāśrame vāsaḥ* ("living in a non-āśramic state").

3. See GDh 5.27–28; ĀpDh 2.8.6; VaDh 11.2; MDh 3.119.

many authorities give him precedence over even a king; if a king meets a *snātaka* on the road it is the king who should salute the latter with respect.[4] The *snātaka* thus occupies totally contrasting positions within the two major Brāhmaṇical systems of sacraments and *āśramas*.

We also encounter two contrasting positions within Brāhmaṇical theology regarding the importance of living in an ā*śrama.* On the one hand, there is a tendency to discount outward appearances and to emphasize internal qualities. Belonging to socially recognized institutions of holiness and wearing the appropriate insignia of such states do not make a person holy. Yājñavalkya says that "an *āśrama* is not the cause of righteousness."[5] Manu echoes the same when he says: "Although he may be censured, let him treat all creatures alike and practice righteousness in whatever *āśrama* he may happen to live, for an emblem is not the cause of righteousness."[6] The *Mahābhārata* (12.112.13) also says that "an *āśrama* is not an index of righteousness" and goes on to ask the rhetorical question dripping with sarcasm: "Should one man kill a Brahmin in an *āśrama* and another present the gift of a cow in a non-*āśrama*, is the former not a grievous sin, and is that gift given in vain?"[7]

On the other hand, there is a growing tendency within Brāhmaṇical theology to regard the *āśrama* scheme as obligatory and to consider non-āśramic states as deficient and even sinful. Yājñavalkya (YDh 3.241) himself, who earlier in his treatise had asserted that an *āśrama* does not cause righteousness, enumerates "living outside an *āśrama*" among the minor sins. Likewise, the *Mahābhārata* (13.24.71) lists "those who are outside the four *āśramas*" among people who go to hell. The *Kūrma Purāṇa* (2.21.36) also calls an *anāśramin* a *paṅktidūṣaka*, that is, a man who defiles others who sit down in the same line as him for a meal.

As living outside the *āśramas* came to be considered a sin, smṛti passages were invented both to demonstrate that doctrine and to prescribe appropriate penances. One of the earliest citations of such a text is made by Śaṃkara: "A Brahmin shall not remain an *anāśramin* even for a single day. If one remains an *anāśramin* for a year, one should perform a single *kṛcchra* penance."[8] Mādhava, likewise, deals with the sin of living outside the *āśramas* in the section on penances and cites a text ascribed to Hārīta:

4. See MDh 2.138–39; GDh 6.25; VaDh 13.59.

5. YDh 3.65: *nāśramaḥ kāraṇaṃ dharme.*

6. MDh 6.66: *dūṣito 'pi cared dharmaṃ yatra tatrāśrame vasan / samaḥ sarveṣu bhūteṣu na liṅgaṃ dharmakāraṇam //* The same verse is repeated in the *Viṣṇudharmottara Purāṇa*, 2.131.33.

7. MBh 12.112.14: *āśrame yo dvijaṃ hanyād gāṃ vā dadyād anāśrame / kiṃ nu tat pātakaṃ na syāt tad vā dattaṃ vṛthā bhavet //*

8. Śaṃkara on VeS 3.4.39: *anāśramī na tiṣṭheta dinam ekam api dvijaḥ / saṃvatsaram anāśramī sthitvā kṛcchram ekaṃ caret //* Thibaut mistranslates the last phrase, "he goes to utter ruin," and thus misses the point of the text, which is to prescribe the penance for living outside the *āśramas*. The opening phrase (*pratīka*) of the same passage is cited in the commentaries of Bhāskara and Rāmānuja on the same *sūtra.* All three cite it anonymously simply as a smṛti. Variants of this verse are cited frequently in medieval texts: see Vaidyanātha Dīkṣita *Smṛtimuktāphala*, I, 123; Bhaṭṭoji Dīkṣita, *Caturviṃśatimatasaṃgraha*, p. 85. *Kṛcchra* is the generic term for a penance, but when the term is used without a qualification it stands for the *prājāpatya* penance: eating once a day for three days during the night and for three days during the day, eating what is received unasked for three more days, and fasting completely during the last three days. See Kane 1973, IV, 132, 145.

> A man who has been an *anāśramin* for a year should perform the *prājāpatya* penance and then enter an *āśrama*. If he has been so for two years, or for three years, or for over three years, he should perform respectively the *atikṛcchra*, or the *kṛcchrātikṛcchra*, or the lunar penance.[9]

The belief in the sinfulness of living outside the *āśramas* is at the root of the prescription regarding the purificatory penance that a person intending to renounce should perform. Sources prescribe different penances, but they are unanimous in enjoining a more severe penance on an *anāśramin* than on a person who is in an *āśrama*.[10] A variant reading found in a manuscript of Rudradeva's *Saṃnyāsapaddhati* indicates that one performs such a penance in order to remove the sin of living outside the *āśramas*.[11]

The controversy regarding the status of those outside the *āśrama* scheme must have been relatively old, because the author of the *Vedāntasūtras*, who probably wrote in the early centuries of the common era, found it necessary to discuss whether such people could attain the liberating knowledge of Brahman. He argues that those who stand between the *āśramas*—that is, those who do not belong to a particular *āśrama*—are nevertheless qualified to acquire knowledge, because it is so stated in the Vedas and the Smṛtis. Notwithstanding that, however, the author asserts that it is far better to be in an *āśrama* (VeS 3.4.36–39).[12] The commentators Śaṃkara, Bhāskara, and Rāmānuja do not add anything substantive to the argument. They mention the widower, however, as the primary example of an *anāśramin* and cite the passage mentioned above forbidding a person to remain even for a day outside the *āśramas* in support of the superiority of living in an *āśrama*.

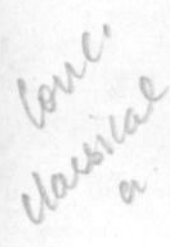

As this discussion shows, the strategy of the creators of the original system to use the concept and the term *āśrama* to evaluate the religious status of different ways of life became successful probably beyond their wildest dreams. Not only did the system they designed become a central institution of Brāhmaṇical theology, the very concept of *āśrama* came to define the theologically proper way to live one's life. By the early middle ages, living outside the four recognized *āśramas* came to be regarded as tantamount to living in sin.

8.2 Atyāśramin: *Transcendence of the* Āśramas

A question parallel to that of living outside the *āśramas* (*anāśrama*) relates to the possibility of living beyond the *āśramas* (*atyāśrama*): is it theologically possible to posit a

9. PāM II, 440. For *prājāpatya* see the previous note. For the variant descriptions of the *atikṛcchra* and the *kṛcchrātikṛcchra*, which involve forms of fasting progressively more severe than the *prājāpatya*, see Kane 1973, IV, 130, 133. The lunar penance consists of reducing and increasing by a mouthful a day the intake of food during the fortnights of the waning and waxing moon, respectively. On the full moon, thus, one eats 15 mouthfuls and on the new moon one observes a total fast.

10. For a detailed discussion of this point, see my note to the translation of Ypra 6.2–3.

11. *anāśramajanitapratyavāyaparihārārtham:* manuscript "I" of my edition. See the critical apparatus to 18.38 (p. 129).

12. Mādhava (PāM I, 533) mentions this passage of the VeS in support of his argument that *anāśramins* such as widowers and *snātakas* are qualified to enter the renouncer's *āśrama* that is devoted to the search for knowledge.

state of life that transcends the totality of *dharma* comprehended by *varṇāśrama*? This was a question that loomed large in medieval Brāhmaṇical theology dealing with liberation, the nature and status of a liberated person, and the highly controversial issue of whether a man can be liberated while he is still alive (*jīvanmukta*).[13]

Whatever may have been the meaning of the term *atyāśramin* in the early literature,[14] during medieval times the term referred specifically to a person who assumed a state of life that was defined as transcending the four *āśrama*s. It has been long recognized that the tendency to classify objects, institutions, and knowledge in general is deeply rooted in Indian culture. Once a classificatory system has been established, moreover, it is common to posit a category that transcends that system, a category that represents a more perfect condition than the ones envisaged within the system—a trait that I would call the X + 1 syndrome. It occurs more frequently in sets of four that are formed by adding one to a preexisting three.[15] Sometimes, as in the fifth Veda,[16] a fifth category is added to a preexisting four. This tendency manifests itself in the discussions regarding the state beyond the four *āśrama*s, namely the fifth *āśrama*.

Beyond that numerological propensity, the issue of *atyāśrama* was inextricably connected to the conflicting views regarding liberation prevalent in medieval theologies. We have seen that in the early literature renunciation as the last *āśrama* was regarded as constituting a state beyond *dharma*, a state devoted solely to the pursuit of liberation. We saw that Manu, accordingly, calls it simply *mokṣa*. The further classification of the fourth *āśrama* that we have examined indicates its growing complexity; not all people living a life of renunciation were either liberated or even aspired to immediate liberation. Renunciation became increasingly another aspect of *dharma*. In this context, liberation or aspiration to liberation was reserved for the highest class of renouncers called Paramahaṃsa. The *Vaikhānasa Dharmasūtra* (VaiDh 1.9), for example, says that Paramahaṃsas are beyond *dharma* and *adharma*, truth and untruth, and all such dualities.

Even though the *Vaikhānasa* does not address this issue, a renouncer who is beyond all dualities of right and wrong inherent in *dharma* is considered in some theological traditions, for example in Advaita Vedānta, as a person who is enlightened, who has attained the liberating knowledge, who is, in other words, liberated while he is still alive (*jīvanmukta*) in the body and visible in this world. It is within these theologies that the claim was made that such individuals are beyond the four *āśrama*s—indeed, beyond the *varṇa*s and beyond the reach of all injunctions and prohibitions that constituted the very heart of Brāhmaṇical *dharma*.

Śaṃkara is the earliest theologian to deal with this subject in a somewhat systematic

13. For a study of the theological debate on these questions between the Advaita and Viśiṣṭādvaita traditions, see Olivelle 1986 and 1987.

14. For a discussion of this issue, see section 1.1.4.

15. For an analysis of this tendency to add one to a preexisting triad, see Malamoud 1982, 34–37, where further bibliography is given. See section 3.5 regarding the applicability of this syndrome to the historical development of the *āśrama* system.

16. Many texts call themselves the fifth Veda, including the *Mahābhārata*, several Purāṇas, and *Tiruvāymoḷi*. See Carman and Narayanan 1989, 4–7; Fitzgerald 1980, 125–40.

manner.[17] He does not, however, always speak with one voice. As we shall see (section 8.5), Śaṃkara, on the one hand, argues against those who would deny the *āśrama* status to renunciation and defends the legitimacy of the celibate *āśrama*s in general and the fourth *āśrama* in particular. On the other hand, there are instances where he appears to affirm that true renunciation, which for him is the renunciation of an enlightened person, is beyond the realm of *varṇa* and *āśrama*, whose *dharma* is part of the illusory phenomenal world constructed by ignorance (*avidyā*).

In the course of explaining the reason why rites are of no use with regard to the acquisition of the liberating knowledge of Brahman and why a seeker after that knowledge should abandon ritual activities as well as ritual accessories such as the top knot and the sacrificial string,[18] Śaṃkara observes:

> If the performance of rites were obligatory and their abandonment undesirable, the (Veda) would not have declared in such unambiguous statements as, "That is the self; you are that" (ChU 6.8.7), the perception of the identity between one's very self and the highest self that is unrelated both to ritual accessories and to ritually caused factors such as castes and *āśrama*s. (*Upadeśasāhasrī* 2.1.31)

Here Śaṃkara lumps *āśrama*s together with castes, rites, and ritual accessories such as the sacrificial string as belonging to the ritual sphere, which is governed by ignorance. *Āśrama*, just like caste, belongs to the illusory body; it is unrelated to one's true self:

> A person who seeks to obtain the perception of this highest truth should abandon the fivefold desire—the desire for sons, wealth, worlds, and so forth—which results from the mistaken identification of oneself with caste, *āśrama*, and the like. (*Upadeśasāhasrī* 2.1.44)

It appears, therefore, that, according to Śaṃkara, a person who considers himself as belonging to a particular *āśrama* cannot by definition possess the knowledge of his true self. An enlightened person—if we follow his argument to its logical conclusion—must be unrelated to and beyond the *āśrama*s. Did Śaṃkara himself draw this conclusion?

In his commentaries on both the *Bṛhadāraṇyaka* and the *Chāndogya Upaniṣad*, Śaṃkara openly admits that a person who possesses the knowledge of Brahman is beyond and outside the *āśrama* system. Commenting on the *Bṛhadāraṇyaka* 3.5.1,[19] he argues that a renouncer should discard ritual accessories such as the sacrificial cord and the normal emblems of the renouncer's *āśrama*. These, he says, are carried by people "who resort to (renunciation) merely as an *āśrama* (*āśramamātra*)." An opponent objects that the text under discussion enjoins renunciation, and renunciation requires the carrying of ritual accessories: "The Vedas and Smṛtis enjoin on the renouncer's *āśrama* both the ritual instruments, such as the sacrificial string, and the (renouncer's) emblem." His

17. I will limit myself to the six works regarding whose authenticity there appears to be a scholarly consensus. They are Śaṃkara commentaries on the *Vedāntasutras*, the *Bhagavad Gīta*, and three Upaniṣads—*Bṛhadāraṇyaka*, *Chāndogya*, and *Taittirīya*—and his independent treatise *Upadeśasāhasrī*. See Paul Hacker's (1978) contributions on Śaṃkara; Nakamura 1983.

18. He concludes the first chapter of the prose section of the *Upadeśasāhasrī* (2.1.44) likewise by saying: "A person who is firmly established in the perception of the highest truth, therefore, should abandon all rites and their accessories, such as the sacrificial string, because they are the result of ignorance."

19. For a translation and study of this passage, see Olivelle 1986, 83–91.

assumption is that the renunciation Śaṃkara is referring to must be the same as the renouncer's *āśrama.* The text under discussion, the opponent therefore concludes, must refer to the abandonment of items other than the sacrificial string and the top knot.

Śaṃkara's answer is illuminating. He asserts that there is a type of renunciation different from the renunciation associated with the acquisition of knowledge.[20] The former type of renunciation "constitutes an *āśrama*" (*āśramarūpaṃ pārivrājyaṃ*) and is directed not at knowledge but at attaining a heavenly world after death. It is with reference to this *āśrama* of renunciation that ritual instruments such as the sacrificial cord are prescribed. Śaṃkara thus emphatically rejects the opponent's identification of renunciation as such with the renouncer's *āśrama*—a common enough assumption though it must have been—and makes a sharp distinction between two types of renunciation: renunciation that results from the knowledge of Brahman and renunciation that constitutes an *āśrama.* It is evident that in the eyes of Śaṃkara the former did not constitute an *āśrama.* Elsewhere in the same passage he identifies such a renouncer as a Paramahaṃsa.[21] All the rules relating to renunciation found in authoritative texts, therefore, refer only to the *āśrama* of renunciation.

Śaṁkara takes a similar position in his commentary on the famous passage (see section 3.5) dealing with the three branches of *dharma* (*dharmaskandha*) of the *Chāndogya Upaniṣad,* 2.23. He includes both the hermit and the renouncer within the third *dharmaskandha* of austerity; this renouncer, however, is characterized as "not established in Brahman but established merely in the *dharma* of that *āśrama*" (*na brahmasaṃsthaḥ āśramadharmamātrasaṃsthaḥ*). It appears, therefore, that here Śaṃkara considers the three *dharmaskandhas* to include all four *āśramas*. The person "established in Brahman" (*brahmasaṃstha*), on the other hand, is the renouncer who stands outside the *āśramas.*[22] For Śaṃkara a person who knows Brahman is by definition a renouncer. He concludes:

> Thus, the term *brahmasaṃstha* should be taken here as referring to the mode of life called Paramahaṃsa that is beyond the *āśramas* (*atyāśramin*) and that refers solely to a renouncer who has given up all rites and ritual accessories. . . . This alone, therefore, is the renunciation declared in the Veda and not the taking of a sacrificial string, a triple staff, water pot, and the like.[23]

Śaṃkara here identifies the renouncer who knows Brahman not only with Paramahaṃsa but also with *atyāśramin.*

20. Śaṃkara does not make any lexical differentiation between these two divergent types of renunciation, calling both by the same name, *pārivrājya.*

21. See numbers 12 and 64 in Olivelle 1986, pp. 80 and 82.

22. Later in the same discussion, however, Śaṃkara disagrees with an opponent who also takes the second *dharmaskandha* of austerity to encompass both the hermit and the renouncer, just as Śaṃkara had done earlier. The reason appears to be that the opponent does not admit a higher type of renouncer who is the person "established in Brahman" and takes the latter to be a person in any *āśrama* who has come to realize Brahman. This explanation of Śaṃkara's opponent is accepted by Rāmānuja in his commentary on VeS 3.4.19. Bhāskara (on VeS 3.4.20), who was probably a contemporary of Śaṃkara, reproduces Śaṃkara's argument but rejects it in favor of the other interpretation.

23. *tathā ihāpi brahmasaṃsthaśabdo nivṛttasarvakarmatatsādhanaparivrāḍekaviṣaye 'tyāśramiṇi paramahaṃsākhye vṛtta iha bhavitum arhati, mukhyāmṛtatvaphalaśravaṇāt. ataś cedam evaikaṃ vedoktaṃ pārivrājyam, na yajñopavītatridaṇḍakamaṇḍalvādiparigraha iti.* Śaṃkara goes on to cite several texts in support of this assertion, including the reference to *atyāśramin* in the *Śvetāśvatara Upaniṣad* (6.21).

In his commentary on the *Bṛhadāraṇyaka Upaniṣad,* 4.5.15, furthermore, Śaṃkara affirms that renunciation is meant not only for those who possess the knowledge of Brahman but also for those who seek to obtain it. In his comments on 4.4.22 of the same Upaniṣad, he also asserts that those who seek the self abandon all rites and become renouncers. It is, however, uncertain what, if any, distinction Śaṃkara made between the renunciation of an enlightened person and that of a person seeking enlightenment. Such a distinction is common in later Advaita literature, especially in the writings of Vidyāraṇya.[24] It is also unclear whether Śaṃkara assumed the renunciation of a seeker after knowledge to be an *āśrama,*[25] and, if so, whether he made a distinction between that and the *āśrama* of renunciation that he had earlier distinguished from the renunciation of the enlightened and characterized as consisting of carrying the emblems of that state and as unrelated to knowledge.

A very different picture of Śaṃkara's position on the relationship between renunciation and *āśrama,* however, emerges in his commentary on the *Vedāntasūtras.* As we shall see in section 8.5, Śaṃkara's main aim there is to refute the Mīmāṃsika objections (VeS 3.4.18) to the celibate *āśrama*s and to establish the vedic basis of all *āśrama*s, especially that of renunciation. In so doing he presents views that stand in sharp contrast to those expressed in the other commentaries we have examined and in his *Upadeśasāhasrī.*

Śaṃkara's main discussion of this topic is found in his commentary on VeS 3.4.20, in which he attempts to demonstrate that the *Chāndogya* (2.23) statement on the three branches of *dharma* has injunctive force with reference to the celibate *āśrama*s. Here

Śaṃkara asserts that "the person established in Brahman" is a reference to the *āśrama* of renunciation and that the three "branches of *dharma*" encompass only the first three *āśrama*s. This assertion directly contradicts the interpretation he gives in his commentary on the same passage in the *Chāndogya Upaniṣad,* where he asserts that the three "branches" include the four *āśrama*s and that a person established in Brahman is beyond all *āśrama*s.[26] In his commentary on the *Taittirīya Upaniṣad,* 1.12 also, which I shall examine in section 8.5, Śaṃkara defends the existence of *āśrama*s other than that of the householder and assumes that renunciation, in which alone knowledge is possible, is indeed an *āśrama.*

There are several possible explanations for these discrepancies in so vital an area of theology that also had significant practical consequences. One can, of course, assume that the ascription of these texts to Śaṃkara is wrong and that they have been composed by different authors with divergent views on this point. This is possible but probably unlikely, given the evidence advanced in support of their unitary authorship. If the com-

24. See his *Jīvanmuktiviveka,* 1–4. Potter (1982) assumes that the distinction was first introduced by Vidyāraṇya and denies that Śaṃkara ever had such a distinction in mind. According to Potter, Śaṃkara identified renunciation with the state of an enlightened and liberated person (*jīvanmukta*). See also his comments in Potter 1981, 34–38. As my study has hopefully demonstrated, Śaṃkara's position is much more complex and much less clear.

25. His comments on *Bṛhadāraṇyaka* 4.5.15, however, appear to indicate that he took the virtues to be cultivated in renunciation as constituting the duties of that *āśrama* (*āśramakarma*).

26. In his commentary on VeS 3.4.49 also, Śaṃkara assumes that renunciation relating to knowledge is indeed the fourth *āśrama* and that people should undertake them either by going through all of them sequentially (*samuccaya*) or by choosing (probably) the *āśrama* of a renouncer (*vikalpa*).

mentaries on the Upaniṣads were written by the author of the commentary on the *Vedāntasūtras*, then we must assume that Śaṃkara either changed his views or was inconsistent.

Even though Śaṃkara undoubtedly considered at least some form of renunciation to be beyond the modes of life comprehended by the *āśramas*, he nowhere asserts that such renouncers are not bound by conventional morality or that theirs was a totally antinomian state—a view ascribed, as we shall see, to the Advaita tradition in later theological debates. It is, furthermore, extremely unlikely that he would have espoused such a radical view. In spite of the fact that he advocated the total renunciation of rites and such central symbols of the Brāhmaṇical life as the top knot and the sacrificial string, Śaṃkara was not a radical thinker as evidenced by his insistence that only Brahmins are qualified to become renouncers, a position far more conservative than that of most later Advaitins.

Śaṃkara's view that true renunciation prescribed in the Veda does not fall within the scheme of the *āśramas*, so clearly asserted in his commentary on the *Bṛhadāraṇyaka* 3.5.1, appears to have caused some embarrassment to at least a section of later Advaita thinkers. Ānandagiri, the medieval commentator of Śaṃkara,[27] for example, commenting on this passage attempts to explain away Śaṃkara's statement. When Śaṃkara says that the texts alluded to by his opponent refer to the *āśrama* of renunciation, Ānandagiri says, what Śaṃkara really means is that such a type of renunciation is "regarded as an *āśrama*, even though in reality it is not an *āśrama* but has only the appearance of an *āśrama*."[28] The implication is that the renunciation of the enlightened is in fact the true *āśrama*. Ānandānubhava, the thirteenth-century Advaita theologian, also regards the highest state of renunciation, that of an enlightened renouncer, to be an *āśrama* and denounces Bhāskara for not having considered it as such: "How does this miserable scoundrel, the blockhead from Karṇāṭaka, not see that he is contradicting the said authorities even when he reviles a well-known *āśrama*."[29]

The term *atyāśramin* is used with some frequency in several medieval documents with Advaita leaning to characterize a person who is enlightened and who has attained the liberated state while still in the body—the *jīvanmukta*. In attempting to demonstrate the scriptural basis for the existence of such individuals, Vidyāraṇya (JMV, pp. 203–4, 231) says that smṛti texts use a variety of epithets to denote a *jīvanmukta*, among which is *ativarṇāśramin* ("person beyond *varṇa* and *āśrama*"). One of the longest passages in praise of the *atyāśramin* is found in the *Sūta Saṃhitā*, which is traditionally accepted as part of the *Skanda Purāṇa*.[30] Parameśvara here tells Viṣṇu the different types of teachers

27. He is ascribed by some to the end of the thirteenth century: see Potter 1970, 198.

28. *āśramatvena rūpyate vastutas tu nāśramas tadābhāsa iti yāvat*. In *Bṛhadāraṇyaka Upaniṣad* with Śaṃkara's commentary (ĀnSS 15), p. 461.

29. *Nyāyaratnadīpāvali*, ed. Olivelle 1986, 115. See also ibid., 117.

30. Verses from this passage are cited by Vidyāraṇya (JMV, pp. 33–35). A few of them are cited anonymously in the *Nāradaparivrājaka Upaniṣad*, 193–94. References to the *ativarṇāśramin* is found also at SūS 3.7.5, 73. The *Aṣṭāvakra Saṃhitā*, 1.5, also states that the liberated person is beyond *varṇa* and *āśrama*. The *Kūrma Purāṇa* (1.2.83) gives *atyaśramin* (the *Garuḍa Purāṇa*, 1.49.19, reads *antyāśramin*) as a subcategory of Yogin: see section 6.1.2 and note 28 there. See also MBh 12.12.6; 12.285.194–95.

belonging to different classes and *āśrama*s: "The highest type of teacher, O sage, is said to be fivefold: student, householder, hermit, mendicant, and *ativarṇāśramin*, listed in ascending order of superiority" (SūS 3.5.9–10). Here the *ativarṇāśramin* is clearly distinguished from the mendicant and constitutes a fifth category, even though it is not termed the "fifth *āśrama*" (see section 8.3). The text goes on to show that the criterion for the relative superiority of these teachers is the respective level of their knowledge. The highest knowledge achievable by definition is the liberating knowledge of Brahman, which is possessed only by the *ativarṇāśamin*, who is the teacher of all and can never be the pupil of anyone.

> An *ativarṇāśramin*, it is said, is the teacher of teachers. There is no one in this world equal, much less superior, to him. (SūS 3.5.15)
>
> He is an *ativarṇāśramin* who knows the highest reality, which is different from the body, the senses, and the like, which is the witness of all, absolute consciousness, and self-effulgent, and whose self is bliss. (SūS 3.5.16–17)
>
> He is an *ativarṇāśramin* , O Keśava, who by the study of just the Great Sayings of the Upaniṣads has come to know his self as the Lord. (SūS 3.5.17–18)
>
> He is an *ativarṇāśramin* who knows the great God who transcends and witnesses the three states.[31] (SūS 3.5.18–19)
>
> He is an *ativarṇāśramin* who knows by means of the Upaniṣads: "*Varṇa*s, *āśrama*s, and the like have been contrived in the body by cosmic illusion. They never belong to me, who am the self, which is pure consciousness." (SūS 3.5.19–20)
>
> He is an *ativarṇāśramin* who knows by means of the Upaniṣads: "As people carry on their activities on their own in the presence of the sun, so the entire universe carries on its activity in my presence."[32] (SūS 3.5.21–22)
>
> When a man attains the vision of his self and the rules of *varṇa* and *āśrama* consequently melt away, he transcends all *varṇa*s and *āśrama*s and abides in his own self. (SūS 3.5.31)
>
> That man is an *ativarṇāśramin* who abides in his very self after transcending his *varṇa*s and *āśrama*s: so state those who know all the Upaniṣads. (SūS 3.5.32)
>
> Therefore, O Keśava, *varṇa*s and *āśrama*s belong elsewhere. They are all, indeed, mistakenly ascribed to the self; they do not pertain to one who knows the self. (SūS 3.5.36)
>
> There are no rules or prohibitions, O Janārdana, no laws on what is allowed and what is forbidden, nor anything else for those who know the self. (SūS 3.5.37)
>
> He who, by means of the Upaniṣads and by his own experience, knows thus for certain the self that is non-dual, changeless, spotless, eternal, pure, without any false appearance, pure consciousness, and highest immortality—he is truly an *ativarṇāśramin*, he alone is the supreme teacher. (SūS 3.5.41–42)

31. The three states of consciousness are waking, dreaming, and deep sleep. The fourth state beyond these three is identified with absolute consciousness that constitutes Brahman (see pp. 229–30 for a discussion of the fourth state and the state that transcends the fourth). The JMV reads "who transcends the *varṇa*s and *āśrama*s and who witnesses the three states."

32. The meaning appears to be that people perform their respective activities during the day when the sun is shining, but their activities do not relate to or affect the sun. In like manner, the appearance of the universe to a liberated person while he is still in the body does not truly affect him.

The *ativarṇāśramin* is thus free from all rules and prohibitions that constitute the Brāhmaṇical *dharma*. If he is not bound by *dharma*, he can act as he pleases, which is the same as the antinomian and libertine position ascribed to the Advaita tradition by Vedānta Deśika which we shall presently examine.

Śaṃkara, as we have seen, appears to assume that the enlightened renouncer is both an *ativarṇāśramin* and a Paramahaṃsa. He does not provide a classification of renouncers, and it is not clear whether he was aware of or accepted the classical fourfold division of renouncers and whether he considered the Paramahaṃsa to be part of such a classification. Medieval authors, such as Vidyāraṇya, subdivide Paramahaṃsas into those who are seekers after knowledge and those who are enlightened, the latter alone being the *ativarṇāśramin*. The medieval text, *Nāradaparivrājaka Upaniṣad* (174–205), as we have seen, presents a sixfold division of renouncers, adding Turīyātīta and Avadhūta to the traditional four.[33] Even though the exact distinction between the two is somewhat obscure, they are considered to be enlightened; the *Nāradaparivrājaka* reserves the epithet *ativarṇāśramin* to these. Turīyātīta literally means "one who has transcended the fourth," and in this context it means that such a renouncer is beyond the fourth, that is the Paramahaṃsa. There appears to be a conscious effort here to draw a parallel between "fourth" and "beyond the fourth" within the context of this classification and the traditional four states of consciousness—waking, sleeping, deep sleep, and the fourth. The fourth state traditionally has been taken to be the absolute state of consciousness that constitutes Brahman. The *Nāradaparivrājaka* (190), however, presents the fourth state also as part of relative consciousness and posits a "state beyond the fourth" (*turīyātīta*) as the absolute. Thus the final and absolute state of consciousness that is "beyond the fourth" parallels and in some way coincides with the final state of renunciation that is Turīyātīta—"beyond the fourth." The *Turīyātītāvadhūta Upaniṣad*, which belongs to a period somewhat later than the *Nāradaparivrājaka*, collapses the Turīyātīta and the Avadhūta into a single category and gives an informative description of the behavior of such an individual:

> Staff, water pot, waistband, loincloth, and garment—all these he throws into water after performing the rites prescribed in his own rule. He then becomes naked, giving up even the use of discolored old clothes, bark garments, or antelope skins. Thereafter he functions without mantras. He gives up shaving, inunction, bathing, the vertical sectarian marks and the like. He does away with all worldly and vedic rites. Everywhere he avoids pious and impious deeds. He gives up even knowledge and ignorance. He overcomes cold and heat, pleasure and pain, respect and disrespect. He burns up blame, praise, pride, jealousy, deceit, arrogance, desire, hate, lust, anger, greed, delusion, excitement, impatience, indignation, self-protection, and the like, together with the three mental impressions. He regards his body as a corpse. Remaining the same both when he receives and when he does not, he sustains his life in the manner of a cow, without effort, without regard to rules, without greed, and eating just what he happens to come by. He reduces to ashes the entire body of learning and scholarship. He conceals his true nature. He repudiates the distinction between the superior and the inferior. He contemplates the non-dual (Brahman), which is superior to all and which is the essence of all. This divine secret and ancient treasure he draws into himself: "There is no one else different from me." He does not fear pain. He does

33. For this and other classifications of renouncers, see section 6.1.2.

not rejoice at pleasure. He longs not for love. He is not attached anywhere either to the pleasant or to the unpleasant. All his senses have come to rest. He does not call to mind the prominence he had formerly attained with respect to *āśrama*, conduct, learning, or virtue. He abandons the conducts associated with classes and *āśrama*s. He never dreams, for he always remains the same during day and night. He is always given to wandering. He is left with just his body. A place of water is his water pot. Although he is sane, he wanders always alone as if he were a fool, a lunatic, or a goblin. He is not given to conversation. By meditating on his own nature, he finds support in (Brahman), which has no support. In keeping with his concentration on his self, he gives up everything. In the guise of a Turīyātītāvadhūta he is intent on concentrating on the non-dual (Brahman). He abandons his body by realizing that he has the nature of OṂ. Such a man is an Avadhūta. He has done all there is to do.[34]

As we see from this passage, such renouncers abandon even the normal rules of begging and the like that govern the life of ordinary renouncers and that are expounded in texts on the *dharma* of ascetics. Their eating habits are compared to those of cows and pythons: they eat what people throw on the ground, picking it up with their mouths in imitation of animals. Those who follow the python vow remain in one place and eat only what is given to them unasked. They do not carry any emblem symbolic of their state, such as a bamboo staff and a begging bowl, and it appears that they went naked. Some texts even advise them to adopt loathsome habits so that people would not recognize them as holy men and would instead insult and persecute them (Olivelle 1992, 107–12).

The Viśiṣṭādvaita tradition was the major opponent of the Advaita understanding of renunciation during the medieval period.[35] One of the keenest minds within the Viśiṣṭādvaita tradition was the fourteenth-century theologian Vedānta Deśika, also known as Veṅkaṭa Nātha. He combats the Advaita position vigorously in the sixty-fourth and sixty-fifth chapters of his *Śatadūṣaṇī*,[36] entitled *Yatiliṅgabhedabhaṅgavāda* and *Alepakamatabhaṅgavāda*, respectively. It is in the latter chapter that he deals with the Advaita assertion that an enlightened renouncer is beyond all *āśrama*s and free from all rules of *dharma*.

Ascribing to Advaita an extreme view regarding the status of an enlightened renouncer, Vedānta Deśika says that according to Advaitins such a man may act as he pleases and calls such a view "libertinism" (*svaira*):

> In this world there are some people who reject the duties of all *varṇa*s and *āśrama*s, and resemble the Cārvākas ["materialists"]. They have become one even with the Cāṇḍālas ["outcastes"] and do not pay any heed to the restraints contained in the injunctions and prohibitions. (Abh 2)

In his refutation of the view that such a form of renunciation is legitimate and authorized by scripture, he asks the Advaitin: "Is this condition of yours that is repudiated by all learned men an *āśrama* or not an *āśrama*?" (Abh 11). Vedānta Deśika goes on to demonstrate how it cannot be either the one or the other.

If the Advaitins consider the status of their liberated renouncers an *āśrama*, he asks,

34. For explanatory comments on this passage, see my translation: Olivelle 1992.

35. For a study of the debate between these two traditions, see Olivelle 1986 and 1987.

36. For editions and translations of these, see Olivelle 1987.

"is it something different from the four *āśrama*s, or something not different from them?" (Abh 12). He dismisses the first possibility, "because we do not find a fifth *āśrama* (see section 8.3) laid down in the Vedas, the Smṛtis, the Itihāsas [i.e., epics], the Purāṇas, or other similar treatises" (Abh 13). He dismisses also the second possibility, first because such a state is nowhere admitted and because if such a state is authorized by the scriptures it would put those renouncers under the authority of the Veda (Abh 17), which, of course, would be an implicit denial of their freedom from all rules and prohibitions.

Finally, Vedānta Deśika rejects the contention that the renunciation of an enlightened man is a non-āśramic state. In this context he explains that texts on which the Advaitins base their assertions can be explained otherwise. For example, texts that speak of ancient renouncers who acted aberrantly and even non-rationally do so only to encourage renouncers to be humble and to bring disgrace upon themselves and thus to enhance their inner virtues. He denies that these texts permit Paramahaṃsas to perform forbidden acts, such as adultery (Abh 189). Vedānta Deśika also uses other hermeneutical strategies to explain away passages that appear to support the Advaita position. One significant strategy is borrowed from Āpastamba, who sought to deny that practices of ancient sages that are clear transgressions of *dharma* can be imitated by people living during his time: "Transgression of the *dharma* and violence are found among the ancient sages. They committed no sin on account of the greatness of their luster. A man of later times who, seeing their conduct, follows it, will fall" (ĀpDh 2.13.7–9). This principle is later associated with the ages of the world (*yuga*), according to which different *dharma*s applies to different *yuga*s (see section 8.4).

The Advaita opponent of Deśika puts forward one last argument. Surely the *atyāśrama* state is established by the use of the term *atyāśramin* in the *Śvetāśvatara Upaniṣad*, 6.21? Vedānta Deśika's response is illustrative of the hermeneutical strategies used to explain such texts in accordance with one's own views:

> No, because that term can be explained either as indicating a person belonging to a special *āśrama* that is very eminent, or as indicating a person belonging to a particular *āśrama* that is beyond the three beginning with vedic studentship, or else by using some other cogent reason. Otherwise, the result is that this passage would openly contradict hundreds of vedic, smṛti, epic, and other authoritative texts whose meaning is perfectly clear.[37]

Since scripture cannot contradict itself, passages whose meaning is obscure—and Vedānta Deśika would include here all texts that appear to support the *atyāśrama* position—need to be interpreted in such a way as not to contradict the meaning of clearer texts.

Beyond scoring debating points and engaging in hermeneutical combat, the major issue at the root of these disputes is the divergent theologies of liberation. Viśiṣṭādvaita and other devotional sects did not recognize the possibility of a person attaining liberation while still alive in this world. Much less did they accord any special status to indi-

37. Abh 350–51: *nanu śvetāśvataropaniṣadupasaṃhāre tadadhikāritayā atyāśramitvopapādanād aprāptārthatvena tadvidhir iti cen na, atiśayitāśramaviśeṣaniṣṭha iti vā brahmacaryāditrayātikāntāśramaviśeṣaniṣṭha iti vā anyena vā kena cid aviruddhena nimittena tannirvāhāt. anyathā sphuṭatarārthaśrutismṛtītihāsādiśatakopaprasaṅgaḥ.*

viduals who claimed to be liberated. Further, the rules of *dharma* were for them laid down by God, and a liberated individual does not become independent of God. For the Advaitins, on the other hand, the rules of *dharma*, like everything else in this world, belong to *saṃsāra* and, therefore, are as illusory as the latter. A person who attains enlightenment can no longer be under the power of *dharma*, any more than a person who has seen the rope—to use the famous Advaita illustration of illusory knowledge—can be afraid of the snake. These seemingly trivial debates about the status of the highest type of renouncer, therefore, are based on the most central issues of Brāhmaṇical theology.

8.3 The Question of a Fifth Āśrama

I have already alluded to what I have called the X + 1 syndrome—that is, the Indian propensity to add one to a preexisting set to establish a more perfect set. The importance of three and four in most cultures is well recognized. In ancient India, however, the number five took on theological importance for a variety of reasons, some of which are enumerated in this passage from the *Śatapatha Brāhmaṇa* (1.5.2.16): "There are five ritual utterances . . . ; the sacrifice is fivefold; the sacrificial animal is fivefold; there are five seasons in a year: this is the single measure of the sacrifice and its completion."[38] The assertion of a fifth *āśrama* as the completion and perfection of the four is, therefore, in line with that general Indian propensity.

I have also made reference to the term *turīyātīta*, "the one beyond the fourth." Brahman, according to some medieval theologians, is "the one beyond the fourth"—beyond the four states of relative and illusory consciousness. The Turīyātīta is "the one beyond the fourth"—beyond the four normal classes of renouncers; he is also thereby beyond the four *āśramas*, since the four types of renouncers comprise the fourth *āśrama*. It was only natural, therefore, that at least some Advaita theologians would come to call this "one beyond the fourth" the fifth *āśrama*.

A document belonging to the Advaita renunciatory tradition contains a ritual procedure for discarding all the emblems of a normal renouncer and for becoming a naked Avadhūta. It bears the title *Pañcamāśramavidhāna*, "The Procedure for (Entering) the Fifth *Āśrama*."[39] At the very start the author of this little work asks: "What is the authority for the existence of a fifth *āśrama*?" (3) He cites several texts, such as the *Kaivalya Upaniṣad* (5), that speak of transcending the *varṇas* and *āśramas*, and quotes the following verse from an anonymous Smṛti: "After one has completed the duties of the four *āśramas* in the prescribed manner, one is entitled to adopt the fifth *āśrama* when one has embraced non-corporeal bliss."[40] For this author the state of the *atyāśramin* is identical to that of the fifth *āśrama*. This transcendence of the *āśramas* is effected by the abandon-

38. For a discussion of the significance of number five, see Gonda 1970, 44f, and Malamoud 1982, 34–35.

39. This medieval text also bears the alternate title *Pañcamāśramavidhi.* I have edited and translated it twice: see Olivelle 1980, and 1986, 143–56. I cite from the latter edition.

40. *Pañcamāśramavidhāna*, 9: *caturāśramakarmāṇi samāpya vidhimārgataḥ / videhasukham ālambya pañcamāśramam arhati //*

ment of the emblems that symbolize the renouncer's *āśrama*: "(These authoritative texts) show the transcendence of the *āśramas*; this amounts to a fifth *āśrama*, because the abandonment of the staff and so forth entails the abandonment of renunciation, which is invariably associated with them."[41] The abandonment of the staff, the begging bowl, the water pot, and the ochre garment, therefore, which for other theologians constitutes the advancement to a higher type of renunciation, is for this author the rite whereby renunciation (*saṃnyāsa*) itself is renounced. As after the abandonment of the third *āśrama* one enters the fourth, so after the abandonment of the fourth one enters the fifth *āśrama*. This *āśrama* is associated by the author with what he calls "non-corporeal bliss" (*videha-sukha*):

> As there is no bliss of renunciation and detachment in the householder's *āśrama*, so there is no non-corporeal bliss in the fourth *āśrama*, because permanent and occasional activities, such as the staff *tarpaṇa*,[42] are present in it. For the sake of bliss without activity, therefore, one accepts the fifth *āśrama*. The same is called the path of an Avadhūta. Furthermore, as after abandoning the topknot, sacrificial cord and so forth, and (entering) the fourth *āśrama* one immediately takes possession of the staff and the rest, so after abandoning the staff and the like and (entering) the fifth *āśrama* one takes possession of nothing at all. On the contrary, the very abandonment of everything constitutes the principal state of a Paramahaṃsa.[43]

At one point an opponent objects that, following the advice of the *Bhagavad Gītā* 3.20, "Even if you consider only the welfare of the world, you should work," a renouncer should not abandon the staff and other emblems at least for the welfare of the world. The author retorts: "The welfare of the world (has relevance) only to those who consider the world as real. What does the world's welfare mean to those who regard the world as unreal? It is of no concern to one whose self is pure consciousness" (14–16). The author then goes on to present a brief rite for discarding the staff, the water pot, the loincloth, the girdle, and the robe (48–71).

Even though this brief text is unique, it is evident that at least some sections of the Advaita tradition supported the notion of a fifth *āśrama*. I have already cited the authoritative testimony of Vedānta Deśika, who ascribes such a view to his Advaita opponent. The statement of the *Sūta Saṁhitā* (3.5.9) I have already cited that calls the *ativarṇāśramin* "the fifth" after the four *āśramas* appears also to support such a view, even though the *Sūta* does not call this the fifth *āśrama*.

Several Purāṇas, moreover, indirectly support the existence of such a view by vigorously combatting it. The *Viṣṇu Purāṇa*, for example, regards the doctrines associated with naked ascetics and the fifth *āśrama* as belonging to Buddhists and Jains disguised as Brāhmaṇical ascetics. It shows how the Daityas, rivals of the gods, were defeated

41. Ibid., 11–12: *āśramātikramaṇaṃ bhāsate. tac ca pañcamāśrame ghaṭate, daṇḍādiparityāgena tadvyāptasaṃnyāsaparityāgāt.*

42. This term normally refers to the water offerings given to deceased ancestors and sometimes to gods and other beings. Renouncers do not offer water but use the staff to perform *tarpaṇa* by saying: "OṂ I satiate the gods," "OṂ I satiate the seers," and "OṂ I satiate the ancestors," at the bottom, at the middle, and at the top of the staff, respectively. Cf. Ypra 49.17–47.

43. The last is a clear reference to the *Paramahaṃsa Upaniṣad*, 47. Our author here appears to identify his fifth *āśrama* with both the Avadhūta and the principal or higher type of Paramahaṃsa.

when Viṣṇu disguised as a naked Jain ascetic persuaded them to give up the path of the Veda (ViP 3.18). Then it declares :

> The student, the householder, and the hermit belong to *āśramas*, of which the fourth is the renouncer—there is no fifth. The naked man who after giving up the householder's life does not become either a hermit or a renouncer is, indeed, a sinner.[44]

It goes on to advise people not to have any dealing with such ascetics. The mere sight of them causes loss of purity. The *Kūrma Purāṇa*, likewise, considers a fifth *āśrama* to be illegitimate: "One should, therefore, understand that there are only four *āśramas*. A fifth is not to be found in all the Vedas."[45]

It appears from the statements of its opponents that the theology of a naked ascetic, whether that state is considered as merely beyond the *āśramas* or as constituting a fifth *āśrama*, was considered by many as smacking of Buddhist and/or Jain ideologies. Advaita ascetics of this type are openly vilified as Buddhist monks in disguise. The opening stanza of Vedānta Deśika's *Yatiliṅgabhedabhaṅgavāda* (Ybh 1), for example, calls Advaita renouncers "Buddhist frauds, who tread not the Veda's path." A group of verses ascribed to Hārīta and Dattātreya by Viśiṣṭādvaita writers, but which the Advaitin Ānandānubhava[46] claims was composed by Bhāskara himself, claims that the appearance of these naked ascetics, who are Buddhists in disguise, to pervert those who follow the vedic tradition is a sure sign of the dawn of the Kali age:

> When the horrible Kali age dawns, there will appear other men who bear the mendicant's emblem. All these men are inflamed by the fire of Gautama [i.e., the Buddha]. In the Kali age, moreover, they will falsely explain the entire meaning of the Veda. These naked men are Buddhists in disguise, and they insult the triple Veda. They will eat the food of Śūdras, thinking: "We are liberated." In the Kali age they will surely cause even those who are established in their proper *dharma* to deviate from the right path. There are many twice-born men who live by resorting to a single bamboo staff. By abandoning rites they fall into the dreadful Raurava hell. Let a wise man, therefore, neither talk with them nor even look at them. After looking at them one is purified by gazing at the sun. By feeding a twice-born who is naked or is without a sacrificial string at a funerary offering, a man offers to his manes semen, urine, excrement, and the like.[47]

8.4 Āśrama *and the Doctrine of* Yuga

At least by the beginning of the common era, the four *yugas* came to constitute the major division of cosmic time in Hindu mythology, the division that had the greatest impact on

44. ViP 3.18.36–37. A very similar verse is found in the *Saura Purāṇa*, 17.6: "There are four *āśramas*: student, householder, hermit, and renouncer. A fifth is not found among them."

45. *Kūrma Purāṇa*, 1.2.85. At 1.2.83, however, the *Kūrma*, as we have seen, refers to *atyāśramin*. Evidently it did not consider the latter to constitute a separate *āśrama*.

46. See his *Nyāyaratnadīpāvali*, nn.154–58. (Olivelle 1986, 115).

47. See Varadācārya's *Yatiliṅgasamarthana* (ed. in Olivelle 1987), III. 38–43. A longer version of this text is given by Ānandagiri in his commentary on Ānandānubhava's *Nyāyaratnadīpāvali*, pp. 330–31.

Brāhmaṇical hermeneutics and the theology of *dharma*.[48] There are four *yugas*—Kṛta, Tretā, Dvāpara, and Kali—each succeeding one being worse than each preceding. The life span, intelligence, strength, and virtue of people decrease with each succeeding age. Each *yuga*, consequently, has its own unique properties, its own specific *dharma*. Beginning with Manu, *yugadharma*, the law and morality specific to different *yugas*, became an important section of Brāhmaṇical treatises on *dharma*: "In accordance with the decrease in their length, one set of *dharmas* is applicable to men in the Kṛta *yuga*, different sets in Tretā and Dvāpara, and yet another in the Kali *yuga*" (MDh 1.85).

The Kṛta *yuga* was the golden age of perfection when people were naturally good, nature was bountiful, and *dharma* attained its full perfection. The gradual decline of *dharma* in keeping with the growth of evil among people as the *yugas* progress is often portrayed as the loss of one foot of *dharma* during each succeeding *yuga*.

> *Dharma* and truth possess all four feet and are whole during the Kṛta *yuga*, and people did not obtain anything unrighteously (*adharmeṇa*). By so obtaining, however, *dharma* has lost one foot during each of the other *yugas* and righteousness (*dharma*) likewise has diminished by one quarter due to theft, falsehood, and deceit. (MDh 1.81–82)

Dharma, therefore, is standing precariously on one leg in the present Kali age. That as time passes the world gradually deteriorates is a belief that finds expression also in texts composed several centuries before the common era.[49] These texts do not invoke the doctrine of *yugas*, but the same principle is at the heart of the *yugadharma* theory, especially as it is used within Brāhmaṇical hermeneutics to invalidate and for all practical purposes annul past laws and customs while maintaining the illusion of an unchanging and eternal *dharma*. The latter theory probably did not reach its full articulation until the first centuries of the common era. It is in texts composed after this time that the *yuga* theory is applied to both the *varṇa* and the *āśrama* systems.

The idyllic condition of the Kṛta *yuga* is often depicted as a time when there were no distinctions among people, all being equally good and virtuous (LiP 39.15–16). For example, it is stated that in the Kṛta *yuga* there was a single *varṇa* and that the system of four was created at the dawn of the Tretā.[50] Likewise, there was only one Veda in the Tretā and it was divided into four during the Dvāpara (MatsP 144.10). The same principle of creeping distinctions is applied also to the *āśramas*. Thus, the *Mahābhārata* (3.148.17–18) says that in the Kṛta *yuga* people of all four *varṇas* followed the same

48. For an accessible account of the doctrine of *yugas* and its relation to other cosmic time scales such as *manvantara* and *kalpa*, see Kane 1974, V.1, 686–718. For the history of the *yuga* doctrine, the relationship of the *yuga* doctrine to *dharma*, and the *dharma* of the Kali age, see Kane 1973, III, 885–968, and Lingat 1962. For further bibliography, see Rocher 1986, 124, n. 48.

49. Yāska (*Nirukta* 1.20), for example, distinguishes between the ancient sages who had the direct perception of *dharma* and later ones who did not possess such powers and had to be taught. Gautama (GDh 1.3) and Āpastamba (ĀpDh 2.13.7–9) use the principle of a gradually weakening and deteriorating humanity as a hermeneutical principle to show that people living today should not follow the example of ancient sages, whom the scriptures record as acting contrary to *dharma*.

50. See MatsP 144.78; *Brahma Purāṇa* 229.52.

āśrama.[51] The *Kūrma Purāṇa* (1.27.48) states explicitly that the fourfold division of the *āśramas*, just like that of the *varṇas*, was created at the beginning of the Tretā *yuga*. As their creation was a sign of decline, so the fact that people fail to adhere to the *dharma* of their respective *varṇas* and *āśramas* is a sure sign of the dawn of the Kali *yuga.*[52]

The most significant connection between the *yugas* and the *āśramas*, however, concerns the question whether all the four *āśramas* are operative in the present Kali *yuga*. With reference to the *varṇas* some authors assert that in the Kali there are no true Kṣatriyas, while others go as far as to assert that only Śūdras are left in this age.[53] In a similar way, the number of *āśramas* that people can legitimately follow decreases in the Kali *yuga*.

There are many institutions and practices that were proper in former times, but that are prohibited in the Kali. These are referred to as *kalivarjya*—things that are forbidden in the Kali *yuga.*[54] Among them is entering the hermit's *āśrama*. This institution, as we have seen, became obsolete at least by the first centuries of the common era and continued its existence only as the stuff of legend and poetry. It came to be considered a *kalivarjya* at least by the twelfth century when Śrīdhara in his *Smṛtyarthasāra* (p. 2) includes the hermit's *āśrama* together with living as a student for a long time in a list of things forbidden in the present age. The latter prohibition would include lifelong studentship, the first *āśrama* of the original system and still mentioned as a legitimate mode of life by the authors of the classical Dharmaśāstras.

There are a few instances where even renunciation is considered an institution forbidden in Kali. A verse ascribed to Vyāsa prohibits renunciation after 4400 years of the Kali *yuga* have elapsed. "When 4400 years of the Kali *yuga* have elapsed, a wise Brahmin should neither establish the three sacred fires nor enter renunciation."[55] Another verse again ascribed to Vyāsa lists renunciation among five practices forbidden, although texts that cite it also provide an exception: people may continue to renounce so long as the Vedas and the division of society into *varṇas* continue to exist: "The establishment of the three sacred fires, killing cows, renunciation, offering meat at an ancestral oblation, and levirate: one should avoid these five in the Kali age."[56]

That these hermeneutical squabbles were not left merely at the ethereal levels of theological abstraction but were used in very practical matters of significant financial

51. The expression *samāśrama* may also mean that the *āśramas* were equally distributed among the *varṇas*, as van Buitenen takes it in his translation, but it is more likely that the text wants to point out that all the people had the same *āśrama*, just as at verse 19 it says that they had the same Veda and mantra.

52. See MBh 12.230.14, 17; MatsP 144.70–72; ViP 6.1.32–33.

53. For the disappearance of Kṣatriyas, see Kane 1974, II.1, 380–82, where references to primary sources are given. For the belief that only Śūdras exist today, see the MatsP 144.78, which says that just as there was only one *varṇa* in the Kṛta *yuga*, so there will be only one, namely Śūdra, in Kali. Cf. Kane 1973, III, 892.

54. For a list of such practices, see Bhattacharya 1943; Kane 1973, III, 926–68.

55. Kane 1974, II.2, 953; 1973, III, 960. See Kamalākarabhaṭṭa's *Nirṇayasindhu*, p. 441.

56. Vaidyanātha Dīkṣita, *Smṛtimuktāphala*, Varṇāśramadharmakāṇḍa, p. 176; Viśveśvara Sarasvatī, *Yatidharmasaṃgraha*, pp. 2–3. Kamalākarabhaṭṭa (*Nirṇayasindhu*, pp. 264, 441) and Kāśīnātha Upādhyāya (*Dharmasindhu*, p. 976) interpret these prohibitions as directed only at the Kuṭīcaka type of renouncers who carry triple staffs and not at single-staffed Paramahaṃsas.

importance is revealed in a fascinating inscription dated 1584 C.E. from South India studied by Derrett.[57] This inscription is a defense of an extraordinary event: the succession of a married householder to the leadership position (*mahant*) of a Pāśupata monastery with all its power, social prestige, and financial rewards, a position which until that time had been filled by a celibate renouncer. Part of the defense of this transition consists in the claim that lifelong celibacy and renunciation are explicitly forbidden in the Kali *yuga.* In support of this claim the author of the inscription cites a verse recorded in Mādhava's *Pārāśaramādhavīya* that forbids, among other things, "prolonged studentship" (*dīrghakālaṃ brahmacaryam*) during the Kali *yuga* and interprets this prohibition to include renunciation.[58] The argument, therefore, was that in the present Kali age renunciation is illegitimate and all contemporary renouncers are in violation of this *kalivarjya.* Since there are only householders in existence, therefore, a householder may legitimately head a monastery.

An interesting departure from this pattern of including the renouncer's *āśrama* among things forbidden in Kali is found in the *Mahānirvāṇatantra* (8.8), according to which, in the Kali *yuga* only two *āśrama*s are legitimate, the householder's and the renouncer's, whereas those of the student and the hermit are forbidden.

The inclusion of the celibate *āśrama*s, especially renunciation, among things forbidden in the Kali *yuga* points to the continuing tension between the ideals of celibate asceticism and procreative ideology centered on the married householder. The creation of the *āśrama* system did not eradicate this tension. A millennium or more after its creation the system was not fully accepted by all and needed to be legitimized over again. It is to this continuing debate over the legitimacy of the celibate *āśrama*s that we turn in the concluding section of this volume.

8.5 The Legitimcay of the Āśrama *System: The Continuing Debate*

In the spring of 1978, while I was in Poona, India, conducting research on the history of the *āśrama* system, the following report of a speech by the then vice-president of India appeared in the *Indian Express* (May 8, 1978) under the headline "Sanyasis are parasites:"

> Who is better—the householder or the sanyasi? Of course, the householder, according to Vice-President B. D. Jatti. While the householder willingly renounces all that he earns to his wife and children for their love and affection, the sanyasi depends on others for his milk and fruits. Parasites, who are a mere burden on society, are sinners. If man has to progress, everybody must work. This message was given by Mr. Jatti while inaugurating the 846th Basava Jayanti Celebration in Bombay on Sunday.

The patient reader of this book will no doubt note that Vice-President Jatti was engaging in a debate that had been going on in Indian culture for a couple of millennia and that he was echoing rhetoric that is over 2,000 years old. The *Mahābhārata* already claimed that

57. Inscription no. 135 from Jambukēśvaram reported in 1940 by C. R. Krishnamacharlu in his *Annual Report on South Indian Epigraphy* for 1936–37, 79. See Derrett 1974.

58. See PāM I, 123 and Derrett 1974, 69–70.

the householder was the true renouncer, the true "eater of what is left over."[59] The legitimacy of renunciation has been always at the heart of the debate on the legitimacy of celibate *āśrama*s in general and on the relative value of celibacy and marriage.

The creation of the *āśrama* system and especially of its classical formulation was intended to resolve this controversy and to blunt the opposition between the two ideologies. Many modern scholars, such as Müller (1878, 343) and Deussen (1909, 131), as we have seen (section 1.3.2), appear to have accepted that the *āśrama* system indeed resolved the issue. A closer examination of the history of the system, however, shows that the issue was never fully settled and that old battles had to be fought over and over again even after the *āśrama*s had become part of the mainstream Brāhmaṇical theology.

The main opponents of the *āśrama* system, at least of the legitimacy of the celibate *āśrama*s, appear to have been the conservative core of the Brāhmaṇical tradition represented by the adherents of Pūrva Mīmāṃsā, the school of vedic exegesis and hermeneutics. They continued the tradition of the early conservative experts of *dharma* represented by Gautama and Baudhāyana in upholding the vedic values of marriage, procreation, and ritual against the onslaught of ascetic ideologies.

The earliest extant work and the basic text of Mīmāṃsā is the *Pūrva Mīmāṃsāsūtra* (PMS) ascribed to Jaimini, which may have been composed around the beginning of the common era. There Jaimini does not engage the issue of the legitimacy of celibate *āśrama*s explicitly. In dealing with the theology of debts, however, he emphatically rejects the possibility of lifelong celibacy, saying that for a Brahmin the performance of the Soma sacrifice, acquisition of knowledge, and procreation are compulsory because they are prescribed by the statement on debts (PMS 6.2.31). Śabara (sixth century C.E.) in his commentary on this *sūtra* leaves no doubt that these duties are obligatory on all twice-born people, including the Kṣatriyas and Vaiśyas, even though the vedic statement on debts (TS 6.3.10.5) speaks explicitly only of Brahmins.

In his commentary on PMS 1.3.3, moreover, Śabara adduces three examples of injunctions found merely in the Smṛtis which, because they contradict explicit vedic injunctions, should be considered as unauthoritative. One of them is the rule that a person should remain as a vedic student, that is in a celibate condition, for 48 years. Śabara rejects this rule because it contradicts the vedic injunction that a person should establish the sacred fire, which implies marriage, while his hair is still black. Commenting on the very next *sūtra*, Śabara goes a step further, saying: "Some lived as vedic students for forty-eight years in order to hide their impotence. From this practice, we assume, arose the smṛti rule to that effect." This must surely have been intended as a jab—clearly below the belt—at ascetic celibates of his time!

Kumārila, the great seventh- or eighth-century Mīmāṃsist, in his *Tantravārttika*, the subcommentary on Śabara, has a long section on this question. He admits that the requirement to establish the fire while the hair is still black is extremely vague with regard to the person's age. He concludes, nevertheless, that the injunction must require a person to do so while he is in his youth or at the very least while he is middle-aged. Remaining a student for 48 years would mean that a person would be in his 50s—and

59. See Wezler 1977 for a study of this question, together with Bodewitz's review of it in WZKS 24 (1980): 239–42.

probably much older—before he is able to marry and establish a fire, and that would clearly contradict the vedic injunction. In his more extensive reflection on the problem of the relative authority of the Vedas and the Smṛtis,[60] however, Kumārila prefers to defend the authority of both the vedic and the smṛti injunction by showing that the latter applies to people who are not qualified to marry or to perform sacrifices: "... this rule [i.e., 48-year studentship] applies to the blind, the lame, and other such men who are incapable of assuming the life of a householder. They are required to become either perpetual students or renouncers."

Kumārila thus resolves the conflict by restricting lifelong celibacy to those who are not qualified to follow vedic injunctions because of a physical defect. Even though his position would still leave open the possibility of an ordinary person becoming a renouncer after he has fulfilled his ritual and procreative obligations, it appears from the writings of Advaita opponents of the Mīmāṃsā position that at least some Mīmāṃsists totally rejected the legitimacy of celibate *āśramas* for ordinary people, reserving them for the blind, the lame, the impotent, and other ritually incompetent people.

The *Vedāntasūtras*, ascribed to Bādarāyaṇa and composed at a time not long after the *Pūrva Mīmāṃsāsūtras*, contain a vigorous defense of the celibate *āśramas*,[61] in the course of which Bādarāyaṇa ascribes to Jaimini the view that scriptural passages referring to celibate *āśramas* are merely references and not proper injunctions, and that in any case such modes of life are explicitly forbidden (VeS 3.4.18). According to the normal exegetical rules, therefore, these texts cannot be taken as the basis of *dharma*. Jaimini also denies any independent status to knowledge that would necessitate the abandonment of rites, both because of the example of sages such as Janaka, who possessed knowledge but continued to perform rites, and because of explicit vedic statements that prescribe the performance of rites until death (VeS 3.4.2–7).

In his commentary on these *sūtras*, Śaṃkara presents in greater detail the arguments of Jaimini, or at least of the Mīmāṃsists, in support of rejecting the legitimacy of the celibate *āśramas*. Indian theologians generally present their opponents' views accurately, and it is safe to assume that, although written by an adversary, these arguments reflect the views of the Mīmāṃsists.

Jaimini's major point is that vedic texts mentioning celibate modes of life are merely references aimed at glorifying something and not proper injunctions, because these texts do not contain verbs with injunctive power.[62] These *āśramas* are enjoined only in Smṛtis and by custom. They are, therefore, to be disregarded when they contradict the explicit injunctions of the Veda.[63] I cite the entire argument of Jaimini as reported by Śaṃkara (on VeS 3.4.18), an argument reminiscent of the early debates recorded by Gautama and Baudhāyana that took place when the *āśrama* system was still in its infancy and over a millennium before the time of Śaṃkara.

60. This is found after his commentary on PMS 1.3.4; in the ĀnSS edition, pp. 110–11.

61. See the fourth *pāda* of the third *adhyāya*, especially *sūtras* 17–26.

62. Generally such Sanskrit verbal forms are the gerundive, the imperative, and the optative. Injunctions alone are be the basis of *dharma*, while mere references or laudatory remarks are meaningful with reference to *dharma* only in so far as they relate to an explicit injunction.

63. We have already seen this principle of interpretation enunciated in PMS 1.3.3: see section 3.2.1.1.

[JAIMINI] Now, vedic passages, such as "There are three branches of *dharma*" (ChU 2.23.1), have been cited[64] to demonstrate the existence of celibate *āśramas*. However, they do not have the power to establish them, because, according to the teacher Jaimini's view, these passages contain only references[65] to other *āśramas*[66] and not injunctions.

[OPPONENT] Why?

[JAIMINI] Because they do not contain even one of the injunctive verbal forms. The purport of every one of them, moreover, we find to be something quite different. Now, the passage "There are three branches of *dharma*," contains only a reference to the *āśramas*.

[OPPONENT] But surely, even though it is only a reference, we do gather from it the existence of the *āśramas*?

[JAIMINI] Yes, we do gather that, but they are established[67] not by an express vedic text[68] but by smṛti and custom. Consequently, given that they contradict express vedic statements, they are either to be disregarded[69] or to be taken as directed at those who are unqualified.[70]

[OPPONENT] Surely, even the householder's state is only referred to along with those of the celibates in the statement: "Sacrifice, study, and giving constitute the first."[71]

[JAIMINI] That is indeed true. Nevertheless, it is only on the householder that rites such as the daily fire sacrifice are enjoined, and therefore his existence alone is established by vedic texts. Consequently, the present reference is solely for the purpose of praise, and it is not intended as an injunction. Express vedic texts such as the following, furthermore, do indeed forbid other *āśramas*:[72] "A slayer of the hero among gods, indeed, is he who extinguishes the sacred fire" (TS 1.5.2.1); "Having brought a choice gift to the teacher, do not cut off your line of progeny" (TU 1.11.1); "A sonless man has no world: all the beasts know this" (AitB 7.13). Likewise, the teaching of passages such as the following also concern the path to the gods and not other

64. This passage and ChU 5.10.1, MuṇU 1.2.11, BāU 4.4.22, and JU 64, were cited by Śaṃkara in his commentary on the previous *sūtra*, VeS 3.4.17, that seeks to demonstrate that knowledge belongs only to people in celibate modes of life.

65. Rāmānuja employs the technical term *anuvāda* ("illustrative reference") to explain the term *parāmarśa* used by Bādarāyaṇa.

66. Namely, to *āśramas* other than that of the householder. On *āśramāntara*, see section 1.1.4.

67. The Sanskrit *prasiddhi* is rather vague and can mean "well known." In the present context, however, it probably refers to their establishment by clear injunctions. *Prasiddha* with the latter meaning also occurs in the paragraph after next.

68. The Sanskrit *pratyakṣaśruti* refers to a vedic text that is presently available for inspection, as opposed to a text that needs to be inferred (*anumitaśruti*) to have at one time existed on the basis of practices authorized by smṛti or custom. See section 3.2.1.1.

69. This is precisely the argument used by Gautama to reject the fourfold division of *āśramas* and to defend the sole legitimacy of the householder's *āśrama*: see section 3.2.1.1.

70. That is, those who are disqualified from procreative and ritual activities of a householder due to blindness, impotency, and the like, an issue I will discuss below.

71. The intention of the objector is to place the householder on the same level as the others. If all are merely referred to in the passage under question (ChU 2.23), then all are equally legitimate.

72. After dealing with the first part of the *sūtra* that these vedic texts are merely references, the Mīmāṃsist now turns to the second part that notes the existence of vedic texts explicitly prohibiting celibate *āśramas*.

> *āśramas*: "Those in the wilderness here who worship with the thought 'Faith is our austerity'" (ChU 5.101); and "Those in the wilderness who practice austerity and faith" (MuṇU 1.2.11). It is, moreover, doubtful whether other *āśramas* are in fact spoken of in passages such as "Austerity alone is the second" (ChU 2.23). Likewise, the statement "Desiring this very world ascetic wanderers wander forth" (BāU 4.4.22) is an eulogy of a world and not an injunction regarding the ascetic life.

As part of his argument against celibate *āśramas*, Jaimini (Śaṃkara on VeS 3.4.3) holds up the examples of ancient sages, such as Janaka, the king of Videha, and Uddālaka, whose eminence in knowledge is beyond doubt, to demonstrate that householders engaged in procreation and ritual activities can indeed attain the knowledge revealed in the Vedas.

There are, moreover, definite rules in the Vedas that require a person to perform rites all his life, such as the statement in the *Īśa Upaniṣad* (2), that instructs a man to desire to live a hundred years while performing rites, and the declaration of the *Śatapatha Brāhmaṇa* (12.4.1.1) that the daily fire sacrifice is a ritual undertaking from which one is freed either in old age or by death (Śaṅkara on VeS 3.4.7).[73]

Medieval authors also cite a vedic text with an implied prohibition of celibate *āśramas*: "He offers the daily fire sacrifice all his life."[74] Since only a householder is able to offer the daily fire sacrifice, this text implies that it is not legitimate to abandon that life and to assume a celibate *āśrama* in which ritual activities are rendered impossible. Mādhava, indeed, acknowledges that these latter-day opponents of celibacy are following in the footsteps of ancient sages such as Gautama and gives a succinct account of their argument:[75]

> Some do not approve of *āśramas* other than that of the householder. In support of that they cite the smṛti of Gautama: "But the Venerable Teacher (prescribes) a single *āśrama*, because the state of the householder is prescribed in express (vedic texts)" (GDh 3.36). The Venerable Teachers,[76] however, are of the opinion that there is no *āśrama* apart from the one, that of the householder. And they give the reason, namely that the householder's state is enjoined in express vedic texts, whereas the others lack such injunctions. . . . For this very reason the vedic text: "He offers the fire sacrifice

73. Śaṃkara commenting on VeS 3.4.18 and 19 admits that the entire debate between Jaimini and Bādarāyaṇa is carried on without taking into account the explicitly injunctive statement regarding celibate *āśramas* found in JU 64. From a historical standpoint, it appears that the *Jābāla Upaniṣad* was either not composed or was not considered as a vedic text during the time of the composition of the *Pūrva Mīmāṃsāsūtra* and the *Vedāntasūtra*.

74. *yāvajjīvam agnihotraṃ juhoti.* See PāM I, 523; Vaidyanātha Dīkṣita, *Smṛtimuktāphala*, Varṇāśramadharmakāṇḍa, p. 121. This text is often simply referred to as *yāvajjīvaśruti:* see Śaṃkara on BāU 4.5.15 (p. 716); Viśvarūpa on YDh 3.45 (II, p. 20). I have been unable to identify the source of this text.

75. For other accounts, see Śaṃkara on BāU 4.5.15 (pp. 714–23); Viśvarūpa on YDh 3.45 (II, pp. 19–22); Vijñāneśvara on YDh 3.56–57; Vaidyanātha Dīkṣita, *Smṛtimuktāphala*, Varṇāśramakāṇḍa, p. 121. The entire first chapter of Yādavaprakāśa's *Yatidharmasamuccaya* is devoted to this question. He presents first the arguments of the opponents who seek to establish that renunciation is not a *śrauta* or vedic *āśrama* but only a *smārta*—that is, one based on the Smṛtis—and therefore illegitimate, because it contradicts explicit vedic injunctions regarding procreation and lifelong ritual activity. Yādava then proceeds to establish the vedic basis of the renouncer's *āśrama*.

76. What follows appears to be a commentary on Gautama's statement.

all his life," assigns the entire life span of a man solely to the performance of rites. (PāM I, 523)

As we have seen in the citation from Śaṃkara, the central aim of the Mīmāṃsists was to deny vedic authority to celibate modes of life. Their back-up position was that the injunctions dealing with celibate *āśrama*s, if they had any validity at all, are directed not at normal people who are capable of marrying but at the handicapped—the blind, the lame, the impotent—whom these texts provide with an alternative mode of life.

As if taking their cue from such arguments, the supporters of the celibate *āśrama*s turn the the tables on the opponents by interpreting the texts such as those prescribing lifelong ritual activities as directed not at people who are detached from the world but at those who are full of desires and wish to attain a heavenly world. For Śaṃkara all injunctions regarding the performance of rites are aimed at people who are still under the power of ignorance, for rites and knowledge, just like knowledge and ignorance, and light and darkness, cannot coexist in the same person.[77] Vijñāneśvara, as we have seen (section 6.2.2), restricts all such injunctions, including the statements regarding the three debts with which humans are born, to people who are still attached to this world. The Advaita response during the Middle Ages generally follows that line of argument.

In his commentary on the *Taittirīya Upaniṣad* (1.12), Śaṃkara presents an opponent as arguing that, since knowledge arises through rites or actions (*karma*), there is only a single *āśrama*, namely that of the householder.[78] Śaṃkara in refuting him offers a completely new argument. The daily fire sacrifice and similar rites should not be regarded as the only rites (*karma*). Celibacy, austerity, truthfulness, self-control, non-injury, and the like that are practiced by renouncers are also *karma*, and they are powerful instruments for attaining knowledge. Thus the injunctions relating to the performance of *karma* do not support merely the householder's mode of life but also the legitimacy of all *āśrama*s. It appears that Śaṃkara here attempts to redefine *karma* to include also the moral activities of renouncers, an attitude in marked contrast to that adopted by him in his commentaries on the *Bṛhadāraṇyaka* and the *Chāndogya* that we examined earlier.

The supporters of renunciation unanimously reject the Mīmāṃsaka interpretation that that *āśrama* is meant for people unqualified for marriage.[79] Medhātithi (on MDh 6.36), for example, rejects this interpretation out of hand, because people who are disqualified from marriage would be disqualified for those very reasons—for example, blindness and impotency—also from renunciation. Vijñāneśvara (on YDh 3.56–57) puts it succinctly:

> As the lame and other such people are disqualified from vedic rites because of their inability to perform acts such as the Viṣṇukramaṇa and gazing at the clarified butter,[80] so also are they disqualified from rites given in the Smṛtis, because of their inability to perform acts such as carrying a water pot and going on the begging

77. See, for example, Śaṃkara on BāU 4.5.15 (p. 724).

78. This position is referred to explicitly as *aikāśramya*.

79. See Śaṃkara on VeS 3.4.20; Sureśvara, *Bṛhadāraṇyakopaniṣadbhāṣyavārttika*, 4.4: v. 1144; Vaidyanātha Dīkṣita, *Smṛtimuktāphala*, Varṇāśramadharmakāṇḍa, p. 121.

80. Three steps that the sacrificer takes between the altar and the Āhavanīya (eastern) fire. A lame man would not be able to do this, while the blind will not be able to look at the clarified butter.

round.[81] Therefore, how can one overcome the problem of the *āśramas* of lifelong celibates and the like by taking them as referring to the lame and so forth?

The controversy regarding the legitimacy of celibate and ascetic ways of life and the relative value of domesticity and asceticism thus continued throughout Indian history. At the heart of these debates was the *āśrama* system. Traditions that I have not fully explored in this study, such as Tantrism and the medieval *bhakti* movements, added new dimensions and novel arguments against asceticism. As recent sociological studies show, the debate apparently continues.[82]

81. Accepting hypothetically the opponent's contention that renunciation is an institution based only on Smṛtis, Vijñāneśvara shows that it cannot be restricted to the handicapped, because their disabilities affect the performance of activities relating to renunciation just as much as those relating to vedic rites.

82. For a sociological analysis of this controversy in modern times, see Madan 1987. For the total absorption of a renouncer sect into the caste system, see Bouillier 1979.

Epilogue

In this book I have examined an institution that has been—and that has been accepted by native theologians and modern scholars alike as being—a cornerstone of what we have conveniently come to call "Hinduism." Ghurye (1964, 2) and others have suggested that the best native equivalent of "Hinduism" is *varṇāśramadharma*—the *dharma* of *varṇa*s and *āśrama*s—the unchanging core of that broad and ill-defined tradition. We have seen, however, that, when we scratch below the surface, even an institution seemingly as immutable as the *āśrama* system has undergone drastic changes over time and has been the subject of continuous controversy and debate. How is it then that, despite such historical changes and controversies in the case of even its most central institutions, there is the pervasive and almost unconscious assumption among natives and foreigners alike that India—especially Indian religion and its major institutions and beliefs—is unchanging? If it is an illusion, who has created it? If the illusion has been a lasting one—and the theological speculations regarding *dharma* and the Vedic tradition appear to indicate that it has been—then what social or human purpose did it serve?

I have had occasion in this study to refer to the sociological theory enunciated by Berger and Luckmann (1967). Humanly created worlds—that is, the symbolic frameworks and social structures that permit humans to understand and control their environment—lack the stability of genetically created worlds. Their inherent instability, on the one hand, permits rapid change and creativity, opening the door to the historical progress we observe in human culture, science, and technology. The same instability, on the other hand, carries with it the danger of dissolving a culture and a society into disorder, anarchy, and chaos. Strategies for legitimating the inherited world—strategies in which religious doctrines and institutions play a central role—therefore, are found in every human culture. These strategies, no doubt, are primarily intended to defend the inherited world, to render it more plausible especially to new generations, and to guard it against novelty and change. An important outcome of the same strategies, especially those relating to exegesis and hermeneutics, is to create a perception—even if it is an illusory perception—of the immutability of that world. These strategies and the illusion of immutability they create are as essential for the continuity of human society and culture as are change and innovation.

However much the keepers of the inherited world may try to keep that world intact and immune to change, change inevitably comes. A major element of the legitimating process, therefore, consists in techniques of integrating the new elements into the scheme of the old world—of grafting new branches onto the old trunk—as smoothly as possible and without revolutionary upheavals. These techniques primarily consist of exegesis and hermeneutics that seek to find new meanings in old texts and traditions. In modern times, especially in the United States of America, the exegetical enterprise is carried out most notably by the Supreme Court: changes in law and society are presented as "interpretations" of the fundamental document of the society, the Constitution, thus blunting the effects of novelty and change. In India and in most traditional societies, however, the exegetical enterprise has been carried out by religious experts who interpret the authoritative texts of the tradition.

The fact that Indian culture and religion have been perceived as unchanging by both Indians themselves and outsiders is a tribute to the efficacy and success of the Indian exegetical tradition. It was especially the Brāhmaṇical tradition that cultivated the exegetical techniques both formally as the Mīmāṃsā and informally in presenting all their religious texts—the epics, Purāṇas, Dharmaśāstras, philosophical texts, and the like—as explicating the Vedic *dharma* and as deriving their authority from the Veda. The Veda thus stands as the mythical font—unchanging and eternal—of the tradition, every change and every new doctrine or institution being "discovered" within it through laboriously elaborated techniques of interpretation.

A historian, I believe, has to pay attention both to the changes and their causes that constitute history and to the exegetical and interpretive techniques through which those changes were appropriated by the society. If we ignore the latter, we will miss one of the most significant and interesting aspects of human culture and history. Specifically within the history of religion, Jonathan Z. Smith (1982, 43) has drawn the attention of scholars to the significance of the exegetical traditions for the study of religion:

> I have come to believe that a prime object of study for the historian of religion ought to be theological traditions, taking the term in its widest sense, in particular, those elements of the theological endeavor that are concerned with canon and its exegesis. That is to say, bracketing any presuppositions as to its character as revelation (and from this question, the historian of religion must abstain), the radical and arbitrary reduction represented by the notion of canon and the ingenuity represented by the rule-governed exegetical enterprise of applying the canon to every dimension of human life is that most characteristic, persistent, and obsessive religious activity. It is, at the same time, the most profoundly cultural, and hence, the most illuminating for what ought to be the essentially anthropological view point of the historian of religion and a conception of religion as human labor. The task of application as well as the judgment of the relative adequacy of particular applications to a community's life situation remains the indigenous theologian's task, but the study of the process, particularly the study of the comparative systematics and exegesis, ought to become a major preoccupation of the historian of religion.

The general indictment that historians of religion have paid little attention to the theological and exegetical traditions of the religions they study is particularly true in the case of historians of the religions of India. Few are acquainted with even the most basic rules of exegesis and interpretation of Mīmāṃsā, even though it is impossible to read most philosophical or religious texts, replete as they are with arguments based on those very rules, without an adequate grasp of Mīmāṃsā.

We have seen that the *āśrama* system was initially presented by its proponents not as something new but as an institution already sanctioned in the Vedas. A new institution was presented within the context of an exegesis of a Vedic text. Objections to the system, as well as subsequent controversies and changes, we have also seen, were carried out within an exegetical setting. Indeed, the entire history of this central institution appears as a long and continuous series of exegetical endeavors by both the proponents and the opponents of the system. The history of the *āśrama* system—indeed the history of the "Hindu" tradition—can be adequately understood only within what Jonathan Z. Smith calls "the human labor" of theology and exegesis, the same labor whose efficiency and success has produced the marvelous illusion of *sanātanadharma* and changeless India.

Bibliography

1. Primary Sources

Note: Commentaries are listed under the appropriate text.

Āgniveśya Gṛhyasūtra. Ed. L. A. Ravi Varma. Trivandrum Sanskrit Series 144 (Trivandrum: 1940).

Ahirbudhnya Saṃhitā. Ed. M. D. Ramanujacharya. 2nd ed. revised by V. Krishnamacharya. 2 vols. (Madras: Adyar Library, 1966).

Aitareya Āraṇyaka.. Ed. with Sāyaṇa's commentary by Bābā Śāstrī Phaḍke (ĀnSS 38, 1898). Tr. A. B. Keith (Oxford: Oxford University Press, 1909).

Aitareya Brāhmaṇa. Ed. with Sāyaṇa's commentary by Kāśīnātha Śāstrī Āgāśe. 2 vols. (ĀnSS 32, 1896). Tr. M. Haug 1863. Reprint (Delhi: Bharatiya Publishing House, 1976–77). Tr. A. B. Keith (HOS 25, 1920).

Amarasiṃha, *Nāmaliṅgānuśāsana* (*Amarakośa*). Ed. with *Amarakośodghāṭana* of Kṣīrasvāmin by K. G. Oka 1913. Reprint (Delhi: Upāsanā Prakāshan, 1981). Ed. with the commentary of Bhānuji Dīkṣita by H. Śastrī (KSS 198, 1970).

Ānandānubhava, *Nyāyaratnadīpāvali.* Ed. with Ānandagiri's commentary by V. Jagadisvara Sastrigal and Kalyanasundara Sastrigal (Madras: Government Oriental Manuscripts Library, 1961). Partially translated in Olivelle 1986.

Aṅguttara Nikāya of the *Sutta Piṭaka.* Ed. R. Morris and E. Hardy. 5 vols. (PTS, 1885–1900). Tr. F. L. Woodward. 5 vols. (London: Luzac, 1951–55).

Āpadeva, *Mīmāṃsānyāyaprakāśa.* Ed. and tr. F. Edgerton (New Haven: Yale University Press, 1929).

Āpastamba Dharmasūtra. Ed. G. Bühler. 3rd ed. (BSS 44, 50, 1932). Ed. with Haradatta's commentary *Ujjvalā* by Umeśa Chandra Pāṇḍeya (KSS 93, 1969). Tr. G. Bühler (SBE 2, 1879).

Āpastamba Śrautasūtra. Ed. R. Garbe 1882–1902. 3 Vols.; Reprint (Delhi: Munshiram Manoharlal, 1983).

Āruṇi Upaniṣad. Ed. in SUS. Tr. in Olivelle 1992.

Āśrama Upaniṣad. Ed. in SUS. Tr. in Olivelle 1992.

Aṣṭāvakra Saṃhitā. Ed. and tr. Swami Nityaswarupananda (Calcutta: Advaita Ashrama, 1975).

Aśvaghoṣa, *Buddhacarita.* Ed. and tr. E. H. Johnston 1936. Reprint (Delhi: Motilal Banarsidass, 1984).

Āśvalāyana Gṛhyasūtra. (ĀnSS 105, 1939). Tr. H. Oldenberg (SBE 29, 1886).

Atharvaveda Saṃhita. Ed. with Sāyaṇa's commentary by Vishva Bandhu. Vishveshvaranand Indological Series 13–17 (Hoshiarpur, 1960–64). Tr. M. Bloomfield (SBE 42, 1897). Tr. W. D. Whitney (HOS 7–8, 1905).

Atrismṛti. Ed. in *Smṛtīnaṃ Samuccayaḥ* (ĀnSS 48, 1929).

Bāṇa, *Harṣacarita*. Ed. K. P. Parab (Bombay: Nirnayasagar Press, 1946).

Bāṇa, *Kādambarī*. Ed. and tr. M. R. Kale. 4th ed. (Delhi: Motilal Banarsidass, 1968).

Baudhāyana Dharmasūtra. Ed. E. Hultzsch. 2nd ed. Abhandlungen für die Kunde des Morgenlandes, XVI,2, 1922. Reprint (Nendeln, Liechtenstein: Kraus Reprint Ltd., 1966). Ed. with Govinda Svāmī's commentary by U. C. Pāṇḍeya (KSS 104, 1972). Tr. G. Bühler (SBE 2, 1879).

Baudhāyana Gṛhyasūtra with the *Gṛhyaparibhāṣāsūtra*, *Gṛhyaśeṣasūtra*, and *Pitṛmedhasūtra*. Ed. R. Shama Sastri. University of Mysore Oriental Library Publications, Sanskrit Series 32/55 (Mysore: 1920).

Baudhāyana Śrautasūtra. Ed. W. Caland 1904–13. 2 vols. Reprint (New Delhi: Munshiram Manoharlal, 1982).

Bhagavad Gītā, with commentaries and subcommentaries of Śaṃkara, Ānandagiri, Nīlakaṇṭha, Dhanapati, Śrīdhara, Abhinavagupta, Madhusūdana, and Śrīdharmadattaśarma. Ed. Wasudev Laxman Śāstrī Panśīkar. 2nd ed. (Delhi: Munshiram Manoharlal, 1978). Tr. with Śaṃkara's commentary by C. V. Ramachandra Aiyar (Bombay: Bharatiya Vidya Bhavan, 1988). See also van Buitenen 1981, Zaehner 1969.

Bhāgavata Purāṇa. Ed. Nārāyaṇa Rāma Ācārya (Bombay: Nirnaya Sagar Press, 1950).

Bhāradvāja Gṛhyasūtra. Ed. H. J. W. Salomons (Leyden: E. J. Brill, 1913).

Bhāsa, *Pratimānāṭaka*. Ed. C. R. Devadhar. Poona Oriental Series 54 (Poona: Oriental Book Agency, 1937).

Bhaṭṭoji Dīkṣita, *Caturviṃśatimatasaṃgraha*. (Benares Sanskrit Series, No. 137; Benares: 1907).

Bhavabhūti, *Uttararāmacarita*. Ed. and tr. M. R. Kale (Bombay: G. Narayan & Co., 1911).

Bhaviṣya Purāṇa (Bombay: Venkatesvara Press, 1959).

Brahmāṇḍa Purāṇa. Ed. J. L. Shastri (Delhi: Motilal Banarsidass, 1973).

Bṛhadāraṇyaka Upaniṣad. Ed. in EPU. Tr. in TPU. Ed. with Śaṃkara's commentary by Vināyak Gaṇeś Āpte (ĀnSS 15, 1939). Tr. with Śaṃkara's commentary by Swāmī Mādhavānanda. 4th ed. (Calcutta: Advaita Ashrama, 1965).

Bṛhadavadhūta Upaniṣad. Ed. in SUS. Tr. in Olivelle 1992.

Bṛhaddevatā. Ed. and tr. A. A. Macdonell (HOS 5–6, 1904).

Bṛhaspatismṛti. Ed. K. V. Aiyangar (GOS 85, 1941).

Caraka Saṃhitā. 2 vols. (Delhi: Motilal Banarsidass, 1975).

Chāndogya Upaniṣad. Ed. in EPU. Tr. in TPU. Ed. with Śaṃkara's commentary in Śrīśāṃkaragranthāvali, no. 5 (Śrīraṅgam: Śrīvāṇīvilasa Mudrāyantrālaya, n.d.).

Corpus Inscriptionum Indicarum. Vol. III: *Inscriptions of the Early Gupta Kings and their Successors*. Ed. J. F. Fleet 1988. Reprint (Benares: Indological Book House, 1970).

Critical Pāli Dictionary. Ed. V. Trenckner (Copenhagen: Munksgaard, 1924—).

Dakṣasmṛti, in *Smṛtīnāṃ Samuccayaḥ* (ĀnSS 48, 1929).

Devaṇṇabhaṭṭa, *Smṛticandrikā*. Ed. and tr. J. R. Gharpure. Collections of Hindu Law Texts (Bombay: 1917).

Dhātupāṭha. Included in Pāṇini, *Aṣṭādhyāyī*. Ed. and tr. O. Böhtlingk 1887.

Dīgha Nikāya of the *Sutta Piṭaka*. Ed. T. W. Rhys Davids and J. E. Carpenter. 3 vols. (PTS, 1890–1911). Tr. T. W. and C. A. F. Rhys Davids (SBB 2–4, 1899–1921).

Durgasiṃha, *Liṅgānuśāsana*. Ed. D. G. Koparkar (Poona: Deccan College, 1952).

Edicts of Aśoka. Corpus Inscriptionum Indicarum, Vol. I. Reprint (Benares: Indological Book House, 1961).

Eighteen Principal Upaniṣads. Ed. V. P. Limaye and R. D. Vadekar (Poona: Vaidika Saṃśodhana Maṇḍala, 1958).

Gaṇapāṭha. Included in Pāṇini, *Aṣṭādhyāyī*. Ed. and tr. O. Böhtlingk 1887.

Garuḍa Purāṇa. Ed. R. Bhattacharya (KSS 165, 1964).

Gautama Dharmasūtra. Ed. with Haradatta's commentary (ĀnSS 61, 1910). Ed. with Maskarin's commentary by Veda Mitra (New Delhi: Veda Mitra & Sons, 1969). Tr. G. Bühler (SBE 2, 1879).

Gobhila Gṛhyasūtra. Ed. with Bhaṭṭanārāyaṇa's commentary by Chintamani Bhattacharya 1936. Reprint (New Delhi: Munshiram Manoharlal, 1982). Tr. H. Oldenberg (SBE 30, 1892).

Gopatha Brāhmaṇa. Ed. R. Mitra and H. Vidyabhusana (Calcutta: Bibliotheca Indica, 1872).

Hiraṇyakeśi Gṛhyasūtra. Tr. H. Oldenberg (SBE 30, 1892).

Īśa Upaniṣad. Ed. in EPU. Tr. in TPU.

Jābāla Upaniṣad. Ed. in SUS. Tr. in Olivelle 1992.

Jaiminīya-Upaniṣad-Brāhmaṇa. Ed. and tr. H. Oertel (New Haven: 1894 [= JAOS 16,1894, pt. 1]). See also Bodewitz 1973.

Jaina Sūtras. Tr. H. Jacobi. 2 vols. (SBE 22, 1884; SBE 45, 1895).

Jātaka. Ed. V. Fausböll. 7 vols. (London: Trübner, 1877–97). Tr. E. B. Cowel et al. 6 vols. (Cambridge: Cambridge University Press, 1895–1907).

Jayākhya Saṃhitā. Ed. E. Krishnamacharya (GOS 54, 1969).

Kaivalya Upaniṣad. Ed. in *Upaniṣadaṃ Samuccayaḥ*.

Kalhaṇa, *Rājataraṅgiṇī*. Ed. M. A. Stein (Leipzig: O. Harrassowitz, 1892). Tr. M. A. Stein 1900. 2 vols. Reprint (Delhi: Motilal Banarsidass, 1979).

Kālidāsa, *Abhijñānaśākuntalam*. Ed. and tr. M. R. Kale. 10th ed. (Delhi: Motilal Banarsidass, 1969).

Kālidāsa, *Kumārasaṃbhava*. Ed. Nārāyaṇ Rām Ācarya "Kāvyatīrtha" (Bombay: Nirnaya Sagar Press, 1946).

Kālidāsa, *Raghuvaṃśa*. Ed. with Mallinātha's commentary by K. P. Paraba. 3d ed. (Bombay: Nirnaya Sagar Press, 1886).

Kālidāsa, *Vikramorvaśīya*. Ed. and tr. C. R. Devadhar. 3rd ed. (Delhi: Motilal Banarsidass, 1966).

Kamalākarabhaṭṭa, *Nirṇayasindhu*. Ed. Nārāyaṇa Rāma Ācārya "Kāvyatīrtha" (Bombay: Nirnaya Sagar Press, 1949).

Kaśīnātha Upādhyāya, *Dharmasindhu*. Ed. Pandit Sudāmā Miśra Śāstrī (KSS 183, 1968).

Kāṭhaka Saṃhitā of the *Yajur Veda*. Ed. L. von Schroeder. 3 vols. (Leipzig: F. A. Brockhaus, 1900–10).

Kaṭhaśruti Upaniṣad. Ed. in SUS. Tr. in Olivelle 1992.

Kaṭha Upaniṣad. Ed. in EPU. Tr. in TPU.

Kātyāyanasmṛti. Ed. P. V. Kane (Bombay: 1933).

Kauṣītaki Upaniṣad. Ed. in EPU. Tr. in TPU.

Kauṭilya, *Arthaśāstra*. Ed. and tr. R. P. Kangle. 3 vols. University of Bombay Studies, Sanskrit, Prakrit and Pali, nos. 1–3 (Bombay: University of Bombay, 1960–65).

Khadira Gṛhyasūtra. Tr. H. Oldenberg (SBE 29, 1886).

Kuṇḍikā Upaniṣad. Ed. in SUS. Tr. in Olivelle 1992.

Kūrma Purāṇa. Ed. A. S. Gupta (Varanasi: All-India Kashiraj Trust, 1971).

Laghu-Saṃnyāsa Upaniṣad. Ed. in SUS. Tr. in Olivelle 1992.

Lakṣmīdhara, *Kṛtyakalpataru*. Ed. V. Rangaswami Aiyangar. 12 vols. (GOS, 1941–53).

Liṅga Purāṇa (Bombay: Veṅkateśvara Press, 1906).

Mādhava, *Pārāśaramādhavīya*. Ed. Chandrakanta Tarkalankara. 3 vols. Reprint (Calcutta: The Asiatic Society, 1973–74).

Mahābhārata. Ed. V. S. Sukthankar et al. 19 vols. (Poona: Bhandarkar Oriental Research Institute, 1927–59). Ed. with Nīlakaṇṭha's commentary by Pandit R. Kinjawadekar. 6 vols. Reprint (New Delhi: Oriental Books Reprint Corp., 1979). Tr. van Buitenen 1973–78.

Mahānārāyaṇa Upaniṣad. Ed. and tr. J. Varenne. 2 vols. Série in-8, 11–12 (Paris: Institut de Civilisation Indienne, 1960).

Mahānirvāṇatantra (Bombay: Venkatesvara Press, 1985). Tr. A. Avalon 1913. Reprint (New York: Dover Publications, 1972).

Maitrāyaṇīya Saṃhitā of the *Yajur Veda.* Ed. L. Von Schroeder. 4 vols. (Leipzig: F. A. Brockhaus, 1881–86).

Maitrī (Maitrāyaṇī) Upaniṣad. Ed. in EPU. Tr. in TPU.

Majjhima Nikāya of the *Sutta Piṭaka.* Ed. V. Trenckner and R. Chalmers. 3 vols. (PTS, 1888–99). Tr. R. Chalmers (SBB 5–6, 1926–27).

Mānava Dharmaśāstra (*Manusmṛti*). Ed. with the commentaries of Medhātithi, Sarvajñanārāyaṇa, Kullūka, Rāghavānanda, Nandana, Rāmacandra, and Govindarāja by V. N. Mandlik. 3 vols. (Bombay: Ganpat Krishnaji's Press, 1886). Ed. and tr. with Bhāruci's commentary by J. D. M. Derrett. 2 vols. (Wiesbaden: Franz Steiner, 1975). Tr. G. Bühler (SBE 25, 1886).

Mānava Gṛhyasūtra. Ed. F. Knauer (St. Petersburg: J. Glasounof, 1897). Tr. M. J. Dresden (Groningen: J. B. Wolters, 1941).

Mānava Śrautasūtra. Ed. and tr. J. M. van Gelder. 2 vols. Reprint of 1963; Sri Garib Dass Oriental Series 31–32 (Delhi: Sri Satguru Publications, 1985).

Maṇḍūkya Upaniṣad. Ed. in EPU. Tr. in TPU. Ed. tr. with Gauḍapāda's *Kārikā* by R. D. Karmarkar 1953. Reprint (Poona: Bhandarkar Oriental Research Institute, 1973).

Markaṇḍeya Purāṇa. Ed. J. Vidyasagara (Calcutta: Saraswati Press, 1879).

Matsya Purāṇa (ĀnSS 54, 1907).

Milinda Pañho. Ed. V. Trenchner (PTS, 1962). Tr. T. W. Rhy Davids. 2 vols. (SBE 35–36, 1890, 1894).

Mīmāṃsā Koṣa. Ed. Kevalānanda Sarasvatī. 7 vols. (Wai: Prājña Pāṭhaśālā Maṇḍala, 1952–66).

Moggallāna. *Abhidānappadīpikā.* Ed. Swami Swarikadas Shastri (Benares: Bauddhabharati, 1981).

Muṇḍaka Upaniṣad. Ed. in EPU. Tr. in TPU.

Nāradaparivrājaka Upaniṣad. Ed. in SUS. Tr. in Olivelle 1992.

Nāradasmṛti. Ed. and tr. Richard W. Lariviere. 2 pts. University of Pennsylvania Studies on South Asia, vols. 4–5 (Philadelphia: University of Pennsylvania, 1989).

Nīlakaṇṭha, *Saṃskāramayūkha.* Ed. Nārāhāri Shastri Shende (Bombay: Gujarati Printing Press, 1969).

Nṛsiṃha Purāṇa. Ed. Uddhavācārya Aināpure (Bombay: Gopal Narayan, 1911).

Pāli Tipiṭakaṃ Concordance. Ed. E. M. Hare et al. (London: Pāli Text Society &Luzac, 1952—).

Pañcamāśramavidhāna. Ed. in Olivelle 1986.

Pañcaviṃśa Brāhmaṇa. Ed. Ānandachandra Vedāntavāgīśa. 2 vols. (Calcutta: Bibliotheca Indica, 1869–74).

Pāṇini, *Aṣṭādhyāyī.* Ed. and tr. O. Böhtlingk 1887. Reprint (Hildesheim: Olms, 1964). Tr. S. C. Vasu 1891. 2 vols. Reprint (Delhi: Motilal Banarsidass, 1962).

Paramahaṃsa Upaniṣad. Ed. in SUS. Tr. in Olivelle 1992.

Pāraskara Gṛhyasūtra. Ed. Mukunda Panta Puṇatāmakara (KSS 11, 1920). Tr. H. Oldenberg (SBE 19, 1886).

Patañjali, *Mahābhāṣya.* Ed. F. Kielhorn 1880. 3rd ed. revised by K. V. Abhyankar. 3 vols. (Poona: Bhandarkar Oriental Research Institute, 1962–72).

Praśna Upaniṣad. Ed. in EPU. Tr. in TPU.

Pūrva Mīmāṃsāsūtra of Jaimini. Ed. with the commentaries of Śabara and Kumārila

(*Tantravārtika*). 7 vols. (AnSS 97, 1971–81). Tr. G. Jha. 3 vols. (GOS 66, 70, 73, 1973–74).

Rāmāyaṇa. Ed. G. H. Bhatt et al. 6 vols. (Baroda: Oriental Institute, 1960–71). Tr. Goldman 1984.

Ṛgveda Saṃhitā. Ed. with Sāyaṇa's commentary by F. Max Müller. 6 vols. (London: Wm. H. Allen & Co., 1849–74). Tr. Geldner 1951–57.

Rudradeva, *Saṃnyāsapaddhati*. Ed. P. Olivelle (Madras: Adyar Library and Research Centre, 1986).

Sāmaveda Saṃhitā. Ed. with commentaries of Mādhava and Bharatasvāmin by C. Kunhan Raja. Adyar Library Publications 26 (Madras: Adyar Library, 1941).

Śaṃkara, *Upadeśasāhasrī*. Ed. S. Mayeda (Tokyo: Hokuseido Press, 1973). Tr. S. Mayeda (Tokyo: University of Tokyo Press, 1979).

Saṃnyāsa Upaniṣads. Ed. F. Otto Schrader (Madras: Adyar Library, 1912). Tr. Olivelle 1992.

Saṃyutta Nikāya of the *Sutta Piṭaka*. Ed. M. L. Feer. 6 vols. (PTS, 1884–98).

Sanatkumāra Saṃhitā. Ed. V. Krishnamacharya (Madras: Adyar Library, 1967).

Śāṇḍilya Saṃhitā. Ed. Gopinath Kaviraj. Princess of Wales Saraswati Bhavana Texts 60 (Benares: Eureka Printing Works, 1935).

Śāṅkhāyana Āraṇyaka (ĀnSS 90, 1922).

Śāṅkhāyana Gṛhyasūtra. Ed. S. R. Seghal. 2nd ed. (Delhi: Sri Satguru Publications, 1987). Tr. H. Oldenberg (SBE 19, 1886).

Śāṅkhāyana Śrautasūtra. Ed. A. Hillebrandt 1885. Reprint (New Delhi: Meharchand Lachhmandas, 1981). Tr. W. Caland 1953. Reprint (Delhi: Motilal Banarsidass, 1980).

Śatapatha Brāhmaṇa. Ed. A. Weber 1855. Reprint. Chowkhamba Sanskrit Series 96 (Varanasi: 1964). Tr. J. Eggeling (SBE 12, 26, 41, 43, 44, 1882–1900).

Śāṭyāyanīya Upaniṣad. Ed. in SUS. Tr. in Olivelle 1992.

Saura Purāṇa (ĀnSS 18, 1911).

Somadeva, *Kathāsaritsāgara*. Ed. Pandit Durgāprasād and Kāsināth Pāndurang Parad. 4th ed. revised by Laxman Śastri Pansikar. (Bombay: Jāwajī, 1930). Tr. C. H. Tawney 1880. Reprint. 2 vols. (New Delhi: Munshiram Manoharlal, 1992).

Śrīdhara, *Smṛtyarthasāra*. (ĀnSS 70, 1912).

Sureśvara, *Bṛhadāraṇyakopaniṣadbhāṣyavārtika*. 3 vols. (ĀnSS 16, 1892–94).

Suśruta Saṃhitā. Ed. J. Trikamjī and Nārāyaṇa Rāma Ācarya "Kāvyatīrtha." 3rd ed. 1938. Reprint (Varanasi: Chaukhamba Orientalia, 1980).

Sūta Saṃhitā of the *Skanda Purāṇa*. 3 pts (ĀnSS 25, 1924–25).

Suttanipāta. Ed. D. Anderson and H. Smith (PTS, 1913). Tr. V. Fausböll (SBE 10, 1881).

Śvetāśvatara Upaniṣad. Ed. in EPU. Tr. in TPU. Ed. and tr. L. Silburn (Paris: Adrien Maisonneuve, 1948).

Taittirīya Āraṇyaka. Ed. with Sāyaṇa's commentary by Bābā Śāstrī Phaḍka. 2 vols. (ĀnSS 36, 1898).

Taittirīya Brāhmaṇa. Ed. with Sāyaṇa's commentary by Nārāyaṇa Śāstrī Goḍabole. 3 vols. (ĀnSS 37, 1898).

Taittirīya Saṃhitā. Ed. with Sāyaṇa's commentary by Kāśīnātha Śāstrī Āgāśe. 9 vols. (ĀnSS 42, 1900–08). Tr. A. B. Keith (HOS 18–19, 1914).

Taittirīya Upaniṣad. Ed. with Śaṃkara's commentary by Vināyak Ganeś Āpte (ĀnSS 12, 1929). Tr. in TPU.

Theragāthā and *Therīgāthā*. Ed. H. Oldenberg and R. Pischel (London: H. Frowde, 1883). Tr. Mrs. Rhy Davids (London. H. Frowde, 1909–13).

The Thirteen Principal Upanishads. Tr. R. E. Hume. 2nd ed. (Oxford: Oxford University Press, 1931).

Turīyātītāvadhūta Upaniṣad. Ed. in SUS. Tr. in Olivelle 1992.

Upaniṣadāṃ Samuccayaḥ (ĀnSS 29, 1925).

Vaidyanātha Dīkṣita, *Smṛtimuktāphala*. Ed. J. R. Gharpure. Collection of Hindu Law Texts 25 (Bombay: 1937–40).

Vaikhānasa Dharmaṣūtra. Ed. and tr. in VaiSm.

Vaikhānasa Gṛhyasūtra. Ed. and tr. in VaiSm.

Vaikhānasa Smārtasūtra. Ed. and tr. W. Caland. Bibliotheca Indica 242, 252 (Calcutta: Asiatic Society of Bengal, 1927–29). Tr. Eggers 1929.

Vājasaneyi Saṃhitā. Ed. A. Weber (Berlin: Ferd. Dümmler's Verlagsbuchhandlung, 1852).

Vāmana Purāṇa. Ed. Anad Swarup Gupta (Varanasi: All-India Kashiraj Trust, 1968).

Varāhamihira, *Bṛhajjātaka*. Tr. Swami Vijnananda 1912. Reprint (New York: AMS Press, 1974).

Varāhamihira, *Bṛhatsaṃhitā*. Ed. and tr. M. Ramakrishna Bhat. 2 vols. (Delhi: Motilal Banarsidass, 1981–82).

Vasiṣṭha Dharmasūtra. Ed. A. A. Führer. 3rd. ed. (BSS 23, 1930). Tr. G. Bühler (SBE 2, 1879).

Vāsudevāśrama, *Yatidharmaprakāśa*. Ed. and tr. P. Olivelle. 2 vols. De Nobili Research Library 3–4 (Vienna: University of Vienna Institute for Indology, 1976–77).

Vātsyāyana, *Kāmasūtra*. Ed. Gosvāmī Dāmodar Shastri (KSS 29, 1929). Tr. R. F. Burton 1883. Reprint (New York: Arkana, 1962).

Vedānta Deśika, *Śatadūṣaṇī*. Ed. V. Srivatsankachar (Madras: 1974). Ch. 64 *Yatiliṅgabhedabhaṅgavāda* and ch. 65 *Alepakamatabhaṅgavāda*, ed. and tr. in Olivelle 1986–87.

Vedāntasūtras of Bādarāyaṇa. Ed. with Śaṃkara's commentary by Nārāyan Rām Ācārya (Bombay: Nirnaya Sagar Press, 1948). Tr. with Śaṁkara's commentary by G. Thibaut. 2 pts. (SBE 34, 1890; SBE 38, 1896). Ed. and tr. with Rāmānuja's commentary by R. D. Karmarkar. 3 pts. University of Poona Sanskrit and Prakrit Series, vol. 1 (Poona: 1959–64). Ed. with the commentary of Bhāskara. Chowkhambā Sanskrit Series 70, 185, 209 (Benares: 1915).

Vidyāraṇya, *Jīvanmuktiviveka*. Ed. and tr. S. Subrahmanya Sastri and T. R. Srinivasa Ayyangar (Madras; Adyar Library, 1978).

Vinaya Piṭaka. Ed. H. Oldenberg. 5 vols. (London: Williams and Norgate, 1879–83). Tr. I. B. Horner (SBB 10, 11, 13, 14, 20, 25, 1938–66). Tr. T. W. Rhys Davids and H. Oldenberg (SBE 13, 17, 20, 1855–82).

Viṣṇu Dharmasūtra (*Viṣṇusmṛti*). Ed. with Nandapaṇḍita's commentary by V. Krishnamacharya. 2 vols. Adyar Library Series 93 (Madras: 1964). Tr. J. Jolly (SBE 7, 1880).

Viṣṇudharmottara Purāṇa. (Bombay: Veṅkaṭeśvara Press, 1912).

Viṣṇu Purāṇa. Ed. Śrīrāma Sarmā Ācārya. 2 vols. (Barelī: Saṃskṛta Saṃsthāna, 1967). Tr. H. H. Wilson 1840. Reprint (Calcutta: Punthi Pustak, 1972).

Viśveśvara Sarasvatī, *Yatidharmasaṃgraha*. Ed. V. G. Apte (ĀnSS 60, 1928).

Vṛddha-Hārītasmṛti. Ed. in *Smṛtīnaṃ Samuccahaḥ*. (ĀnSS 48, 1929).

Yādavaprakāśa, *Yatidharmasamuccaya*. Ed. Śrī Bhagavadācārya (Baroda: 1937).

Yājñavalkya Dharmaśāstra. Ed. with Vijñāneśvara's commentary (*Mitākṣarā*) by U. C. Pandey (KSS 178, 1967). Ed. with Aparāditya's commentary (*Aparārka*). 2 vols. (ĀnSS 46, 1903–04). Ed. with Viśvarūpa's commentary (*Bālkrīḍā*) by T. Ganapati Sastri 1921–22. Reprint (New Delhi: Munsiram Manoharlal, 1982). Ed. with Śūlapaṇi's commentary by J. R. Gharpure (Bombay: 1939). Ed. with Mitra Miśra's commentary (*Vīramitrodaya*). 7 vols. (Benares: Chowkhamba Sanskrit Series, Benares).

Yāska, *Nirukta*. Ed. V. K. Rajavade (Poona: Bhandarkar Oriental Research Institute, 1940).

2. Secondary Literature

Allchin, B. and Allchin R. 1982. *The Rise of Civilization in India and Pakistan.* Cambridge: Cambridge University Press.

Altekar, A. S. 1955. "The Ashrama System." *Professor Ghurye Felicitation Volume,* ed. K. M. Kapadia. Bombay: Popular Book Depot.

Apte, V. M. 1951. "Religion and Philosophy." Ch. XXVI of *The Vedic Age.* History and Culture of the Indian People, ed. R. C. Majumdar. Vol. 1. London: George Allen & Unwin.

———. 1954. *Social and Religious Life in the Gṛhya-sūtras.* Bombay: Popular Book Depot.

Babb, L. A. 1970a. *The Divine Hierarchy: Popular Hinduism in Central India.* New York: Columbia University Press.

———. 1970b. "Marriage and Malevolence: The Uses of Sexual Opposition in a Hindu Pantheon." *Ethnology* 9: 137–48.

Banerjee, S. C. 1962. *Dharma-Sūtras: A Study in Their Origin and Development.* Calcutta: Punthi Pustak.

Barnett, L. D. 1913. *Antiquities of India.* London: P. L. Warner.

Barua, M. B. 1921. *A History of Pre-Buddhistic Indian Philosophy.* Calcutta: University of Calcutta.

Basham, A. L. 1951. *History and Doctrines of the Ājīvikas: A Vanished Indian Religion.* London: Luzac.

Basu, Jogiraj. 1969. *India of the Age of the Brāhmaṇas.* Calcutta: Sanskrit Pustak Bhandar.

Basu, Jyotirmayee. 1964. "The Role of Asramas in the Life of Ancient Hindus." *Journal of Indian History* 42: 847–76.

Belvalkar, S. K. and Ranade, R. D. 1927. Reprint 1974. *History of Indian Philosophy—II. The Creative Period.* New Delhi: Oriental Books Reprint Corporation.

Bergaigne, A. 1878–97. *La religion védique d'après les hymnes du Ṛig-veda.* 4 vols. Paris: F. Vieweg.

Berger, P. L. 1969. *The Sacred Canopy.* Garden City, New York: Doubleday.

Berger, P. L. and Luckmann, T. 1967. *The Social Construction of Reality.* Garden City, New York: Doubleday.

Bhagat, M. G. 1976. *Ancient Indian Asceticism.* Delhi: Munshiram Manoharlal.

Bhagwat, D. 1939a. *Early Buddhist Jurisprudence.* Poona: Oriental Book Agency.

———. 1939b. "Origin of Indian Monachism." *Journal of the Bombay University* 8.2: 104–30.

Bhandarkar, D. R. 1940. *Some Aspects of Ancient Indian Culture.* Sir William Meyer Lectures 1938–39. Madras: University of Madras.

Bhandarkar, R. G. 1933. "The Latest Limit of the Date of the Origin of the Conception of the Ten Avatāras of Viṣṇu and of the Widow Marriage Text." In Vol. 1 of *Collected Works of Sir R. G. Bhandarkar,* ed. N. B. Utgikar and V. G. Paranjpe. Poona: Bhandarkar Oriental Research Institute.

Bhattacharya, B. 1943. *The "Kalivarjyas" or Prohibitions in the "Kali" Age.* Calcutta: University of Calcutta.

Biardeau, M. 1982. "The Salvation of the King in the *Mahābhārata.*" In Madan 1982, 75–97.

Biardeau, M. and Malamoud, C. 1976. *Le sacrifice dans l'Inde ancienne.* Paris: Presses Universitaires de France.

Blair, C. J. 1961. *Heat in the Rig Veda and Atharva Veda.* American Oriental Series, 45. New Haven: American Oriental Society.

Bloch, T. 1989. *Über das Gṛhya- und Dharmasūtra der Vaikhānasa.* Leipzig: G. Kreysing.

Bloomfield, M. 1899. Reprint 1978. *The Atharvaveda and the Gopatha Brāhmaṇa.* New Delhi: Asian Publication Services.

———. 1908. *The Religion of the Veda.* New York: G. P. Putnam's Sons.

———. 1924. "On False Ascetics and Nuns in Hindu Fiction." JAOS 44: 202–42.

Bodewitz, H. W. 1973. *Jaiminīya Brāhmaṇa I, 1–65.* Translation and Commentary with a Study *Agnihotra and Prāṇāgnihotra.* Leiden: E. J. Brill.

———. 1976. *The Daily Evening and Morning Offering (Agnihotra) according to the Brāhmaṇas.* Leiden: E. J. Brill.

Bouillier, V. 1978. "L'ascétisme dans le code Népalais." *Journal Asiatique* 266: 133–52.

———. 1979. *Naître renonçant: une caste de sannyāsī villageois au Népal central.* Nanterre: Laboratoire D'Ethnologie.

Bradford, N. J. 1985. "The Indian Renouncer: Structure and Transformation in the Lingayat Community." In *Indian Religion,* ed. R. Burghart and A. Cantlie, 79–104. London: Curzon Press.

Brown, N. 1970. *Man in the Universe: Some Continuities in Indian Thought.* Berkeley: University of California Press.

Bühler, G. 1887. *Über die indische Secte der Jaina.* Vortrag gehalten in der feierlichen Sitzung der Kaiserlichen Akademie der Wissenschaften. Vienna.

Cantlie, A. 1977. "Aspects of Hindu Asceticism." In *Symbols and Sentiments,* ed. J. Lewis, 247–67. London: Academic Press.

Cardona, G. 1976. *Pāṇini: A Survey of Research.* Delhi: Motilal Banarsidass.

Carman, J. and Narayanan, V. 1989. *The Tamil Veda: Piḷḷāṉ's Interpretation of the Tiruvāymoḻi.* Chicago: University of Chicago Press.

Chakladar, H. C. 1929. *Social Life in Ancient India: Studies in Vātsyāyana's Kāmasūtra.* Calcutta: Greater India Society.

———. 1962. "Some Aspects of Social Life in Ancient India." In *The Cultural Heritage of India,* II, 557-81. Calcutta: Ramakrishna Mission Institute.

Chakraborti, H. 1973. *Asceticism in Ancient India: In Brahmanical, Buddhist, Jaina and Ajivika Societies.* Calcutta: Punthi Pustak.

Chanda, R. 1934. "Śramaṇism." *Proceedings of the Twenty-first Indian Science Congress, Sec. VIII.* Bombay. Cited from reprint in *Indian Museum Bulletin,* Jan.–July, 1977: 89–111.

Chatterjee, H. 1971. *The Law of Debt in Ancient India.* Calcutta: Sanskrit College.

Chattopadhyaya, S. 1965. *Social Life in Ancient India (in the Background of the Yajñavalkyasmriti).* Calcutta: Academic Publishers.

Collins, S. 1982. *Selfless Persons: Imagery and Thought in Theravāda Buddhism.* Cambridge: Cambridge University Press.

Das, K. 1943. "The Four Ages of Man." *Vedanta Kesari* 30.1: 29–35.

Das, R. M. 1962. *Women in Manu and His Seven Commentators.* Varanasi: Kanchana Publications.

Della Santina, P. 1989. "Conceptions of Dharma in the Śramaṇical and Brāhmaṇical Traditions: Buddhism and the Mahābhārata." In Matilal 1989, 97–115.

Deo, S. B. 1956. *History of Jaina Monachism from Inscriptions and Literature.* Deccan College Dissertation Series, 17. Poona.

Derrett, J. D. M. 1968. *Religion, Law and the State in India.* London: Faber.

———. 1974. "Modes of Sannyāsis and the Reform of a South Indian Maṭha Carried Out in 1584." JAOS 94: 65–72.

Deshpande, M. 1985. "Historical Change and the Theology of Eternal Sanskrit," *Zeitschrift für vergleichende Sprachforschung* 98: 122–49.

Deussen, P. 1905. *Sechzig Upanishads des Veda aus dem Sanskrit übersetzt und mit Einleitun-*

gen und Anmerkungen versechen. Leipzig: F. A. Brockhaus. Tr. V. M. Bedekar and G. B. Palsule, *Sixty Upaniṣads of the Veda.* 2 vols. Delhi: Motilal Banarsidass, 1980.

———. 1906. Reprint 1966. *The Philosophy of the Upanishads.* Tr. A. S. Gedan. New York: Dover.

———. 1909. "Āśrama." In *Encyclopedia of Religion and Ethics*, ed. J. Hastings, II, 128–31. Edinburgh: T & T Clark.

Devahuti, D. 1970. *Harsha: A Political Study.* Oxford: Clarendon Press.

Devasthali, G. V. 1965. "Religion and Mythology of the Brāhmaṇas." *The Bau Vishnu Ashtekar Vedic Research Series* I. Poona.

Dharmadeva. 1961. "Kyā vedon men vānaprastha saṃnyāsa āśramon kā vidhāna nahīn hai?" *Vedavāṇī* 14.1: 89–95.

———. 1963. "Saṃnyāsāśrama kā veda-brāhmaṇa-upaniṣad ādi men spaṣṭa vidhāna." *Vedavāṇī* 15.5: 5–9.

———. 1966. "Prācīna vaidika āśramavyavasthā." *Gurukula Patrikā* (Haridwar) 18.

———. 1970. "Catechism on the Vedic Dharma and Arya Samaj." *Vedic Light* (New Delhi), 4.3: 79–81.

Douglas, M. 1982. *Natural Symbols: Explorations in Cosmology.* New York: Pantheon.

Dumont, L. 1960. "World Renunciation in Indian Religions." *Contributions to Indian Sociology* 4: 33–62.

———. 1970. *Homo Hierarchicus: The Caste System and Its Implications.* Tr. M. Sainsbury. Chicago: University of Chicago Press.

Dutt, S. 1960. *Early Buddhist Monachism.* Rev. ed. London: Asia Publishing House.

———. 1962. *Buddhist Monks and Monasteries of India.* London: George Allen & Unwin.

Edgerton, F. 1927. "The Hour of Death." *Annals of the Bhandarkar Oriental Research Institute* 8: 219–49.

Eggers, W. 1929. *Das Dharmasūtra der Vaikhānasas. Übersetzt und mit textkritischen und erklärenden Anmerkungen versehen. Nebst einer Einleitung über den brahmanischen Waldeinsiedler-Orden und die Vaikhānasa-Sekte.* Göttingen: Vandenhoeck & Ruprecht.

Erdosy, G. 1988. *Urbanization in Early Historic India.* BAR International Series 430. Oxford: B.A.R.

Farquhar, J. N. 1913. *The Crown of Hinduism.* Oxford: H. Milford.

———. 1920. *An Outline of the Religious Literature of India.* Oxford: Oxford University Press.

———. 1925. "The Organization of the Sannyasis of the Vedanta." JRAS 45: 479–86.

Feldhaus, A. 1982. "Bahiṇā Bāī: Wife and Saint." JAAR 50: 591–604.

Filliozat, J. 1972. *Un Texte Tamoul de Dévotion Vishnouite: le Tiruppāvai d'Āṇṭāḷ.* Pondichéry: Institut Français d'Indologie.

Fitzgerald, J. 1980. "India's Fifth Veda: The Mahābhārata's Presentation of Itself," *Journal of South Asian Literature* 20: 125–40.

Frauwallner, E. 1973. *History of Indian Philosophy.* Tr. V. M. Bedekar. 2 vols. Delhi: Motilal Banarsidass.

Fris, O. 1950. Review of "Skurzak 1948." *Archiv Orientální* (Prague) 18: 385–88.

Gangadharan, N. 1976. "The Antiquity of the Institution of the Four Āśramas." *Bulletin of Traditional Cultures* (University of Madras): 149–59.

Garbe, R. 1917. *Die Sāṃkhya-Philosophie.* 2nd. ed. Leipzig: H. Haessel.

Geldner, K. F. 1951-57. *Der Rig Veda.* 4 vols. HOS 33–36.

Ghosh, A. 1973. *The City in Early Historical India.* Simla: Indian Institute of Advanced Study.

Ghosh, B. 1927. "Āpastamba and Gautama." *Indian Historical Quarterly*, 3: 607–11.

Ghosh Chaudhury, S. K. 1967. "Chaturasrama—A Composite Feature of Life in Pre-Buddhist India." *Proceedings of the Indian History Congress* (37th session, 1965): 130–33.

Ghurye, G. S. 1964. *Indian Sadhus.* 2nd ed. Bombay: Popular Prakashan.

Goetz, H. 1966. *Mira Bai: Her Life and Times.* Bombay: Bharatiya Vidya Bhavan.

Goldman, R. P. 1978. "Fathers, Sons and Gurus: Oedipal Conflict in the Sanskrit Epics," *Journal of Indian Philosophy* 6: 325–92.

———. 1984. Tr. *The Rāmāyaṇa of Vālmīki.* Vol. I: Bālakāṇḍa. Princeton: Princeton University Press.

Gombrich, R. 1988. *Theravāda Buddhism: A Social History from Ancient Benares to Modern Colombo.* London: Routledge & Kegan Paul.

Gonda, J. 1957. *Some Observations on the Relations between "Gods" and "Powers" in the Veda, A Propos of the Phrase sūnuḥ sahasaḥ.* The Hague: Mouton.

———. 1960, 1963. *Die Religionen Indiens.* 2 vols. Stuttgart: W. Kohlhammer.

———. 1961. "Ascetics and Courtesans." ALB 25: 78–102.

———. 1965. *Change and Continuity in Indian Religion.* Disputationes Rheno-Trajectinae 9. The Hague: Mouton.

———. 1966. *Loka: World and Heaven in the Veda.* Amsterdam: North-Holland.

———. 1969. *Ancient Indian Kingship from the Religious Point of View.* Leiden: E. J. Brill.

———. 1970. *Viṣṇuism and Śivaism: A Comparison.* London: Athlone Press.

———. 1976. *Triads in the Veda.* Amsterdam: North-Holland.

———. 1980. *Vedic Ritual: The Non-Solemn Rites.* Handbuch der Orientalistik, II.1.1. Leiden: E. J. Brill.

———. 1984. *Prajāpati and the Year.* Verhandelingen der Koninklijke Nederlandse Akademie van Wetenschappen, Afd. Letterkunde, Nieuwe Reeks, Deel 123. Amsterdam: North-Holland.

———. 1986. *Prajāpati's Rise to Higher Rank.* Leiden: E. J. Brill.

Gopal, R. 1959. *India of the Vedic Kalpasūtras.* Delhi: National Publishing House.

Haberlandt, M. 1885. "Uber den dritten ācrama der Inder." *Mittheilungen der Anthropologischen Gesellschaft in Wien* 15: 10–12.

Hacker, P. 1978. "'Topos' und 'chris'." In *Kleinen Schriften,* ed. L. Schmithausen, 338–59. Wiesbaden: Franz Steiner.

Halbfass, W. 1988. *India and Europe: An Essay in Understanding.* Albany: SUNY Press.

Hall, F. 1982. *Sāṃkhyasāra.* Reprint. Calcutta: Bibliotheca Indica.

Hauer, J. W. 1927. *Der Vrātya. Untersuchungen über die nichtbrahmanische Religion Altindiens.* Stuttgart: W. Kohlhammer.

Heesterman, J. C. 1957. *The Ancient Indian Royal Consecration.* Disputationes Rheno-Trajectinae 2. The Hague: Mouton.

———. 1962. "Vrātya and Sacrifice." *Indo-Iranian Journal* 6: 1–37.

———. 1964. "Brahmin, Ritual and Renouncer." WZKS 8: 1–31.

———. 1968. "The Return of the Veda Scholar (samāvartana)." In *Pratidānam: Indian, Iranian and Indo-European Studies presented to Franciscus Bernardus Jacobus Kuiper on his Sixtieth Birthday,* ed. J. C. Heesterman et al., 436–47. The Hague: Mouton.

———. 1982. "Householder and Wanderer." In Madan 1982, 251–71.

———, 1985. *The Inner Conflict of Tradition: Essays in Indian Ritual, Kingship, and Society.* Chicago: University of Chicago Press.

Hopkins, E. W. 1969. *The Great Epic of India.* Reprint. Calcutta: Punthi Pustak.

Jacobi, H. 1884. *Jaina Sūtras.* 2 vols. SBE 22, 45.

Jaini, P. S. 1991. *Gender and Salvation: Jaina Debates on the Spiritual Liberation of Women.* Berkeley: University of California Press.

Jha, G. 1964. *Pūrva-Mīmāṁsā in its Sources.* Benares: Benares Hindu University.

Jolly, J. 1928. Reprint 1975. *Hindu Law and Custom.* Tr. B. Ghosh. Calcutta: Bharatiya Publishing House.

Kaelber, W. O. 1989. *Tapta Mārga: Asceticism and Initiation in Vedic India.* Albany: SUNY Press.

Kakar, S. 1968. "The Human Life Cycle: The Traditional Hindu View and the Psychology of Erik Erikson." *Philosophy East and West* 18: 127–36.

Kane, P. V. 1942. "The Meaning of Ācāryāḥ." *Annals of the Bhandarkar Oriental Research Institute,* 23: 206–13.

———. 1962–75. *History of Dharmaśāstra.* I.1 (1968), I.2 (1975), II.1–2 (1974), III (1973), V.1 (1974), V.2 (1962). Poona: Bhandarkar Oriental Research Institute.

Kangle, R. P. 1960–65. *The Kauṭilīya Arthaśāstra.* Three Parts. University of Bombay Studies, Sanskrit, Prakrit and Pali, Nos. 1–3; Bombay: University of Bombay.

———. 1968. "The Relative Age of the *Gautamadharmasūtra.*" In *Mélanges d' Indianisme à la mémoire de Louis Renou,* 415–25. Paris: Éditions E. de Boccard.

Keith, A. B. 1925. *The Religion and Philosophy of the Veda and Upanishads.* HOS 31–32.

———. 1928. *A History of Sanskrit Literature.* Oxford: Oxford University Press.

Kern, H. 1898. Reprint 1968. *Manual of Indian Buddhism.* Varanasi: Indological Book House.

Khare, R. S. 1976. *Culture and Reality: Essays on the Hindu System of Managing Foods.* Simla: Indian Institute of Advanced Study.

Klostermaier, K. K. 1989. *A Survey of Hinduism.* Albany: SUNY Press.

Knipe, D. M. 1975. *In the Image of Fire.* Delhi: Motilal Banarsidass.

Kosambi, D. D. 1965. Reprint 1975. *Culture and Civilisation of Ancient India in Historical Outline.* Delhi: Vikas.

Krishnan, Y. 1969. "Was It Permissible for a Saṁnyāsī (Monk) to Revert to Lay Life?" *Annals of the Bhandarkar Oriental Research Institute* 50: 73–89.

———. 1989. "The Meaning of the Puruṣārthas in the Mahābhārata." In Matilal 1989, 53–68.

Larson, G. J. 1969. *Classical Sāṃkya: An Interpretation of Its History and Meaning.* Delhi: Motilal Banarsidass.

Larson, G. J. and Bhattacharya, R. S., eds. 1987. *Encyclopedia of Indian Philosophies,* Vol. IV. Saṃkhya. Delhi: Motilal Banarsidass.

Law, B.C. 1918. "A Short Account of the Wandering Teachers at the Time of the Buddha." *Journal of the Asiatic Society of Bombay,* New Series 14: 399–406.

Leslie, I. J. 1989. *The Perfect Wife: The Orthodox Hindu Woman according to the Strīdharmapaddhati of Tryambakayajva.* Delhi: Oxford University Press.

Lévi, S. 1898. *La doctrine du sacrifice dans les Brahmaṇas.* Paris: Ernest Leroux.

Liebich, B. 1936. *Die vier indischen Āçramas.* Breslau: Preuss & Jünger.

Ling, T. 1976. *The Buddha: Buddhist Civilization in India and Ceylon.* Harmondsworth: Penguin.

Lingat, R. 1962. "Time and Dharma." *Contributions to Indian Sociology* 6: 7–16.

———. 1973. *The Classical Law of India.* Tr. J. D. M. Derrett. Berkeley: University of California Press.

Lorenzen, D. N. 1972. *The Kāpālikas and Kālāmukhas: Two Lost Śaivite Sects.* Australian National University Centre of Oriental Studies, Oriental Monograph Series, XII. New Delhi: Thompson Press.

———. 1978. "Warrior Ascetics in Indian History." JAOS 98: 61–75.

Macdonell, A. A. and Keith, A. B. 1912. Reprint 1967. *Vedic Index.* 2 vols. Delhi: Motilal Banarsidass.

Madan, T. N. 1982. *Way of Life: King, Householder, Renouncer. Essays in Honour of Louis Dumont.* New Delhi: Vikas Publishing House.

———. 1987. *Non-Renunciation: Themes and Interpretations of Hindu Culture.* Delhi: Oxford University Press.

Majumdar, R. C. 1922. *Corporate Life in Ancient India.* Calcutta: Calcutta University.

———. 1960. Reprint 1981. *The Classical Accounts of India.* Calcutta: Firma KLM.

Malamoud, C. 1972. "Obervations sur la notion de 'reste' dans le brāhmanisme." WZKS 16: 5–26.

———. 1976a. "Terminer le sacrifice: remarques sur les honoraires rituels dans le brahmanisme." In Biardeau and Malamoud 1976.

———. 1976b. "Village et forêt dans l'idéologie de l'Inde brâhmanique." *Archives Européennes de Sociologie* 17: 3–20.

———. 1977. *Le svādhyāya: recitation personnelle du Veda. Taittirīya-Āraṇyaka, Livre II.* Paris: Institut de Civilisation Indienne.

———. 1980. "Théologie de la dette dans les Brāhmaṇa." *Puruṣārtha: Science Sociales en Asie du Sud* 4: 39–62.

———. 1982. "On the Rhetoric and Semantics of Puruṣārthas." In Madan 1982, 33–54.

Marglin, F. A. 1985. "Female Sexuality in the Hindu World." In *Immaculate & Powerful: The Female in Sacred Image and Social Reality,* ed. C. W. Atkinson, C. H. Buchanan, and M. R. Miles, 39–59. Boston: Beacon Press.

Matilal, B. K. 1989. *Moral Dilemmas in the Mahābhārata.* Shimla/Delhi: Indian Institute of Advanced Study and Motilal Banarsidass.

Mayrhofer, M. 1953-76. *Kurzgefasstes etymologisches Wörterbuch des Altindischen—A Concise Etymological Sanskrit Dictionary.* Heidelberg: Carl Winter Universitätsverlag.

McKenzie, J. 1922. Reprint 1971. *Hindu Ethics: A Historical and Critical Essay.* New Delhi: Oriental Books Reprint Corporation.

Mees, G. H. 1935. *Dharma and Society: A Comparative Study of the Theory and the Ideal of Varna ("Natural Class") and the Phenomena of Caste and Class.* The Hague: N. V. Servire; London: Luzac.

Meyer, J. J. 1927. *Über das Wesen altindischen Rechtsschriften und ihr Verhältnis zu einander und zu Kauṭilya.* Leipzig: Otto Harrassowitz.

———. 1930. *Sexual Life in Ancient India: A Study in the Comparative History of Indian Culture.* London: Routledge & Kegan Paul.

Miller, D. M. and Wertz, D. C. 1976. *Hindu Monastic Life: The Monks and Monasteries of Bhubaneswar.* Montreal: McGill-Queen's University Press.

Modi, P. M. 1935. "The Development of Āśramas." *Proceedings and Transactions of the Seventh All India Oriental Conference* (Baroda, 1933), pp. 315–16.

Morgan, K. W. 1953. *The Religion of the Hindus.* New York: Ronald Press.

Müller, F. Max. 1878. *Lectures on the Origin and Growth of Religion as Illustrated by the Religions of India.* Hibbert Lectures. London: Longmans, Green.

Nakamura, H. 1983. *A History of Early Vedānta Philosophy.* Tr. T. Leggett et al., Pt. 1. Delhi: Motilal Banarsidass.

Nandi, R. N. 1986. *Social Roots of Religion in Ancient India.* Calcutta: K. P. Bagchi.

Obeyesekere, G. 1990. *The Work of Culture: Symbolic Transformation in Psychoanalysis and Anthropology.* Chicago: University of Chicago Press.

O'Flaherty, W. 1973. *Asceticism and Eroticism in the Mythology of Śiva.* London: Oxford University Press.

Ojha, C. 1981. "Feminine Asceticism in Hinduism: Its Tradition and Present Condition." *Man in India* 61: 254–85.

Oldenberg, H. 1882. *Buddha: His Life, His Doctrine, His Order.* Tr. W. Hoey. London: Williams & Norgate.

———. 1919. *Die Weltanschauung der Brāhmaṇa-Texte.* Göttingen: Vandenhoeck & Ruprecht.

Olivelle, P. 1974a. "The Notion of Āśrama in the Dharmasūtras." WZKS 18: 27–35.

———. 1974b. *The Origin and the Early Development of Buddhist Monachism.* Colombo: M. D. Gunasena.

———. 1975. "A Definition of World Renunciation. " WZKS 19: 75–83.

———. 1978a. "The Integration of Renunciation by Orthodox Hinduism." *Journal of the Oriental Institute* (Baroda) 28: 27–36.

———. 1978b. "Ritual Suicide and the Rite of Renunciation." WZKS 22: 19–44.

———. 1980. "*Pañcamāśramavidhi:* Rite for Becoming a Naked Ascetic." WZKS 24: 130–45.

———. 1981. "Contributions to the Semantic History of Saṃnyāsa." JAOS 101: 265–74.

———. 1984. "Renouncer and Renunciation in the Dharmaśāstras." In *Studies in Dharmaśāstra,* ed. Richard W. Lariviere, 81–152. Calcutta: Firma KLM.

———. 1986–87. *Renunciation in Hinduism: A Medieval Debate.* Vol. 1 (1986): *The Debate and the Advaita Argument.* Vol. 2 (1987): *The Viśiṣṭādvaita Argument.* De Nobili Research Library, Vols. 13-14. Vienna: University of Vienna Institute for Indology.

———. 1987. "King and Ascetic: State Control of Asceticism in the Arthaśāstra." In *Festscrift for Ludo Rocher,* ALB 51: 39–59.

———. 1990. "Village vs. Wilderness: Ascetic Ideals and the Hindu World." In *Monasticism in the Christian and Hindu Traditions,* ed. Austin Creel and Vasudha Narayanan, 125–160. Lewiston, N.Y.: Edwin Mellen.

———. 1991. "From Feast to Fast: Food and the Indian Ascetic." In *Problems of Dharma: Rules and Remedies in Classical Indian Law,* ed. I. Julia Leslie, 17–36. Panels of the VIIth World Sanskrit Conference, ed. J. Bronkhorst. Vol. IX. Leiden: E. J. Brill.

———. 1992. *Saṃnyāsa Upaniṣads: Hindu Scriptures on Asceticism and Renunciation.* New York: Oxford University Press.

Pancholi, B. P. 1965. "Kyā saṃnyāsa āśrama avaidika hai?" *Vedavāṇī* 17.9: 7–15.

Pande, G. C. 1957. *Studies in the Origins of Buddhism.* Allahabad: University of Allahabad.

———. 1978. *Śramaṇa Tradition: Its History and Contribution to Indian Culture.* Ahmedabad: L. D. Institute of Indology.

Pandey, R. B. 1969. *Hindu Saṁskāras: Socio-Religious Study of the Hindu Sacraments.* Delhi: Motilal Banarsidass.

Parpola, A. 1980. "On the Primary Meaning of the Sacred Syllable OṂ." *Studia Orientalia* (Helsinki) 50: 195–213.

Parry, J. 1982. "Sacrificial Death and the Necrophagous Ascetic." In *Death and the Regeneration of Life,* ed. M. Bloch and J. Parry, 74–110. Cambridge: Cambridge University Press.

———. 1985. "The Aghori Ascetics of Benares." In *Indian Religion,* ed. R. Burghart and A. Cantlie, 51–78. London: Curzon Press; New York: St. Martin's Press.

Potter, K. H. 1963. *Presuppositions of India's Philosophies.* Englewood Cliffs, N. J.: Prentice-Hall.

———. 1970. *The Encyclopedia of Indian Philosophies.* Vol. 1: *Bibliography of Indian Philosophies.* Delhi: Motilal Banarsidass.

———. 1981. *The Encyclopedia of Indian Philosophies.* Vol. 3: *Advaita Vedānta up to Śaṃkara and His Pupils.* Delhi: Motilal Banarsidass.

———. 1982. "Śaṃkarācārya: The Myth and the Man." JAAR, Thematic Studies, 48, nos. 3–4: 111–25.

Prabhu, P. N. 1954. *Hindu Social Organization with Reference to Their Psychological Implications.* 2nd ed. Bombay: Longmans, Green.

Radhakrishnan, S. 1929. *Indian Philosophy.* 2nd ed. 2 vols. London: George Allen & Unwin.

———. 1953. *The Principal Upaniṣads.* London: George Allen & Unwin.

Ramanujan, A. K. 1973. *Speaking of Śiva*. Baltimore: Penguin.

———. 1983. "The Indian Oedipus." In *Oedipus, A Folklore Casebook*, ed. L. Edmunds and A. Dundes, 234–61. New York: Garland Publishing Company.

Ranade, R. D. 1926. *A Constructive Survey of Upanishadic Philosophy: Being a Systematic Introduction to Indian Metaphysics.* Poona: Oriental Book Agency.

Rau, W. 1957. *Staat und Gesellschaft im alten Indien nach den Brāhmaṇa-Texten dargestellt.* Wiesbaden: Otto Harrossowitz.

Renou, L. 1955–69. *Études védiques et pāṇinéennes.* 17 vols. Paris: Publication de l'ICI.

Renou, L. and Filliozat, J. 1947. *L'Inde classique: manuel des études indiennes.* 2 vols. Paris: Bibliothèque de l'École Francaise d'Extreme-Orient.

Rhys Davids, T. W. 1903. Reprint 1971. *Buddhist India.* Delhi: Motilal Banarsidass.

Rocher, L. 1986. *The Purāṇas.* In *A History of Indian Literature*, ed. J. Gonda, II.3. Wiesbaden: Otto Harrassowitz.

Sadasivaiah, H. M. 1967. *A Comparative Study of Two Viraśaiva Monasteries.* Mysore: University of Mysore.

Sarkar, B. K. 1917. "Varṇāśrama Dharma and Race Fusion in Ancient India," *Modern Review*, February, 211–15

Schrader, F. O. 1916. Reprint 1973. *Introduction to the Pāñcarātra and the Ahirbudhnya Saṃhitā.* Madras: Adyar Library.

Seltur, S. S. ed. 1911. *A Complete Collection of Hindu Law Books on Inheritance.* Madras: V. Kayanaram Iyer.

Senart, E. 1930. Reprint 1975. *Caste in India: The Facts and the System.* Tr. E. D. Ross. Delhi: Ess Ess Publications.

Settar, S. 1986. *Inviting Death: Historical Experiments on Sepulchral Hill.* Dharwad: Karnatak University Press.

Sharma, A. 1982. *The Puruṣārthas: A Study in Hindu Axiology.* East Lansing: Asian Studies Center, Michigan State University.

Sharma, H. D. 1939. *Contributions to the History of Brāhmaṇical Asceticism (Saṃnyāsa).* Poona Oriental Series 64 (= The Poona Orientalist 3.4, 1–76). Poona.

Sharma, R. S. 1983. *Material Culture and Social Formations in Ancient India.* Delhi: Macmillan.

Sharma, S. 1962. "Khā saṃnyāsāśrama kā vedon men vidhāna hai?" *Vedavāṇī* 14.12: 8–11.

Shastri, A. M. 1975. "The Bhikṣu-sūtra of Pārāśarya." *Journal of the Asiatic Society*, Calcutta, 14 (1972; issued May 1975): 52–59.

Shukla, S. J. B. 1966. "Vedeṣu gṛhasthāśramavarṇanam." *Surabhāratī* (Baroda Sanskrit College), pp. 31–33.

Singh, S. 1972. *Evolution of the Smṛti Law: A Study in the Factors Leading to the Origin and Development of Ancient Indian Legal Ideas.* Varanasi: Bharatiya Vidya Prakasana.

Sivapujanasimha. 1963. "Saṃnyāsāśrama kī vaidikatā." *Vedavāṇī* 15.3: 7–8, 17–19.

Skorpen, E. 1971. "The Philosophy of Renunciation—East and West." *Philosophy East and West* 21: 283–302.

Skurzak, L. 1948. *Études sur l'origine de l'ascétisme indien.* A, no. 15. Wroclaw: Societé des Sciences et de Lettres.

———. 1958. *Études sur l'épopée indienne.* A, no. 61. Wroclaw: Societé des Sciences et de Lettres.

———. 1967–68. "Indian Asceticism in its Historical Development." ALB 31/32: 202–10.

Smart, N. 1970. "Āśramas." In *A Dictionary of Comparative Religion*, ed. S. G. F. Brandon, 108. New York: Scribner.

Smith, B. K. 1989. *Reflections on Resemblance, Ritual, and Religion.* New York: Oxford Uni-

versity Press.
Smith, H. D. 1975. *A Descriptive Bibliography of the Printed Texts of the Pāñcarātrāgama.* Vol. 1. GOS 158, 1975.
Smith, J. Z. 1982. *Imagining Religion: From Babylon to Jonestown.* Chicago: University of Chicago Press.
Sprockhoff, J. F. 1976. *Saṃnyāsa: Quellenstudien zur Askese im Hinduismus. I—Untersuchungen über die Saṃnyāsa-Upaniṣads.* Abhandlungen für die Kunde des Morgenlandes 42,1. Wiesbaden: Franz Steiner.
———. 1979. "Die Alten im alten Indien: Ein Versuch nach brahmanischen Quellen." *Saeculum* 30: 374–433.
———. 1980. "Die feindlichen Toten und der befriedende Tote." In *Leben und Tod in den Religionen: Symbol und Wirklichkeit,* ed. G. Stephenson, 263-84. Darmstadt: Wissenschaftliche Buchgesellschaft.
———. 1981. "Āraṇyaka und Vānaprastha in der vedischen Literatur: Neue Erwägungen zu einer alten Legende und ihren Problemen." Pt. 1. WZKS 25: 19–90.
———. 1984. Idem. Pt. 2. Ibid. 28: 5–43.
———. 1987. "Kaṭhaśruti und Mānavaśrautasūtra—eine Nachlese zur Resignation." *Studien zur Indologie und Iranistik* 13/14: 235–57.
———. 1991. "Āraṇyaka und Vānaprastha." Pt. 3. WZKS 35: 5–46.
Strauss, O. 1911. "Ethische Probleme aus dem 'Mahābhārata'." *Giornale della Società Asciatica Italiana* 24: 193–335. Reprint 1912. Florence: Tipografia Galileiana.
Thakur, U. 1963. *The History of Suicide in India.* Delhi: Motilal Banarsidass.
Thapar, R. 1966. *A History of India.* Harmondsworth: Penguin.
———. 1978. *Ancient Indian Social History: Some Interpretations.* New Delhi: Orient Longman.
———. 1979. "Dissent and Protest in the Early Indian Tradition." *Studies in History* (Center for Historical Studies, Jawaharlal Nehru University), 1.2: 177–96.
———. 1982. "Householders and Renouncers in the Brahmanical and Buddhist Traditions." In Madan 1982, 273–98.
———. 1984. *From Lineage to State: Social Formations in the Mid-First Millennium B.C. in the Ganga Valley.* Bombay: Oxford University Press.
Tilak, S. 1989. *Religion and Aging in the Indian Tradition.* Albany, N.Y.: SUNY Press.
Trautmann, T. R. 1971. *Kauṭilya and the Arthaśāstra: A Statistical Investigation of the Authorship and Evolution of the Text.* Leiden: E. J. Brill.
Tull, H. W. 1989. *The Vedic Origins of Karma: Cosmos as Man in Ancient Indian Myth and Ritual.* Albany: SUNY Press.
van Buitenen, J. A. B. 1973–78. Tr. *The Mahābhārata.* 3 vols. Chicago: Chicago University Press.
———. 1981. *The Bhagavadgītā in the Mahābhārata: A Bilingual Edition.* Chicago: Chicago University Press.
van Gennep, A. 1960. *The Rites of Passage.* Tr. M. R. Vizedom and G. L. Caffee. Chicago: University of Chicago Press. (French ed. 1909).
Van Troy, J. 1964. "The Origin of Asceticism and of the Āśrama Dharma." *Bhāratī* (Benares Hindu University) 8.1: 1–26.
Vyas, S. N. 1967. *India in the Rāmāyaṇa Age.* Delhi: Atma Ram.
Wayman, A. 1963. "The Stages of Life According to Varāhamihira." JAOS 83: 360–61
Weber, M. 1958. *The Religion of India: The Sociology of Hinduism and Buddhism.* Tr. H. H. Gerth and D. Martindale. New York: Free Press.
———. 1964. *The Sociology of Religion.* Tr. E. Fischoff. Boston: Beacon Press.
Weinrich, F. 1928. *Das "Gokapilīyam." Ein philosophisches Gespräch zwischen Kapila und*

Syūmaraśmi aus dem Mahābhārata. Göttingen: Dieterich.

———. 1929. "Entwicklung und Theorie der Āśrama-Lehre im Umriss." *Archiv für Religionswissenschaft* 27: 77–92.

Wezler, A. 1977. *Die wahren "Speiseresteesser" (Skt. vighasāśin).* Beiträge zur Kenntnis der indischen Kultur- und Religionsgeschichte I. Akademie der Wissenschaften und der Literatur. Abhandlungen der Geistes- und Sozialwissenschaftlichen Klasse, Jahrgang 1978. Nr. 5. Wiesbaden: Franz Steiner.

———. 1979. "Śamīka und Śṛṅgin. Zum Verständnis einer askesekritischen Erzählung aus dem Mahābhārata." WZKS 23: 29–60. Paul Hacker's reply, ibid. 23: 61–62.

Wiltshire, M. G. 1983. "The 'Suicide' Problem in the Pāli Canon." *Journal of the International Association of Buddhist Studies* 6: 124–40.

Winternitz, M. 1923. "Ascetic Literature in Ancient India." *Calcutta Review* October: 1–21.

———. 1926. "Zur Lehre von den Āśramas." In *Beiträge zur Literaturwissenschaft und Geistesgeschichte Indien. Festgabe Hermann Jacobi,* ed. W. Kirfel, 215–27. Bonn: F. Klopp.

———. 1927. Reprint 1977. *A History of Indian Literature.* Tr. S. Ketkar. 2 vols. New Delhi: Oriental Books Reprint Corporation.

Zaehner, R. C. 1966. *Hinduism.* 2nd ed. Oxford: Oxford University Press.

———. 1969. *The Bhagavad-Gītā.* London: Oxford University Press.

Index